The Color Management Handbook for Visual Effects Artists

Victor Perez brings together the research and expertise of world-leading color scientists to create a comprehensive guide for visual effects (VFX) artists in color management. This book explores the latest standards of high dynamic range (HDR) and Academy Color Encoding System (ACES) workflows, in an easily digestible and widely applicable resource. Its purpose is to make artists confident and familiar with color management and its science, to improve the quality of visual effects worldwide.

Without assuming any previous knowledge, this self-contained book builds the reader's understanding from the ground up, exploring all the elements of the color workflow at a scientific level. It covers how to set up a consistent pipeline in relation to other departments, inside and outside visual effects, from camera to screen, so everybody is aligned to the same standards, preserving color qualities and consistency while maintaining the artistic intent end to end. It also delves into all the integral concepts for color management, ranging from color theory to digital image fundamentals, and much more.

This book is an invaluable resource for VFX students and professionals who want to be well-informed about the latest HDR and ACES pipelines, as well as those at every level of production wishing to gain a deeper understanding of managing color in visual effects projects.

Victor Perez is a multi-award winning film director, screenwriter, and VFX with over 25 years of combined experience, who has worked on a number of Hollywood films, including Christopher Nolan's *The Dark Knight Rises*, *Rogue One: A Star Wars Story*, and *Harry Potter and the Deathly Hallows*, among many others. He received the Italian Academy Award for his outstanding work as VFX supervisor on *The Invisible Boy: Second Generation* in 2019.

The Color Management Handbook for Visual Effects Artists

Digital Color Principles, Color Management Fundamentals & ACES Workflows

Victor Perez

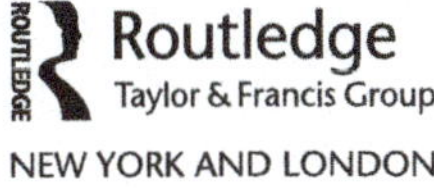

NEW YORK AND LONDON

First published 2024
by Routledge
605 Third Avenue, New York, NY 10158

and by Routledge
4 Park Square, Milton Park, Abingdon, Oxon, OX14 4RN

Routledge is an imprint of the Taylor & Francis Group, an informa business

Library of Congress Cataloging-in-Publication Data
Names: Perez, Víctor (Film director), author.
Title: The color management handbook for visual effects artists : digital color principles, color management fundamentals & ACES workflows / Victor Perez.
Description: New York. NY : Routledge, 2023. | Includes bibliographical references. |
Identifiers: LCCN 2022061893 (print) | LCCN 2022061894 (ebook) |
ISBN 9781032383606 (hardback) | ISBN 9781032383613 (paperback) |
ISBN 9781003344636 (ebook)
Subjects: LCSH: Cinematography—Special effects—Handbooks, manuals, etc. |
Digital cinematography—Handbooks, manuals, etc. | Color cinematography—
Handbooks, manuals, etc. | Color computer graphics—Handbooks, manuals, etc.
Classification: LCC TR858.P46 2023 (print) | LCC TR858 (ebook) | DDC
777—dc23/eng/20230213
LC record available at https://lccn.loc.gov/2022061893
LC ebook record available at https://lccn.loc.gov/2022061894

ISBN: 9781032383606 (hbk)
ISBN: 9781032383613 (pbk)
ISBN: 9781003344636 (ebk)

DOI: 10.4324/b23222

Typeset in Sabon LT Pro
by codeMantra

Dedicated to all the colors of my life: Red, Green, Blue, and James (my son).

Contents

Foreword

Color management and visual effects often have a difficult relationship, shrouded by misunderstandings and misinformation. Sometimes, it's like we're trying to put together a puzzle by using a hammer to fit the pieces together. There's certainly a need for better strategies to fix this troubled relationship. If you ever feared having to deal with color management, gasped at words like Bayer pattern, chroma sub-sampling, linear workspace, DPX, and EXR, or never completely understood the workings of an ACES pipeline, then this might be the book you're looking for. Victor Perez has managed to decipher some of the cryptic nature around color management, color principles, and the ever-impenetrable ACES workflow. Complex topics are presented in a clear and organized way, offering "production-ready" methods and technical language which will easily be understood by visual effects artists at any level. In other words, this book is written by an artist for artists, as it attempts to demystify and democratize color management for the visual effects industry.

This book would have been a lifesaver when I started my VFX career in 1999. Back then, without all the available resources we have today, such as YouTube and online communities of artists sharing experiences and ideas, we had to learn VFX by trial and error, often alone, many times successfully, but in other instances, leading to frustrating dead ends. This meant that without such readily available information, long hours were spent experimenting, making assumptions and lucky guesses on how to control the color space and the delivery formats of projects. In this sense, a valuable resource like this book would certainly have made all the difference when we were creating a color pipeline at The Mill London when I was the head of Nuke™. Together with the other heads of departments, we set out on a quest to create a color pipeline for the company to define what color space, file formats, and processes would be used from ingesting, conforming, CG, compositing, all the way to grade and delivery. But let's be honest, making color pipelines can be difficult. Not only we had countless meetings and endless experimentation, but we were also too busy with clients' projects to have enough time to go deeper into setting a proper and efficient pipeline. But in the end, probably like most companies, the outcome was achieved, to a great extent, by brute-forcing the process.

Without understanding the full color pipeline of a production we can't create convincing VFX, but the problem is *where do we start?* Many of us don't have the time to study and experiment during a production. Sometimes we go through a job hoping we've picked the correct color space and trusting that the LUT's given by the colorists and DIT's have the correct provenance. This is the only way we can be sure that the delivery has the correct specs for the project. We try to make sense of it all, but most of the time we deal with color like it's a game of chance; we never know if we have the winning numbers! That is because our knowledge is usually flawed or incomplete and often, we don't admit this, since some of us simply don't like to talk about color and don't give it the time it deserves. Just try to mention "color management" in a visual effects meeting and see what happens!

So many times I've been asked by my own students, "How do I become a great VFX artist? Where do I start? Should I learn Nuke, Fusion™, After Effects™, Natron, or skip them altogether and just learn Unreal Engine?" My reply is always the same. Don't focus only on software, also focus on developing your core skills by learning photography, color, cameras, lenses, composition, and light. And go outside, take photos, and experience the real world, not just what's in front of your screen!

One of the problems is that most artists starting their careers are sometimes too concerned with learning shortcuts for a specific software, thinking this will be the deciding factor to make a great VFX shot. But the truth is, you can only make a good-looking image if you know what a real image looks like in the first place. We also often fail to see the big picture within the production pipeline, focusing too much attention on our solo VFX shot without fully understanding how it was filmed, what color space was used, and what file format should be created after a shot is finished. This may cause in the end confusion and a lack of understanding of the whole visual effects process. But what if it was possible to understand better the color pipeline?

In this book, you will find suggestions and some of the necessary tools to understand and build an agnostic color management pipeline. Take note of the word "agnostic". It's important to understand that color management and color spaces do not belong to one single software. It's a system, a pipeline, existing from the moment we start filming with a camera, to the final grade, delivery, and everything in between. One of the strengths of this book is that it's not just a scientific or academic text. It also seeks to be a practical book that you can use in a real production environment. The fact that Victor works in the industry as an active professional means that he's not just an academic, he's also a creator of visual effects, a filmmaker, and a storyteller. Don't get me wrong, there's no problem with a good scientific book, but good visual effects usually combine art and science. Just look at some of the Oscar®-winning movies for the best VFX category of the last 15 years: *Ex Machina*, *First Man*, *Interstellar*, *Gravity*, *Tenet*, *Dune*, and *Avatar*. We could all agree that these films achieve a symbiosis of practical, digital, technical, and artistic elements, making them artistic and technical accomplishments.

As I see it, VFX artists usually fall into two camps. On one side we have the "physically accurate" folks. For example, they would move a 3D object in a scene using a command prompt on a terminal. There's nothing wrong with a good terminal command, but sometimes it seems a bit overcomplicated. On the other side, we have the "artists", the ones that would move the 3D object around, blur it, shake it, and use *gaffer tape* to make it look real, as long as you don't look behind that object! Again, nothing wrong with *gaffer tape*, most blockbuster films were probably saved by this classic method. Fix it in post? I say, fix it with gaffer tape! (Anyway, you get my point …). The first approach can be a bit overcomplicated sometimes and could suppress creativity. But the second one perhaps lacks some structure and procedural methodology. None of these two approaches is incorrect, I would say, they are both correct. It's a pointless debate that leads nowhere, the old battle of the two sides of the brain. As you will find in this book, visual effects combine both technical and artistic endeavors. I'm sure Victor will make your VFX journey easier, helping you find your creative voice while you set up your own agnostic pipeline.

–Hugo Guerra, Director & VFX Supervisor

Preface

Color management relies on an empirical system of capture, process, and reproduction of images. This is a scientific approach to an elementary component of visual arts: color; something that we artists are used to address in a very different way – less "regulated" and more "emotional" – however this system implies the use of the universal language of science: mathematics … Wait! Don't close the book just yet! I know it might sound boring or complicated when you just read above the words "scientific approach" or "mathematics", but it is not at all, at least not on these pages. I know very well you are an artist, and believe me, I kept you in mind when I wrote every single word on this book.

Indulge me, I want to demystify in this book a few myths: first of all, science is not boring, and second, you do not need to be a color scientist to understand color management, as you do not need to be an automotive engineer to drive a car, but let's face it, understanding how "the car" works is essential to drive it (chose your fuel carefully at the pump!). I am not a color scientist myself; I am a visual effects artist and an expert in artistic formative processes. The knowledge I share with you is based on my experience on the field (with the help of many people way better prepared than me in their respective fields), where I had developed professionally for the past 25 years based mainly in need to learn things to solve my own – and others' – problems (the healthiest form of curiosity). My work ethics rely on knowing what you are doing and then pass your knowledge to others, as others helped me in my way up (making sure you do not spread misinformation, as it would slap you back in the face sooner or later), so I must be extremely rigorous to precisely understand every aspect of my job from three different perspectives: **science, technology,** and **art**. Those three elements are interlinked in the visual effects craft and sometimes the lines where one ends and the other starts are quite blurry. Well, those grey areas are precisely the ones that I am most interested in, the ones that required this book. Color management is at the center of the intersection between these three elements, you cannot explain it to an artist just from the scientific point of view ignoring the art component in a framework where technology is influencing its development. So, expect this book to be oriented to artists, not for scientists, yet I will use basic scientific grounds to understand the necessary elements, however, in plain language. Everything is focused to provide practical knowledge applicable on your field. I also added a set of fundamentals about color in general to expand your skills and consolidate a platform for you to develop your digital image skills. Know your craft. By the moment you turn the last page of this book, color management will be a clear topic, so you know what is going on and what you need to do to ensure every link of the chain is preserved, remember: a chain is as strong as its weakest link.

In my early career – as many artists out there – I had to wear many hats: photographer, graphic designer, colorist, filmmaker, compositor … and they all have one thing in common, the existential question to self: *"Do the rest of the world see in their monitors what I see in mine?"* Now, do not tell me you never asked yourself this question before. Furthermore, if you continue the overthinking flow, you could even question – terrified – if you are actually seeing the right colors in your own monitor. Doubts are the enemy of artists and color management, being handled without knowledge is the perfect place to find doubts everywhere … please do not become a philosopher of color management, try the scientific method (it is way easier). Welcome to the White Rabbit hole. But fear not, this is when you are going to love the mathematic precision I mentioned above, because using color management – hence an empirical approach to color values – you can do things in only two ways: right or wrong, easy. With the same clarity that 2 + 2 = 4. Only 4 is the right answer, anything else that is not 4 is plainly a wrong answer. Understanding color management will provide you the peace of mind of knowing you are doing things right and to be able to point the finger to the problem when things are wrong … but most importantly, you will have the answer to the "existential" question: you are looking at the <u>right</u> color and the rest of the world will see the best approximation[1] to that color on their displays. Color management is accessible to everyone in the industry end-to-end, and many talented color scientists collaborate to provide the tools we need for an efficient workflow, collectives like ACES or OCIO which offer an open-source set of tools are setting the golden standard for handling color, software and hardware are embracing these new workflows, so at the end of the day it is all up to the user to press the right buttons. So this book will not focus on pressing buttons, it is not a tutorial to showcase how to do things in a particular software (for that matter you have already the documentation and manuals of the software), I want to dig deeper and to provide you with the knowledge to understand how color management works so you will know automatically what is the purpose of all buttons of any software regarding color management. You will decide which buttons to press depending on what you need: a form, not a formula. I have carefully prepared every chapter to be software-agnostic, but I admit that sometimes, for the sake of being clear to illustrate my point, I used the industry-standard compositing and image processing software Nuke, instead of drawing abstract graphics; my aim is to be clear and useful, not pedant. In the additional materials that accompany this book online, you will find a few tutorials for well-known software of different kinds to set up them up in an ACES color managed pipeline.

I am going to be honest, color as a science can be overwhelming. The level of complexity can spiral into lots of data for precision, and that level of precision is what is expected from a color scientist, who I deeply admire, to make the difference and advance our technology by striving for excellence. But as I mentioned earlier, this book is not aimed at scientists but for artists, and while precision is still required maybe the omission of certain aspects or the simplification of others would help you, the artist, to grasp my point and to understand better the concepts and lessons to be acquired. As artists we have different needs and different mindsets than scientists. We made a silent pact in the beginning of our careers to let technology condition our ways to work and science to command our approach to the representation of reality, and sadly sometimes, when learning the technicalities of our craft, we focus so much on the science-technology binomial expecting the art to be a consequence of those two. I do not think so. Art is a way to interpret and apply science and technology. Know the rules to understand when to break them in your favor, and that is what I did here. Based on my experience I know I can oversimplify a few concepts to help you see the big picture and to focus on what is important for us, artists. Let me make an example of healthy simplification: "Earth is rounded", well, not exactly, the diametral distance between the poles is shorter than the diameter measured at the equator, but we can affirm that Earth is rounded without offending anyone. Some other times I will cite elements without developing much into the argument to enable your curiosity to prompt you for an active research and keep learning if you desire. Other times, at my discretion, I will omit data that will just unnecessarily complicate the examples, or simply use theoretical applications of oversimplified data to make the concept easier to apprehend without sacrificing the outcome or the quality of the knowledge, returning to the example of "Earth is rounded", do you know that if you measure your weigh at the poles and on the equator you will discover that you weigh differently? That's a fun fact unless you need infinitesimal calculations of weigh difference for your craft.

After all, 2.0 + 2.0 = 4.0 and 2 + 2 = 4 are practically the same thing, and still someone could argue they are not – and they would be right depending on the context – but for the purpose here I would say they are the same. So no worries, I will write only what it would serve you to work as an artist (and maybe a bit more, but just a bit).

I would invite you to continue your research beyond this book into the fascinating world of color science, hoping that this volume was the spark that ignited your curiosity. I consider this text contains everything you need to know to understand and deal yourself with color management, HDR, and the ACES workflows for VFX. By no means this book intends to disrespect any color scientist or their craft by the simplifications or voluntary omissions made on the text. Science should be available to anybody. I wrote this book to be concise and still easy to handle and digest, in a language and style near to artists, tested on the field, to be kept near for future reference and most importantly, to be fun to read while learning.

–Victor Perez

Note

1 Of course it depends on the quality of their display, but if you did your work right you would not have to worry about it. I will elaborate this point when I discuss about displays.

Acknowledgments

The task of writing a comprehensive handbook for visual effects artists on a complex subject such as color management, which is constituted by science, technology, and art, is somehow intimidating. In order to deliver everything I consider fundamental, I relied on personal wisdom gathered from the field, working in the collaborative art of visual effects on different positions, where I have the privilege to learn from the experience and knowledge of my peers, project after project, while adapting to the ever-changing technology. Through conversations with colleagues in the context of preparing this book, including color scientists, software developers, and artists, they helped me finding the constant line of common understanding necessary to develop a solid ground knowledge of color management, artist-friendly, software agnostic*(ish)* but technology-oriented, as the visual effects industry is. They must be acknowledged for their efforts and dedication have shaped this book.

First of all, my second family at Foundry® for always supporting me, especially Jennifer Goldfinch for her tenacious support and patience, without her presence, this book would not exist. Juan Salazar for helping me focus the content without falling into the *Rabbit Hole*. Mark Titchener, Nigel Hadley, Christy Anzelmo, and the whole Nuke team for their invaluable cooperation.

Thomas Mansencal was particularly supportive to achieve the scientific precision this book required. As always, Thomas was welcoming and willing to share his vast wisdom with the community and improve the visual effects industry.

Carol Payne and Bhanu Srikanth at Netflix® are other key players who require special thanks for thrusting me to write this book. They fueled the idea of helping visual effects artists and facilities to get educated into the subject of the book.

Other good people whose contributions helped me improve this book are Nick Shaw, Steve Wright, Kevin Shaw, Mark Pinheiro, Ian Failes, Walter Arrighetti, Simon Yahn, and Scott Dyer.

And finally, I would like to thank Dr. Mike Seymour for being a role model in the noble art of researching, learning, and teaching visual effects.

Section I

Optics and Perception of Color

Elements of Optics

As visual effects artists we observe reality not just through our eyes but most importantly through the lens of a camera. This fact set the rules of the game to start digging into the journey of light to be perceived as color. Understanding the very process of perception of color is key to comprehend the system we use to capture color. Therefore, I decided to start our journey of color management far from the *management* part and closer to the *color*. We need to get familiar with lights, cameras, supports, lenses and ultimately with the physiognomy of the most wonderful organ in our body: the eye. I believe that in order to understand the process of color acquisition and management, it is important to put into context the very fundamental notions about physics of light, color and how this is captured. Everything is within a historical context.

This chapter explores those basics to start building your color knowledge from the ground up.

Light

From a physics point of view, the first question that pops in our mind when we need to approach color is very simple: "*What is color?*" However, since color is intrinsically related to light, before finding an answer to that question maybe we should understand one of the fundamental properties of light: *wavelength*.

Light is much more than we can observe, light itself is an *electromagnetic radiation*, and it behaves, contemporarily, as both *particles* ("packages" of energy: photons) and *waves*, with a huge span of wavelengths inside every single ray of light. Actually, there is more light that we cannot see than the fraction that we can (Figure 1.1).

The wavelength is a characteristic of any kind of wave. It is the distance over which the shape of a wave repeats, measured on any given point on the wave.

The figure above illustrates this concept. A given *sinusoidal wave*[1] – right now we do not need to care about the distance or the value in this example, just the mere concept of wavelength. If we select a point in the wave, for instance where y reaches its maximum value – let's name this point A – and we continue moving in the x axis until next time y repeats the same value as in point A – let's name this other point B – the distance between A and B describes the wavelength for this wave. That is what makes color as we will see below.

Light could contain, depending on its wavelength: *gamma rays, x-rays, infrared, ultraviolet, microwaves, radio waves* and, of course, the *visible spectrum*: what we see. The wavelength range of the visible spectrum goes approximately from 300 to 700 nm. The nanometer is part of the International System of Units (SI) and its standard symbol is *nm*

DOI: 10.4324/b23222-2

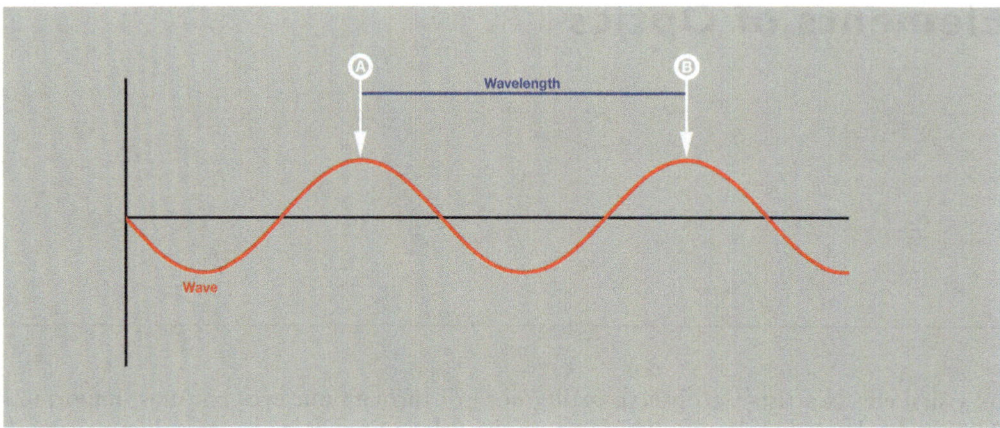

Figure 1.1 Wavelength of a sinusoidal wave

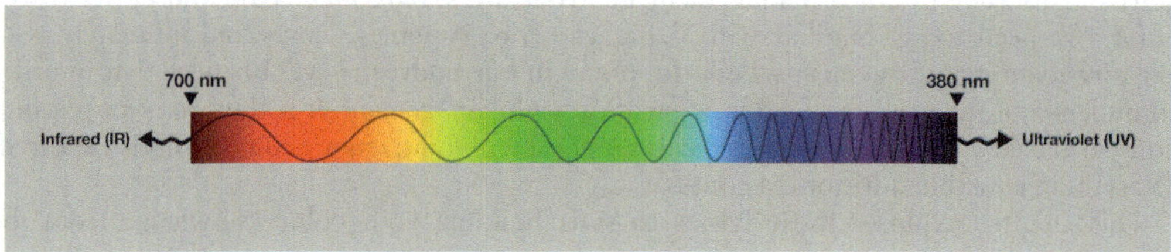

Figure 1.2 The visible spectrum

(now you can read the measurements of the visible spectrum!) and do not forget that a nanometer is as small as one billionth of meter … let me put it in a number to help you picture it: the 0.000000001 portion of a meter. Maybe numbers are not representing well in your mind how small a nanometer is, let me give you a piece of information to visualize it yourself: a human hair is approximately 90,000 nm wide. But not all wavelengths of light are that small, for instance the wavelengths of Radio waves can range from 30 cm to thousands of meters. Of course, we are going to focus on the aspects of light we can see: the visible spectrum. Beyond that range I mentioned above our eyes can see nothing, but certain animals can (and so certain special cameras) like the case of blood-sucking insects, such as bedbugs and mosquitoes, that can see infrared – certain wavelengths longer than 750 nm – while others, such as bees, can see ultraviolet – certain wavelengths shorter than 390 nm – so our vision is not the only model that exists in the world, but until we start producing films and TV shows for bees and mosquitos to enjoy I would focus on our *visible spectrum* (Figure 1.2).

The figure above shows a representation of the visible spectrum. From red, the biggest wavelengths, to violet, the smallest, with every color in between. Beyond the boundaries of red there are infrared, x-rays, etcetera; and over violet, as you guessed: ultraviolet, microwaves, and so on. But what defines the colors within the visible spectrum?

I think it is time I tell you the truth. Do you remember the riddle: "If a tree falls in a forest, and there's no one around to hear it, does it make a *sound*?" You might have heard that there's no definitive answer to this question. However, there is an answer but it depends on what we mean by "sound". If we consider sound just the vibration of air (or any other medium) then the answer is *yes*. But I would lean more toward sound being the sensation we experience when our ears detect those vibrations and send information about those vibrations to the brain. In this case the answer is the opposite, *no*. For me, if nobody hears it, there is no *sound*, but just a process of vibration in different mediums. I think you already got my point about what I meant with "the truth", and I am going to make a bold statement in the same style of the riddle above: "*color does not exist without our eyes*". I am not interested in studying the electromagnetic radiations of the visible spectrum without keeping account of how human beings perceive those wavelengths. So, it is time to talk about the perception of color.

Perception of Color

Now that we have our "color palette", we are ready to start answering the original question: "*What is color?*" Well, for the time being we can say that color is the *perception* of certain wavelengths of the radiation of light in the range known as the visible spectrum. This statement takes us to consider three elements in the process of color perception: *light, observed object*, and *receptor*.

A ray of light could reach our eye directly from the source of light itself or after it had been bounced from an object, what we call *reflected light*. So, I could say a ray of light is not visible until it is reflected by a surface and arrives to our eye – or an optical capturing device but I will refer to this as just The eye to simplify the explanation – with this I mean we only *see* those rays of light incoming into the eye, those other radiations that expand in all directions are invisible. For instance a ray of light passing in front of your eyes, side by side, would not be visible, unless there is dust in the air, or some sort of thick atmosphere, then you would see the reflected light of that dust or the particles of atmosphere, but light itself can travel in the vacuum, like the space, and be invisible unless it hits the surface to bounce to our eyes.

There are different aspects that will condition the perception of a color, for instance, it will depend on the relation between the color of the light – or the range of wavelengths radiated by the source – and the color of the surface of the observed object, as I will discuss later in this book. But since we have already mentioned the human eye quite a few times, I think the next natural question would be: "*How the human eye receives and perceives this stimulation of the visible spectrum?*"

First of all, the human eye can distinguish around 10 million variations from the range of the visible spectrum; as I mentioned above, wavelengths of light radiation ranging from 390 to 750 nm.

How? Inside the human eye there are two kinds of photo-sensitive cells that interest us: *cones* and *rods*. *cone cells* are responsible for the color stimulation, and *rod cells* are sensitive to critical luminosity variations without accounting for color variations (monochromatic). To oversimplify the concept: cones see color, rods perceive brightness. We have millions of both kinds, and they are all found in the retina, which is the back wall inside the ocular globe (the eye), receiving the light passing into the eye through the pupil. In other words, if we can make the analogy between a digital camera and the human eye: the retina is the "sensor" of the human eye.

Humans are *trichromatic*,[2] which means our brain recreates every visible color variation as the result of the mix of three monochromatic spectral stimuli. In other words: all colors we can see are reconstructed by mixing three primary colors, the mix depends on the intensity of each primary. I am sure you are familiar with the RGB sliders, that is a trichromatic system.

Every single response – of the three available for this type of photoreceptor cell – is generated by a different kind of cone cell, of which we have three kinds in our eyes:

- *Small (S) cones*: reacting to wavelengths around 420 nm, which generate what we can define as the Blue component;
- *Large (L) cones*: sensitive to wavelengths around 564 nm, resulting the Red component; and
- *Medium (M) cones*: stimulated by wavelengths around 534 nm, the green component.

Just to be clear and avoid any confusion, the stimulation of those photoreceptors is not made by "colors" but merely by certain wavelengths for each kind of cell, in a certain combination of intensities that are "deciphered" by the brain and interpreted resulting in the visualization of color. So "color" itself does not belong to the light entering the eye, I mean the wavelengths perceived are just achromatic, color happens as a sensorial response to radiations in a portion of light (the wavelengths ranging in the visible spectrum). Coming back to the simple examples related to digital imaging: if I give you three numbers, like for instance 100, 0 and another 0, well they are just numbers, and numbers have no colors, but if I tell you those three numbers are meant to be interpreted as percentages values of RGB, then you have: R = 100%, G = 0%, and B = 0% (1.0 0.0 0.0), and now a red color appears in your mind (Figure 1.3).

Yes, we recreate colors in our brain in a similar way we handle color in our monitors digitally, using the RGB system with an analogic system coming from the S, M, and L cones. In the digital image every pixel has three color values, one for red, one for green, and one for blue. If you think about it, they are just three values, an array of three numbers that are ultimately processed by displays as the result the represent one single color. We will review this subject in depth in the next chapter, but I wanted to put you into the perspective that the displaying system of our monitors and the human eye are quite aligned.

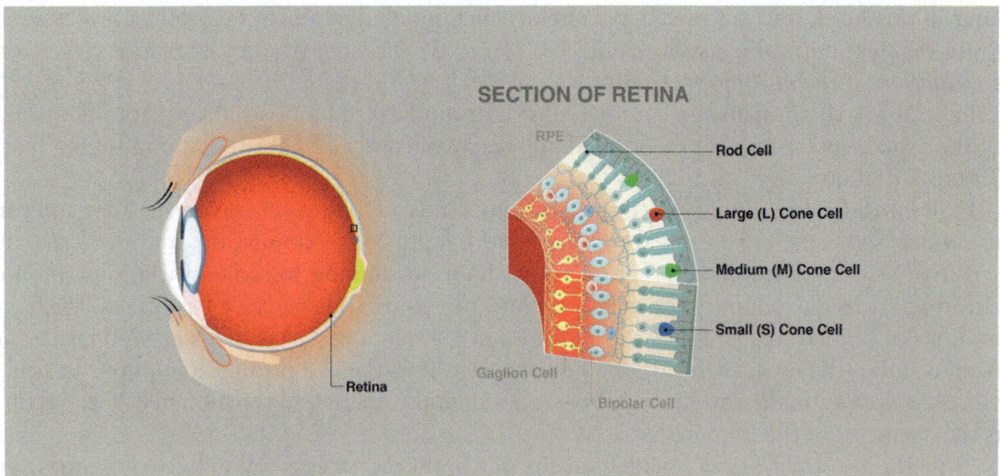

Figure 1.3 Eye anatomy – section of retina

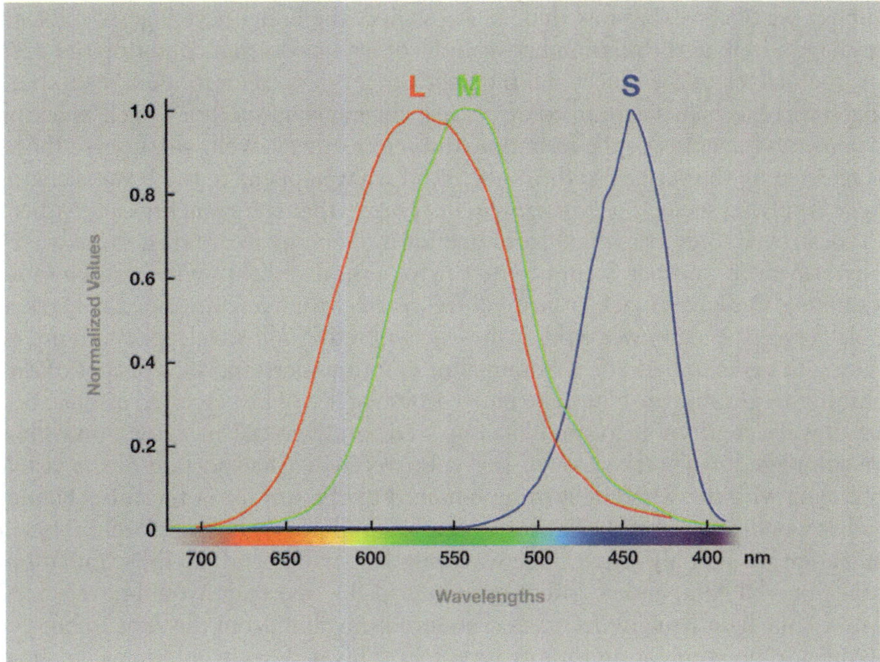

Figure 1.4 Normalized response of human cone cells

But back in our eyes, not all three kinds of cone cells react with the same amount of response (Figure 1.4).

In the figure, we can see a normalized response of human cone cells. The response curve for S cones – the blue color – is narrower than the other two, and as you can see, there is a gap of response between S cones and M cones corresponding approximately around the 475 nm area (this is the blue zone). On the other hand, L and M cones are quite broad with an area of superposition around the 555 nm area, which means both L and M are sensitive to certain green wavelengths in common. Something worth mentioning is that not all three stimuli have the same response in term of brightness[3] (amount of light perceived), some components contribute with higher brightness than others.

Something as apparently trivial as measuring the perception of brightness could spiral quickly down the Rabbit Hole (as you can already notice by the number of endnotes on this page!), depending on the definition we use of "brightness of a light source". For instance, we might require radiometric[4] units for *Human Visual System* neutral "physical" units defined based on *Watts*, while photometric[5] units are *Human Visual System* weighted units defined based on *Lumens*. So, once again let's simplify, I will use display-oriented examples to render the concept clear without needing to dig down too much. So, to showcase an instance of conversion from RGB to luma[6] to understand the imbalance between the perception of luminance[7] for each component of color: the *ITU BT.709*, a standard for photometric/digital calculation of the luminance (Y), stablishes that Y = 0.2126 R + 0.7152 G + 0.0722 B. In simpler words, the green component carries almost three quarters of the luminance, the red carries less than a quarter; and blue does not even reach a tenth.

As you probably know white light contains the whole visible spectrum, and as we mentioned earlier, our perception of color depends on the relation between light and the surface of the object we observe. So now that we know how the human eye ingests color information let's have a look at the relation between the other aspects that condition our perception of color: the surface of the object and the light being reflected on it bouncing to our eyes.

We perceive objects in a certain color because their surface qualities, such as texture, that absorb some wavelengths of the radiation and reject others. Well, we observe those wavelengths rejected by the surface of the object. And what happens to those wavelengths being absorbed? Applying the *law of conservation of energy* that states energy can neither be created nor destroyed, only converted from one form of energy to another, those wavelengths are transformed on another form of energy, for instance: heat. Which is why under the strong summer sunlight a black t-shirt will feel warmer than a white one; the black absorbs the whole visible spectrum while the white one will reflect all wavelengths (Figure 1.5).

I'm going to make a theoretical example for you to understand the concept of the reflective light. In this graphic the blue cube under white light will be perceived as blue, because it absorbs all wavelengths able to stimulate our "red" and "green" receptors, only blue receptors are stimulated to *see* the color of this cube, receiving that portion of the visible spectrum traveling with the white light being bounced by the surface of the cube (Figure 1.6).

But what would happen if the light was pure red and not white as before. In this case our blue cube, that would only reject "blue wavelengths", will absorb all those radiations emitted by the pure red light, and no radiations of the visible spectrum would be rejected, which means no visible light being reflected and bounced traveling from the cube to our eyes and, in consequence, no stimulation for any receptors. This way we would perceive the cube as black, no color.

No matter how complex a particular color, the human eye elaborates light from three independent components that are combined and processed by our brain, to simplify it, the three kinds of *photoreceptors* (cone cells) match the RGB color model: one receptor for red, one for green and one for blue. This is not a coincidence, the RGB color model was actually built for the purpose of sensing, representation, and display of images in electronic systems based in human perception of colors. We are going to use this model a lot in the next, and you have

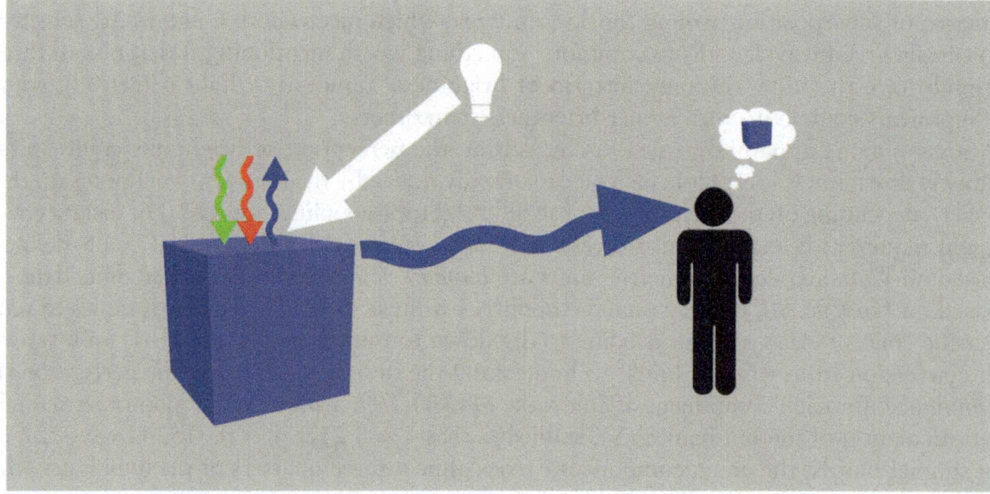

Figure 1.5 Reflective light and wavelength absorption – the blue cube instance

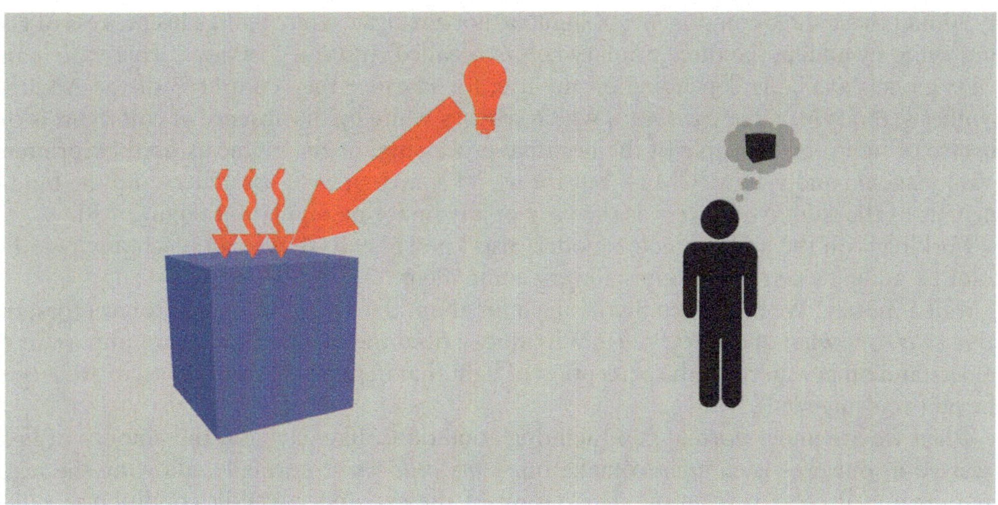

Figure 1.6 Reflective light and wavelength absorption – the black cube instance

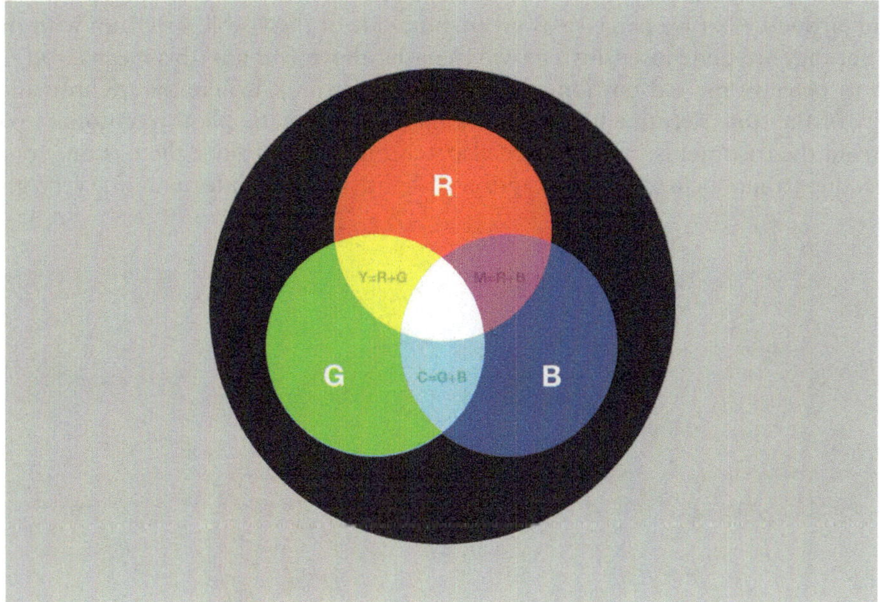

Figure 1.7 Additive synthesis of light

to be familiar with it, but no worries, being a visual effects (VFX) artist, you are already using it every day, in every software, in your monitor … it is all about RGB values, now it is time to be aware of it and know how does it work (it will make your life way easier). As we are talking about the RGB color model, it takes us to discuss the *synthesis of color* (Figure 1.7).

Following the same parameters as the human eye to split off light, we can define a color model based on the addition of three values, one for red, one for green, and one for blue.

By adding those three components of light we got again the white light. This process of getting white by adding the three primary colors is called *Additive Synthesis*. There are many color models available depending on the use, for instance the "contrary" of the Additive Synthesis, the *Subtractive Synthesis*, which reaches white by the absence of color, this is the inverse of light, the principle of the negative processing, or the pigments used by printers: cyan, magenta and yellow (CMY). But for us, VFX artists, we must understand the fundamentals of the Additive process as the base of any image manipulation (Figure 1.8).

Working with the additive color model, also known as RGB we can reach any possible color by adding a certain amount of every component.

Wait a minute! We have been discussing a lot about the Trichromatic photoreceptors, the *cone cells*, but what about *rod cells*? Why do we need them? I think they are important to understand other aspects of the perception of light that might enlighten you as an artist (yes, the pun was intended).

When we are under normal good lighting conditions, like daylight, the amount of light received in our eyes is enough to make our *cone cells* work normally, allowing the regular function of color perception. This vision of the eye under well-lit condition is called *Photopic Vision*. However, under low light conditions, *cone cells* do not receive enough intensity to be stimulated to perceive any wavelength, it is then when *rod cells* become very handy. This is called *Scotopic Vision*. *rod cells* are most sensitive to wavelengths around 500 nm (around what we perceive as green–blue side of the visible spectrum with the *cone cells*), but they are quite insensitive to wavelengths above 640 nm (this means: *rod cells* are unable to perceive the red portion of the visible spectrum). Unlike the trichromatic functionality of the *cone cells* due to the three kinds of achromatic photoreceptors to conform color from the tristimulus, *rod cells* are also achromatic, and since there is only one kind, they produce a monochromatic perception of light (no color information), very good for

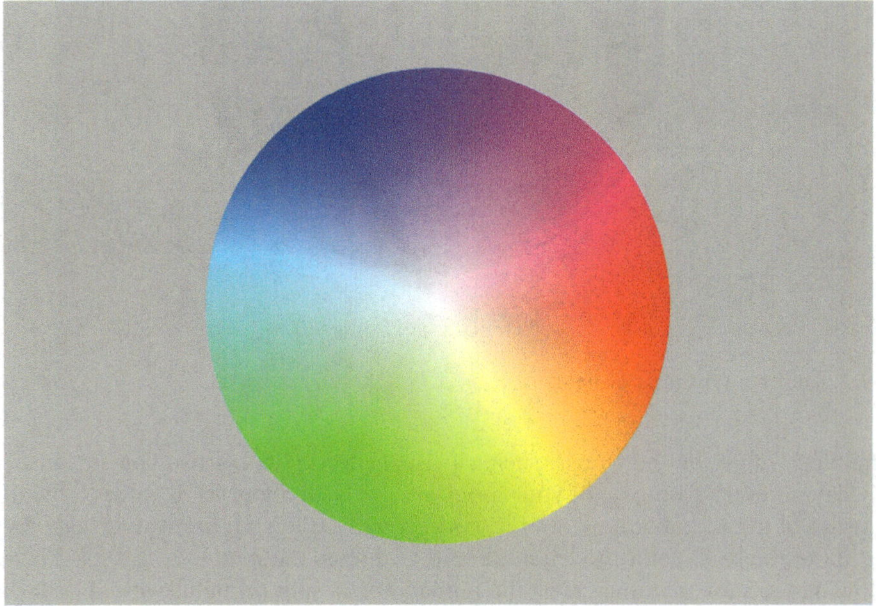

Figure 1.8 Color wheel (RGB colors mixed)

accurate changes of intensity in low-light conditions, making you able to distinguish shapes, but not helpful for color. The best example of this is when you arrive late to the cinema, the film already started, you can see the seats and the numbers on them but probably you would not be able to see the color of the seats and the walls of the room. Now you know why. For a good perception of color we need good light conditions, to enable the *photopic vision.*

It is important to understand how *photopic* and *scotopic* vision works to replicate, in an artistic way, the behavior of color under any light conditions. For instance, one of the key steps in a day-to-night process would be right alchemy of contrast and saturation (specially the luminance for the former red tones), just as cone and rod cells react, if you do not have enough light to saturate colors you should keep that in mind: low light means low intensity, low contrast, hence low saturation.

Many of the features of the human eye appear in the mechanism of light capture of a camera. In the next part of this chapter, we are going to explore how a camera works in terms of light and color.

Capturing Light

A camera is a device to capture light in a similar way the human eye does. But in terms of color, *how could we capture light on a physical support?*

Let's wind the clocks back to 1694, when a natural philosopher named *Wilhelm Homberg* noticed that light darkens some chemicals (what we know today as the *photochemical effect*). Together with the invention of the *pinhole camera* –a box with a small hole in one face that projects inside it, at the opposite face, the image in front of the hole, the discovery of the *photochemical effect* settled the principles of photography (Figure 1.9).

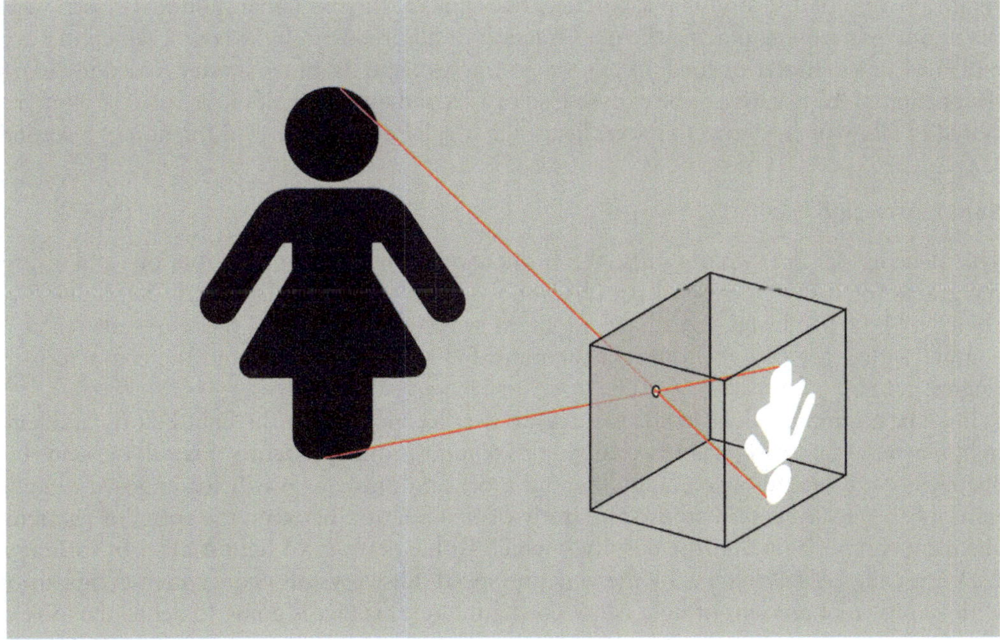

Figure 1.9 Pinhole camera

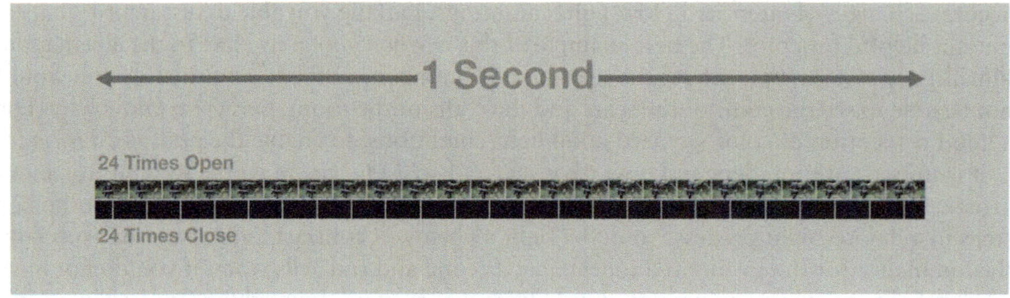

Figure 1.10 Film shutter opening cycle in one second at 24 fps

The importance of Homberg's discovery in relation with color resides in how light modifies the composition of the photo-sensitive chemicals used in photography film: *silver halide salts*. We are now talking about *exposure*.

The key difference, from the camera point of view, between still photography and moving pictures is the limitation of the time of exposure due to the frames needed to be exposed every second. In a still photograph the time of exposure –I mean the time the shutter is open, and light enters and impacts onto the film negative or the digital equivalent – has no restrictions: from a small fraction of a second to several minutes if you like, as the photographer wishes. However, in *motion pictures* there is a limitation on top, because the shutter must be opened and closed at least 24 times every second to generate 24 frames per second, the standard for capturing real time in cinema (Figure 1.10).

Hence we need a film stock "sensitive" enough to be correctly exposed in about a forty eighth fraction of a second – in a film negative camera, the mechanic shutter is closed when the negative is moving placing the next fraction of film ready to be exposed, which in a second is 24 times shutter opened (to expose 24 frames), and 24 times shutter closed to change the portion of the negative to be exposed, so in a second, usually half of the time the shutter is closed to allow the negative to move, hence the regular exposition 1/48 fraction of a second.

Sensitometry

The alchemy of *silver halide salts*, the proportion, composition, distribution, and size of the grains for every color-sensitive (also known as *chromogen*) layer will determine how color will be reproduced. Let's have a look at how a single grain of these crystals reacts in contact with a ray of light, this is a theoretical example to understand the characteristics (Figure 1.11).

Imagine a grain of silver halide salt crystal that has never seen the light before. Suddenly light reaches it … slowly it starts changing its composition, apparently it is still the same but chemically it is latently becoming different, more and more, as it is being exposed to light, until its chemical reaction stops. The study of this relation between the speed of changing chemical composition and the density – which is the quantity of light it absorbs turning it dark – is called *sensitometry*. By the way, the speed those crystals change their composition with a consistent amount of light is not constant, and this fact is going to define the look of the picture massively.

If you expose this crystal too fast it will not react at all as it needs time to unchain the reaction, and, on the other hand, if you expose it for too long, after a while it reaches its

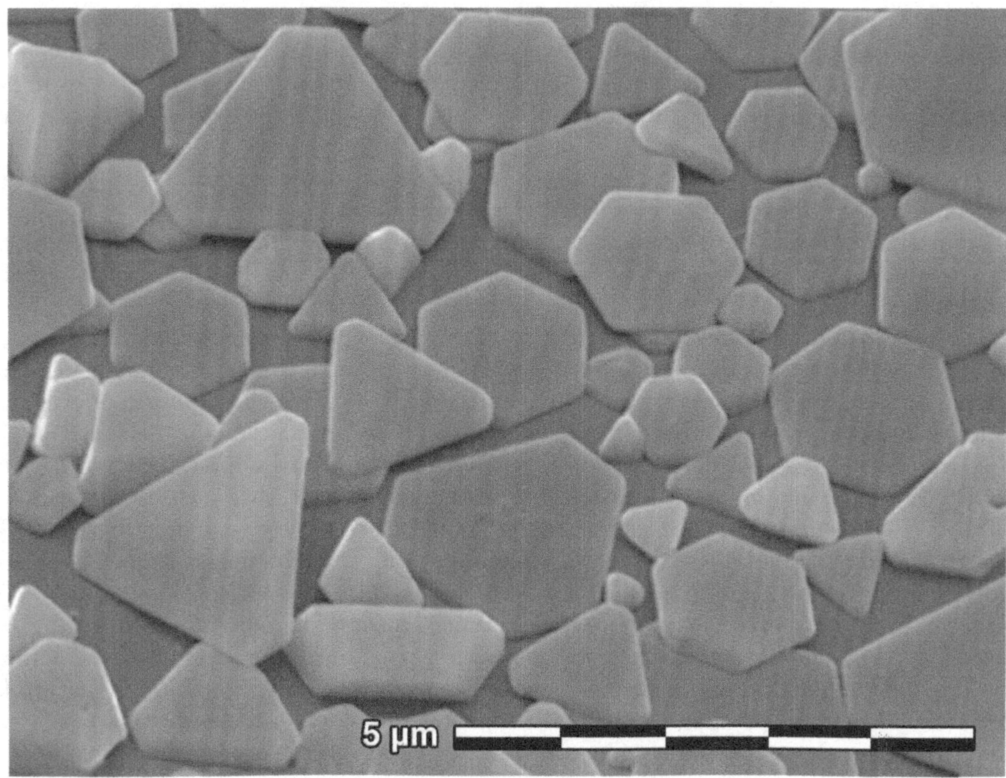

Figure 1.11 Kodak T-Grain silver halide crystals of black & white film under the scanning electron microscope (the scale represents 5 µm)

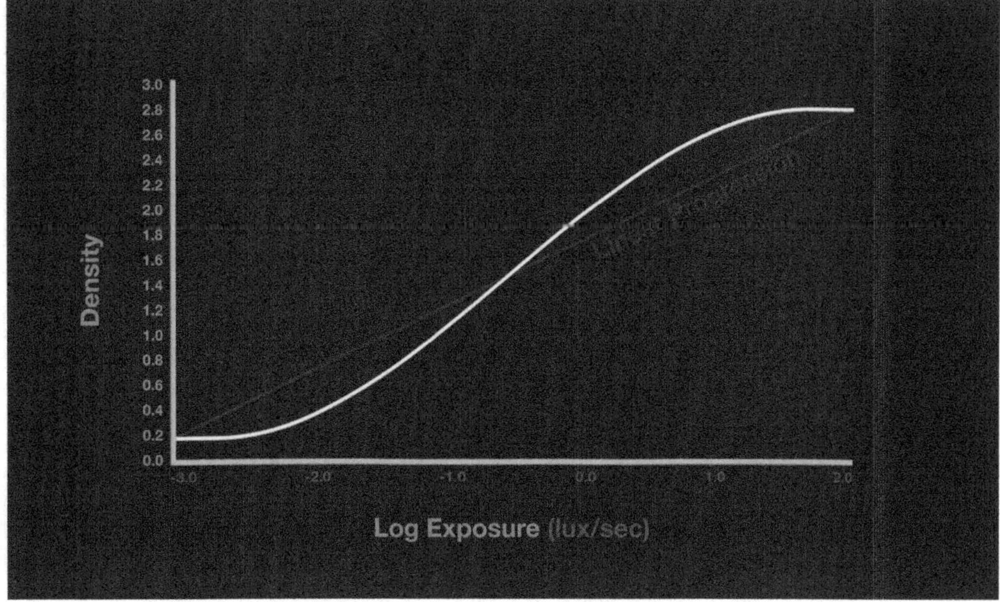

Figure 1.12 S-Curve

maximum and it stop changing. This model of exposition is known as the S-curve for the characteristic graphic representation of exposure against density.

Let's have a look at this interesting graphic: the representation of the relation between the density (vertical axis) and the time it has been exposed to light (exposure, in the horizontal axis) (Figure 1.12).

The result is a curve with the shape of an "S" I mentioned above. The first appreciation we can see is that the progression is not arithmetically linear.

A linear progression means a constant arithmetic proportion of both x and y axis, that, in a graphic representation returns a straight line. Meaning the increments are equal, measured at any point of the curve for the same segment length.

But back to our *sensitometric curve*, it is clearly not linear. This is important to understand one of the fundamentals of computer generated images (also known as computer-generated imagery (CGI), you already knew that). In an analogic world, like film negative, or even inside our eyes, the proportion between the density and exposure is never linear (Figure 1.13).

I overexaggerated the representation of the curve in order to appreciate the different parts. We need a minimum of exposure[8] to start capturing light, that starts at the bottom of the *s-shaped* curve, this is called *toe*, after that articulation there is an area more or less linear around the center of the curve, the *straight part* of the curve, then it tends to stop, as you see in the top area and so it bends until it becomes constantly horizontal, that top bend of the curve is the Shoulder. But notice that our curve has no origin on the absolute value 0, instead it starts slightly above, this first point is known as the *lift* that extends horizontally, the *base and fog*, until reaching the *toe*. The higher the base, the more "milky" is our black level (usually not a good thing for cinematographers), but we can address this as we will see later with the color manipulators, like for instance an look up table (LUT).[9]

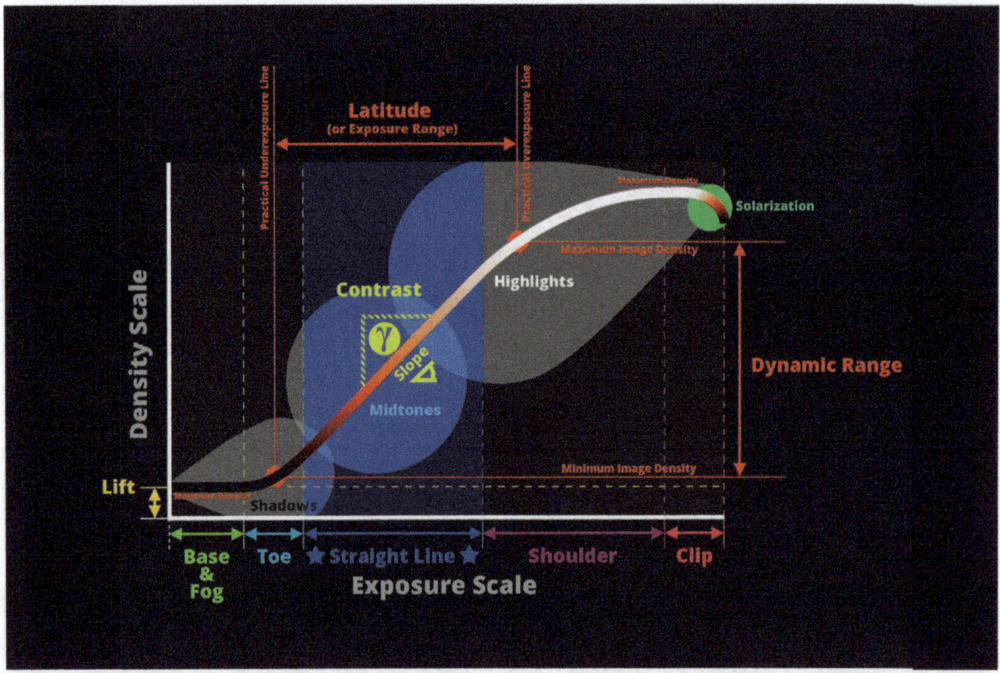

Figure 1.13 Characteristic curve breakdown

Another important feature of the curve is the slope of the *straight part*: it determines the gamma, which is the non-linear proportion between the black and the white levels, distributing the mid-tones: the flatter this line is the more shades of grays you get (less contrast), the higher inclination, the harder the step rises from black to white (higher contrast). The range of increments of exposure horizontally distributed in this curve is known as *latitude*. The relation of extent of the straight part vertically and horizontally will define the dynamic range and the contrast ratio.

In terms of exposure, we define a point right above the beginning of the *Toe* as the reference *minimum image density*, so everything below this point will be regarded as just black, with no detail in it; and the same way, we define a reference point right below the end of the Shoulder as the *maximum image density*, so any value above it will be read as plain white. This creates a nice look of the whites and the blacks, but the information beyond those points is still there it can turn very useful when we perform color manipulations.

From the minimum image density to the maximum image density we have defined the *dynamic range*, the range of densities a support can capture, in other words, the number of steps available to effectively capture details from the lightest white to the darkest black.

An easy experiment to understand the dynamic range, without the need of any device, is to simply fire a match under the bright Sun: you may be able to barely see just the flame; but if you fire another match in a dark room in the middle of the night you could probably see the whole room illuminated with just that tiny light. This means that our eyes have a marvelous high dynamic range (HRD) and the ability to adapt to different ranges of light. For the first case of the example, under daylight the portion of the curve we were viewing was more toward the high area of the curve and in the second, the dark room, we find ourselves at the bottom in the dark areas. By opening or closing the *diaphragm* of the lens we allow more, or less, light to pass though, deciding "what portion" of the sensitometric curve we like to use for the subject in our exposure, the closer the diaphragm, the lower we are going set our portion of the curve (less light), and the other way around for the high part (more light). In optics, this is called *aperture* and can be measured in *f-stops*.

The *f*-stop, also known as *relative aperture,* expresses the diameter witch light pass through a lens. It's related to the focal length of the lens and the *effective* aperture diameter (Figure 1.14).

This is a graphic for *f*-stops, in one stop increments: *f*-stop indicates the ratio of the *focal length* to the *diameter of the entrance pupil*. Notice that because we are calculating the area of a circle those numbers are in an exponential progression, since the area of a circle is π times the radius square ($A = \pi r^2$).

Between $f/1.4$ and $f/2$ there is one stop of difference, which means half the light gathering area to the first one. Same between $f/2$ and $f/2.8$ … and so on (yes, the proportion is: the higher the number below the *f* the less light you get, because it's a fraction). So, when we say a *stop up* or *stop down*, we are actually talking about the amount of light we like to capture through the lens in increments relative to the current exposition: precisely double the light relative to the current aperture for a stop up, or half the light for one stop down.

Still, before we started talking about *stops*, we were analyzing the sensitometric curve to understand how light behaves with halide salts, but we used only one curve, a monotone. In color film, the negative has three different kinds of halide salts that reacts differently to certain wave lengths. The principle is exactly the same, but every layer is sensitive to one of the primary colors: red, green, and blue, each in a different way. So, the combination of all three together generates the color image. This is known as *chromogenic process*. It means you will get three S-curves, one for each color, together they define the fidelity of the colors for every exposure level.

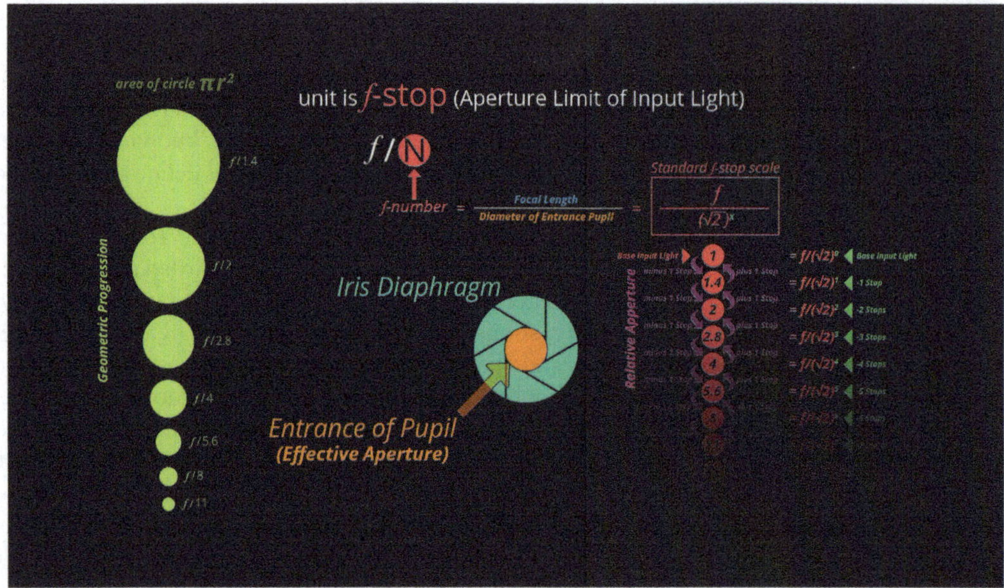

Figure 1.14 f-stop

Capturing Color

Let's have a look at a bit of history of color film. I think it will help to better understand the process of capturing color.

The Technicolor® Tripack

In the beginnings of the commercial color film there were various options available, one of the most popular was the *Technicolor Tripack*,[10] where a prism separates and distributes light onto three monochrome film strips, each one sensitive to each of the three primary colors. Literally three filmstrips running inside a single very big and heavy camera. Then the emulsion of every single primary monochrome filmstrip was printed over one final master filmstrip using a process similar to the modern *offset* printers, applying "ink" from each original filmstrip like a stamp. One of the most famous films using this process was *The Wizard of Oz* in 1939 (Figure 1.15).

However, this system had many issues – without even taking into account the massive camera to contain the three strips rolling concurrently, the costs of rolling three filmstrips to be later developed, and the noise it generated – the biggest problem was the amount of light it needed to be correctly exposed because of the splitting of light in three beams plus the light the prism itself absorbs (Figure 1.16).

Kodak® Kodachrome

Imagine, one day, after a period where studios and companies were in continuous research and development of new systems to capture color, striving for image excellence – a time very similar to our days in the era of digital cameras – the Eastman Kodak Company presented

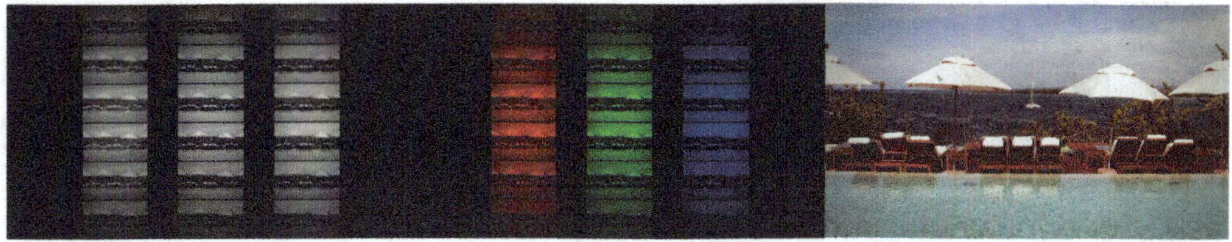

Figure 1.15 Technicolor tripack (simulation)

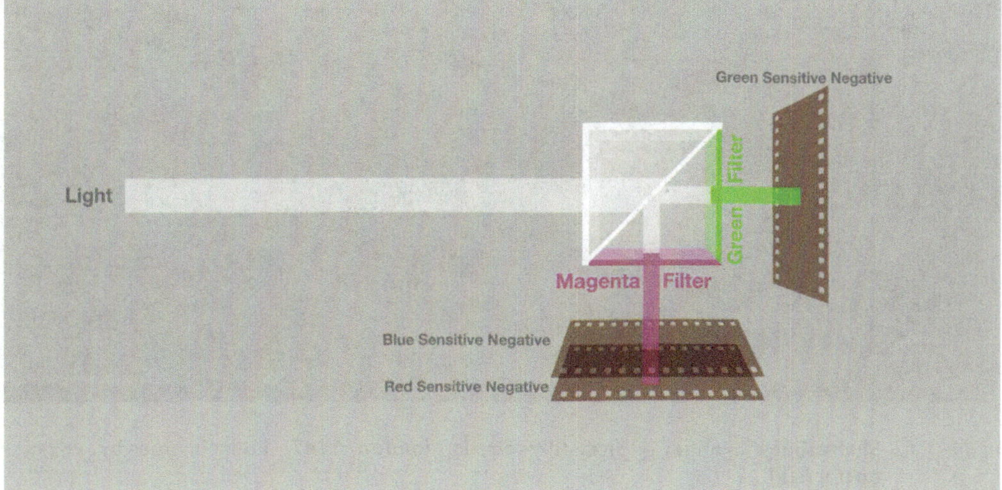

Figure 1.16 Technicolor dichroic prism

the *Kodachrome*, the first economical single-strip 35 mm negative-recording *monopack*,[11] and everything changed. It was 1950 and since then the film-negative technology has evolved and developed, with finer grain, higher sensitivities ... but the system itself and the standards are quite the same for film today (Figure 1.17).

This is a section of a monopack negative with its layers:

- A clear protective topcoat
- UV filter
- Blue layer
- Yellow filter (to cut all blue light beyond this layer)
- Green layer
- Inter layer
- Red layer
- Clear triacetate Base
- Anti-halation backing

All you need to capture color images in a single film strip, slightly thicker than a tenth of a millimeter. I personally find this very impressive (Figure 1.18).

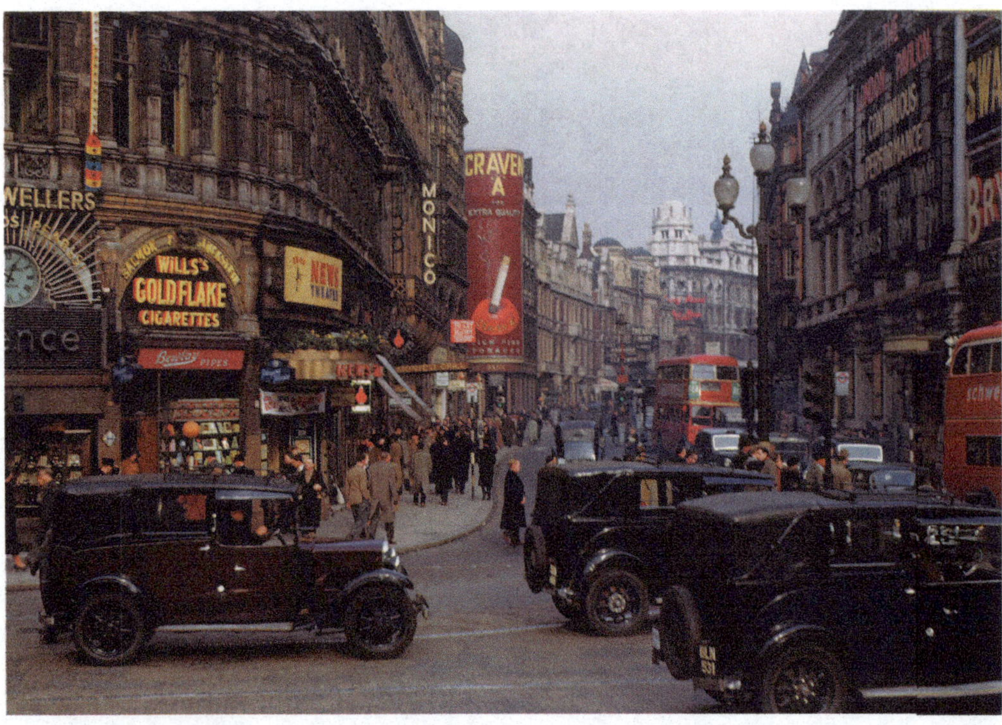

Figure 1.17 Shaftesbury avenue – piccadilly circus, london 1947, kodachrome by chalmers butterfield

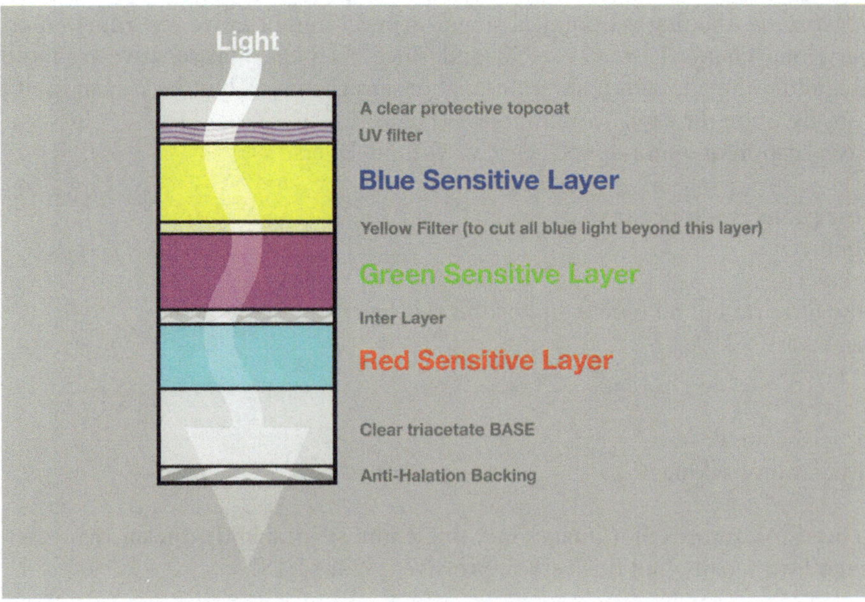

Figure 1.18 Monopack film negative layers (section view)

Color Temperature

There is only one factor we are still missing here: the balance between colors, or to be precise: the *white balance*. Why? Because the nature of light is radically different when you film, for instance, indoors (studio) or outdoors (under the sunlight). It is time to have a look at *color temperature*.

As humans, our brain is used to adapt the stimuli perceived by our eyes in order to make sense of the world. The perception of color, as the perception of luminosity is relative to the environment – and even influenced by our cultural background – so our brain interprets colors making assumptions, in the case of color temperature, assuming what is the color of light by aligning the appearance of the white. And this happens without you noticing, and you cannot even control it. For instance, in an overcast day, if you walk on the streets you might not pay much attention that the color of the light has a high component of blue (what we identify with "cold"), so every object you observe under that natural light condition will appear naturally bluish, still your brain, understanding the environmental lighting conditions would not trigger the idea that the object is blue, instead you will interpret it with its regular color; and the most curious thing is that if you enter in a building that has the lights on – let's imagine the typical tungsten lights[12] that have a very orangish tone – you brain will adapt its perception of what is white to make sense of the new lighting conditions, so if you take a look at the object again it will look consistent in color, even if there is a real absolute measurable difference between the object under the overcast light and the artificial tungsten light. Our brains are great doing this white balance, constantly and unnoticeably, so anything observed keeps a perceptive consistence of the aspect of its color.

So as our brain constantly "tricks" us to see things in a certain way, we need a measurable system to interpret this aspect. Let's look at a more scientific approach to the white balance so we can understand and use it. This is something that is going to stick with us when we are managing color, so you will need to be sure everyone is aligned with the same aspect of white (and in consequence the relation of all colors).

Color temperature is a characteristic of *visible light*. In physics a so-called *black body*[13] (theoretically something that absorbs all incident light), will radiate light – glow – when it is heated. The spectrum of this light, and therefore its color, depends on the temperature of the body. For instance, you can make this experiment (be careful!), if you heat a needle with a lighter, in the beginning it will eventually glow dark red ("red hot"), if you continue applying heat it will eventually turn yellow (more or less like the filament of a lightbulb but obviously way less intense) eventually bluish-white … (at this point you should stop applying heat now or you are going to get burned and I think you already have got my point!) (Figure 1.19).

Color temperature is conventionally stated in the unit of absolute temperature, the Kelvin[14] (K). Be careful with the terminology here because in the Kelvin scale higher temperature means the color moves from "warm" (reddish) towards "cold" (bluish), this is not like the artistic cold-warm convention, but actually the other way around, and by the way, this scale of temperature is not measured in degrees (so, no ° symbol), just Kelvin. A reddish white will be around 3000 K while bluish whites are on color temperatures over 5000 K.

Let me illustrate a few examples of conventional color temperatures:

- Candle: 1800 K
- Lightbulb: 3000 K
- Studio lamps: 3200 K
- Moonlight: 4100 K
- Daylight: 5500 K
- Overcast Daylight: 6500 K

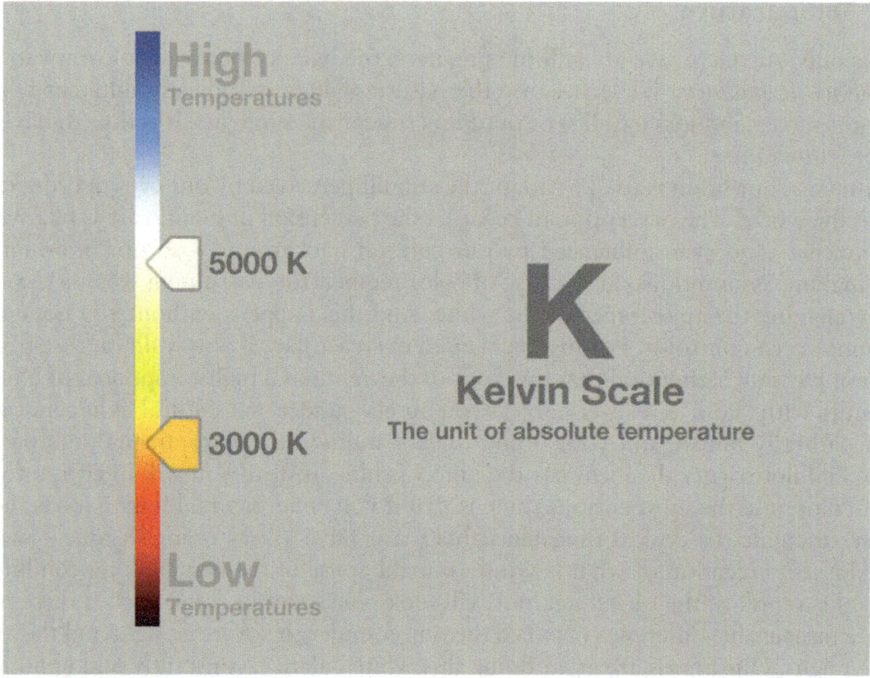

Figure 1.19 The kelvin scale with a temperature gradient simulation

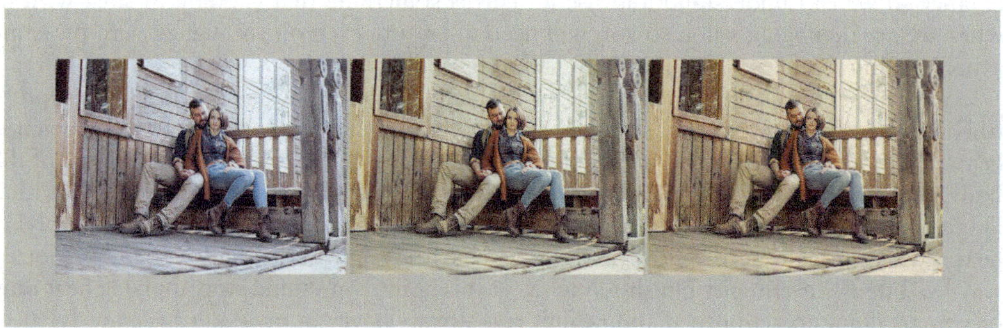

Figure 1.20 Three different white balances for the same image

By changing the balance of the sensitivity of the negative color layers, the film stock could have a white point set for indoors, where lightbulbs conventionally with a filament of tungsten corresponds to 3200 K. And in the other hand, for outdoor a "cooler" white point, set at exactly 5600 K (because under daylight the blue-sky light raises the color temperature of the scene). The idea of using different white points allows cinematographers to faithfully represent the neutrality of the white color, for instance photographing a white piece of paper that will look plainly white, with not abnormal warmer or cooler tones, but simply white. Further adjustments in the color temperature are done by using filters in front of the lens. This is the alchemy of neutrality: white balance (Figure 1.20).

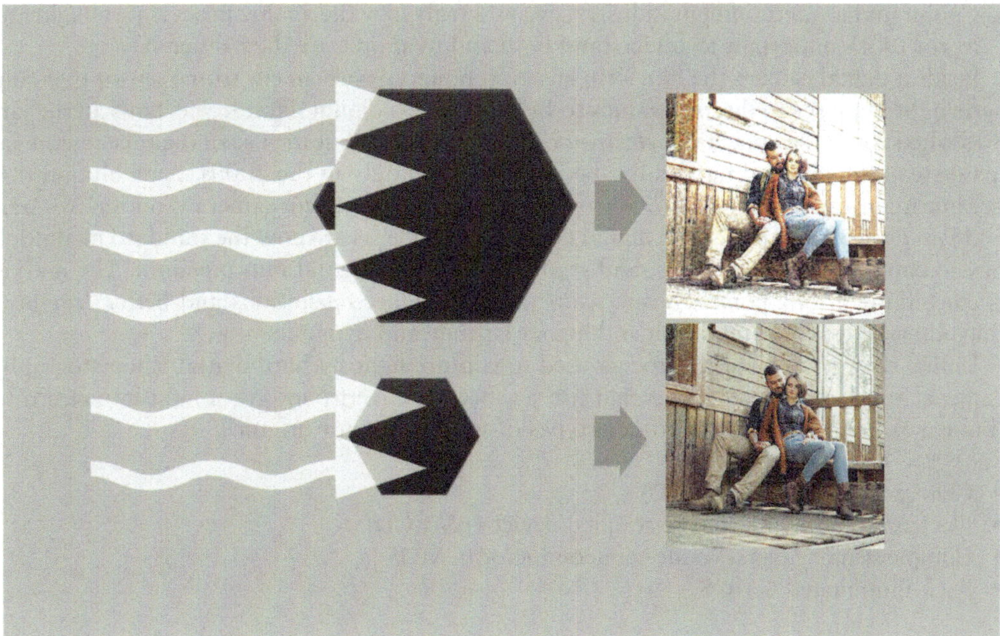

Figure 1.21 Grain size – bigger grain captures more light

Grain Size & Film Speed

This sensitivity of the white point has nothing to do with the ISO,[15] the standardized film speed or sensitivity to light of film stocks. The film speed usually is proportional to the grain size: the faster a film stock is the bigger the grain. Why? Because if the grain is bigger, it will be exposed (hit) by more rays of light so its latent reaction changes faster. But with bigger grain there is a loss in the definition of fine detail (more or less like the concept of pixel resolution, the more pixels – or the smaller the pixels – the more detail you can capture). Another characteristic you can expect is the blue layer to be the noisiest because, as I mentioned before, like in the human eye, the blue sensitive layer needs more light to be correctly exposed, so usually the blue channel would be the noisiest (Figure 1.21).

Film vs Digital Cinema

Before we start discussing this subject let me ask a question that has been around for a long time … *Is film better than digital cinema?* The answer to this question depends on what you consider "better", both have different features, their pros and cons. Hence, I do not like to consider one better than the other but two different capturing mediums. Let me ask you this: *Is watercolor or color pencil better?* Indeed, the question makes no sense. Very important artists are well known for a certain pigment over others, but make no mistake, it is not the brush that makes the artist. As VFX artist you are expected to know both so you can create effects as is they were shot by either of those cameras: film or digital.

Now let's leave aside film negative and let's talk about the digital process. I think we can all agree that digital cameras have contributed to the democratization of visual storytelling in motion, as it's way cheaper and faster than analog film negative process, and this is the key point in the entertainment industry, even if I truly love the analog process results. In any case, for us it's important to understand both and to appreciate their differences.

Inside a digital camera the film strip has been replaced with an electronic sensor that converts light impulses to discreet values to be recorded as digital data. It was Sony in the late 80's who started the concept of *electronic cinematography* but the use of digital cameras for mainstream Hollywood movies has become common only in the 2000s. A revolution that became mainstream with *RED®*, *Silicon Imaging®* or historic film camera vendors like *Arri®* and *Panavision®* that joined the digital era. Digital cameras are now the standard methodology to capture motion pictures, and studios have entire digital film pipelines. The market is converging at one point: cheaper cameras with higher resolutions and better "quality" (including better color rendition and higher latitude and dynamic range).

Unlike the photochemical process used to capture light by film, digital cinematography cameras are electronic machines that use sensors to convert photons of light into electrons (known as photoelectrons). Different types of sensors are, for instance:

- Charge-coupled device (CCD)
- Electron-multiplying charge-coupled device (EMCCD)
- Complementary metal-oxide-semiconductor (CMOS)
- Back-illuminated CMOS

All those sensor types above work using an important property: all electrons have a negative charge. This means that electrons can be attracted using a positive voltage, allowing electrons to be moved around a sensor by applying a voltage to certain areas of the sensor

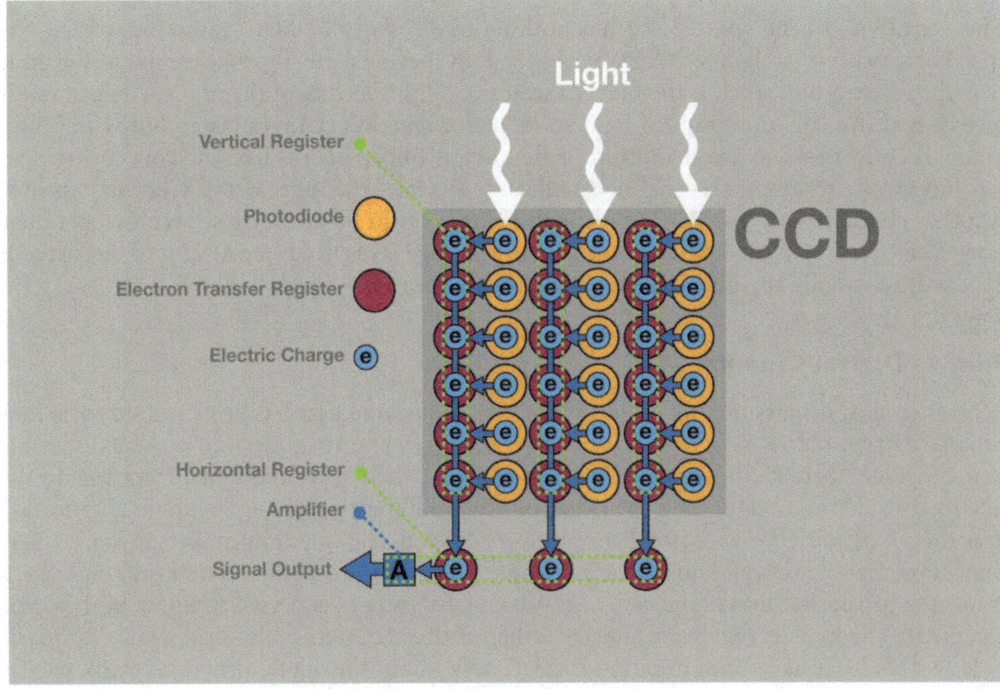

Figure 1.22 Charge-couple device (CCD) structure

where they can be amplified and converted into a digital signal, and ultimately to be processed and displayed as an image. This process happens differently in each type of camera sensor. I would like to dig further into two of the most popular types: the *CMOS* and the *CCD* sensors, so you can see how they work and what are the main difference between them. Even if they are not the only technology available right now and I am sure this technology will continue evolving, the principle of "capturing" photons is mainly the same, I think it is interesting to understand how they work to comprehend the process of image acquisition. Let's have a look at their properties.

The principle of both sensors is somehow similar to how solar panels/cells work; they both convert light into electricity. An oversimplified way to think about a camera sensor is to think of it as an array of thousands of tiny "solar cells", each of which transforms one small portion of light (ray of light) into electrons, then everything is about how to transfer and interpret the accumulated charge of electrons of each photosensitive cell in the image. Let me show you the difference between these two kinds of sensors (Figure 1.22):

CCD

In a CCD, the charge is transported across the chip and read at one corner of the array. An analog-to-digital converter turn each sensor pixel value into a digital value (Figure 1.23).

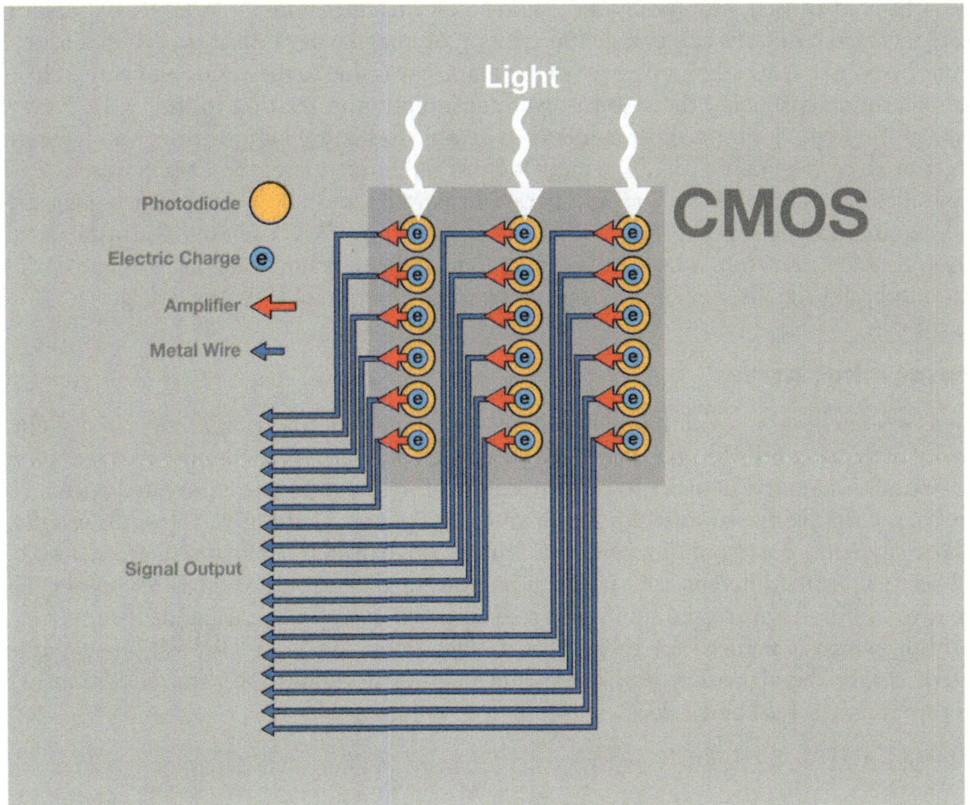

Figure 1.23 Complementary metal-oxide semiconductor (CMOS) structure

CMOS

In most CMOS devices there are several transistors at each pixel that amplify the charge using more traditional wires.

CCD vs CMOS

The CMOS method is more flexible than the CCD because each pixel can be read individually, but CCD sensors have the ability to transport charge across the chip without distortion. CCD sensors were the first available in digital cameras in the 1970s.

Oversimplifying this subject, to avoid the risk of falling into the Rabbit Hole of electronics, the main difference for us, in terms of quality of the image, is that CCD creates "low-noise" images at the expense of lack of speed and sensitivity, making it a challenge to perform low-light imaging or to capture dynamic moving samples. The reason for the low speed is given because there is only one output node per sensor; this means that millions of pixels of signal must be transferred through one node, creating a bottleneck, slowing the capture. Also, if electrons are moved too quickly, it introduces error and read noise, so most CCDs decide to move electrons slower than maximum speed to attempt to reduce noise; and lastly, the whole sensor needs to be cleared of the electron signal before the next frame can be exposed.

In the other hand, CMOS (that existed well before the CCD but became popular after these) have also been adopted by the commercial imaging industry at large, so much that nearly every smartphone camera, digital camera, or imaging device uses a CMOS sensor. The main reason to explain their takeover of the market was due to the easier, and hence cheaper, manufacturing costs, and the lower power consumption in relation to the CCD. New versions of the CMOS sensor allow cameras to be able to feature large sensors and have much larger fields of view than CCD. The main factor that differentiates the CMOS from the CCD is parallelization, as CMOS sensors operate in parallel and allow for much higher speeds and require less power and produce less heat. In addition, CMOS sensors, for instance when shooting RAW, can store a larger dynamic range and could simultaneously image dark signals and bright signals, not subject to saturation or blooming like with a CCD.

Sensor Filter Array

There is something in common between all traditional photosensors: they detect light intensity with just a little to no wavelength specificity, and therefore cannot separate color information. Therefore, in order to capture color information they are provided with a color filter array that is placed over the sensor filtering light at a certain wavelength, usually, as you can imagine, corresponding with our famous three primary colors: red, green, and blue.

There are many different arrays, depending on the disposition of the three colors. Then, the raw capture is processed and converted to a full-color image using a *demosaicing* algorithm, which is tailored for each type of color filter. The color disposition of the filter together with the algorithm of demosaicing highly determines the *color rendition* of the capture (Figures 1.24 and 1.25).

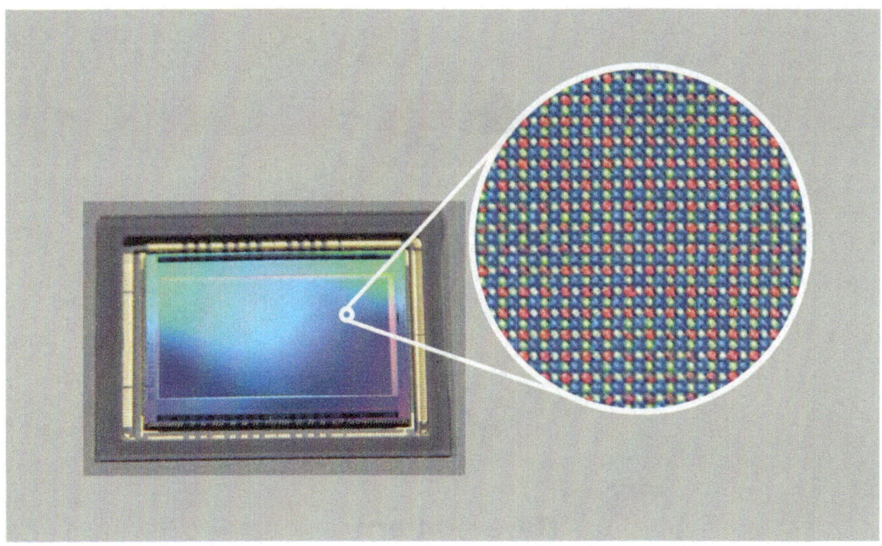

Figure 1.24 Sensor filter array

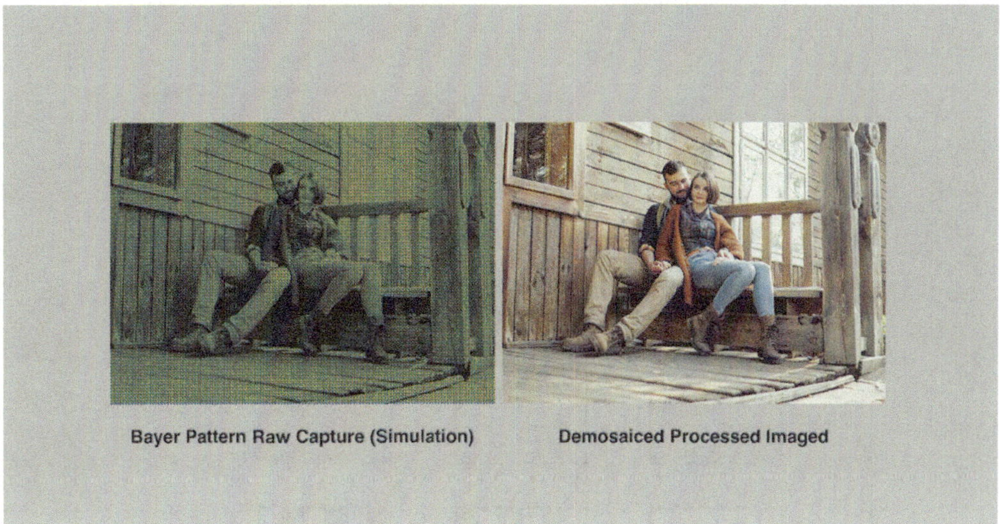

Figure 1.25 Simulation of the image before the demosaicing process

Bayer Pattern

Let's have a look at one of the most famous RGB color filter mosaic: the Bayer pattern (Figures 1.26 and 1.27).

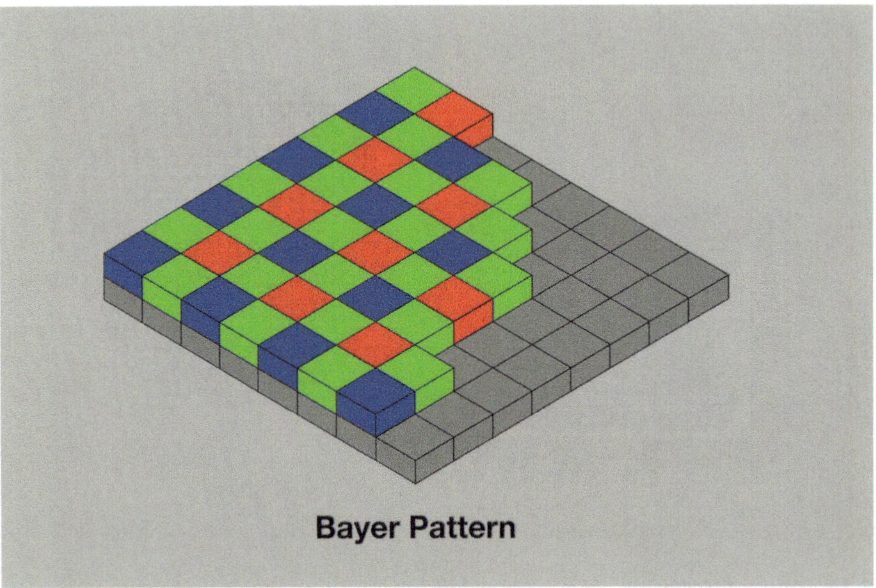

Figure 1.26 The Bayer pattern array. Illustration by colin M. L. Burnett

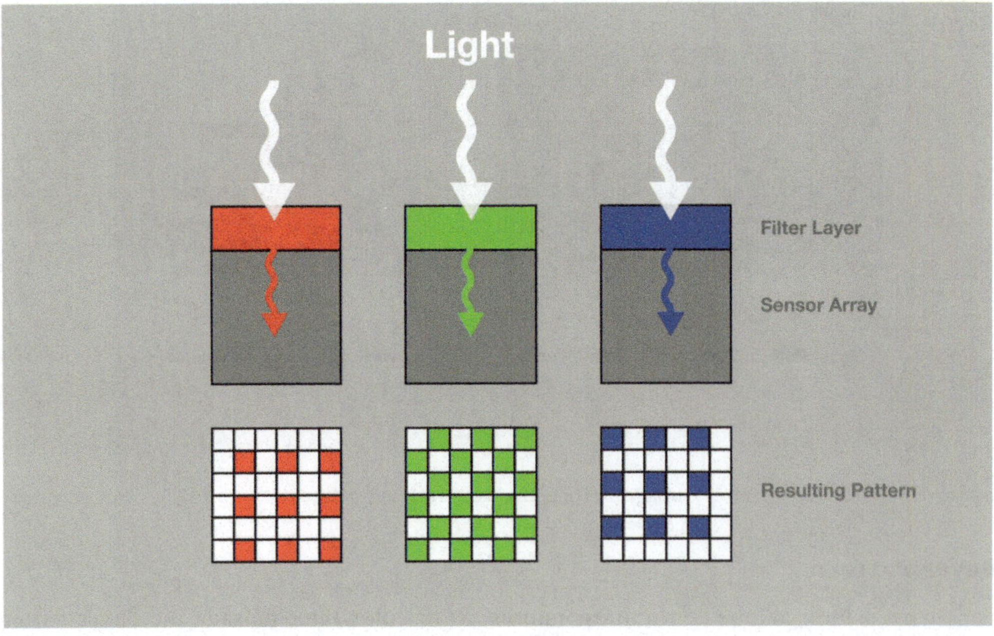

Figure 1.27 Bayer pattern array by components

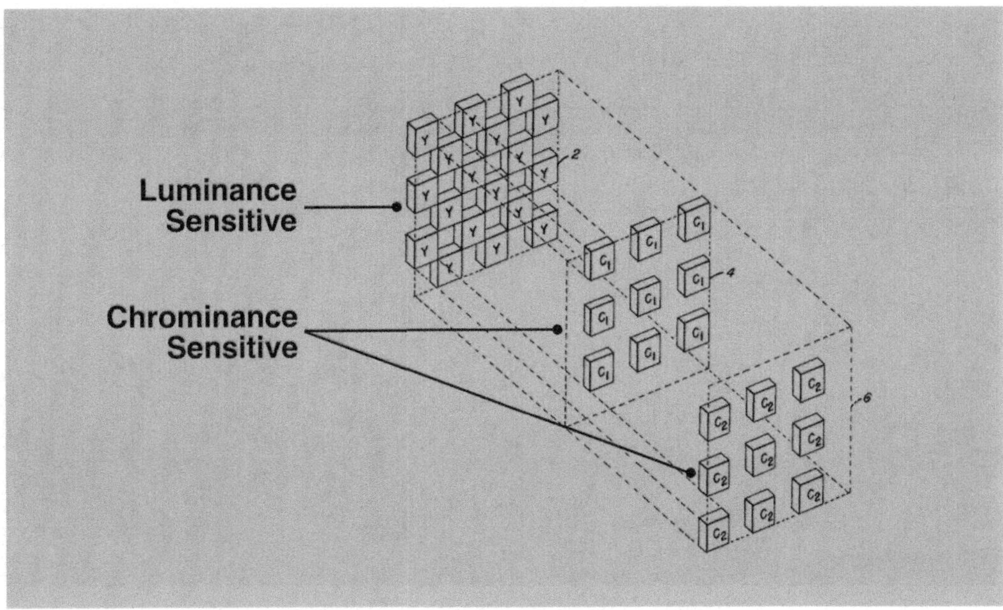

Figure 1.28 Bayer pattern as described in the patent filed by bryce E. Bayer for the eastman kodak company in 1976

Patented in 1976 by Bryce E. Bayer for the Eastman Kodak Company. In his system Mr. Bayer used twice as many green elements as red or blue to mimic the physiology of the human eye, that is much more sensitive to green than the other two wavelengths (Figure 1.28).

He called the green photosensors *luminance-sensitive* and the other red and blue ones *chrominance-sensitive*. In his algorithm the green color drives the luminosity and then the variations of the other two stimuli create the chromatic information.

Luminance vs Chroma

In order to visualize how differently we perceive luminance in relation to chroma information I am going to do an experiment with you. Here is an example of how the human eye is much more sensitive to luminance than chroma information:

In Figure 1.29, there is a FullHD image (1920 × 1080 pixels) with a blur size of 300 pixels applied just in the luminance. The chromatic information is exactly as the original, but you can barely distinguish any shape on the picture.

Let's inverse the process, Figure 1.31 showcases the image with the same amount of blur as before, 300 pixels size, but applied to the chroma components, preserving the luminosity intact. Of course, the color accuracy is not good at all, but your brain is able to decode it and so you can see the picture much clearer than before.

Figure 1.31 displays the original, you can notice not "as much" difference from de blurred chroma than the blurred luma.

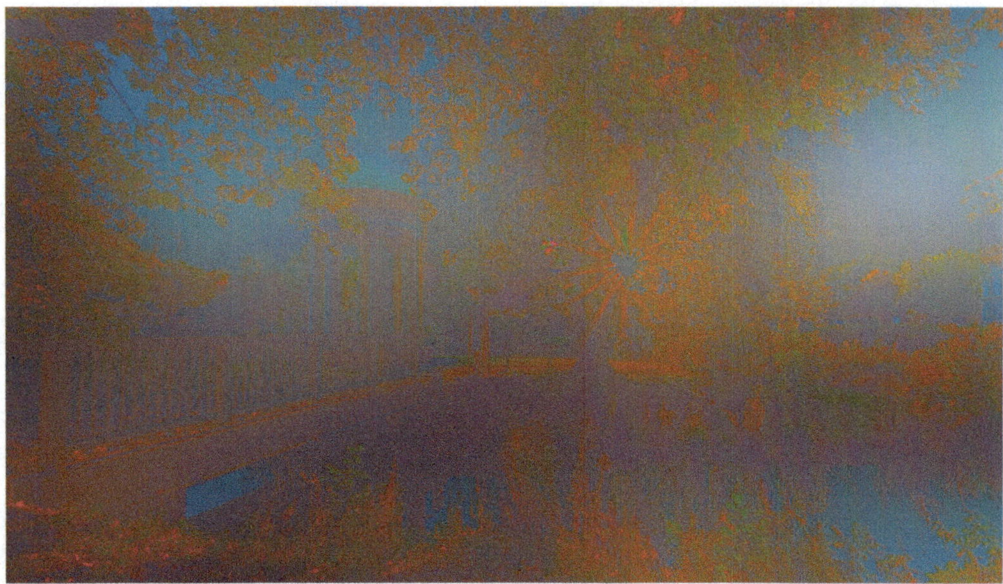

Figure 1.29 FullHD image with 300 pixels size blur applied to its luma information

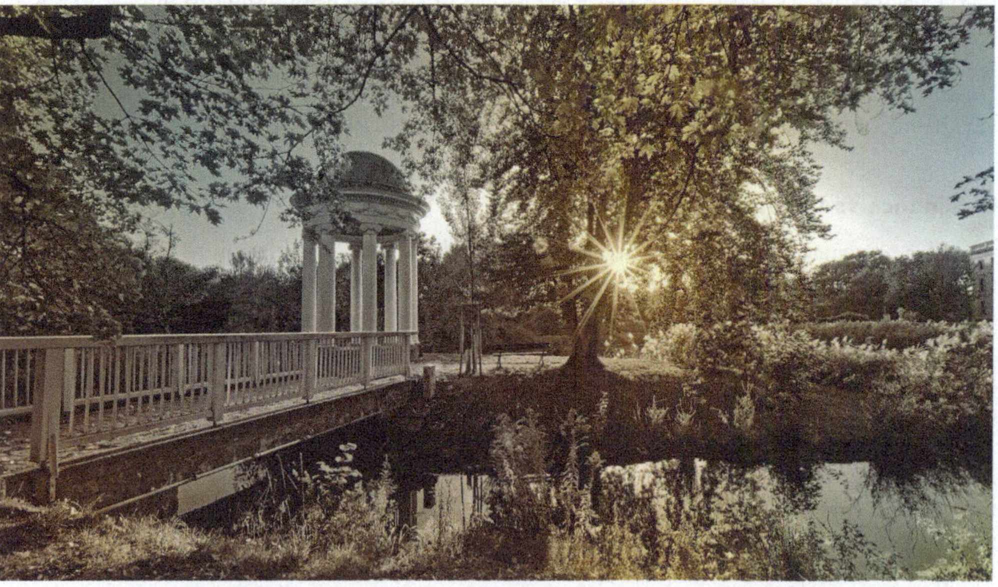

Figure 1.30 The same fullhd image as before but with 300 pixels size blur applied to its chroma information instead

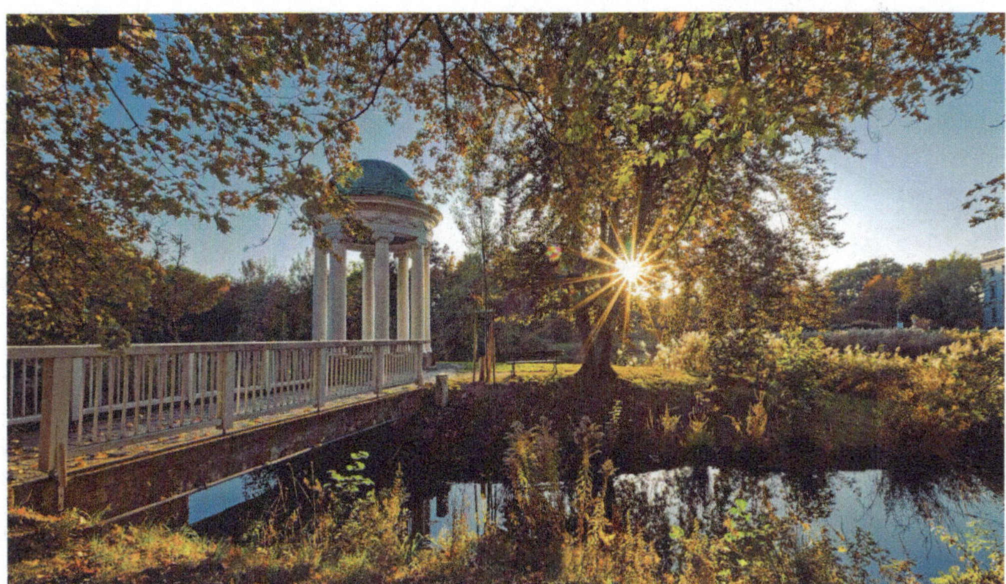

Figure 1.31 Original image

Chroma Sub-Sampling

With the subject of the perception accuracy of luminance (brightness) vs chroma (color) in mind, let's have a look at a useful application. What if we use our perception (or lack of it) to "compress" images in a way that the loss is less noticeable? This takes advantage of the fact that the human eye perceives spatial changes of brightness more sharply than those of color, by averaging or dropping some of the chrominance information in the image. But first of all, why do we need to compress images? Think about it, when talking about the color in an image representation we refer to storing three precise RGB values for every single pixel. In a high definition (HD) image, for instance, with a resolution of 1920 × 1080 pixels we have 2,073,600 pixels; and if we talk about the current high-end TV standards, we have 4K ultra high definition (UHD) with its 3840 × 2160 pixels we reach 8,294,400 pixels … and we are still striving for higher resolutions. So, our 4K UHD imaging systems need to process and interpret over 8 million pixels, each one with its own RGB values, 24 frames per second (also known as *fps*) and higher frame rates! So sometimes it can be overwhelming for cameras or any image data processor to work with so many values, either for electronic reasons or computing capacity. Of course, it can be done, and in fact it is done but it is expensive as we need sophisticated machines to do so. So, is there a way to reduce the amount of data? There are many, but one is especially good because it solves many problems from the top, by disregarding information. The principle is simple: we do not need as much precision for color than for brightness, so we are going to preserve the brightness (luminance/luma) intact, while alternating the collection of color samples between pixels maintaining a practical approximation to color processing and perceptual uniformity so red, green, and blue are processed into *perceptually meaningful* information. In other words, a lower resolution for the color than for the full-resolution capture of brightness. This is chroma subsampling.[16]

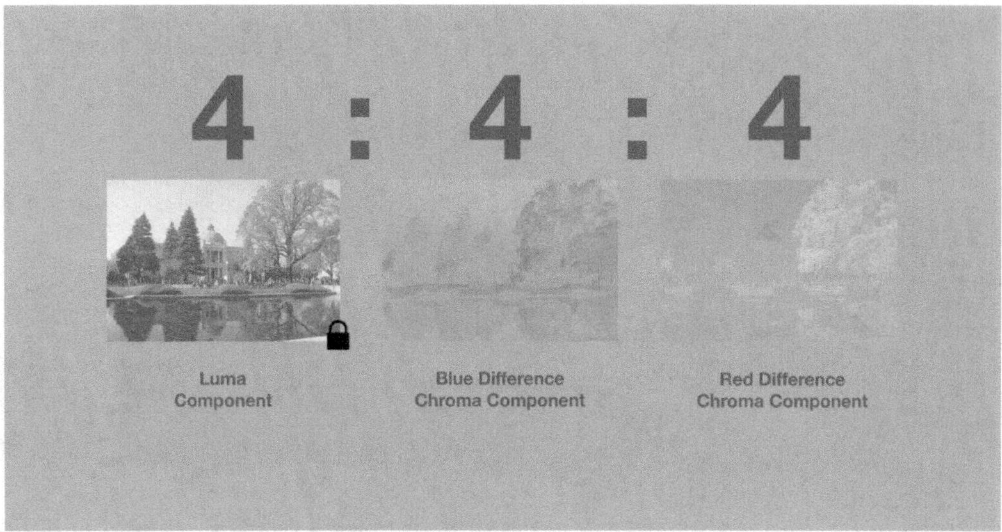

Figure 1.32 Chroma subsampling 4:4:4 (luma component is preserved intact)

Using the RGB model color scientists and engineers developed the YCbCr[17] color space to convert RGB values into luminance Y (or Luma[18] Y′) and chroma C values (C_B for the chroma-difference blue and C_R for the chroma-difference red). The combined luminance data of RGB is encoded separately to create one luminance channel. This data alone makes up a complete and sufficient black and white image. Next, all we need to do is add the color to that curve based on chroma differences from the luminance curve. This way color can be bandwidth-reduced, subsampled, compressed, or otherwise treated separately for improved system efficiency. By storing luminance and chroma data separately, compression algorithms can retain more information where humans are most sensitive and drop information in color where the changes would be "imperceptible". Spoiler alert: for VFX we need all chroma information with no compression or subsampling, especially if we are pulling a key from a green or blue screen, because humans might not notice the missing color information but the tools we use for processing the image, for instance a chromakey will detect the lack of the detail in form of artefacts.

Usually, with top digital cinema cameras, every single frame is captured with this chroma ratio: 4:4:4. The first number stands for the number of luminance samples (remember letter Y); the second for the chroma blue difference number of samples (C_B) and the third for the number of samples in the chroma red difference component (C_R) (Figure 1.32).

A ratio of 4:4:4 means full chroma information. Literally four chroma red samples and four chroma blue samples for every four luma samples. Which is a ratio of 1 to 1.

But this ratio is not common at all in "consumer" cameras, such as smartphones. This 4:4:4 ratio belongs only to high standard digital cinema cameras and film scanners. Capturing a full subsampling image is a heavy process, and a digital film camera has to do it for a high-resolution image at least 24 times every second, which means ultra-fast processors, conductors and drives inside the camera, making them very expensive to manufacture. However, camera manufacturers found the solution to decrease the price, to make it more consumer oriented, just because not everybody needs this high level of chromatic precision to film their cats at home. So just by removing "a little" amount of information from the chroma, where "no one" would notice, making the process much lighter.

With these other ratios were introduced, like the 4:2:2 chroma sub-sampling, adopted for when the chroma subsampling was not so critical, for instance live broadcast events. This means half chroma information than luma (Figure 1.33).

Or even further: 4:1:1 a quarter of chroma in relation to luma or 4:2:0, which is a quarter of chroma but in this case the red chroma difference and the blue ones are alternate in vertical lines, which means, in comparison with 4:1:1, double information in horizontal lines but half in vertical, another way to array the information. 4:2:0 chroma Subsampling is quite popular among consumer cameras, including smartphones (Figures 1.34 and 1.35).

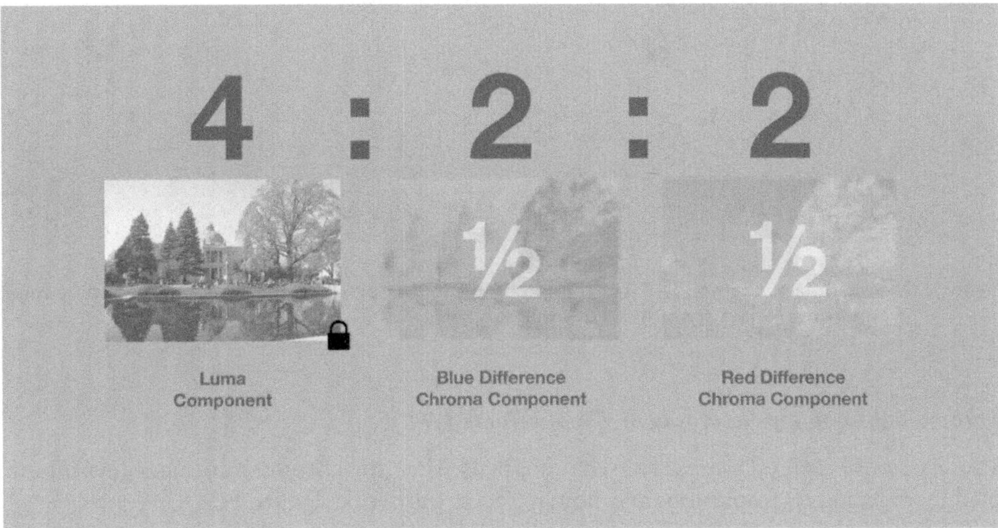

Figure 1.33 Chroma subsampling 4:2:2 (luma component is preserved intact)

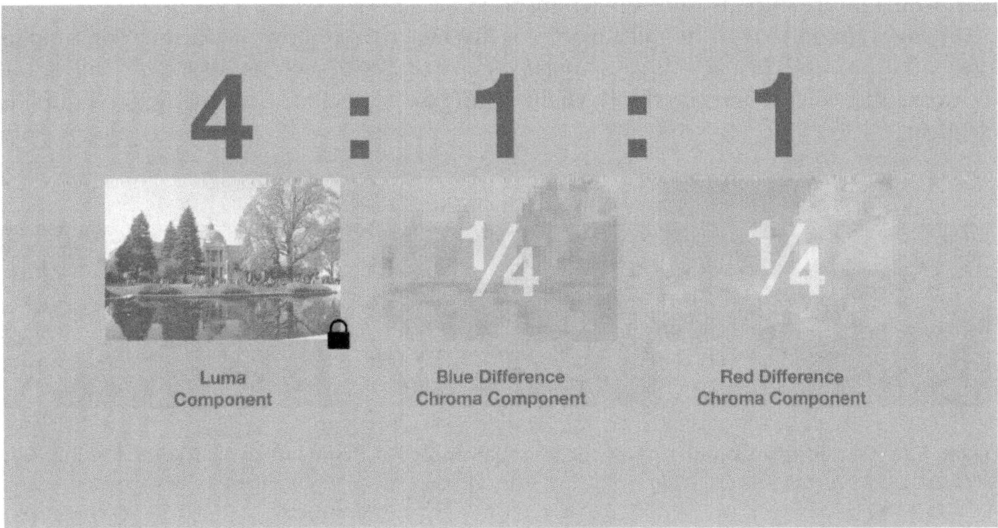

Figure 1.34 Chroma subsampling 4:1:1 (luma component is preserved intact)

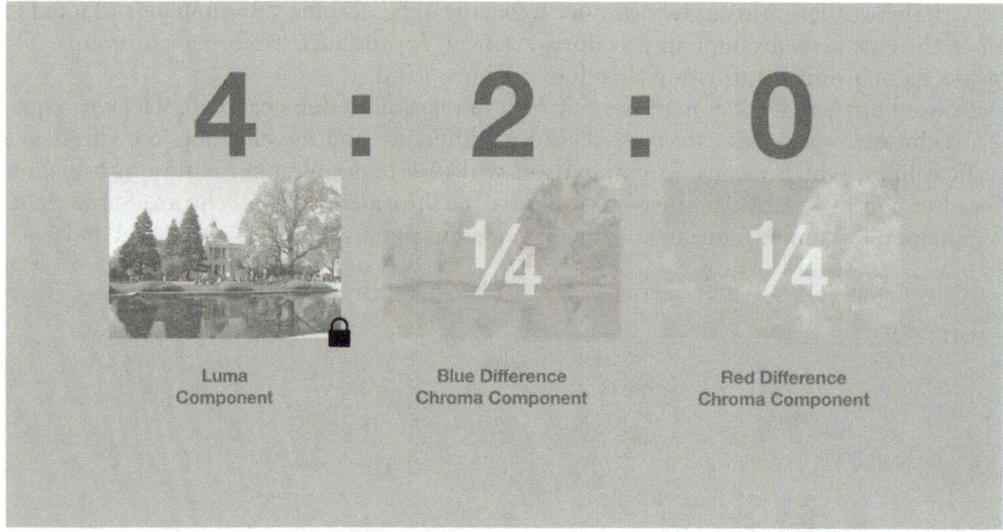

Figure 1.35 Chroma subsampling 4:2:0 (luma component is preserved intact and chroma component alternates from line to line)

Chroma Subsampling Artefacts in visual effects (VFX)

These series of images[19] showcase what happens when the chroma information is subsampled by reducing its resolution, and how it affects our work (Figure 1.36).

The figure above shows a section of the previous image we used for the luma vs chroma Blur experiment. The same detail is illustrated with three different chroma subsamplings: 4:4:4, 4:2:2, and 4:1:1. They all look quite the same, don't they? If you try to find the difference with the original … can you see the difference? I guess you cannot. And, believe me, the chroma information is radically compressed.

Do you want me to try a to pull a matte for this image to see how the chroma subsampling affects the process? Just a simple *channel difference keyer* such as *Keylight®* will do. To showcase the exact difference the Keylight setup has been cloned, so the target values are identical.

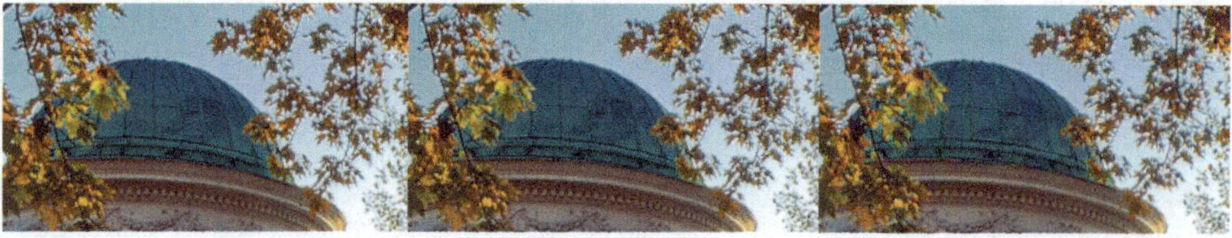

Figure 1.36 Detail with a simulation of chroma subsampled at (from left to right): 4:4:4, 4:2:2, 4:1:1

This first example below displays the original 4:4:4 key pull (Figure 1.37):

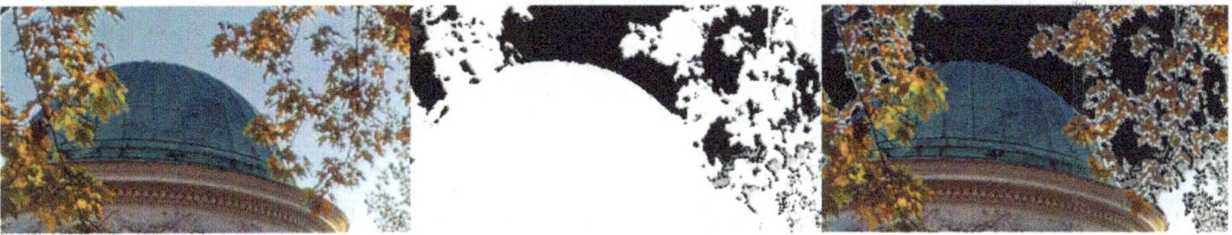

Figure 1.37 Color difference keyer matte extraction at simulated 4:4:4 (from left to right: source, matte, premultiplied result)

The second instance shows the same process applied to the 4:2:2 image (Figure 1.38):

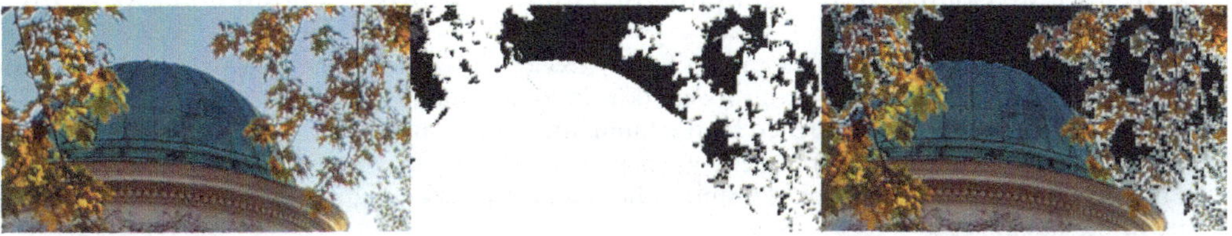

Figure 1.38 Color difference keyer matte extraction at simulated 4:2:2 (from left to right: source, matte, premultiplied result)

The last example represents the keying results of the 4:1:1 (Figure 1.39).

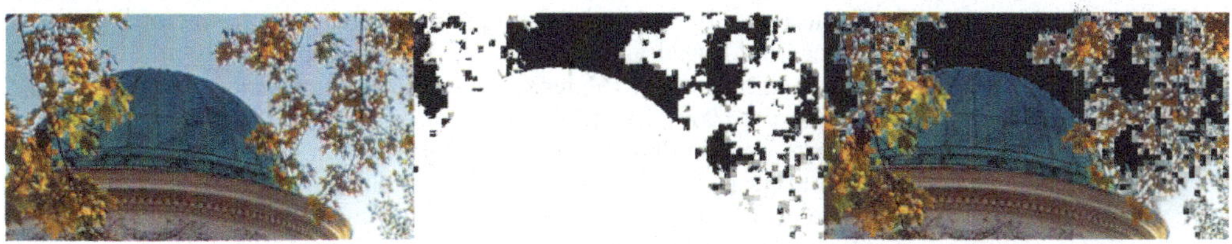

Figure 1.39 Color difference keyer matte extraction at simulated 4:1:1 (from left to right: source, matte, premultiplied result)

Here are the mattes, not very accurate to the edges. The same *Keylight* setup applied to the original image where the colors are the same, but the chroma subsampling had no compression: the edges were smooth and accurate to the shapes of the objects.

That is why we need full information from the capture to manipulate the image. No compression, including no chroma subsampling.

With this we have finished the first chapter about optics elements and the basics of how cameras capture color. We will discuss further elements in the next chapters, but I believe this section has already helped you clarify some concepts that may have already been floating in your mind – because I am sure you heard about them – and maybe you even used them without fully understanding them. Now we are ready to dig deeper into the core of the digital image.

Notes

1 Typically, light is made up of the sinusoidal waves of the electric and magnetic components propagating at right angles to each other; such a light is commonly referred to as nonpolarized light. However, when light is polarized, there is only one direction or plane of vibration. Light that is completely polarized propagates in a sinusoidal uniform helical motion and can be visualized as an ellipse at the end; this is known as elliptically polarized light. Chaudhery Mustansar Hussain, … Maithri Tharmavaram, in *Handbook of Analytical Techniques for Forensic Samples*, 2021. https://www.elsevier.com/books/handbook-of-analytical-techniques-for-forensic-samples/hussain/978-0-12-822300-0?country=IT&format=print&utm_source=google_ads&utm_medium=paid_search&utm_campaign=italyshopping&gclid=CjwKCAjw3POhBhBQEiwAqTCuBlt_EpliH4l1gYIB

2 *Trichromatic*: consisting of three colors. From Greek, *Tri-* comes from τρεῖς (treîs) which means "three"; and *chromatic* comes from χρῶμα (khrôma), meaning "color".

3 *Brightness* is the perception elicited by the luminance of a visual target.

4 *Radiometry* is the measurement of energy or power in electromagnetic radiation fields or light.

5 Photometry is the measurement of visible light in units that are weighted according to the sensitivity of the human eye.

6 *Luma* in video represents the brightness of the current video signal (achromatic, the image without color information), and it is formulated by the contribution of each gamma-compressed color primary to the perception of amount of light. There are different systems to calculate the Luma depends on the standard adopted.

7 *Luminance* is a photometric measure of the luminous intensity per unit area (for instance, reflective light) of the light travelling in a given direction. It describes the <u>amount of light</u> that passes through, is emitted from, or is reflected from a particular area, and falls within a given solid angle.

8 The increments of *exposure* here can be applied by either increasing the amount of light or the time of exposition. For instance, adding double the light – by either physically adding another equal light source or opening the aperture of the lens by double the surface of entrance – would have the same result as exposing the frame for double the time.

9 *LUT*: Look Up Table. It is a term used to describe a predetermined array of numbers that provide a shortcut for a specific computation. In the context of color manipulation, a LUT transforms color input values (for instance camera values) to your desired output values (display ready values to visualize the footage). The subject of LUTs is discussed later in this book.

10 *Tripack* indicates one film strip per color component. Technicolor created also another color capturing process with two-strips system.

11 *Monopack*. All color sensitive layers were contained in a single film strip.

12 *Tungsten light* refers to the most common kind of incandescent lightbulb used to provide artificial light to indoor areas such as your home or office. It features a tungsten filament housed within an inert gas, when a current is passed through the filament, the naturally high resistance of tungsten causes the filament to glow and output an "orange" light. The color temperature of a tungsten light is around 3200 K. Failure to address this in your camera's white balance settings will result in images with a high color temperature, and an overall orange tone.

13 *Black Body*: «An ideal body is now defined, called a blackbody. A blackbody allows all incident radiation to pass into it (no reflected energy) and internally absorbs all the incident radiation (no energy transmitted through the body). This is true for radiation of all wavelengths and for all angles of incidence. Hence the blackbody is a perfect absorber for all incident radiation.» Siegel, R., & Howell, J. R. (2002). *Thermal Radiation Heat Transfer* (Vol. 1, 4th ed.). Taylor & Francis. https://www.routledge.com/Thermal-Radiation-Heat-Transfer/Howell-Menguc-Daun-Siegel/p/book/9780367347079?gclid=CjwKCAjw3POhBhBQEiwAqTCuBk7bHIiMdPAc9LMpgw8nMQ1_aaBjgIRKIHfzfhDV5tNIIjZlfaNXzBoCuEQQAvD_BwE

14 *Kelvin* (symbol *K*): The primary unit of temperature in the International System of Units (SI). Named after engineer and physicist William Thomson, 1st Baron Kelvin (1824–1907). The Kelvin scale is an absolute thermodynamic temperature scale, meaning it uses *absolute zero* as its zero point.

15 *ISO* followed by a number (for instance 400 or 800) represented the sensitivity of a given film emulsion to light, often referred to as "film speed". Higher ISO numbers indicated a greater sensitivity to light.

16 We will discuss the subject of file compression with all its methodologies in the next chapter.

17 *YCbCr, Y'CbCr*, or *Y Pb/Cb Pr/Cr* (also written as $YC_B C_R$ or $Y'C_B C_R$) is a family of color spaces used as a part of the color image pipeline in video and digital photography systems. Y' (with prime) indicates *luma* and is distinguished from Y, that stands for *luminance*. The difference between *luma* and *luminance* is that in *luma* light intensity is nonlinearly encoded based on gamma corrected RGB primaries.

18 *Luminance* vs *Luma*: *Luminance* is the brightness of light as seen by the human eye at a specific angle from a specific surface area; it is regarded as the *perception* or *catching power* of the human eye. *Luminance* is frequently determined by the *brightness* of a surface, and according to the *International Commission on Illumination (CIE)*, it is the linear components sum of the RGB components. Whereas *Luma* is the modified form of the *Luminance*, the prime (') is the *gamma-corrected* component sum of the *Luminance*. *Luma* is the "grayscale" intensity of the image, it is the *brightness* of the present screen or the visual or the black and white image section. As a result, we may say that *Luminance* is the capturing power of brightness, and *Luma* is the determining power of brightness.

19 *Note about Chroma-Subsampling Examples*: To make the concept of Chroma-Subsampling clearer I simulated all examples filtering the Chroma information without any interpolation to showcase the clusters of sub-sampled chroma information. In real case scenarios interpolation and filtering is applied in the various methodologies of encoding resulting in a smoother distribution of the samples improving its appearance but nonetheless resulting in similar artefacts of the exact same kind due to the lack of luma/chroma samples alignment precision.

2

Elements of Digital Color Manipulation

This chapter is oriented to the technologic building blocks of digital color. Here we are going to discuss everything that relates to data representing color to understand how this data can be manipulated. Before we start managing color digitally, we need to know the elements that makes digital data, including some fundamentals of informatics related to digital imaging. I want to make sure you do not get lost in terminology or technology holes when we start discussing complex elements like color spaces or data structures.

Color Data

I strongly believe our language shapes our knowledge. Understanding the origin of words contributes to defining and cataloging new facts, transforming information into knowledge; with this book, I aim to convert knowledge into practical resources. That is why the very first question I need to pop into your mind is, *what the word "digital" actually means?* Once you are a master of the language of our craft, your ability to learn would not be limited by your words. Formulas and facts are as important as terminology.

Digital is a word that nowadays belongs to our everyday vocabulary. It is a term derived from the Latin word *digitum* which means *finger*. But, what is the relation between the fingers of the ancient Romans and the modern computer world? It is thought that **the Roman numbers, I, II, III, IV and V** were born as a convention to write down the number of fingers someone indicates in commerce (imagine the stock market in Wall Street but with togas). A primordial way to express the numbers, how little children express the number of years old they are before even understanding the numerical concept. So, one line (I), like one finger, two lines (II), like two fingers, three (III), even four were noted down with four lines (IIII) – before the more modern sign IV was introduced – the V stays for five, like a hand wide open so the thumb opposite the other fingers forms the V shape of the hand (Figure 2.1).

Therefore, the word *digital* was assigned to things related with numbers, and computers are nothing more, and nothing less, than very sophisticated calculators able to process a massive number of digits … much faster than Romans with their fingers for sure.

Our digital images are arrays of numbers that are interpreted and processed to render a picture on a display. The minimum unit of information that compounds the image is the *pixel*, a word that is made of the contraction of two terms: *picture* & *element*.

Every pixel has an address in the image and every single one has stored its own numerical values that will be processed as a color value. The complexity of this number is directly related to the complexity of the color. In color management one of the most important parts

DOI: 10.4324/b23222-3

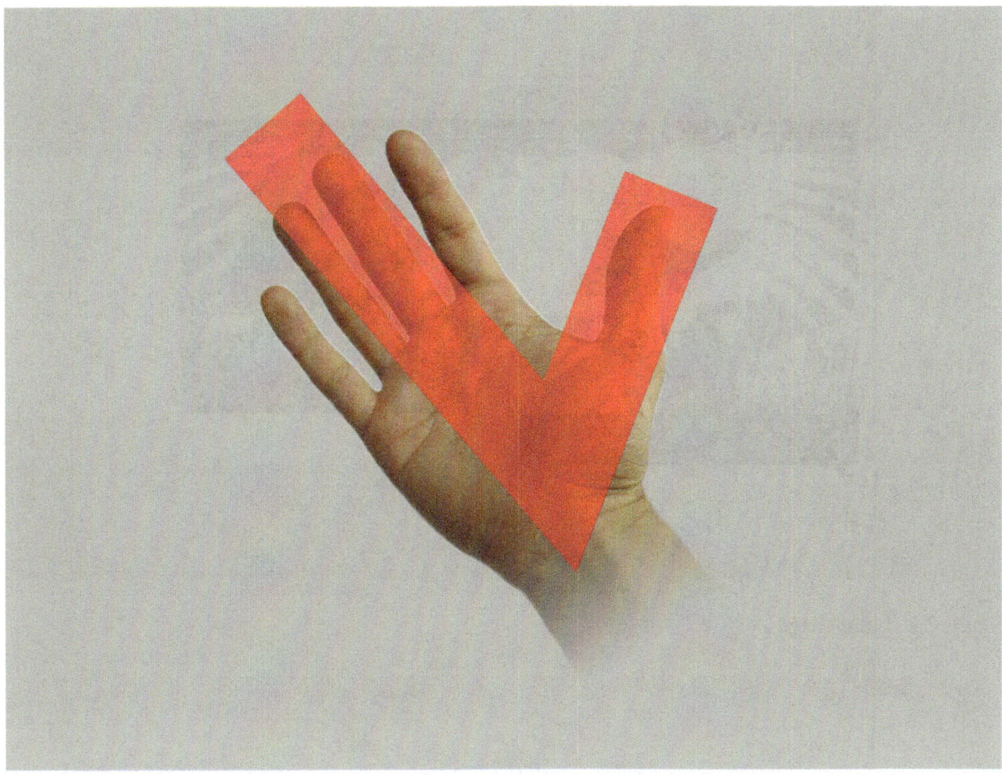

Figure 2.1 Number 5 in roman numeral is V (the whole hand)

is to ensure those values are interpreted the right way, end-to-end, from the way the pixel was generated, manipulated, and depicted.

The basic unit of information a computer can store is the *bit*. A bit, another word made from a contraction: *binary & digit*. It has two possible distinct states, and we usually denote them as 0 and 1. I will discuss this subject later in this book in a deeper manner in Chapter 7, but I think it is a good idea to identify here the very fundamentals of computer data structure in order to proceed with other building blocks of the digital image.

I'm going to arbitrarily assign a "color" to each of my two possible values: black for value 0, and white for value 1. Well, just with one bit to represent "color" we can create a digital image … but we are far from a photorealistic image. We have an image with either black or white pixels. Imagine every pixel as a lightbulb: we can either switch it on or switch it off, because those would be the instructions for the "display", every pixel is a tiny "lightbulb" that we are instructing to switch on or off based on the value of its 1-bit to represent the image. If we want more definition we need gradients, we need more bits to assign "grey" values between white and black (Figure 2.2).

If we add another bit to define color, we will have 2-bit. With this we can reach double the number of possible values resulting from the combination of the two available states (0 and 1). These are the four available combinations: 00, 01, 10, and 11. So we can attach to those values these possible "colors"[1]: black, white and two specified shades of grey (that can

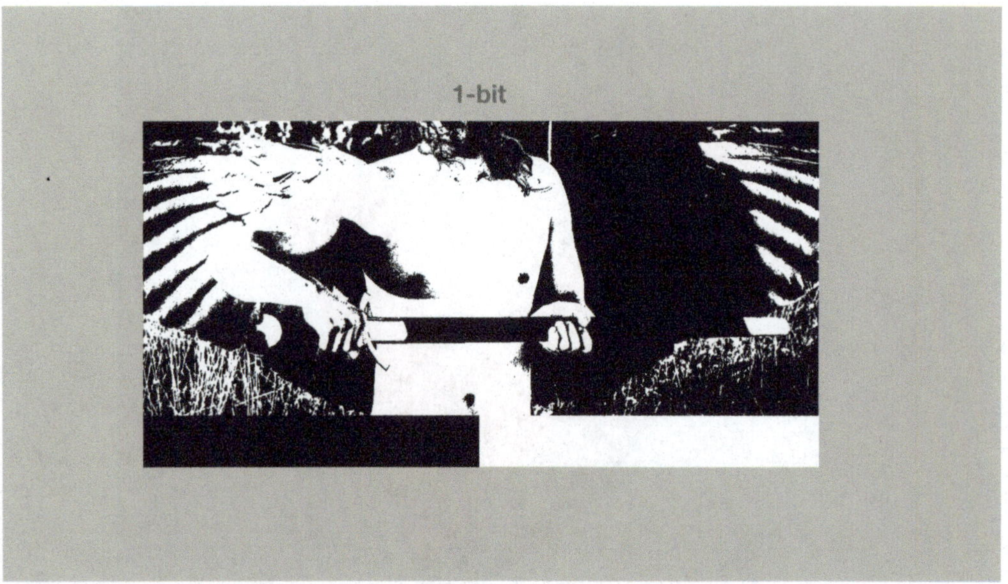

Figure 2.2 **1-Bit image**

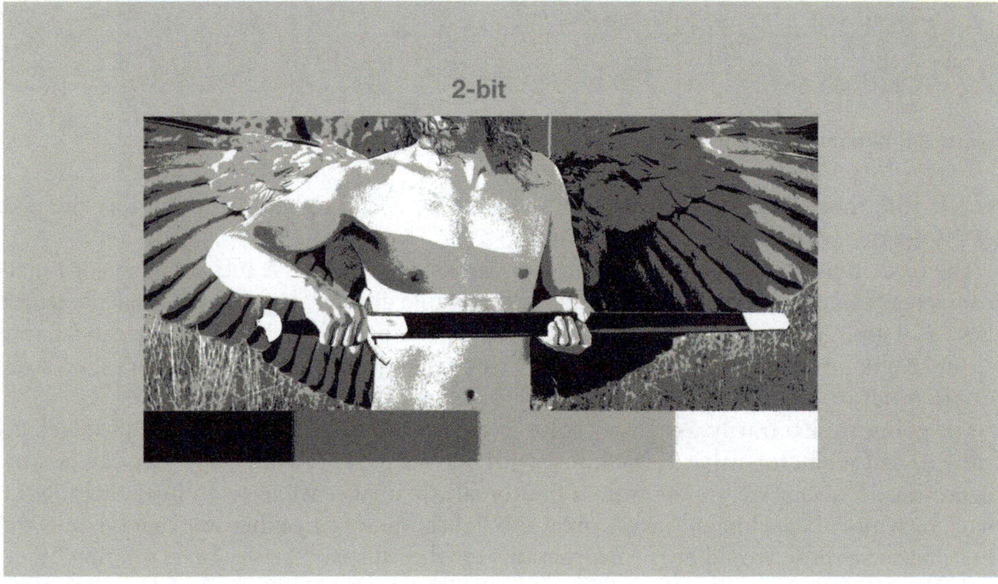

Figure 2.3 **2-Bit image**

be one third of white for one resulting in a dark grey; and two thirds of white for the other resulting in a bright grey) (Figure 2.3).

If we add one more bit, 3-bit, we double again the number of the previously available values, so we now have 16, making available more grey shades between the black and the white (Figure 2.4).

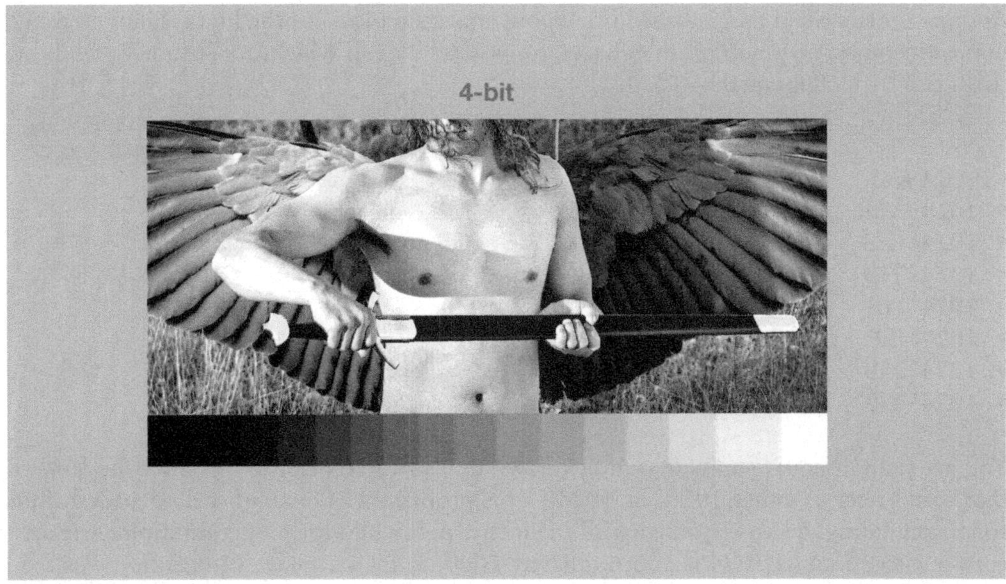

Figure 2.4 **4-Bit image**

And so on, the more bits you have the more intermediate states you have available for the "lightbulb" to be dimmed. But keep in mind the appearance of the end assigned colors, white and black remain always the same, we are just achieving higher precision for intermediate states between fully on (white) and fully off (black), adding more bits would not make you "lightbulb" brighter.

We can arrange bits in so called *words* by grouping bits, combining states, and assigning a different color to any possible *word*, with its unique combination of bit values.

For data storage we use the convention of *bytes*. A *byte* is a unit of digital information that most commonly consists of eight bits (bit-value combination of one byte examples are: "01010101", "11110000", "11001100", "11111111").

Its unit symbol is *B*. Be careful not to confuse *bits* and *bytes*, they are two very different things. The *byte* has two different orders of magnitude to express different multiple-bytes units, one that follows the decimal metric system that goes with exponential increments of 1000, that we will refer to as *Power of 10* units:

                             Metric System Unit

- 1000 kB   kilobyte
- 1000^2 MB   megabyte
- 1000^3 GB   gigabyte
- 1000^4 TB   terabyte
- 1000^5 PB   petabyte
- 1000^6 EB   exabyte
- 1000^7 ZB   zettabyte
- 1000^8 YB   yottabyte

And the other system that is based on exponential increments of the literal binary base (2^x) unit of memory, a system of units based on powers of 2 in which, for instance, 1 kibibyte (KiB) is 2^{10} which is equal to 1024:

	IEC Standard Unit		*Customary Convention Memory Units*	
• 1024 KiB	kibibyte	>>>	KB	kilobyte
• 1024^2 MiB	mebibyte	>>>	MB	megabyte
• 1024^3 GiB	gibibyte	>>>	GB	gigabyte
• 1024^4 TiB	tebibyte	>>>	TB	terabyte
• 1024^5 PiB	pebibyte			
• 1024^6 EiB	exbibyte			
• 1024^7 ZiB	zebibyte			
• 1024^8 YiB	yobibyte			

You are right, there are units that indicate two different numbers, for instance the *terabyte*, that could refer to either 1000^2 or 1024^2. This problem was born in early decades of personal computing, because of the use of the metric prefix kilo for binary multiples arose as a convenience, because 1024 is approximately 1000. The *Customary Convention* was made popular by Microsoft® Windows® operating system and used also by Apple®, before switching to units based on *powers of 10*, with their Mac OS X® 10.6 Snow Leopard and iOS 10®. So, it is normal that there is still a residual amount of confusion with the units, and even the confusion to write the units: is it *kB* or *KB*? Depends on what you meant: *kB* is 1000 bytes; *KB* is 1024 bytes. The trick is that aside from this exception all the other units of bytes – in the *power of 10* scale (and convention) – contain only two letters and they are always uppercase (for instance: MB, GB, TB, ...).

Nowadays the market has been aligning toward the use of the *powers of 10* units to disambiguate any confusion. The IEC[2] further specified that the kilobyte should only be used to refer to 1000. For me it is important that you understand there are two ways to calculate the number of possible values of bit combinations or words, because sometimes we will use powers of 10 (mostly for memory storage) but when referring to the number of bits for color (bit-depth) we will remain with the binary base (2^x) to calculate the number of available "colors".

Returning to the *bit*, we can easily deduce that the higher number of bits in our image to define color data, the more shades – or gradients – we get from "black" to "white". This is called color *bit depth*. Obviously, increasing the bit depth, the size of the file storing the image increases and therefore the process load rises with the same progression. Remember color information is stored for every single pixel so the combination of image bit depth together with image resolution (image size format) will highly influence the file size (Figure 2.5).

Traditional computer monitors display images at 8-bit *per channel* (which means per primary color: R, G and B). If you do the math (2^8) it means 256 values for every channel, which combined are $256^3 = 16,777,216$ different color combinations, yes, over 16 million colors! Keep in mind that, as I mentioned in the previous chapter, the human eye can distinguish about 10 million colors, so in theory less than the color resolution of an 8-bit image. This is very important because it means an 8-bit color bit depth is able to contain enough color values to represent a photoreal picture (Figure 2.6).

Eight bits in every channel makes a total of 24 bits per file, *bit per pixel* (bpp) – or a 32-bit image if we include an 8-bit *alpha channel* to indicate a matte for "transparency" (Figure 2.7).

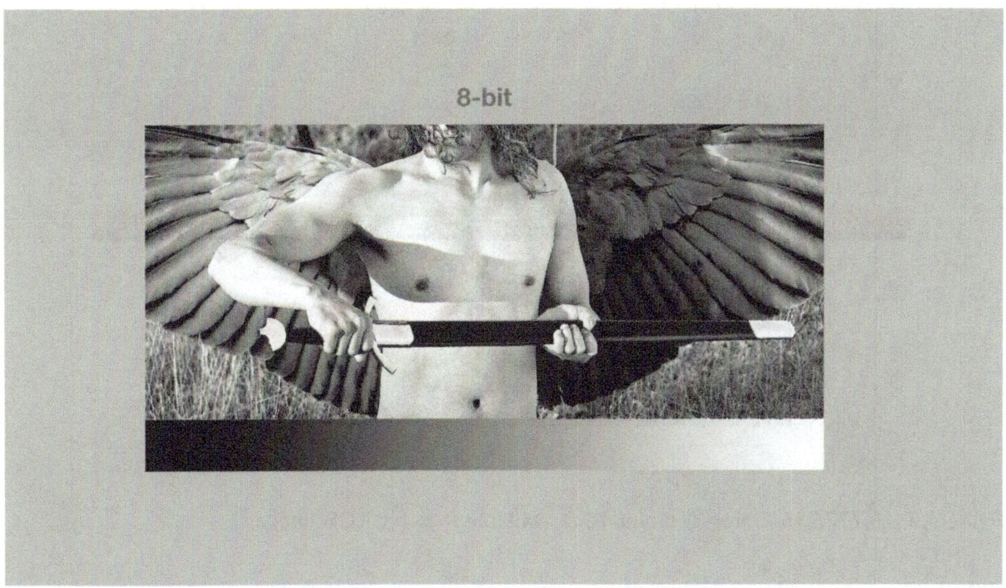

Figure 2.5 8-Bit image

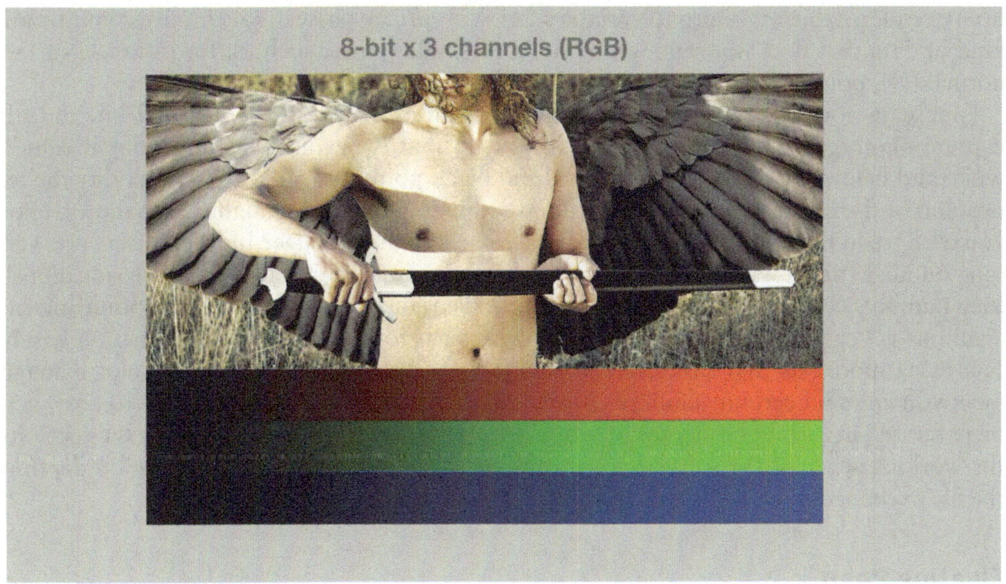

Figure 2.6 8-Bit per channel (RGB) image

However, be careful not to confuse a *32-bit image* with a *32-bit per channel image*, there is a massive difference. Know your bits! When talking about the color bit depth of an image we usually refer to the number of bits as *bit per channel*, so a 32-bit image means: 32-bit for red, 32-bit for green and 32-bit for blue – and for any other channels contained in the image, unless specified otherwise.

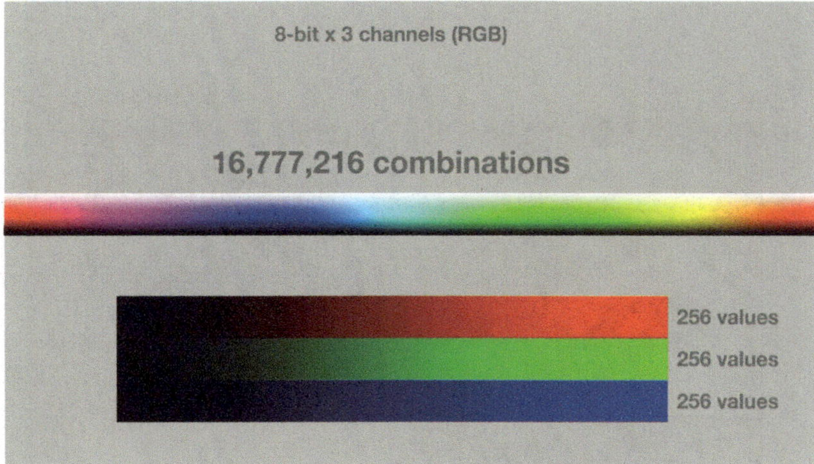

Figure 2.7 16,777,216 Color combinations available in 8-bit RGB image

32-bit *per channel* images have been designed to store extremely accurate *linearly distrib-uted*[3] color information. Not all file formats support this high bit depth. A good example of commonly used 32-bit file format is the *OpenEXR* file (exr), specially used for certain CGI utility render Arbitrary Output Variables (AOVs) (*utility* passes) which only contains any kind of data that does not represent lighting or shading info, such as, for instance, surface normal (N), point (Pixel) position – in the 3D word – (P), depth (Z), …, etc.

Film scans could be captured at 16-bit linear, half of the precision of the 32-bit, and still capture photoreal color information … and data that is beyond the conventional value 1 white and below the value 0 (negative values) black points, so you can even modify the ex-position of the film scan in postproduction revealing details in highlights or shadows. Have you tried to do the math for the result of 32-bit per channel image? Indeed, it is a very, very long number (that I will tell you below). As you can imagine processing those ridiculously long numbers could be very time consuming – even for fast computers – so optimizing cal-culations is key, one good approach to this matter is to use the bits of information wisely. Not using more bits than you need would be a good starting point, but in color manage-ment you will find certain standards for handling files that will constrain data to flow or to be processed in certain bit depths, it would be even normal to have a different bit depth for the working space of the software operating the color manipulations, and the bit depth of the file exchange or delivery to transfer the data.

Floating Point

We have been using the bits of the bit depth to define integer numbers;[4] however, this is not the only way to use those bits to store data and represent values. Let's talk about *float*.

The *float* is a computer number format able to represent a wider range of numeric values than the same use of the 32 bits in integer formulation. Its full name is *single-precision floating-point format*, also known as *FP32* or *float32* – but we will refer to it most of the times as *floating-point* or simply as *float*. A *floating-point* variable can represent a wider range of numbers than a *fixed-point*[5] variable of the same bit width at the cost of precision,

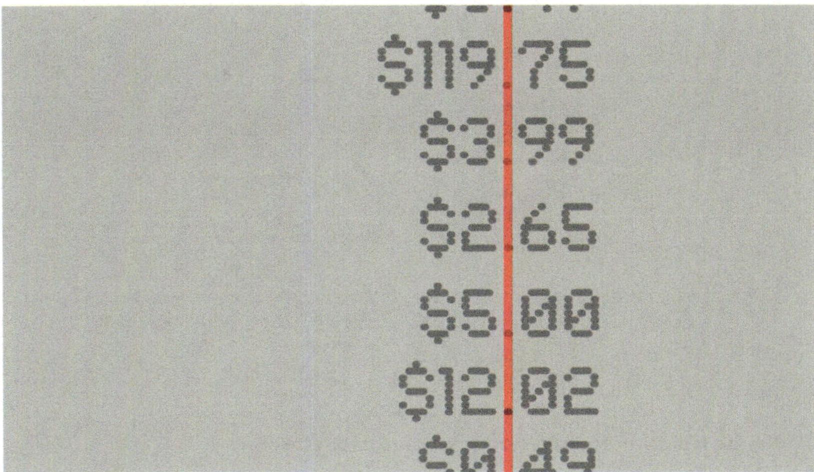

Figure 2.8 Supermarket prices are usually listed in fixed-point format to indicate cents

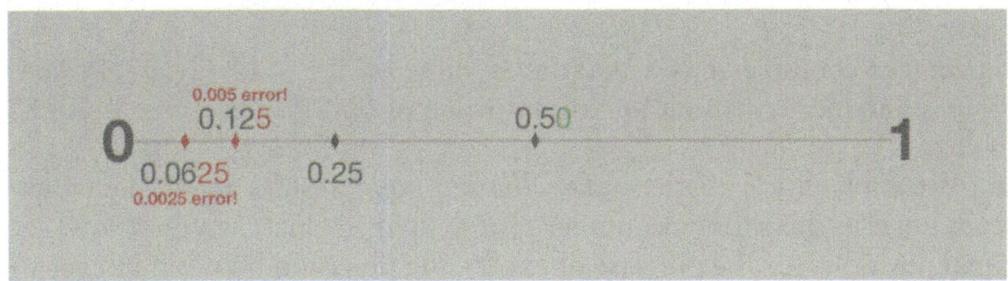

Figure 2.9 The fixed-point precision dilemma

furthermore *fixed-point* number representation is considered to be more complicated and requires more computer resources than the *floating-point* representation: so, *float* is literally faster to calculate than *fixed-point* (Figures 2.8 and 2.9).

So, to avoid confusion between referring to the bits of a 32-bit *per pixel* image, meaning 8-bit per channel in a RGBA image; and a 32-bit floating-point per channel image, we can conventionally refer to the second as just *float*.

The most commonly used floating point standard is the IEEE[6,7] standard, the one we use here.

This is the expression of a 32-bit floating point variable: *significand* (*s*) divided by the *base* (*b*) to the power of the *significant precision* (*p*) minus 1, and the result of that times the *base* to the power of the *exponent* (*e*) width. Maybe the formula this time is easier to read: $(s \div b^{p-1}) \times b^e$ (Figure 2.10).

How are those 32 bits distributed and stored in the computer memory? Let me show you:

- 1 bit for the *sign bit*: to express positive or negative
- 8 bits for the *exponent width*
- 23 bits for the *significand precision*, actually it represents 24 levels, because the *significand precision* = 1 is not required to be accounted (because anything to the power of 1 does not change its resulting value).

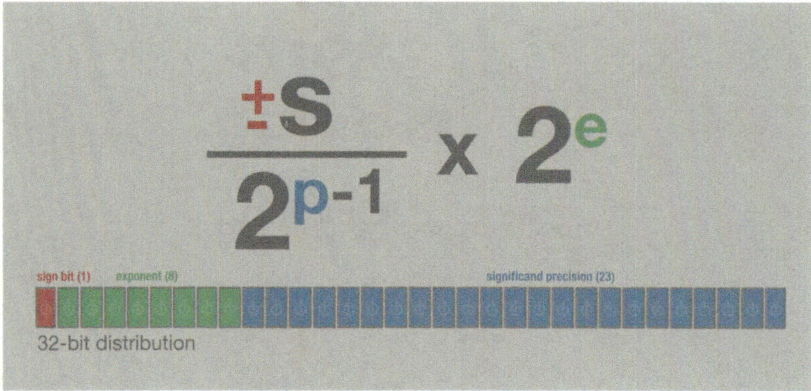

Figure 2.10 Bits distribution for the floating-point data structure

And the space it needs to be stored is 4 *bytes* of memory.

This option offers you from 6 to 9 significant decimal digits precision, for us, in practical terms it allows representing color value increments of 0.00000001 for each component.

A 32-bit *integer* container has a maximum value of: $2^{31} - 1 = 2,147,483,647$; while a *floating-point* container reaches a maximum value of $(2 - 2^{-23}) \times 2^{127} \approx 3.4028235 \times 10^{38}$ per channel![7]

The simplest explanation of the name *floating-point* resides in the fact that the *point* symbol[8] contained in the rational number represented – which as you know, serves to express decimal positions for the purpose of expressing precision between integer values – can move to expand the level of precision as required, opposite to the fixed-point variable that always contains the same number of decimal positions regardless of the precision required. For instance, a number with 7 *fixed* decimals will be limited to the maximum level of precision of its smallest fraction: 0.0000001; while the floating point has a specific control (the *exponent* associated with the *base* of 10 that we use to multiply the *significand* in a scientific notation,[9] as expressed in the formula of the *maximum value* above) to position the *point* symbol moving it – or *floating* above the decimal positions – to accommodate as many decimals as required to express the precision of the represented number; so in the example of the 7 fixed we have 0.0000001 we can say the point has "floated" 7 digits (adding decimal positions) above the number 1, expressed in scientific notation as 1×10^{-7}, where the exponent $^{-7}$ expresses the number of positions the point will "float" over the number – to the left – leaving the *1* to "sink below zeroes". If the exponent was positive instead (1×10^{7}), the *point* symbol would float in the other direction – to the right – becoming an indicator of a big number, making zeroes to sink below the original number *1*. Resulting in 10,000,000. By changing the exponent of the base 10 you make the point symbol to float by a certain number of digits in one direction or another. With the fixed point you will always have the same number of decimal positions regardless of the precision required to express any given number; even to represent just a whole number, and so, following the same previous example of a number with 7 *fixed* decimals: 1 would be represented as 1.0000000, with a consequent waste of digits to express an unnecessary amount of precision (and remember, digits occupy bits of computer storage). I hope this example helps you understand the logic of the *floating-point* name.

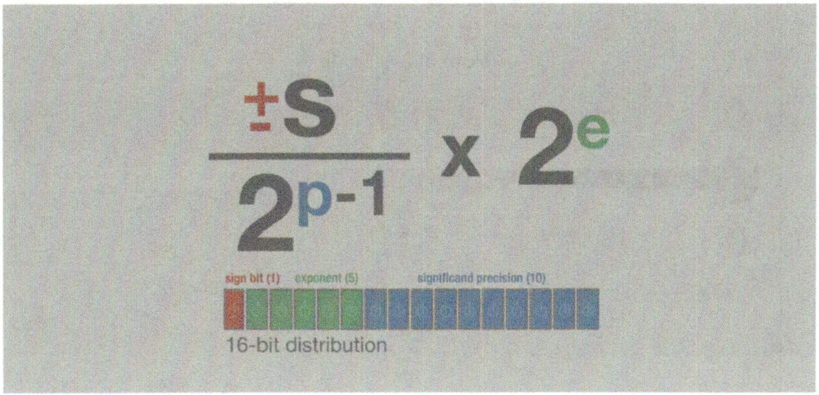

Figure 2.11 Bits distribution for the half-float data structure

Half Float

The high level of precision of the *float* variable is not always necessary, and it is way heavier and slower to process than, for instance, the common 8-bit image; but in the other hand, 8-bit with its mere 256 values, quickly runs out of precision during image processes. Is there a good compromise to reduce the number of bits used while using the same effectiveness of using those bits with a similar *float* methodology to optimize the bits used and increasing their scope of values able to be represented? The answer to this question came in 2002 as the result of the research of *Nvidia* and *Industrial Light & Magic*, establishing the *16-bit half-float*, also known as simply *half-float*. Representing less precision than the 32-bit full float but also half memory storage and consequently fewer processing times (Figure 2.11).

With just 2 *bytes* it stores:

- 1 *sign bit*
- 5 bits for the *exponent width*
- 10 bits of *significand precision*

As you can see, we are now handling gigantic numbers, and this could make it quite difficult to understand the position of certain numbers in the order of scale to represent the magnitude on intensities and their fractions. It is time to discuss normalization.

Normalization

Would it not be easier to find a scale of the scope of brightness values that is friendlier than using the integer scale of 8-bit that ranges from 0 to 255? So in an 8-bit range we have 256 values, so the mid-point would be value 128 … but these numbers are a bit tricky to understand if we move from the conventional halves or doubles, like, what is the percentage of the brightness of value 87 in the same 8-bit scale? Or if I composite an 8-bit with a 10-bit image, the same integer value is going to represent different percentages due to the different scope of the bit depth of the two images. We need a conventional way to express those brightness values to be aligned with a numerical scale that makes sense for all bit depths. That is normalization.

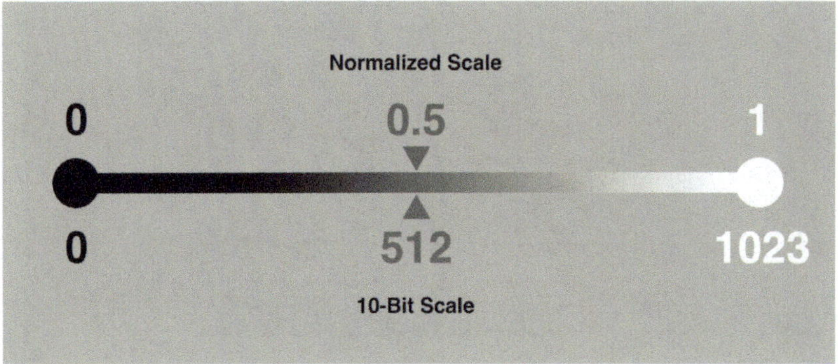

Figure 2.12 Normalized scale vs bits value scale

What I mean with "*normalizing* the values" is to remap the minimum value and set it to 0, and the maximum value of the 8-bit monitor to 1, so we compress all those values between 0 and 1 using decimal positions to express the values in between. Now it is way easier to calculate the mid-point between 0 and 1: indeed, 0.5. This number sits in the same relative position as 128 in the 8-bit scale (Figure 2.12).

In mathematics, in theory, you can divide any number as many times as you like, theoretically even infinite times. However, in more practical terms in our case, we could divide those numbers constrained by the level of precision of the bit depth in use, that in terms of color management, usually we will be handling in a workspace with a minimum of 32-bit float (remember the ginormous maximum value of the *float*? Yes, practically *infinitesimal* number divisions). So, we can do the same "infinitesimal" split of values from the maximum value of our normalized scale: 1. Half of 1 is 0.5; half of 0.5 is 0.25; half of 0.25 is 0.125; half of 0.125 is 0.0625, and so on (by the way, have you notice the *point* "floating" above the decimals). Notice that to define a smaller fraction we require more numbers to be placed, corresponding to the *decimal positions*, more *precision* means more digits in the number represented upon need.

Conventionally, image processing software displays color values in a fixed-point fashion with a certain fixed number of decimals, this does not indicate in any case the way the software is handling color behind the hood. To make a concrete example, Nuke in its viewer, the information displayed for the color average of the sample area is represented by four numbers (corresponding to RGBA) rounded to five fixed decimal positions – which is not precise enough to present the precision of *float*, while the pixel analyzer panel displays the information in *full float* precision up to seven decimal digits that will appear only if required by the rational number displayed; in any case, this software internal workspace is 32-bit float, so every image is handled with that level of precision (Figure 2.13).

We commonly refer to normalization to contextualize the luminance values of an image within the luminance range values of the monitor (usually referenced within a. 8-bit scale), having as a reference 0 as the lowest black achievable by the monitor and 1 as the maximum luminance and any step in between using rational numbers with decimals for precision. The rest of the values above 1 will be scaled proportionally to the luminance scale of the referenced 8-bit scale (the monitor scale).

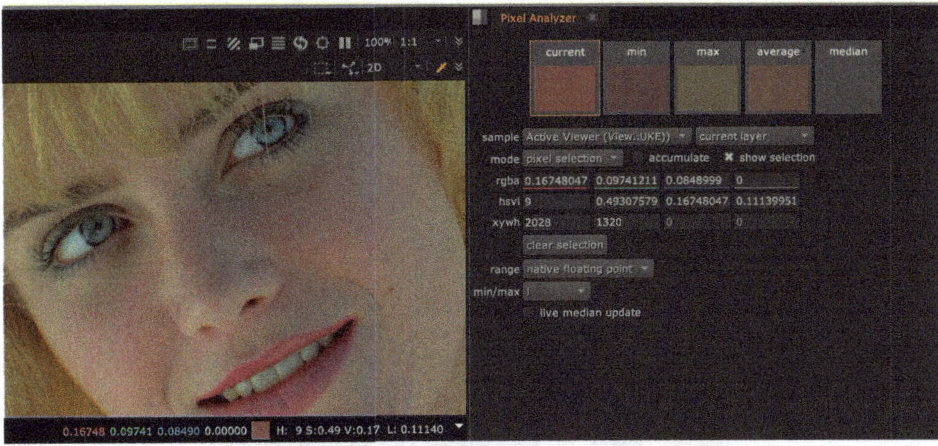

Figure 2.13 Nuke viewer values vs pixel analyzer at its native floating-point range of precision

Linear

Modern image processors and compositing software, like Nuke, as I mentioned above, process images at *32-bit float* bit depth level of color precision, in a *linear light* workspace. I will dive deep into the *linear light* concept later in this book, but for now, in order to comprehend enough the concept of *linear light* for what we need for the time being, all you need to know right now is that any color space is considered linear if by doubling any value in that color space the result is a color that is twice as bright. The linearity refers to the relationship between values and overall brightness of the resulting color.

So, the process of *linearization* of the image refers to the conversion of any color data to reorder the samples to maintain the relationship I mentioned above, so the progression of color values corresponds with the equivalent progression of the overall luminance.

For instance, RAW images (which contain the direct image sensor output) are originally *non-linear* and require a mathematical *function* to "straighten" its original curves. This is a type of linearization that happens before other operations such as white-balance adjustment (to align the RGB curves), black level correction (to set the beginning – lower end – of the curve in the point of 0 value returned in luminance, the black point) (Figure 2.14).

Notice that the linearization here refers only to the "*straightening*" of the original curve of each channel (R, G, and B) to convert the non-linear progression of the *curves* into linear arithmetically progressive straight *curves*[10] ($x = y$).

Another common example of linearization, maybe even closer to our workflows, occurs with the process of counterbalancing the gamma encoded in an image or the logarithmic encoding, by applying the inversed function of that gamma baked in the image or, in the case of *log* images, the logarithmic distribution of luminance sample encoded in the image to nullify in any case its non-linear progression into the neutralized linear progression (Figure 2.15).

But why do we call it *linear*? We refer to a linear light color space meaning that numerical intensity values correspond proportionally to their perceived intensity. Even if we are going to discuss LUTs later in the book when discussing color spaces in depth, I think it would help you picture linearization now, and the 1:1 ratio between input and output ($x = y$).

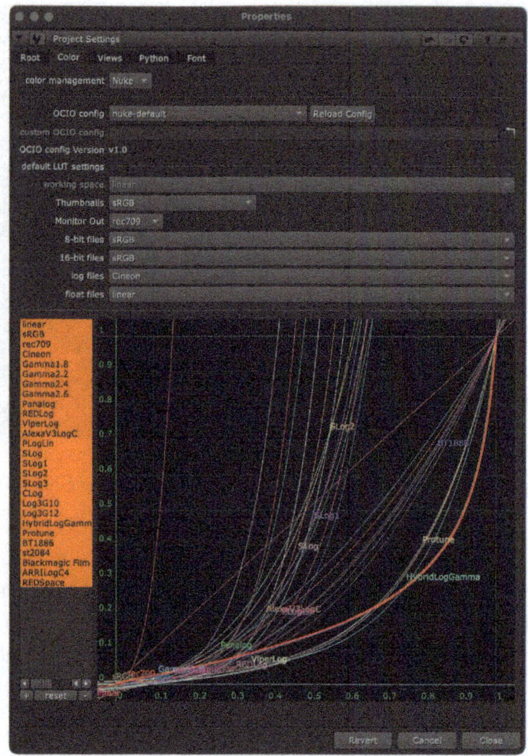

Figure 2.14 Nuke linearization look-up tables (LUTs) to convert from a given color space into the linear light workspace

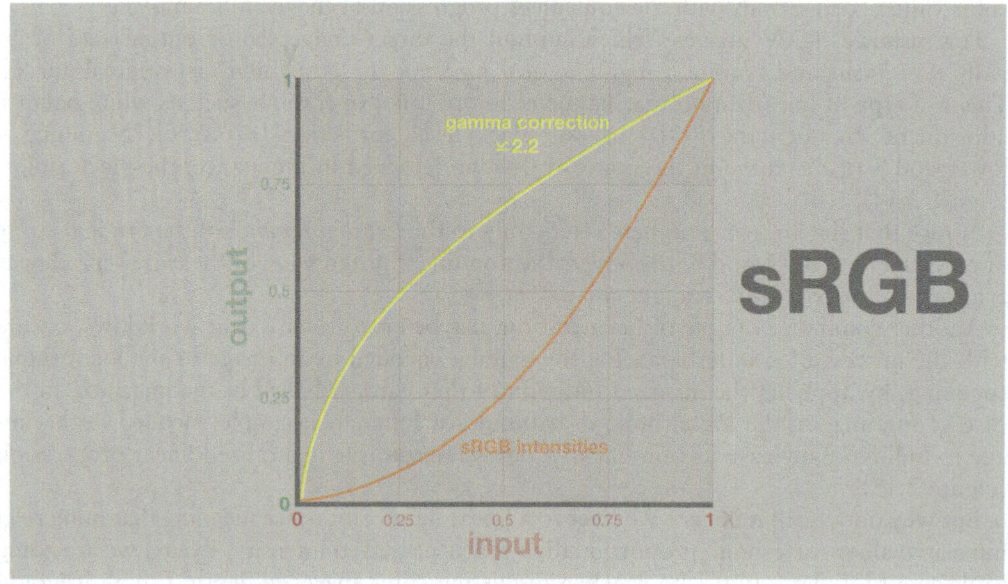

Figure 2.15 sRGB intensities vs its gamma correction – one curve represents the reverse operation of the other resulting in a straight line

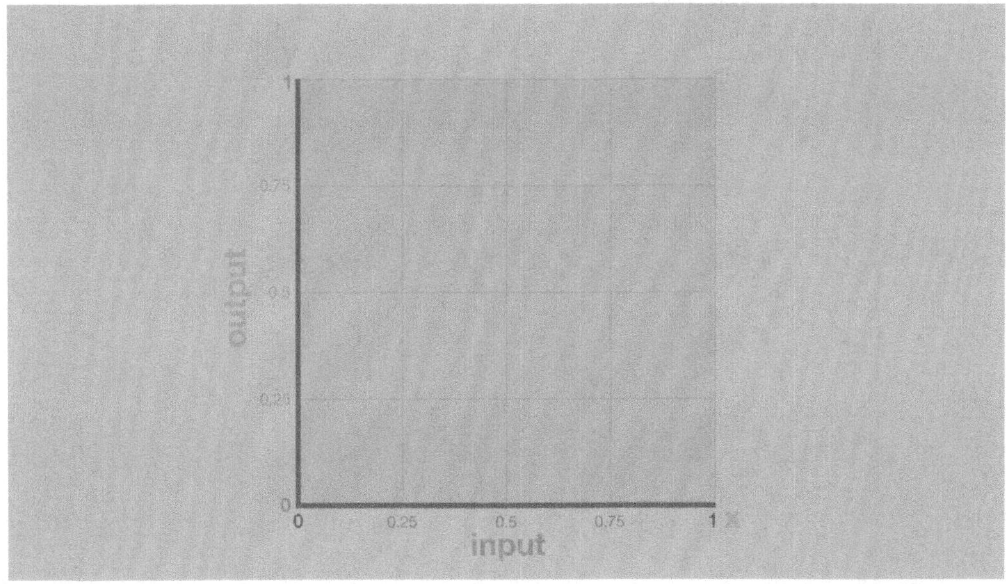

Figure 2.16 The 0 to 1 normalized cartesian diagram

So, let's observe the graphic representation of color values of an LUT, by laying out the 2D cartesian axis (Figure 2.16).

This is a 2D cartesian graphic – we have seen it already many times – showing the normalized values from 0 to 1 in both x, the horizontal (input: given data), and y, the vertical axis (output: the resulting luminance). They are both arranged in an *arithmetic progression*, which means equal distance between all steps in the sequence. The x value is the input – the given values of the original image – and the y the output, the result after the process – usually a function or an array of correspondence. To read a value correspondence we pick a value on the x axis and then we "look up" for the result in y (Figure 2.17).

It's easier to understand the concept of the fixed color manipulation of a LUT using single points: for instance, for a given value of 0.25 (x), I want to return an intensity of 0.5 (y); and for a given value of 0.75 (x) I want a resulting intensity of 1 (y). If we interpolate arithmetically the values in between the results the curve appears as in the figure above.

If we wanted a representation of the values unchanged, what we can refer to as a LUT "*at rest*" (meaning the operation does not alter the result at all), the input and the output values must be the same ($x = y$), a so-called *linear* progression of luminance where every increment of x corresponds to the same increment of luminance represented in y (Figure 2.18).

So, for 0.25 in x we get 0.25 in y, and for 0.5 in x we get 0.5 in y. This means there is no change on the result (y) in relation to the original values (x). By default, this is the state of a lookup table "*at rest*" from an operation before a given function is applied. We modify the y result (*intensity*) for a given x value.

Now that you understand the basics of the LUT, let's get back to the linearization. The linear progression of brightness values corresponding from the color data of the image is essential to applying arithmetic mathematic operations to the image hence fundamental for

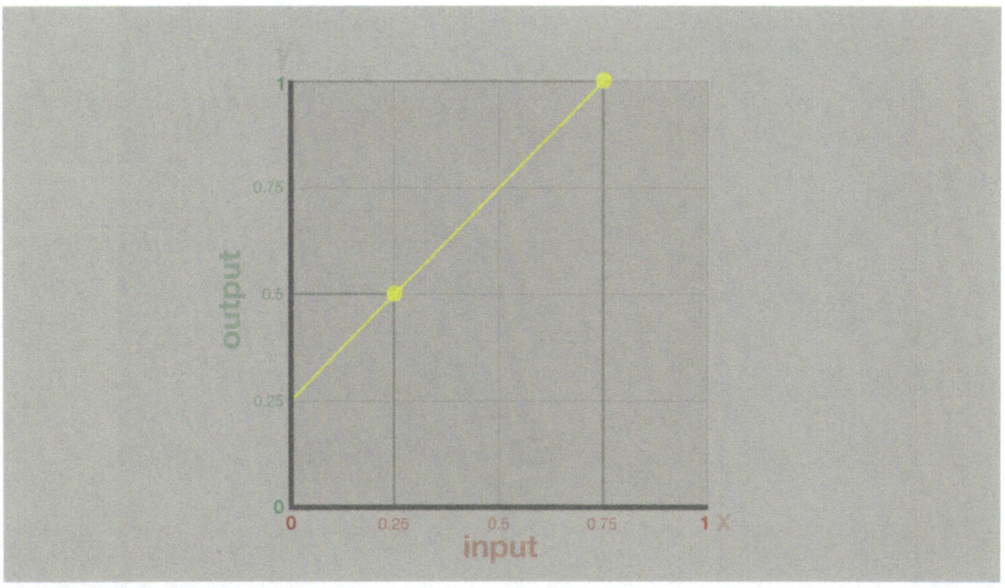

Figure 2.17 A look-up table (LUT) with an offset of +0.25. The result is still a "straight line" but the progression does not represent an equivalence between x and y (1:1).

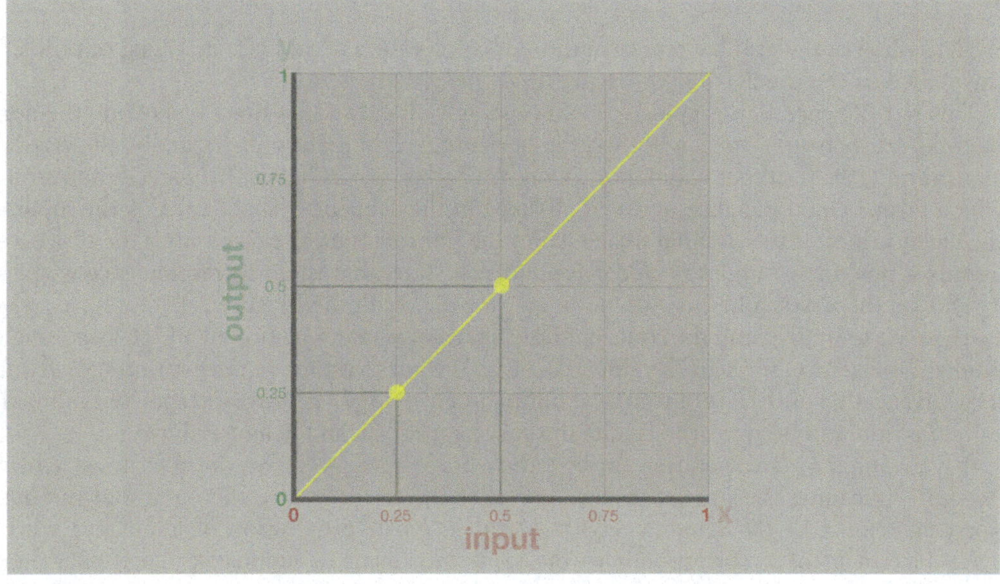

Figure 2.18 A curve with a linear progression of brightness (x = y) 1:1

color manipulation. So, completing the previous example about Nuke working space being 32-bit floating-point let's add the second part of the definition: the working space is *linear light*, so every image entering its environment is being linearized, modifying its original data (input: what you *Read*) to adjust the relationship between its source values and the overall brightness of the resulting color (output: what is *loaded* into Nuke script), so if you double all color values of the image the result would be the whole image twice as bright, as if you added one *f*-stop up. In terms of color management, you need to ensure the process of linearization is done correctly for each *function* encoded in each image.

Color Manipulation

We have been previously focusing on the range of values between 0 ("black") and 1 ("white") which are the values presentable on traditional displays (*sRGB/Rec709*). Of course, the image itself could contain information below 0 (*negative values*) or above 1 (*super-whites*) that are not displayed due to the limitations and standards of that technology and so, conventionally, I do not focus on those extra values in my examples – like in the previous graphic displaying LUTs – and this is just to make things clear, unless it is necessary to visualize features on any of those hidden ends. Of course with the advent of HDR technologies monitors, projectors and TVs are now able to display values beyond the conventional *sRGB* value 1, and it's clear HDR is here to stay and sooner or later it will take over the previous standards, but at the present time there is not a single unified standard for the range of luminance able to be represented on the display, that is now measured in nits, as we will discuss later (p.170), but the principles of the manipulation of the image and the data expressed in this section are quite agnostic of the display and more oriented to the mathematical side of the relation between numbers and color, so no worries about your monitor just yet. We will continue using graphic representations of LUTs later to analyze and explain the math of the color manipulations and *functions*.

In color manipulation for color management, one of the key aspects is that the transformations we apply to the curves, they all must start always, everywhere (on any department) on the same point (black level adjusted: absolute black should be sitting on value 0) and have the same progression (arithmetically linear and preferably using the linear light correlation with the properly white balanced) with the same order of transformations (because it is not the same thing x × 2 + 1 and x + 1 × 2). Something that will be fundamental would be the adoption of standard common rules for all to follow. So, the manipulations happen in a framework that is reproducible by anyone at any point of the workflow.

But there are also other color manipulations that we operate to the image that do not need to be reproducible by other departments and that depend only on certain artists, such as compositors, for instance to match the color features of the CG to look photorealistic, or the absolute color grading colorists operate over the finished film. All manipulations have a set of rules and mathematic operations in common that we all need to know. Math, digital color values and pixels are going to be a constant across all these manipulations. So, we better get familiar with them and what they represent as an idea in our minds, like for instance, the association of the multiplication of color values with brightness. Remember if I multiply the values of the color of all pixels times two, is like increasing the light of my image by one *f*-stop. The color manipulation must be visualized in your head before you display it in the monitor. This will demonstrate you know what is going on at every point in the chain.

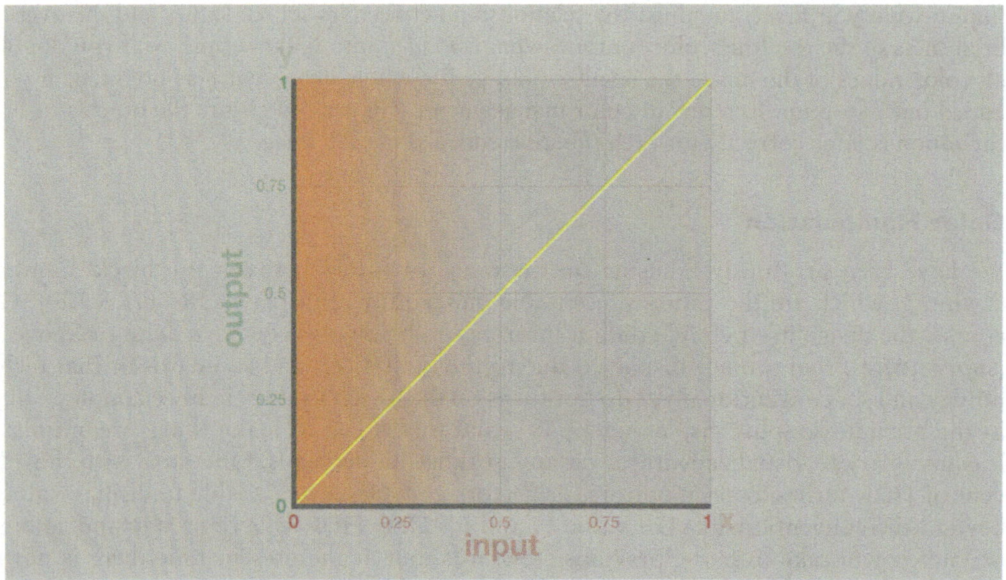

Figure 2.19 Shadows area of the curve

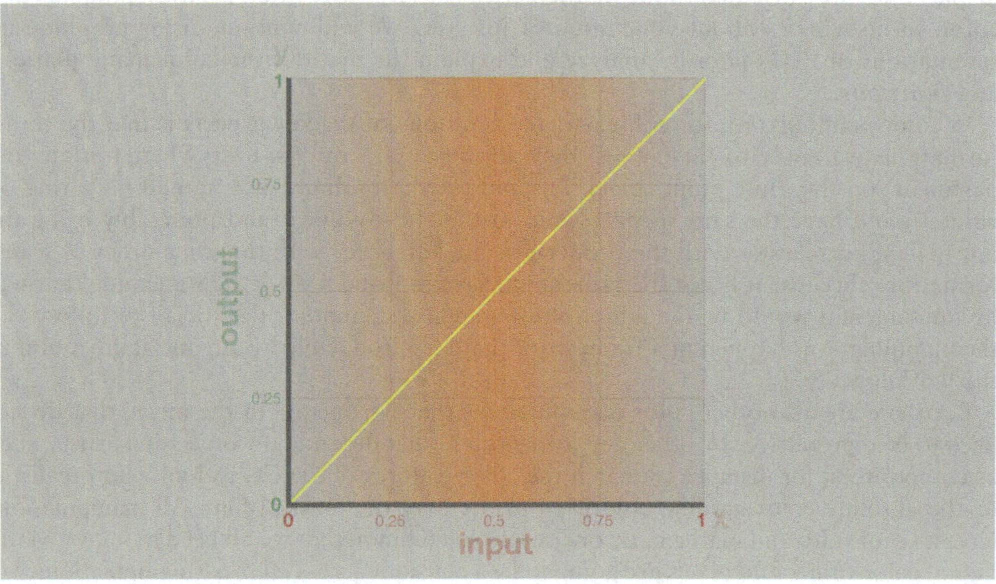

Figure 2.20 Mid-tones area of the curve

Let's get practical, as per the *characteristic curve*, we have seen in the previous chapter that we can define three main areas for this *curve* (or line) (Figures 2.19–2.21):

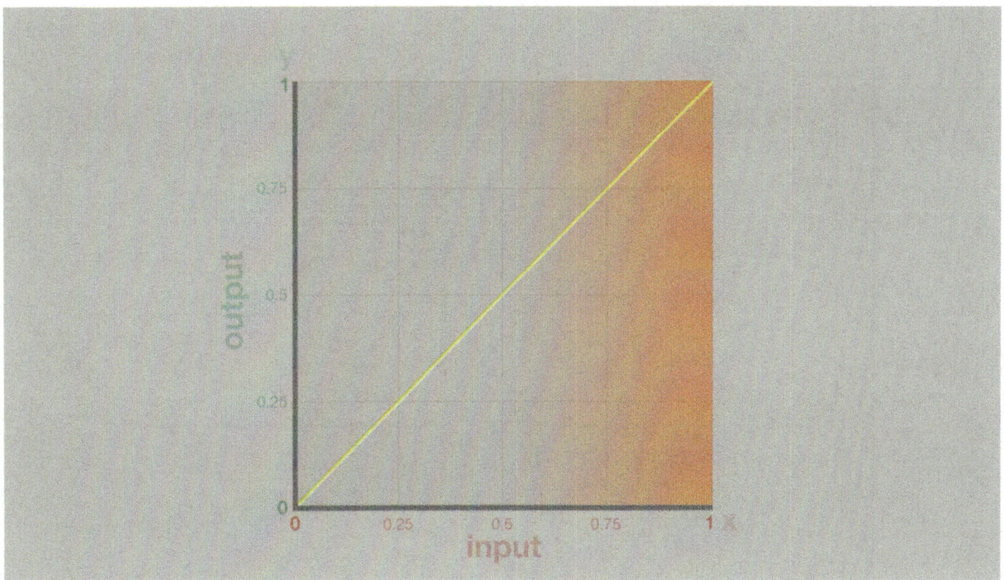

Figure 2.21 Highlights area of the curve

On the three previous figures we have: on the left the shadows, low values; mid-tones around the middle; and highlights on the right (even beyond value 1 as we will see later). Get used to visualizing color manipulations as *curves*.

Display Referred Color Operations

Why is the *linear workspace* a big deal? Because digital images are not always encoded in a *linear* color space. Usually, images ready to be displayed have embedded a color transformation – known as the *Transfer Function* (that we will study later in this book) – to allow them to be correctly displayed on the device they are meant to be shown on, an operation commonly known as *gamma encoding*. The *gamma encoding* is a non-linear operation, and we can reverse it by using the inverted operation process; of course, to do this the gamma curve encoded must be known. However, this is not a problem, since all commercially available devices adhere to certain standards that comply with this function.

Let me illustrate why gamma encoding became necessary years ago, way before TVs became "smart". The first reason was born with the *cathode-ray tube* (CRT) monitors and TVs (Figure 2.22).

CRT has the property of displaying naturally "darkened" images. So, in order to compensate the "lack of brightness" and the color of images being displayed in a CRT monitor, they encoded the video signal with an overall compensation of the gamma around 2.2 to make them look nice in TV and monitors[11], like in this example (Figure 2.23):

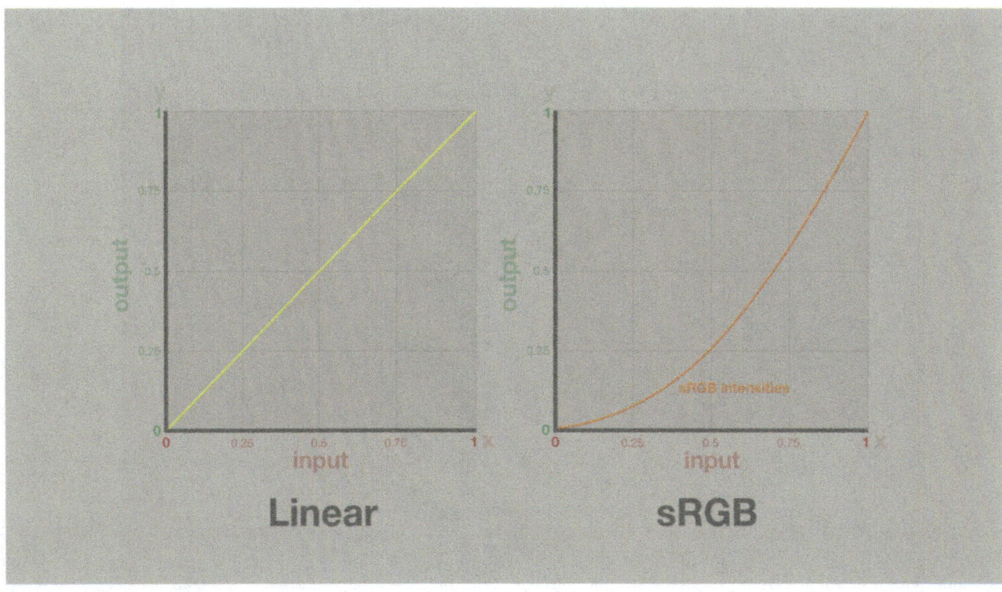

Figure 2.22 Linear light progression vs sRGB gamma-encoded intensities

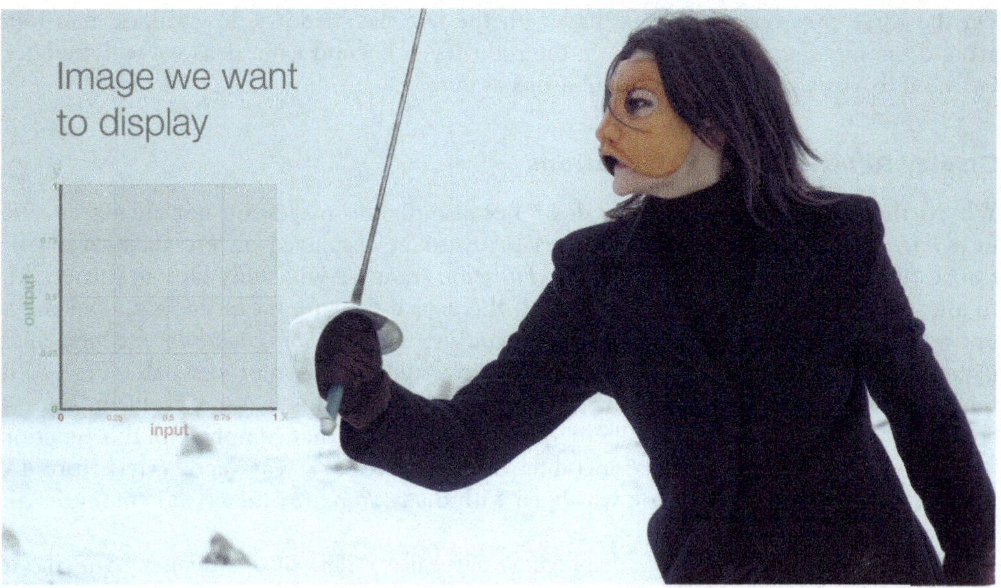

Figure 2.23 Image A – the image intent

- *A* is the image we want to display (Figure 2.23).

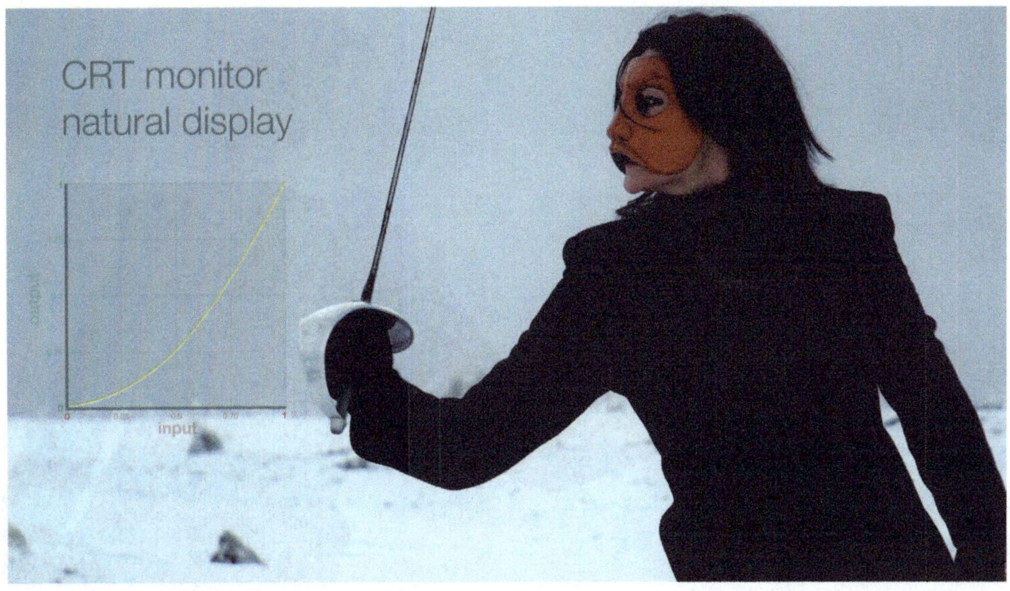

Figure 2.24 Image B – uncompensated image as displayed in a cathode-ray tube (CRT) monitor

- *B* is how a CRT monitor displays the image without any gamma compensation, (obviously dark) (Figure 2.24).

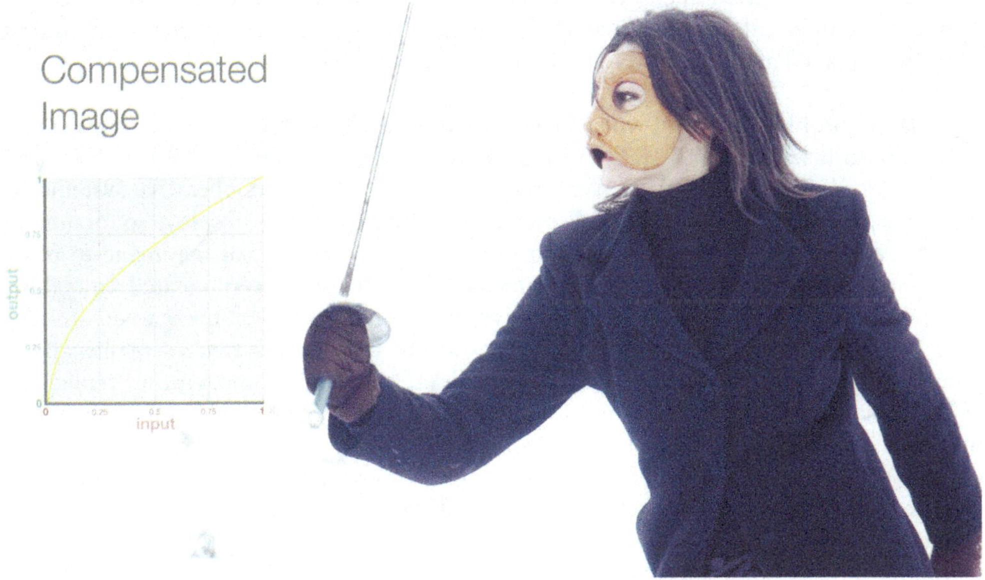

Figure 2.25 Image C – image data with gamma encoded

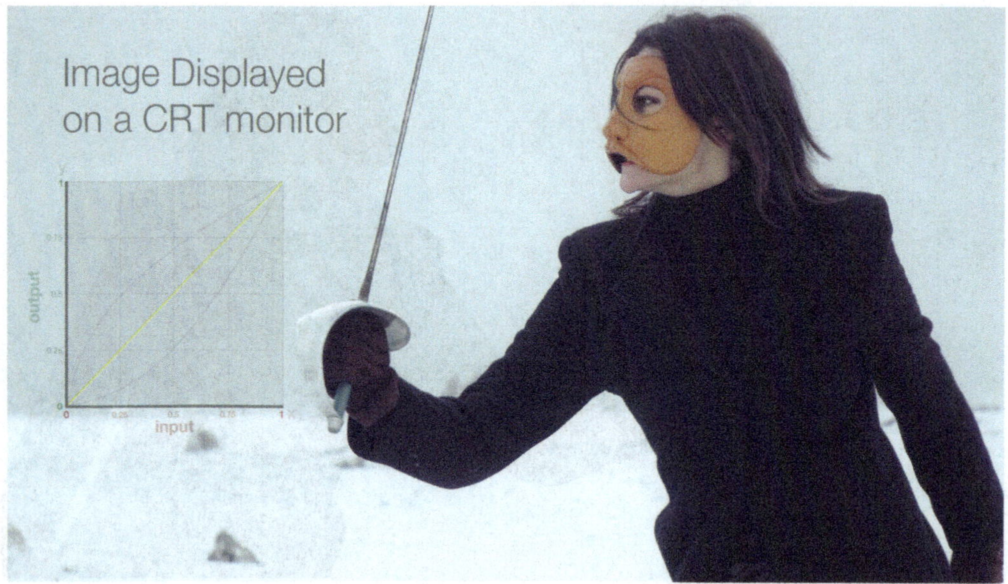

Figure 2.26 Image D – the final compensated image

- Theoretically *C* is the image data compensated (*gamma encoded*) before being shown in the CRT monitor (Figure 2.25).
- And *D* is the image compensated (*gamma correct*) being displayed on a CRT, it looks like in the beginning, the *original intent*. The gamma addresses the "problem" of brightness to be displayed as intended (Figure 2.26).

But a new "problem" arrived when LCD TVs and monitors started populating the world. LCDs do no behave as old CRT TVs displaying images, and do not "darken" the image as CRTs do, however, the TV signal broadcasted, and computers operative systems video signal used the same parameters to display images for any kind of display. So, manufacturers decided to bake inside LCD monitors hardware a correction of the image to respond approximatively with the gamma response of CRTs, so LCD were created embedding a gamma curve to "darken" the image displayed! It might sound a bit crazy to create an "artifact" on the device that does not exist, I know, but if you think twice it makes all sense, you need to align to the technology that was already in every home without replacing the existing devices, so the new ones need to adapt so they all respond the same unified way … of course this will create a few headaches later but we will see later this with the "History of the Color Transfer Odyssey". However, this new color space was easily adopted and both signals and displays were perfectly aligned. Made possible by the cooperation of HP® and Microsoft to create the *sRGB* color space, that was standardized by the IEC in 1996, with its *gamma correction* (a nominal gamma 2.2 function) synchronizing the color of images in monitors, printers, and the World Wide Web. This is still the standard color space for the Web still today: which means that images that had not been originally encoded with this color profile or tagged[12] in sRGB would be automatically interpreted by applying the sRGB gamma transfer function (and other color space features).

Linear vs Logarithmic

We have seen the difference between the *sRGB* and the *Linear* curves but working with film scans the most popular color space used to be the *Cineon*, with this we are going to introduce a neat difference of use of the color bits. First because the *Cineon* is a *logarithmic* color space.

I am aware that the industry is converging into the use of linear (16-bit half-float) EXR files for camera footage, even for film scans, but understanding the logarithmic transfer function will help you as VFX artist to find other applications, like for instance make certain controls with an exponential behavior, instead of the arithmetic linear functioning. This is essential for certain photorealistic operations of compositing, such as, for instance, a non-linear Gaussian blur to mimic the falloff and decay rate following the *inverse square law of light* applied to the diffusion and absorption of light in atmospheric phenomena, like fog (Figure 2.27).[13]

Let's have a look in the next Figure at the difference between *logarithmic* and *linear*, also known as *log* and *lin* respectively (Figures 2.28 and 2.29).

And what is the inverse function of the *l Log* curve? The *exponential* curve. It represents the operation necessary to be applied to a *Log* curve to be converted into a *lin* curve, using the same parameters as the original log curve it will result in a mathematically perfect *linear* progression of brightness values corresponding with the input values (*linear light*). A process known as *log to lin* (also known as *Log2Lin*), or in reverse as *lin to log* (also known as *Lin2Log*) (Figure 2.30).

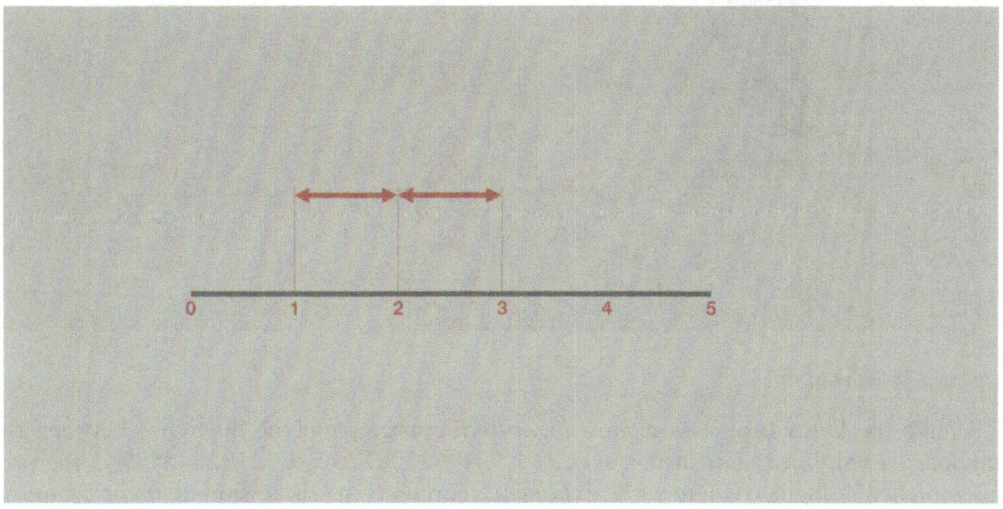

Figure 2.27 Constant arithmetic progression of values

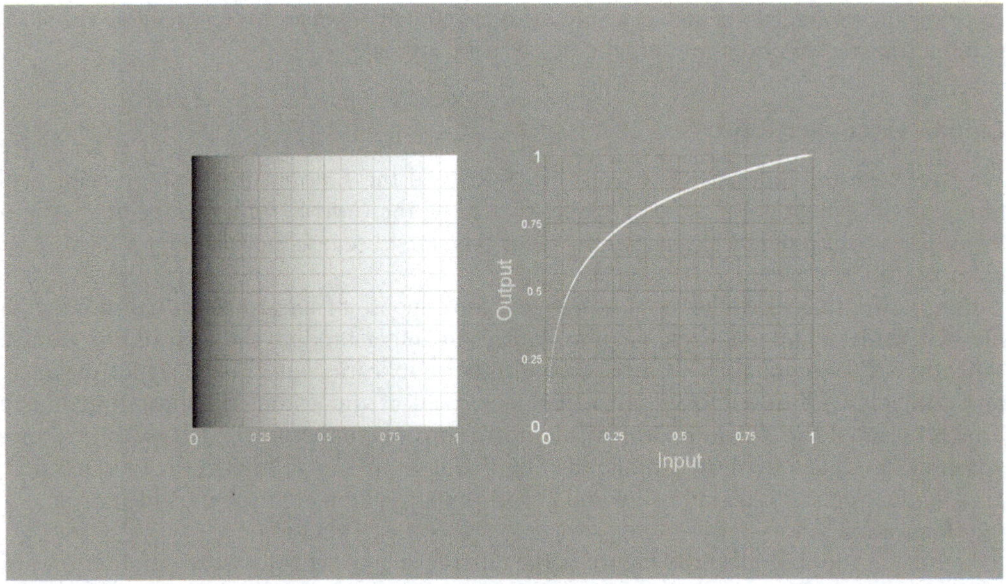

Figure 2.28 Log curve

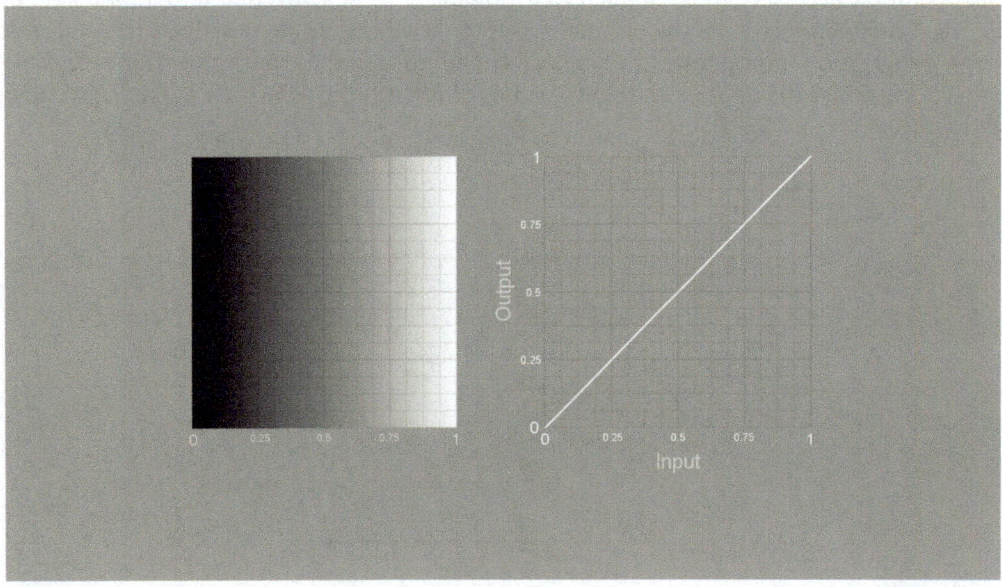

Figure 2.29 Lin curve

Unlike the *linear* progression, in a *logarithmic* progression the difference between the numbers is non-linear. For instance: 0, 1, 1.58496250072, 2, 2.32192809489 ... the progression here is $log_2(x)$, where x (the *exponent*) represents the succession of *integer* numbers starting from 1; 2 is the *base*.

What is the relation between the *exponential* and the *logarithmic* operations?[14] Let me show you the formula, you will see it is really easy to understand: $log_2(x) = y$ and $x = 2^y$. The *logarithm* is the *inverse* function to *exponentiation*.

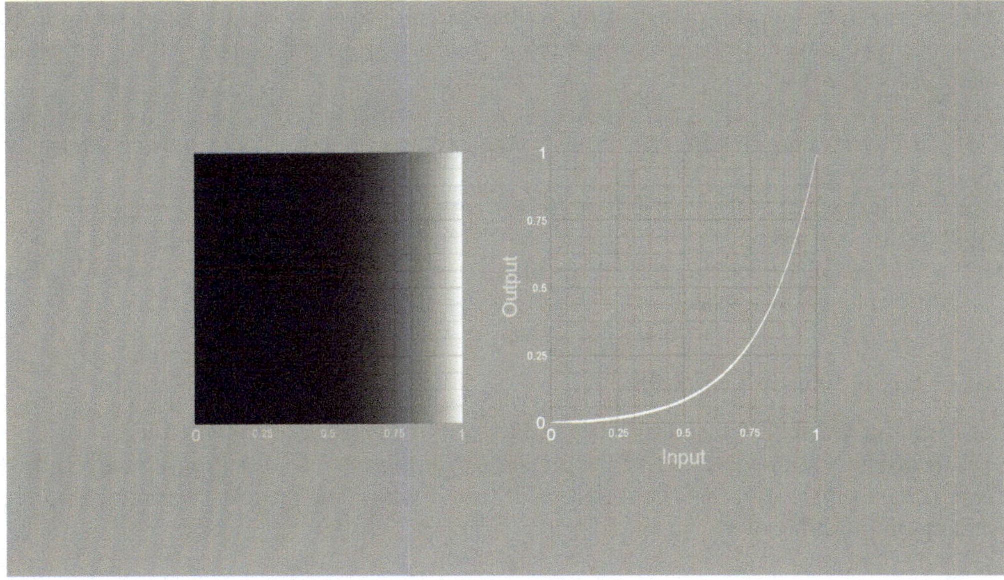

Figure 2.30 The invert function of the log curve: the exponential curve

Exponents, Roots, and Logarithms

Mathematics is the language of science, so do not be afraid of it. I am going to demonstrate how simple these operations are. Exponents, roots (such as square roots, cube roots…, etc.) and logarithms are all related. Understanding their relation is key to grasp the concept of what they do and how.

I'm going to use a very easy example: $3 \times 3 = 9$. Let's represent it graphically – we are visual artists so you will find yourself more comfortable observing the operation … and once you understand it, you would not need the picture anymore as you will visualize it in your head (Figure 2.31).

Using *exponents*, it is expressed as: $3^2 = 9$.

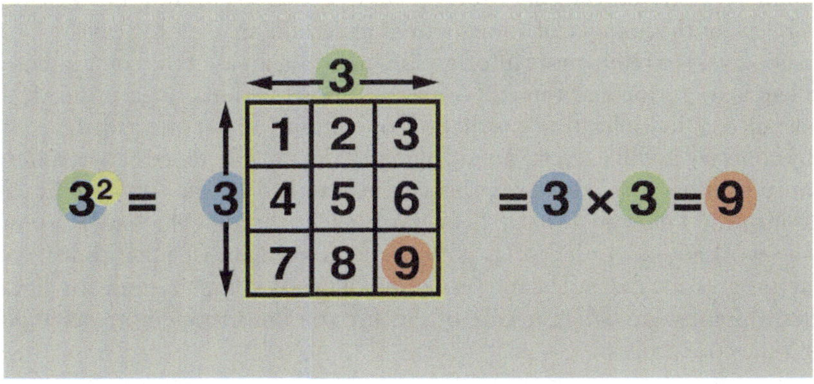

Figure 2.31 $3^2 = 3 \times 3 = 9$

When any of those values are missing, we have an *unknown* to be calculated, therefore an equation to be solved. Depending what piece of information is missing we have a different *notation* to express it:

- $3^2 = x$ Here we are missing the result, so the **exponent** question is *"what is 3 squared?"* Hence: $3^2 = 9$.
- $x^2 = 9$ Here we are missing the base, so the **root** question is *"what is the square root of 9?"* Hence: $\sqrt{9} = 3$.
- $3^x = 9$ Here we are missing the exponent, so the **logarithm** question is *"what is log base 3 of 9?"* Hence: $log_3(9) = 2$.

Log to Lin and Lin to Log *Math*

Let's add the correlation between the x and the y axis to create a lookup table.

To translate the previous linear progression to a *log base 2 of x* progression, we take every value in the output array (y) and substitute it with its logarithm correspondence depending on the value of x:

- $x = 1; y = \log_2(1) = 0$
- $x = 2; y = \log_2(2) = 1$
- $x = 3; y = \log_2(3) = 1.58496250072$
- $x = 4; y = \log_2(4) = 2$
- $x = 5; y = \log_2(5) = 2.32192809489$

We can invert the logarithmic correspondence of the LUT above by applying the inverse function of this logarithm, which is in this case is $y = \log_2(x^2)$, that can be simplified this way: $y = \log_2(x^2)$, hence $x = y$ (the *Linear* progression):

- $x = 1; y = \log_2(1^2) = 1$
- $x = 2; y = \log_2(2^2) = 2$
- $x = 3; y = \log_2(3^2) = 3$
- $x = 4; y = \log_2(4^2) = 4$
- $x = 5; y = \log_2(5^2) = 5$

The main difference in terms of data storage between the *linear* and the *logarithmic* methodologies relies on the number of values stored in certain areas of the curve.

Log is a good way to retain more information in certain areas of the color intensity. But the only problem is to perform arithmetic color operations within a logarithmic framework – like, for instance, a multiplication – is that the operation will not affect all areas of the curve equally, by contrary it will exercise an unbalanced, drastic difference between the highlights in relation to the shadows. However, this can be handled by the software by interpreting the image into the uniformed *linear light* workspace (through the *linearization* process), keeping the workflow in order. That is why the conversion of logarithmic progressions into linear progressions is necessary (using exponential compensation for linearization). No worries, the software will take care of this for you but I thought it was important you understand the core process.

Cineon

In 1990 Glenn Kennel developed the *Cineon* system. The first computer-based system to manipulate film images, end-to-end, from the scanner to the film recorder. Every device aligned to support the *digital intermediate (DI)*. In the film developing world the so-called *intermediate* refers to the physical copy of a negative (either as *positive*, known as *interpositive*, for first generation; or *negative*, known as *internegative*, for second generation copies) to generate subsequent copies, by laying this exposed film strip over another blank unexposed negative strip, and then exposing them together. This analogue process (physical and chemical) was used, for instance to create a *dissolve* transition, by mixing two negatives, exposing them with progressive light densities in every frame (a bit of one and a bit of the other starting with more of one and finishing with more of the other), creating a new intermediate or a master with the transition ... yes, this is how a dissolve was done before film scanners existed, any manipulation was done manually by printing light (*development exposure*).

VFX Commonly Used File Formats

Cineon Log File (.cin)

I am sure you are aware of this, but just in case you are not, for the postproduction of visual effects we usually manage footage and renders using file formats to store one frame per file, also known as frame sequences. Video containers (also known as "wrappers"), such as QuickTime or AVI are not common at all for exchange between departments or to elaborate shots but they become handy for delivery or review in certain limited cases. So, the Cineon file is the first one in the list of file formats I will discuss that is used for frame sequences.

For its scanning/printing system, Kodak created a proprietary file format: the *Cineon* (.cin), used for the first time in production in 1993 at the then recently opened *Cinesite* facility in Los Angeles, California, the film that first used this new technology was Disney's animation classic *Snow White and the Seven Dwarfs*, which became the first film entirely scanned to digital files, to be restored and remastered digitally.

The *Cineon* file format was designed specifically to represent scanned film images, the color encoded in every pixel corresponds to *printing density*. It is a digital reproduction of the film negative, emulating the same response in *gamma*, *color component*, and *crosstalk* (which is the interference of one color from other color channels, or layers if we talk about the physical world; in film negative it occurs when a color sensitive layer absorbs a portion of other wavelengths, in a certain range, it is a normal feature of film negative stock). It was created this way to maintain the same properties from the original negative behavior once it is recorded, and then from the computer to be printed in a film negative strip again (Figure 2.32).

The Cineon Log

A .*cin* file is usually encoded at 10-bit (so 1024 values) for every color channel, and packed in a 32-bit word with 2 bits unused, just RGB (color), no alpha (for transparency indicator matte), for a total of 1,073,741,824 color values.

But for us VFX artists, the most important characteristic about the *Cineon* color space is the *gamma with* logarithmic *encoding*.

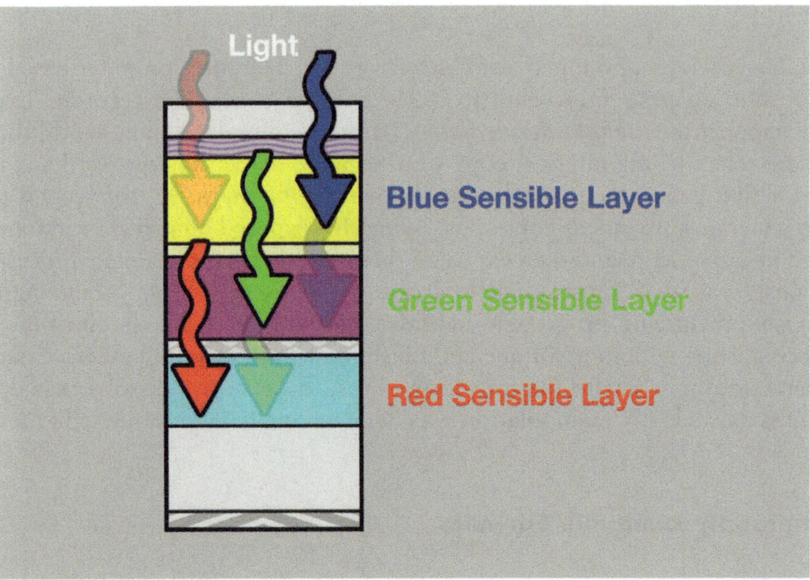

Figure 2.32 Crosstalk

Bit-Depth and Brightness Progression Correspondence for Normalization

Another question to keep in mind, TVs or computer displays have a limited range of color, way less that a film negative. Conventionally, in the 10-bit scale of a *Cineon* file – a scale of values ranging from 0 to 1023 (1024 values in total, because 0 counts as one value) – everything below value 95 in the exposed negative will be read by our computer displays as pure flat black, like the *base plus fog*[15] of the film negative, and in the other side, any value above 685 will be absolute flat white, like a specular reflection of the sun in a chrome surface, a bright lightbulb … everything there will be *clipped*, however this is only a convention to display *log* images in our displays and see colors more naturally, the information is still there available and we can recall it during the manipulation of the image. These are the *superwhites* (values above value 1) we discussed before (Figure 2.33).

If we translate this into a normalized value convention we get our darkest value in 10-bit, 95, as normalized 0 value; and the brightest 10-bit displayed value, 685, as the normalized 1, there are still values present between 685 and 1023 that will return normalized values way above 1 because of the *log* progression. Precisely, as per Kodak official considerations, the brightest value would be 13.53 (although using more efficient ICC[16] color conversions a scanned exposed film negative could reach values above 70). The same way, those values below the nominal 10-bit value 96 will return negative values – values below the display normalized 0 – so there is still a bit of information in the blacks we cannot "see" as they have been placed in the negative range, not much information but still there and nonetheless necessary.

Let's see a representation of the *Cineon* curve using the gradient square we used before for the *sRGB* and *linear* comparison (Figure 2.34).

Look at this curve, it is the standard Cineon transfer function, it is similar to the one we reviewed above for the explanation of the *log* curve.

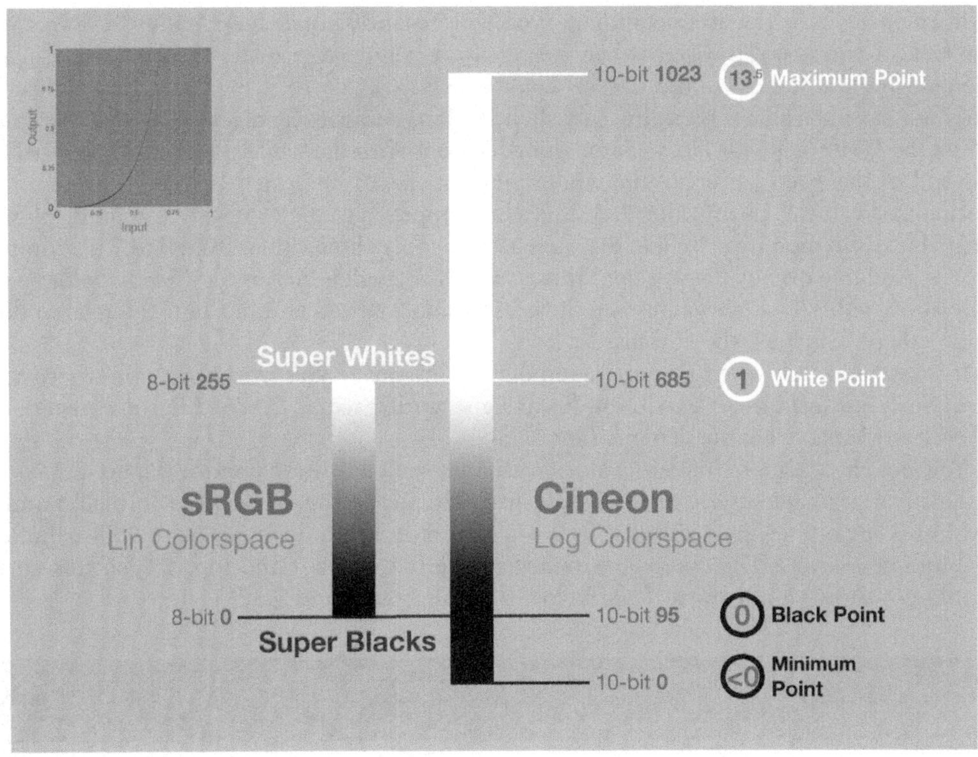

Figure 2.33 Correspondence between sRGB floor and ceiling values within the cineon 10-bit scale

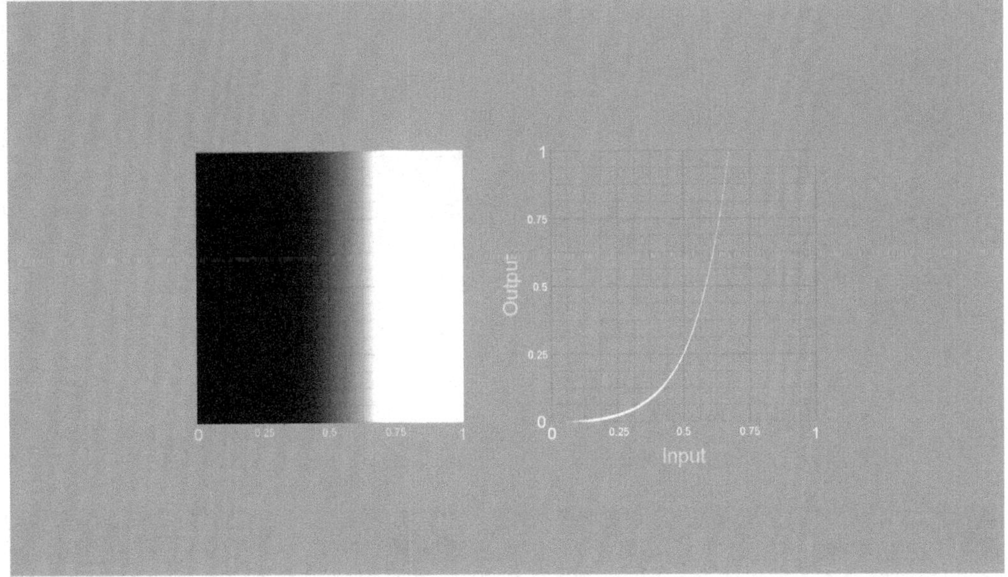

Figure 2.34 The Cineon log curve

If we observe the raw gradient image, you will instantly notice how "milky" it looks and the lack of contrast. However, when we remap its values to reorder the luminance increments using the log curve the *Cineon* color space looks correct. Be aware that the curve does not start at value 0 on *x*, but just slightly after, because the black point is set at value 95 on the 10-bit scale (0–1023). Same thing happens with the white point, it sits way before the end of the *x* axis, because the white point on the 10-bit scale (0–1023) – meaning its normalized value 1 – is on value 685. But what happened to the values we cannot display in our 8-bit sRGB monitor? Well, in the *y* axis we can only show values from 0 to 1 (the output values available on our display) and those superwhite values are in the *Cineon* color space way above value 1, so we cannot see those in this normalized graphic, but rest assured they are up there "outside" the graphic.

It is essential that when you are manipulating the image you work on a non-destructive workflow. For instance, *Nuke* 32-bit linear light workspace or *DaVinci Resolve* own color science workspace. Let me demonstrate it.

You can check those "hidden" values with a virtual exposition control (Figure 2.35).

This is a gradient square at rest, with original values ranging between 0 (black) and 1 (white). The graphic analyzes the value progression of the gradient, its curve of distribution of brightness levels. The curve is normalized, the bottom is 0 and top is 1, so this curve would not show values above 1 nor below 0 (Figures 2.36 and 2.37).

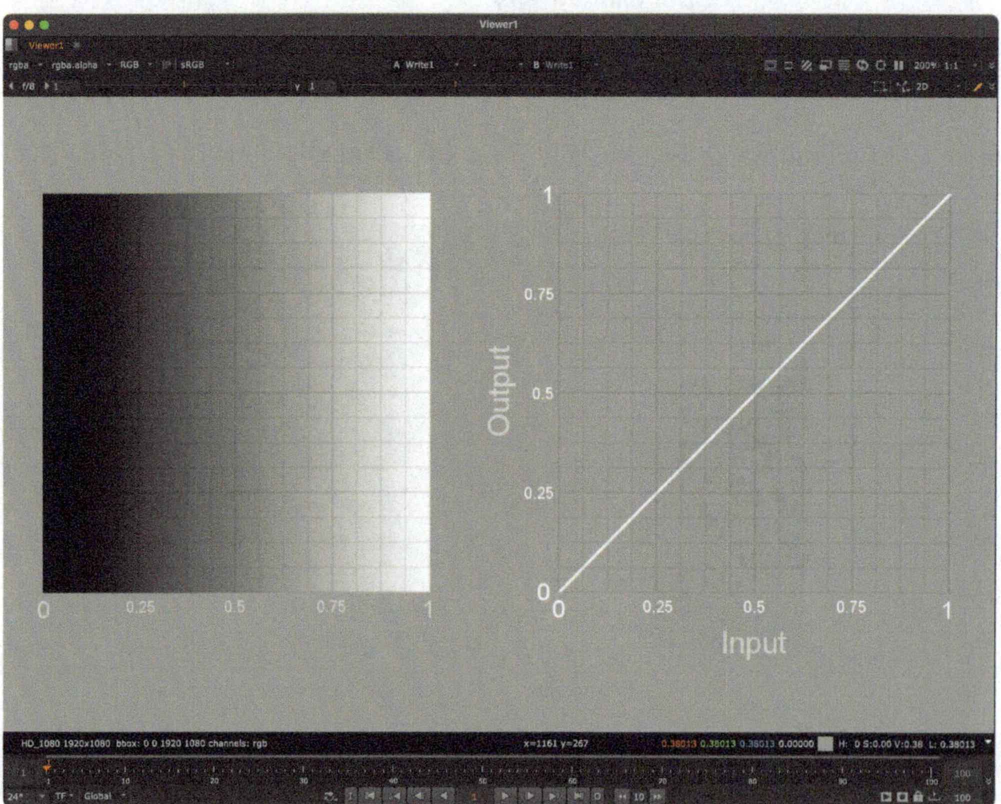

Figure 2.35 Technical image of a gradient from value 0 to value 1 in all rgb channels and its graphic representation – it represents the values an 8-bit srgb monitor represents

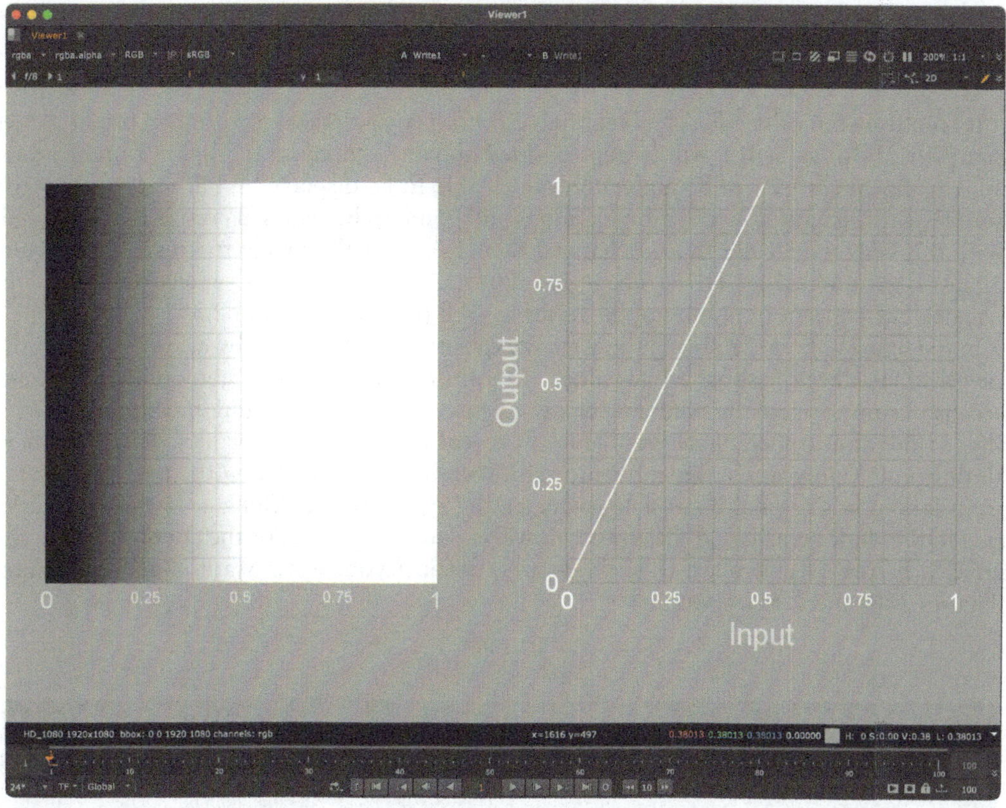

Figure 2.36 Technical image with values greater than 1 – the second half of the gradient goes beyond value 1 – the graphic shows the luminance range of the monitor

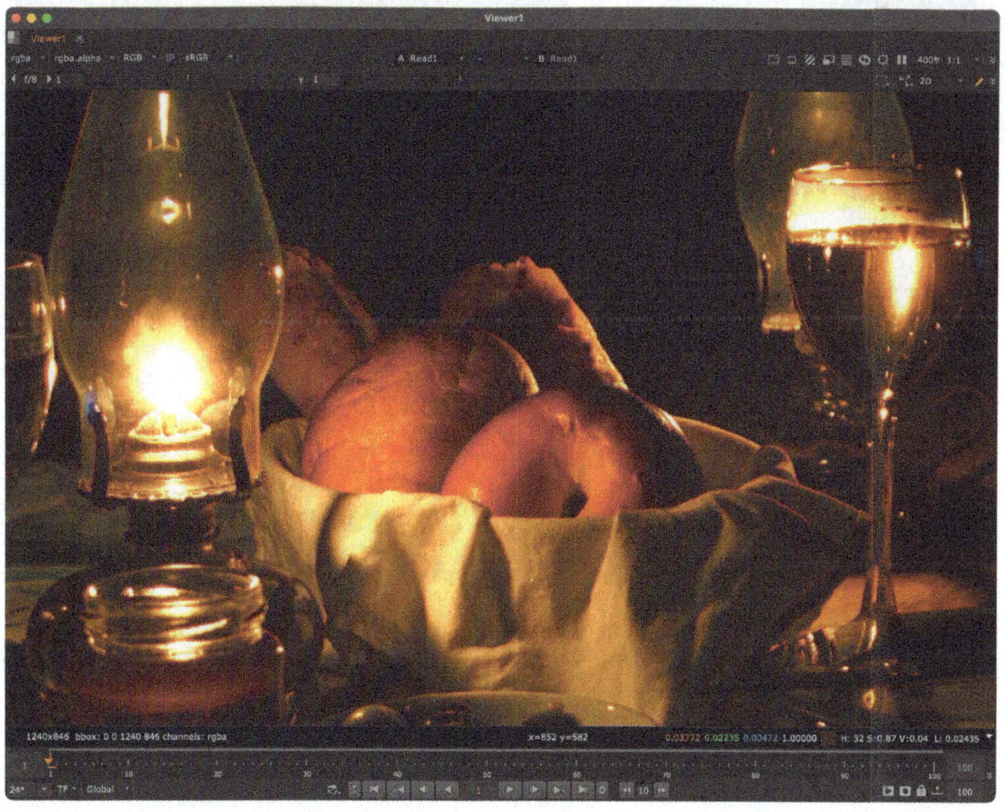

Figure 2.37 HDRI image with values greater than 1 (flames highlights)

If I multiply the value of each pixel times 2 (*multiply* operation) my original bright values that were above value 0.5 will be repositioned above 1 – because 0.5 × 2 = 1 and so anything higher than 0.5 will be above the values able to be displayed – but rest assured in a non-destructive workflow the information is still going to be retained even if not displayed. With this operation I did indeed changed then values of the image to create super-white values. I have added an HDRI image in Figure 2.35, with natural super-white values to visualize the concept in photographic terms as well (Figures 2.38 and 2.39).

In the figures above I reduced the virtual exposition of the image by a few *f*-stops in the viewer to visualize the super-white values. It means the curve on the right would not change because I am not actually changing the gradient values, but changing its exposure virtually, so the appearance of the gradient will reveal the super-white values that were there all this time. Can you see the gradient is still there completely? (Now the dark areas have gone darker, it is normal because by reducing the exposure everything goes darker and details in the dark areas could disappear; however, trust the values of the curve, they are the same as before). Remember: trust the values, not just your eyes. Math is not an opinion (Figures 2.40 and 2.41).

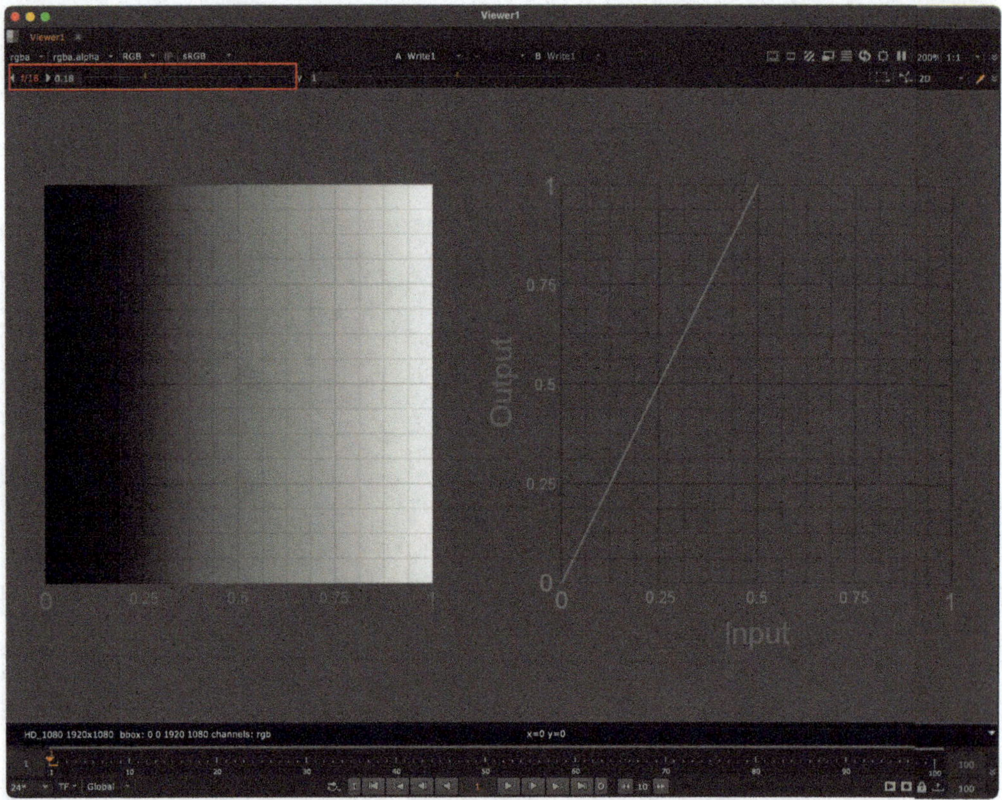

Figure 2.38 Same technical image of figure 2.34 Using the virtual exposition slider to visualize 5 f-stops down (from base f/8 to f/18) revealing the super-white values of the gradient that were clipping on the monitor

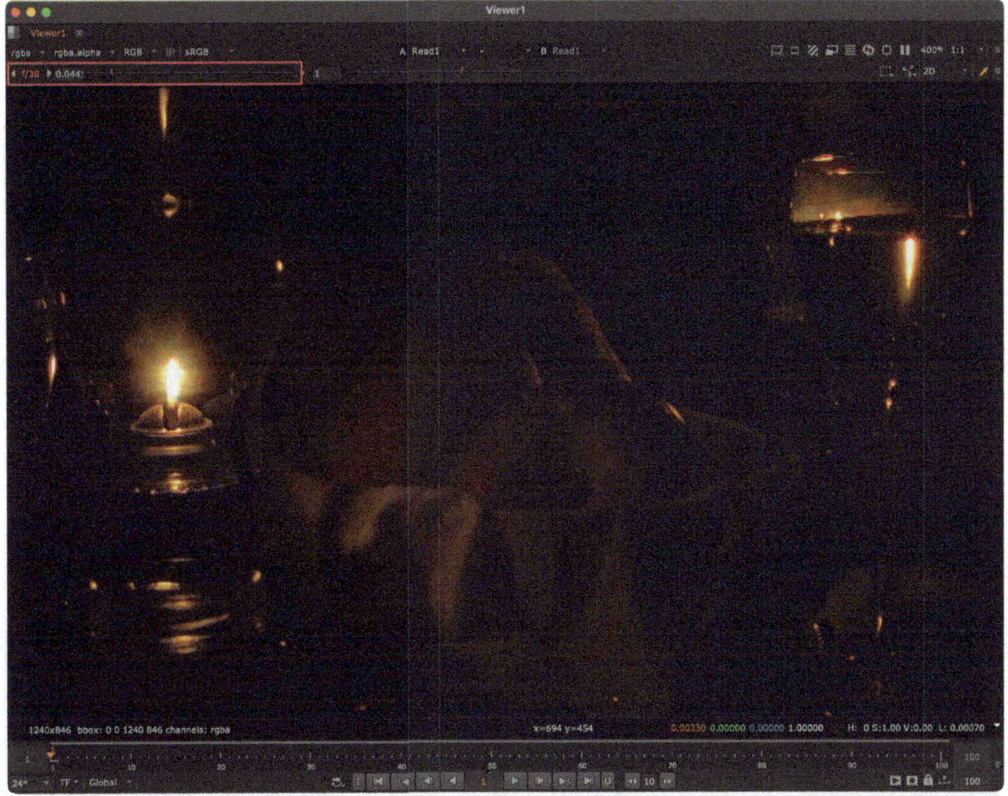

Figure 2.39 Same HDRI image of figure 2.35 Using the virtual exposition slider to visualize 9 f-stops down (from base f/8 to f/38) revealing the super-white values of the flame

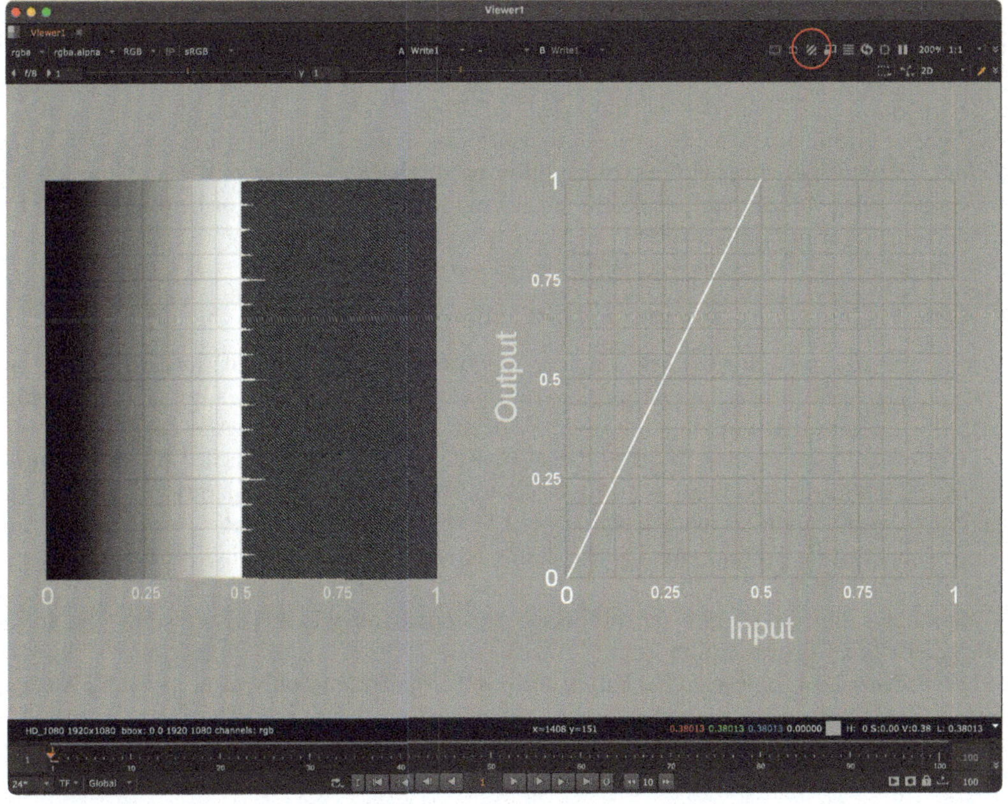

Figure 2.40 The zebra control activated on the viewer

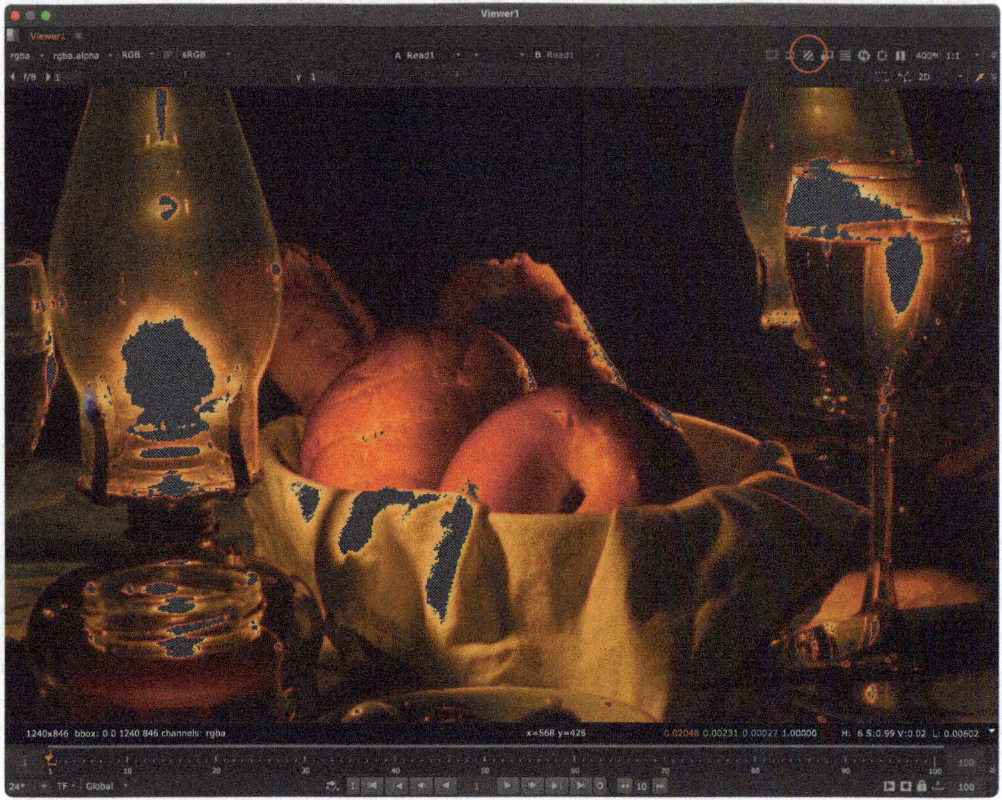

Figure 2.41 The zebra control activated on the viewer displaying the naturally bright-over-value-1 areas of the image

There are other ways to flag values that are not able to be displayed, for instance the *Zebra*, that will evidence with a pattern (alternating diagonal black and white lines, hence the name) those values that go beyond our normalized scale, above 1 or below 0 (out of the range your monitor could display).

Reversibility in a Non-destructive Color Workflow

In a non-destructive color workflow we can always reverse the result of any arithmetical operation, like for instance the *multiply* operation. Let's take the same example I used before with the gradient that I applied the *multiply times 2 operation* (Figure 2.42).

Here my maximum value reaches value 2 while the minimum is still 0 (because 0 multiplied by whatever you want is and will always be 0). After that operation I applied another *multiply* operation with a value of 0.5, to compensate for the previous *multiply times 2* operation, as you can see the result is exactly as the original without any loss of data.

Nowadays the use of the .cin file has been deprecated but his successor – the.dpx – inherited all its feature (and more).

Let's have a look now to other important file formats commonly used in the VFX pipeline, with maybe a piece of advice about how and where to use them (and where not):

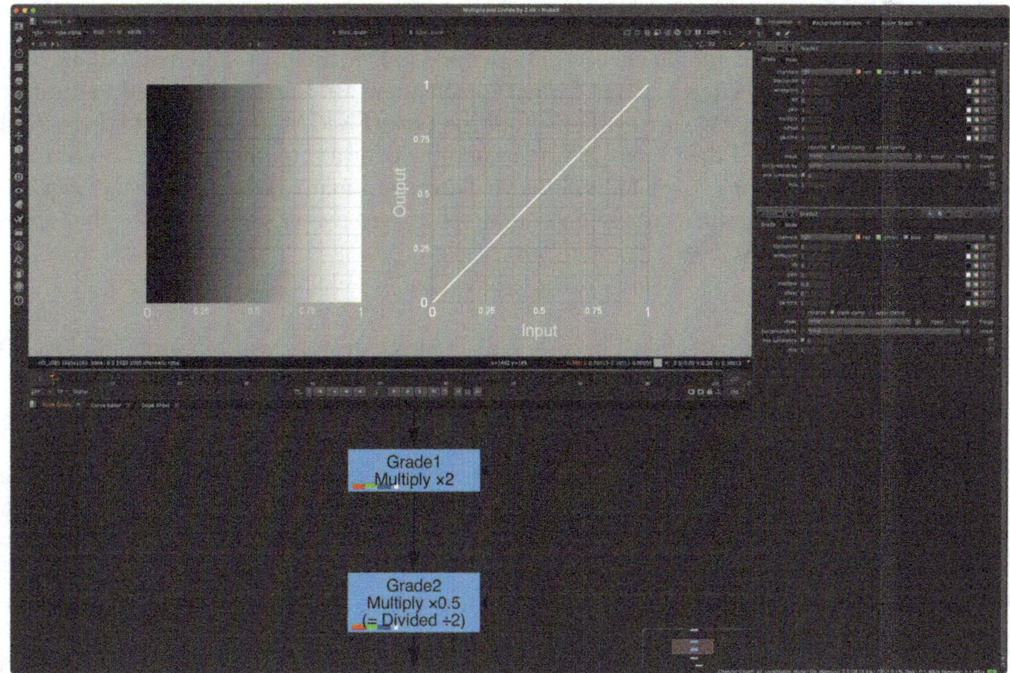

Figure 2.42 In a non-destructive workflow you can multiply ×2 getting values out of the range of your monitor and then divided ÷ 2 to get back the original result.

DPX: Digital Picture Exchange Format (.dpx)

After being awarded with a *Scientific and Technical Academy Award*®,[17] Kodak, in 1997, abandoned the *Cineon* system. But the *.cin* file format still lived for a long while. The *Society of Motion Picture and Television Engineers (SMPTE)* standardized a format for digital intermediate and visual effects based on the late *Cineon*, that was developed before Kodak discontinued the Cineon; in 1994, the first release of the *Digital Picture Exchange* file format, also known as *DPX,* was born. It offers the same feature to encode film scans in uncompressed log format, and even more, it can store not only flexible color information but color spaces, color planes, and other metadata for information exchange between production facilities as well. Since then, it has been widely used for film scans and improved with the newest technologies, like HDR. It is commonly used at either 10-bit or 12-bit depths, but 8-bit and 16-bit options are also available.

TIFF: Tagged Image File Format (.tif/.tiff)

The previous formats are great for film scans, however we needed a good versatile format for our CG renders and other CGI, such as, for instance, digital matte paintings. But not any format, only a format without compression to keep our information safe – a subject we will discuss in a few pages later. We could render, for instance, on *TIF* (also known as *TIFF* or *Tagged Image File Format*) that offers lossless compression if needed, high color-depth (usually 8-bit, 16-bit, or 32-bit), and an *alpha channel* – essential for computer graphics. The colorspaces usually encoded are sRGB for the 8-bit option and Linear for the 16-bit or the 32-bit.

OpenEXR: Open Source Extended Dynamic Range Image File Format (.exr)

There is a file format which offers everything the previous formats do and much more. The king of the files in visual effects … one format to rule them all. Entirely designed for and by the visual effects industry. We are talking about the *OpenEXR*. Starting in 1999, Industrial Light & Magic developed the *OpenEXR*, releasing the code as an open-source C++ library. Today it is a standard for CGI renders, intermediates, and many other uses in the VFX industry, including the container for ACES compliant images (as we will see in the chapter of this book dedicated to ACES).

Its key features are:

- 32-Bit float (or 16-bit half-float), even in half-float it can store without any data loss 30 *f*-stops – where most 8-bit files reach around 7–10 *f*-stops – and this is just the half-float version. This is a very good color resolution that prevent any noticeable color banding after strong color transformations and offers a great margin for color manipulation.
- A single file can store an arbitrary number of *image channels*, not only RGB and alpha (also known as RGBA), but any other kind of *AOVs* render passes, for instance, depth (Z), surface normal (N), motion vector, point position (P), ID pass … and can contain *deep image* data as well.
- Pixels can be stored either as scan lines or as tiles for random-access to rectangular sub-regions, implementing the zooming and panning speeds.
- Metadata: like, color timing information, process tracking data or camera position, and view direction.
- Multiview: storing in one file the left and the right views of a stereoscopic plate, or even other views.
- It can store un-cropped images, storing the information beyond the format ("canvas"), the whole *boundary box*, a.k.a. *bbox*.
- The OpenEXR is the only container able to store ACES compliant images.

Of course, the more information you store, the bigger the file is, but you can keep a lot of information with just one single file per frame, everything is self-contained.

The EXR file format is used pretty much for everything in VFX, always in a linear color space, like for instance, in an ACES color managed pipeline: ACEScg or for delivery and exchange ACES2065-1. It can be use for storing camera scans (that I would recommend to set at 16-bit half-float); or for generating CGI renders (that I would recommend to set at 16-bit half-float for beauty light components, or 32-bit full float for technical AOVs where precision is more critical, for instance: Point Position pass or Z-Depth pass), precomposites, or even deliverables. I would not use the EXR for non VFX related tasks, such as showing a client a picture of a shot sent via email … it will make things unnecessarily complicated, use a JPG for that … but keep in mind the excellence of VFX resides in the attention to detail and then you smash every detail by sending the image compressed in an 8-bit sRGB JPG image. Do not do it, or if you do, think about the artists that were working on the shot, the hours invested, their families … before you destroy it decide to apply the sandpaper of compression over it. I think this introduce you quite well to the concept of compression and the next two file format JPG and PNG.

In 2019 the Academy Software Foundation (ASWF)[18] adopted the OpenEXR project as one of the foundational technologies in computer imaging.

Image Compression: Lossless vs Lossy

Image compression refers to a process to reduce the size of the file containing the data of the image, normally without an apparent or "noticeable" loss of information (Figure 2.43). There are two main types of compression: *lossless* or *lossy*, and each type has various different methodologies to achieve the desired compression.

The lossless compression methodologies restore and rebuild file data in its original form after the file is decompressed. It can be described as a perfectly reversible process. For instance, when the file size of a picture is compressed, its quality remains exactly the same, unchanged, and so the file can be decompressed to its original quality without any loss of data whatsoever. This compression method is also known as *reversible compression*. With this method, although file sizes are reduced, the reduction is less compared to reduction using lossy compression and the process of compression and decompression requires computer resources and time. The most popular form of lossless compression, in everyday personal computer use, is the zip, even though it is not exactly a compressed image file format, but I am sure you are familiar with the process, you put a file into a *.zip* container, so you can transfer it faster, and then, once the file has been transferred, the file can be "unzipped" (decompressed) for its normal usage. This is lossless compression, the file you get after the decompression is the same you had before compressing it … but keep in mind it took time to process the file to be compressed and then more time for the same file to be decompressed, lossless compression uses computer resources, hence time and calculation power.

In *lossy compression*, certain data in a file (considered "unnecessary") is removed and so the original file is not completely restored to its original form after decompression. Specifically, data is permanently destroyed, which is why this method is also known as *irreversible compression*. This data loss is not usually "noticeable". However, the more a file is compressed, the more degradation occurs, and the loss eventually becomes visible. In any case, for the purpose of color management, I would never recommend a lossy methodology for intermediate files (files that are meant to exchange information within

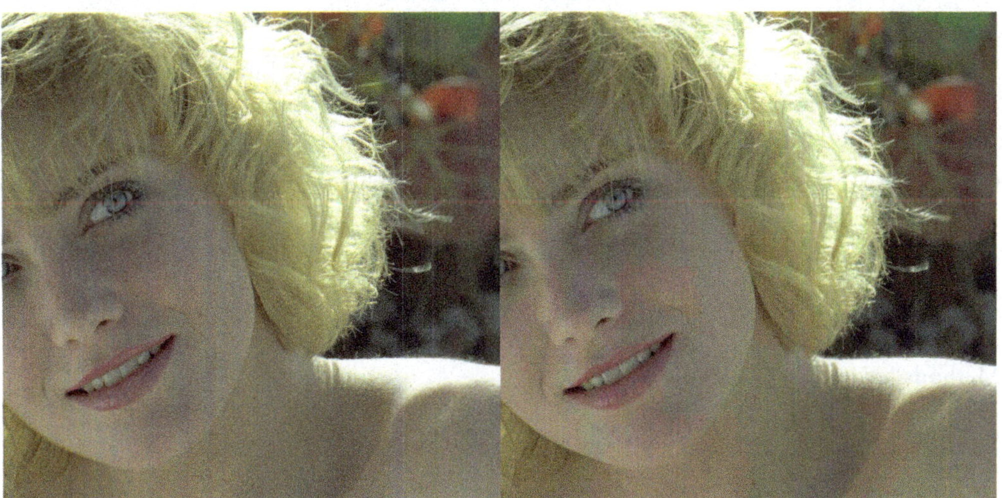

Figure 2.43 Lossless compression (left) vs lossy JPEG compression: heavily compressed (right)

departents, interdepartments, or even interfacilities), reversible compression methods are advised in case the data needed to be compressed. Lossy compression methods could be used to informal exchanges to showcase elements where color precision is not required or the error could be neglected (for instance, thumbnails, contact-sheets …). Lossy compression reduces file size much more than the file size achieved after lossless compression at the expense of image deterioration. The easiest example to understand the lossy compression is the JPEG, which is very effective to reduce the file size of an image … but if you go too far with the compression "quality" settings you will end with an image with poor quality.

Let's have a look at the most representative methods for each type of compression and maybe a few words to contextualize them.

Methods for lossy compression:

- *Transform Coding*: This one is the most popular. It is a combination of both types of compression: lossy and then lossless: first, it discards information naturally unnoticeable based on human perception, hence unnecessary data (reduction of "unappreciable" details), the lossy part; then, the remaining significant information (with its "appreciable" details) is compressed in a perfectly reversible way, the lossless part. It comes in two flavors:

  o *Discrete cosine transform (DCT)*: The one used in the JPEG compression, the most popular lossy format and generally the most efficient form of image compression (at the expense of loss of very valuable data for VFX, so not recommended at all for our pipeline).
  o *Wavelet transform*: It is also popular but being developed more recently the previous, DCT, is more traditionally used.

- *Color quantization*[19]: It operates by reducing the color samples present in the image to a few "representative" colors samples. The limited selection of colors is specified in the color palette in the header of the compressed image. Each pixel references one of the colors specified in the list of available samples of the color palette for this image.[20] This method can be combined with *dithering*[21] to avoid posterization (banding).

  o *Whole-image palette*: Usually 256 colors, used in Graphics Interchange Format (GIF) and PNG file formats.
  o *Block Palette*: Typically, 2 or 4 colors for each block of 4 × 4 pixels.

- *Chroma subsampling*: As I discussed in the previous chapter in depth. Taking advantage of human perception that recognizes more accurate spatial changes of brightness than those of color. So, by averaging or dropping some of the chrominance information in the image you reduce the amount of data store in the image file.
- *Fractal compression.*

Methods for lossless compression:

- *Run-length encoding (RLE)*: available in BMP, TGA, TIFF.
- *Area image compression.*
- *Predictive coding.*
- *Chain codes.*

- *Entropy encoding*: It replaces data elements with coded representations. In combination with the *transformation* and *quantization* forms of compression it results in a significantly reduced data size. The two most common entropy encoding techniques are *arithmetic coding* and *huffman coding*.
- *Adaptive dictionary algorithms*: For instance, *LZW*, available in the GIF and TIFF formats.
- *Deflate* (sometimes written all upper-case *DEFLATE*): Available in the PNG and TIFF formats.

It is possible that at this point you might be asking: "*What is the best choice for compression: lossless or lossy?*" The straight answer is "*it depends*". There is no "right" or "best" answer when it comes to choosing between *compressed* or *uncompressed*, or between *lossless* vs *lossy* compressions. The choice depends on the purpose of the compression and the measure of the consequences of the type of compression, which is why I took this length to explain the subject and provide you with useful knowledge. Let's face the first matter: to be or not to be compressed, that is the question. By deciding not to compress your files you can expect your drives to be flooded with data, make good calculations for the number of frames, its resolution and format because they are going to define the necessary storage, also keep in mind renders and other factors. Without compression the process of writing and reading image information will be faster in terms of CPU usage since there is no process of compression or decompression involved, but you are going to be subjected to the speed of your storage (drives and system) to read and write, sometimes contemporarily, and the ability to access to random sectors of the memory to get the bits and pieces of information required. So, to be clear, with no compression you have a different set of circumstances to handle the matter of reading/writing data. Maybe making a stress test would not hurt anybody if you were unsure. On the other hand, if you decide to go for a compressed workflow you need to know two main things: you should never use a pipeline that relies on a form of compression that deteriorates the aspect of your images on every step, because we have so many steps and, even if at a first look the files look right after one process generation, the result, in the long run, will deteriorate by a lot by the end of the pipeline. On top of that keep in mind that certain technical processes such as tracking and keying require the data structure to be as accurate as possible and maintain the maximum fidelity of the image captured, or what may be imperceptible for the naked human eye would be intolerable for a critical image process such as the extraction of a matte with a keyer or the precision of pattern recognition by a tracker. The pipeline should preserve the data structure integrity end to end. But there are some exceptions when you get out of the pipeline: you could use a lossy compressed image for a quick preview with drawing and annotations for clients or to brief the team, or for thumbnail, or in general for any distribution of the image within the team where color or image precision is not to be evaluated, and never for color accurate evaluations. Of course, those images you exported with a lossy compression are not meant to return to the pipeline ever, so the compression is meant to be unidirectional, never to be back to the pipeline. For your peace of mind, memes and cute photos of your cat could be highly compressed and it would not ruin the fun, for everything else please preserve the data structure integrity, so go lossless.

Now that you are familiar with the image compression methodologies, I think we should continue with other common file formats used in computer graphics that involve a form of compression that characterize them.

Other Commonly Used File Formats

JPEG: Joint Photographic Experts Group (.jpg/.jpeg)

Maybe the most popular lossy compression file format available. The JPEG (also known as JPG) takes its name from the acronym *Joint Photographic Experts Group* which set the standard in 1992, and since then it has become the most popular format for image compression worldwide. Its level of compression is adjustable to trade image quality against file size. It can reach a compression ratio of 10:1 with very little loss of detail able to be perceive.

Many JPEG files embed an International Color Consortium (ICC) color profile, usually *sRGB* and *Adobe RGB*. These color spaces are gamma encoded (non-linear transfer function), hence the dynamic range of an 8-bit JPEG file could represent a maximum dynamic range of about 11 stops. On webpages, if the JPEG image does not specify any color profile information (*untagged*), the color space assumed for displaying purposes is the *sRGB*.

PNG: Portable Network Graphics (.png)

PNG is an image file format that supports lossless data compression. It was developed as an improved, non-patented, replacement for the popular GIF, including the use of the Alpha channel to indicate transparency. It can use an indexed limited palette of colors (up to 256 samples) using 8-bit – not very helpful for us, to be honest; however, it has other features that can be helpful to optimize the use of bits, for instance the registration of one single channel using 1, 2, 4, 8, or 16 bits for that channel, depending on the needs; for *true color*[22] images 8-bit and 16-bit options are available, with or without Alpha. PNG uses the *deflate* lossless data compression format of encoding.

We have been discussing frame sequences (meaning one frame per file, to be interpreted as a "video" sequence) but we still have not discussed the use of video clip files, and since we are getting familiar with image compression, I think it would be good to study video compression and the use of video "containers" in our pipeline.

Video Compression: Inter-Frame Coding

The use of video containers instead of frame sequences is not the regular practice in the VFX pipeline for exchange, they are normally used for final deliveries in a display referred video stream. There are several reasons for video containers not to be preferred over frame sequences, but in order to understand those reasons you need to get to the bottom of a key feature of video compression: the *inter-frame coding*, a method of compression specifically designed for moving pictures.

Inter-frame coding, also known as *inter-frame compression*, is a method of video compression that takes into account what occurs between individual frames. You can retain less data and reduce the overall size of a video file by taking advantage of the fact that many times between a group of frames there are practically very little changes from one frame to the next. So, at certain intervals a whole frame is preserved entirely and used as a reference to be used to annotate the differences of other frames in the animation interval in relation to that reference one, this frame is known as *keyframe*. Those frames in between keyframes are the *interframes*. As a video plays forward, an interframe compression algorithm will only make note of changes that are distinct from the keyframe using *motion vectors* that will be tracking the movement of certain blocks. These motion vectors that relate the "moving" blocks of the image (or the parts of the image that are not moving) from the keyframe is the actual inter-frame information to be stored which is lighter than retaining the whole information of the whole frame for every frame. The only thing that needs to be added afterwards, when the video is decompressed, are the changes that take place in the video from the keyframe that you are comparing it against. In the event that there is a significant alteration in the video, from one frame to the next, such as the beginning of a new scene, then a new keyframe would be generated to serve as the reference point for the subsequent block of frames. Playback will be more seamless with more keyframes, but the resulting video file will obviously be larger.

When it comes to video compression methods that make use of inter-frame compression, there are numerous different kinds of frames that are typically used. These are referred to as the *I*, *P*, and *B* frames:

- *I-frame* means *intra-coded frame*. These are the frames that are totally stored as-they-are and utilized as reference points for the other frames in the video, they are also known as keyframes. This is because keyframes are the only frames in the movie that are not altered in any way. The compression methods available for the I-frames are those that operate on a static image (such as those we reviewed above in the previous section).
- *P-frame* stands for *prediction frame*. Inter-frame prediction involves partitioning the frame into a series of blocks. After that, the encoder searches for blocks that correspond to those in a previously encoded frame (forward encoding) or that are comparable to them – which would then become an I-frame, (keyframe). When there is a match, the block that is being encoded will point to the reference block that the block has a match with. In the future, it would be able to use that reference frame to bring back that matching block to the frame. In situations in which the block does not exactly match, the encoder will compute the difference between the two, and this information will be kept for later use when decoding. In order to carry out the computations and block matching, the P-frame has to have a reference point in the form of an I-frame.
- *B-frame* stands for *bidirectionally predicted frames*, the name is given because the prediction can be produced from either a previous frame or a successive frame, or even from both of them. The function performed by B-frames is analogous to the one that is performed by P-frames; however, these are predicted frames that can be constructed depending on information coming from either direction. B-frames are predicted from information contained in P and I frames (Figure 2.44).

There are different models, sequence types and algorithms to encode video using these kinds of frames, furthermore with the latest developments other functional kinds of frames were introduced for newer codecs.[23] But the most important element you need to grasp from this is the fact that the video containers encode the whole sequence of frames by referencing groups of frames and applying interpolations based on movement and other aspects of resolving data of one frame using information from other frames.

Now imagine the amount of calculations any software needs to perform before accessing to one random frame contained in a video container. It might be useful to reduce the file size of the video but, first of all, predicting frames such as P-frames and B-frames is going to be heavily affected by the quality of the I-frames and the precision of movement in relation to

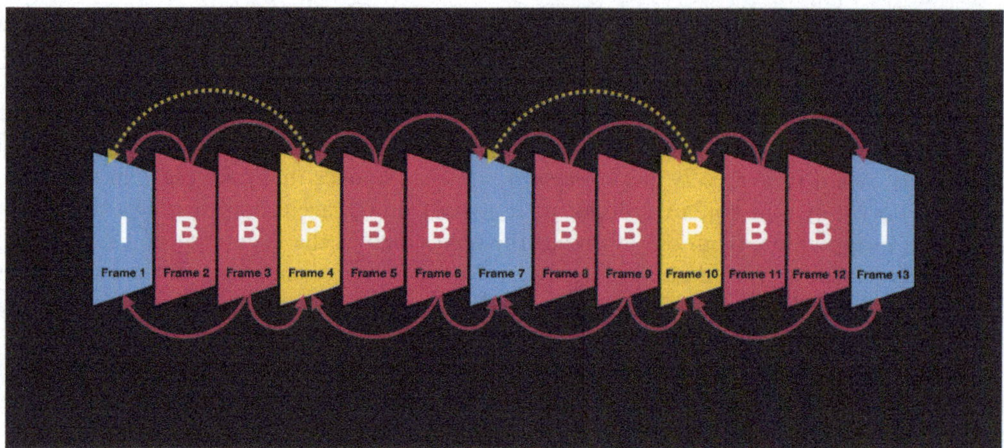

Figure 2.44 I-frame, P-frame, and B-frame sequence

the length of the interval between keyframes ... too many factors that will reduce the quality of our sequence, as for the JPEG, the reduction of detail might not be significant to the human eye but the data quality will be nonetheless severed. Of course you can have a video container with every frame being a I-frame (keyframe on every frame), and those I-frame having a lossless compression... but unless you have a good reason to do that – that you might have – I would recommend to have those frames stored in a frame per file basis. On the other hand, you can find a compromise for very high-quality video containers with very light compression that might be good candidates for masters in a delivery, for instance the Apple ProRes4444.

The last thing relevant for us here to mention about video containers is the *bitrate*. It refers to the amount of video data cap being transferred in a particular amount of time. This is especially relevant for online video streams, but also used in digital video cameras to specify the maximum data flow of a video recording. As usual it will define the file size vs quality of the content. The unit of measurement is bit/s, or bps – bit and not bite – which means bits per second. You can find it specified in kbps (kilobits – or 1000 bits – per second) or more commonly in Mbps (megabits – or 1,000,000 bits – per second). Most codecs allow you to decide if you want a *constant* bitrate, where the quality will adapt to the amount of available data to be use; or *variable* bitrate, where the amount of data will adapt to the amount of detail necessary. The level of detail will be intrinsically linked to the high frequencies of the image as it would require more smaller blocks to describe the content. Even in variable bitrates, sometimes there is a maximum cap for available data to be encoded depending on the device encoding the data on-the-fly, for instance video cameras.

Significant Codecs for VFX Post-Production

As I mentioned earlier the use of video containers is not a usual practice within the production of a VFX shot itself, but for interacting with other departments, for instance Editorial, the use of these wrappers is essential, as they will provide us with editorial reference cuts in the form of video with audio, and they are expecting the VFX department to provide them with temp versions of the VFX shots to be included in the edit while the final shot is being completed, as well as many other tasks ; another instance of the use of video wrappers that is very common is for character animation exports for review containing dialogue, as it might happen that the client needs to review something on-the-fly where audio and video are essential to be well linked; final deliveries for specific media, showreels and other promotional clips … so there is a good use of video containers in the postproduction section of a project and since we belong to it, we are expected to have a good knowledge base of the common codecs in use.

Foremost, please do not confuse *codecs* with *wrappers*. Wrappers are video containers where the information is going to be allocated; a codec is the way the video information is allocated (encoded) inside the containers to be interpreted (decoded) by a software or hardware. There may be codecs available only for certain wrappers, for instance the *Apple ProRes* set of codecs is available only for *QuickTime*; There are other wrappers, such as *Windows Media Video (.wmv)*, with their own proprietary codecs, like the three distinct codecs available for WMV, and by contrast there are codecs that can be placed different wrappers, such as, for instance, *Avid DNxHD* that can be wrapped in a *QuickTime (.mov)* or a *Material Exchange Format (.mxf)*; there are even file formats with different file extensions, like for instance the *MP4 (MPEG-4 Part 14)* used with the extensions: *.mp4*, *.m4a*, *.m4p*, *.m4b*, *.m4r* and *.m4v*, each one with their own features but the same file format (if you think about it, this is similar to what happens with certain image file formats, for instance the TIFF, you can use *.tiff* or *.tif*, they are both the same format but with different extensions). So, in brief, describing the wrapper will not always provide the full information, and since clarity and specificity are integral parts of our work you are advised to be as descriptive as possible, talking with propriety of language.

Specify video files with at least: *Codec* and *Container* (and preferably *Extension* as well), for instance:

- ProRes422, QuickTime (.mov)
  Or for codecs with levels of compression indicate the level of *quality*, for instance:
- H.264, Quality: High, QuickTime (.mov)
  Even though that would be enough to describe the main specs of the video file it would be preferable – as I mentioned above – that you documented yourself about the specifics of the video format available so you can specify the whole string of information required with more control over the data (remember, information is power, so be a powerful artist!), so a more accurate description of the H.264 previous example would be:
- H.264, Codec Profile: *High 4:2:0 8-bit*, Quality: *Best*, YCbCr Matrix: *Rec709*, wrapped in a QuickTime (.mov)
  This indicates pretty accurately all the technical specs of the format… but there is one more thing. There are other aspects, beyond the format of the video that you should specify: resolution, bit depth, color space, sound, and very important – to never just assume – frames per second (fps). The final instance:
- H.264, Codec Profile: *High 4:2:0 8-bit*, Quality: *Best*, YCbCr Matrix: *Rec709*, wrapped in a QuickTime (.mov) @24fps, Resolution: *4K UHD (3840x2160)*, Bit Depth: *8-bit*, Color Space: *Rec709*, MOS[24]

This is a pretty descriptive list of specs. The filename should somehow describe the main specs contained in the clip, but I would not enter in the subject of naming convention, that is for another book. Just keep in mind that every project is different, and you should keep in mind all the possible variations that you should address for the specific project and those that can be assumed because they are not alternative or possible variations. For instance, if you are working with a project that has been shot entirely with spherical lenses there is no need to specify a key piece of information in the specs to indicate if the material is spherical or anamorphic, you can safely assume it is just spherical and the pixel aspect ratio expected is square 1:1. But if the project is mixing anamorphic lenses of different factors of pixel aspect ratios, then you must specify the pixel aspect: "spherical 1:1", or "anamorphic 2:1". Other specifics, maybe less relevant to us, could be the indication of *keyframe* intervals (*I-frames*) or the limitation to certain *bitrates* (useful when the video must be streamed live online, for instance a remote review, usually online review tools such as *ftrack® Review* operate the encoding directly on their platform with all the specifics for optimization of the streaming).

I would like to review the most significant file formats for video containers, but I am going to keep this list quite simple; actually, we are going to review extensively the Apple Quick-Time, which is, in itself, a container with many variations and iterations (actually a multimedia framework), versatile and widely adopted; and the Material Exchange Format (also known as MXF), and then I will mention a few of the most commonly used codecs as well.

QuickTime (.mov)

QuickTime is an extensible multimedia framework developed by Apple Inc., first released in 1991. It is capable of handling various formats of digital video, picture, sound, panoramic images, and interactivity; in here we are going to focus just on the video features. Originally it used only Apple's proprietary codecs but today it supports third-party codecs. I will review the most significant ones here below. Because the QuickTime format was designed for ease of editing, it was chosen as the basis for the MPEG-4 container format. The *Quick-Time* File Format specifies a multimedia container file that contains one or more tracks, each of which stores a particular type of data: audio, video, effects, or text (for instance, subtitles). The usual extension is.*mov*, but rarely you could find.*qt* as well. Let's have a look at the most popular codecs used in the VFX industry.

Commonly Used Codecs

- **Animation**

  Developed by Apple, the *QuickTime Animation* format, also known as *QuickTime RLE*, is a video compression format and codec made for video clips to be played in real time without expensive hardware. It is usually wrapped in the QuickTime container with RLE compression. Data can be encoded either with lossless or lossy compression, and it is one of the few video codecs that supports an Alpha channel and multiple bit depths. These days it is quite obsolete though.

  Commonly used pixel formats:

  o *RGB 8-bit*
  o *RGBA 8-bit*

- **Apple ProRes**

  The flagship codec from Apple, the *ProRes* is a lossy video compression format developed by Apple for use in post-production that supports video resolutions up to 8K.

Apple refers to it as *«visually lossless»*[25] due to its great quality (but still *lossy*, keep it in mind as we already discussed it). It was launched in 2007 as the successor to the *Apple Intermediate Codec* (now obsolete). The *ProRes* family of codecs uses compression algorithms based on the *DCT*. *ProRes* is a popular professional final delivery format.

Available codec profiles:

o *ProRes 4444 XQ 12-bit*

   This profile represents the highest quality option for 4:4:4:4[26] moving pictures in the ProRes family. A very high data rate in order to maintain all the information required for HDR video, produced by digital camera sensors. This format supports up to 12-bits per image channel and up to 16-bit for the alpha channel, just like the regular *ProRes 4444.*[27]

o *ProRes 4444 12-bit*

   This is a very high-quality profile for 4:4:4:4 video sources. Full-resolution, mastering-quality 4:4:4:4 RGBA channels, and perceptually almost identical to the original source. It performs very well even after decoding and reencoding for further generations, even if the RGB channels are encoded with a bit depth of 12-bit, its alpha channel is encoded at 16-bit, making it versatile for motion graphics (usually worked in video clips as opposite to VFX where the regular practice is frame sequences). Compared to the uncompressed 4:4:4 original, this codec has an astonishingly low data rate with a good perception of the image.[28]

o *ProRes 422 HQ 10-bit*

   This one is a higher data rate variant of the *ProRes 422* that maintains the same high degree of visual quality as *ProRes 4444* but for 4:2:2 image sources. *ProRes 422 HQ*, which is widely used in the video post-production business, provides a great preservation of the highest-quality professional HD footage that a single-link HD-SDI signal can carry. This codec can decode and reencode full-width, 4:2:2 video sources at 10-bit while remaining visually lossless over several generations of decoding and reencoding.[29]

o *ProRes 422 10-bit*

   The *ProRes 422* is a high-quality compressed codec that provides virtually all the benefits of *ProRes 422 HQ*, but at 66% of the data rate, making it a good candidate for offline editing in real-time.[30]

o *ProRes 422 LT 10-bit*

   The *422 LT* version is a more compressed format than the ProRes 422 above, with approximately 70% of the data rate and 30% smaller file sizes. This codec is ideal for situations where storage capacity and data rate are limited. In our perspective, its use is intended mainly for editorial purposes.[31]

o *ProRes 422 Proxy 10-bit*

   The *Proxy* option is a codec that is even more compressed than *ProRes 422 LT*, and it is intended for use in offline processes that demand low data rates but full-resolution video, for instance, shot previews in the production database.

- **Avid DNxHD**

   Avid DNxHD (Digital Nonlinear Extensible HD) is a lossy HD video post-production codec created by Avid Technology for multi-generation editorial with low storage and bandwidth needs. It is a video codec designed to be used as both an *intermediate* format for editing and a *presentation* format. DNxHD data is normally wrapped in an MXF container – that we will review later below – but it can also be stored in a QuickTime container, like in this case. DNxHD is quite similar to JPEG, every frame is independent and consists of *VLC*-coded *DCT* coefficients. This codec supports alpha channel data.

Available codec Profiles:

o *DNxHD 4:4:4 10-bit 440Mbit*[32]
o *DNxHD 4:2:2 10-bit 220Mbit*
o *DNxHD 4:2:2 8-bit 220Mbit*
o *DNxHD 4:2:2 8-bit 145Mbit*
o *DNxHD 4:2:2 8-bit 36Mbit*

- **Avid DNxHR**

  Avid DNxHR (Digital Nonlinear Extensible High Resolution) is a lossy UHDTV post-production lossy codec designed for multi-generation editorial purposes with less storage and bandwidth needs. The codec was made for resolutions that are higher than *FullHD* (1080p), such as 2K, 4K, and 8K resolutions. The HD resolutions will still be done with *DNxHD*.

  Available codec Profiles:

  o *DNxHR 444 – Finishing Quality. 12-bit 4:4:4 (Cinema-quality delivery)*
  o *DNxHR HQX – High Quality. 12-bit 4:2:2 (UHD/4K Broadcast-quality delivery)*
  o *DNxHR HQ – High Quality. 8-bit 4:2:2*
  o *DNxHR SQ – Standard Quality. 8-bit 4:2:2 (suitable for delivery format)*
  o *DNxHR LB – Low Bandwidth. 8-bit 4:2:2 (offline quality)*

- **H.264**

  H.264, also known as *MPEG-4 Advanced Video Codec (AVC)* or *MPEG-4 Part 10* is, by a wide margin, the codec that is utilized the most frequently for the encoding, compression, and distribution of video content. The goal of the *H.264/AVC* project was to develop a standard capable of providing good video quality at significantly lower bit rates than previous standards – half or less the bit rate of the previous *MPEG-2, H.263*, or *MPEG-4 Part 2 –*, and easy to implement. Another goal was to provide enough flexibility for the standard to be used in a wide range of applications on a wide range of networks and systems, such as high (and low) resolution video, broadcast, DVD, telecommunications, etc. The *H.264* standard can be thought of as a "family of standards" made up of many profiles, with the *High profile* being by far the most popular. A given decoder interprets at least one profile of those available, but not necessarily all of them. The standard specifies the format of the encoded data and how it is decoded, but it does not specify the techniques for encoding video; this is left up to encoder designers to choose for themselves, and a broad range of encoding schemes have been devised. *H.264* is most commonly used for lossy compression, but it is also feasible to construct completely lossless-coded sections inside lossy-coded images or to accommodate unusual cases where the entire encoding is lossless.

  Commonly used Codec Profiles:
  o *Main*

  Used for digital SDTV[33] (streaming in MPEG-4 format as defined in the *DVB*[34] standard. It is not used for HDTV[35] broadcasts, because in 2004 the *High Profile* (specified here below) was developed for that purpose.

o *High*

The most used profile for disc storage and broadcasting, especially for high-definition television (TV) applications (Blu-ray, DVB HDTV broadcast service)

Quality settings:

o Lossless.
o Lossy, with an adjustable *rate factor* (RF) for balancing file size vs quality.

- **H.265**

H.265, also known as *high efficiency video coding (HEVC)* or *MPEG-H Part 2*, was developed as part of the *MPEG-H* project as a replacement for the popular *Advanced Video Coding*, the *H264*. When compared to *H.264*, *H265* delivers up to a 50% increase in data compression while maintaining the same level of video quality. It supports resolutions up to 8192 × 4320 pixels (including 8K UHD[36]). The high fidelity of the *H.265* profile *Main 10* has been incorporated into nearly all supporting hardware.

Commonly used Codec Profiles:

o *Main*

It allows for an 8-bit color bit depth and 4:2:0 chroma sampling (the most common type of video used with consumer devices).

o *Main 10*

It allows for improved video quality since it can support video at 10-bit color bit depth, while the Main only 8-bit.

Quality settings:

o Lossless.
o Lossy, with an adjustable RF for balancing File Size vs Quality.

- *Motion JPEG* (MJPEG)-*format A* (**MJPEG-A**) & **MJPEG-B**

MJPEG is a type of video codec in which successive frames are encoded using the conventional JPEG technique. There is no interframe compression, thus the resulting encoded data does not achieve the same level of compression as a codec that uses interframe techniques. However, decompression is usually faster, and because there are no dependencies on other frames, any frame can be accessed independently. There are fewer legal restrictions when using the open JPEG standard. It should be noted that the term MJPEG does not refer to a single format. Many entities have created formats that can be classified as MJPEG, however, they differ in subtle ways. MJPEG is available in two variants. The usage of markers distinguishes these two formats. Markers are supported by MJPEG format A but not by MJPEG-B. Each MJPEG-A completely conforms to the standard JPEG specification and, as a result, enables the application of markers.

Usual pixel formats:

o $Y'C_bC_r$ 4:2:0 8-bit
o $Y'C_bC_r$ 4:2:2 8-bit
o $Y'C_bC_r$ 4:4:4 8-bit

Quality settings:

o Lossless.
o Lossy, with an adjustable RF for balancing File Size vs Quality.

- **MPEG-4**

  The *MPEG-4* is a set of international standards for digital audio and video data compression, multimedia systems, and file storage formats. It was first launched in late 1998 as a collection of audio and video coding standards and associated technology. MPEG-4 is used for audiovisual data compression for Internet video, telecommunications, and broadcast TV applications.

  The most commonly use pixel format:

o $Y'C_bC_r$ 4:2:0 8-bit

Quality settings:

o Lossy, with an adjustable RF for balancing File Size vs Quality.

- **Photo – JPEG**

  The Photo JPEG codec uses the Joint Photographic Experts Group image compression technique. In most cases, it is used to store still photographs, but in this case, it is utilized to edit and save high-quality video data. QuickTime has three JPEG-based codecs built in: Photo JPEG, MJPEG-A, and MJPEG-B. MJPEG is identical to *Photo-JPEG* except that the *MJPEG* codecs include translators to support the different capture cards.

  Pixel format:

o $Y'C_bC_r$ 4:2:0 8-bit
o $Y'C_bC_r$ 4:2:2 8-bit
o $Y'C_bC_r$ 4:4:4 8-bit

Quality settings:

o Lossless.
o Lossy, with an adjustable RF for balancing file size vs quality.

- **PNG**

  Well, this is easy to explain: a series of PNG encoded frames wrapped in a video clip.
  Pixel formats:

o RGB 8-bit
o RGBA 8-bit
o RGB 16-bit
o RGBA 16-bit

Quality settings:

o Lossless.

- **Uncompressed**

  It is what it says it is. All data on every single frame, uncompressed and wrapped in a QuickTime container. Yes, it would not require the data to be compressed and then decompressed but do not expect uncompressed videos to run smoothly in real time as it may require some computational time to read all the uncompressed data. In this instance the speed of your drives would make the difference. However, before you go for uncompressed videos, ask yourself if it would not be better to use a lossless codec, if the answer is *no*, then *you are going to need a bigger boat*: start considering getting new bigger drives … because, trust me, you will need them quickly. Uncompressed video data is quite large.

These are just a few samples of codec commonly used but remember technology evolves, so when you find something that you never used before: read its specs, do not guess (please).

MXF: Material Exchange Format (.mxf)

The *MXF* (which stands for *Material "eXchange" Format*) is a container format for professional digital video and audio, described by a set of SMPTE standards, that is widely used in post-production as a *container, wrapper* or *reference* file format. *MXF* files, like in the case of QuickTime, include metadata,[37] which is descriptive information about the media contained within the same file. Frame rate, frame size, creation date, and custom data contributed by a camera operator, assistant, or archivist are all examples of metadata.

Other Relevant Image File Formats

PSD: Photoshop Document (.psd)

PSD files are Adobe Photoshop's native file type. You have probably come across files with the.*psd* suffix, especially if you've used Adobe Photoshop (who doesn't?). Photoshop Documents, which are most typically used by designers and artists, are sophisticated tools for picture data storage and creation. It can store several layers, pictures, and objects. A PSD file can have up to 30,000 pixels in height and width, with a wide variety of image depth and color spread. Even if it is the proprietary format of Adobe Photoshop, other software could read it and interpret it, for instance Nuke, but the file format itself has not been conceived for exchange with other software, hence you could find incompatibilities, shown in the form of the file opened in another software will look different from the original, and that is clearly not a good thing. So my very conservative advice would be not to use PSD files outside Photoshop, and if you really have to, try to keep it simple, rastering all graphics and effects, flattening all layers that could be compacted and just use the PSD file to layout the layers (keeping in consideration that certain blending modes such as "color dodge" or "color burn" for instance, could have different appearances). Keep PSD files for Photoshop, then export using the best suitable file format candidate depending on your needs.

HDR: High Dynamic Range Raster Image (.hdr)

An HDR file is a *raster image*[38] file format for storing digital camera photographs with a HDR. It enables picture editors to improve the color and brightness of digital images with a limited dynamic range. This adjustment helps tone-mapping resulting in a more natural-looking image. Typically, HDR files are saved as 32-bit images.

PIC: Pictor Raster Image

Developed in the 80s, the PIC file is a raster image file saved in *PICtor* format. It was one of the first widely accepted DOS imaging standards (yes, very old), and it is currently primarily used by *Graphics Animation System for Professionals (GRASP)* and *Pictor Paint*. However, unlike other more popular file types such as PNG or JPG, which open when double-clicked, PIC files usually require the assistance of third-party applications to access. There are quite uncommon in regular VFX pipelines.

SGI: Silicon Graphics Image (.sgi)

SGI files are images that have been stored in the *SGI* format. It is usually a color image with three color channels. SGI files contain pictures designed to be displayed on *Silicon Graphics* workstations. Silicon Graphics Computer Systems was a high-performance computing manufacturer that produced hardware and software founded in 1981. Their workstations became the gold standard in the early days of digital visual effects (very expensive but efficient machines), unfortunately, a decline resulting from a series of business strategy moves made SGI less and less popular over time until 2009 when they filed for bankruptcy.

Today a few digital image processor softwares offer compatibility with SGI, but the format itself is not in mainstream use.

TARGA: Truevision Advanced Raster Graphics Adapter (.tga, .icb, .vda, .vst)

TARGA is an acronym for *Truevision Advanced Raster Graphics Adapter*; *TGA* is an initialism for *Truevision Graphics Adapter*. *Truevision, Inc.* created the *TARGA* format for its video boards. The format allows any pixel bit depth up to 255, of which up to 15 bits can be dedicated to an alpha channel, however, in practical terms, the only bit depths used were 8, 15, 16, 24, or 32, with the 16-bit version using 1 bit for the alpha (values that are either "black" or "white"), and 32-bit version using 8-bits for the alpha (256 values).

TARGA files are used to render still images and frame sequences. Different software use different filename extensions, for instance 3DS Max can render *.vda*, *.icb*, and *.vst* variants as well as *.tga*.

XPM: X PixMap (.xpm)

Since its inception in 1989, the *X Window System* has made use of an image file format known as *X PixMap* (XPM). Its primary function is the generation of icon pixmaps, and it supports the use of transparent pixels.

YUV: Luminance (Y) - Chrominance (UV) Encoded Video/Image File (.yuv)

A *YUV* file is a video file encoded in the YUV[39] color model format. It can be saved in the YUV 4:2:0, 4:2:2, or 4:4:4 formats and stores a series of YUV images as a single video file. Both *MPEG-4* and *H.264* decoders can open YUV video files.

GIF: Graphics Interchange Format (.gif)

The format by excellence to store memes and cat pictures, the very fabric of the procrastinating side of the internet is made of gif images. The Graphics Interchange Format, also known as GIF, is a raster file format made simple. Each file can support 256 *indexed* colors and up to 8 bits per pixel. Additionally, rudimentary animations can be made with GIF files by combining images or frames. Do not expect your renders to be stored in a gif but there are other – non-cat related – uses for this light format, for instance, screen captures to showcase others how to find something in a software (in the most elaborated cases, even with animations to create a step-by-step guide), or simply to make annotations.

These are just a few examples of the myriad of file formats available. I am pretty sure you will find others not listed here, it does not really matter. What is really important is that you get familiar with them when you find them. Learn about their features and compatibility. Do not use something if you do not really know it (C'mon: "*I use it because everybody uses it*" or "*I use it because a cousin of mine that works in an important facility told me to use this (even if I don't know why)*", are not excuses). It takes just a few minutes to Google it, find the official resources and learn all the specs you need to know about it for your work. You would be surprised how those minutes invested could shape your career and make your life – and those interacting with you – easier. Spend the time doing things right instead of guessing and fixing errors that would be avoidable if you spent those minutes wisely.

We have focused enough on the data storage, now it is time to "look" at the displays as they are an essential part of color management.

Display White Balance

To understand the color pipeline, we need to understand every element of the digital image process. We had briefly seen the process of capturing the image, the workspace and very simple transformations, and the storage of the imaging data, however, there is a link in the chain we cannot underestimate: the output display, and I mean your monitor (or any other display device you or anybody else uses). We are all supposed to be looking at the same image, that, in theory, must look identical, and this point, believe me, is a big deal and one of the main reasons for color management to exist.

Leaving aside any particular software for manipulating or generating the image and its color handling, a precise color observation requires, first of all, a calibrated color monitor, and a managed – synchronized – color pipeline, everybody involved using the same rules and standards, just to be sure what you see is what your client or collaborators will see on their side, avoiding surprises in your color grade or misleading notes and comments because someone has the wrong perception of the image represented (based on true events).

But let's start from the basics, your hardware, the display (and for display I mean computer monitor, TV, projector ... anything used to watch the content on) should be able to be precise in the way it represents color pixels on screen. One of those elements that will affect the overall look of the represented image is the *white point*. Many modern displays have the ability to apply different standard white points or even to customize it.

The white point is one of the three foundations of any color space (together with the *primaries* and the *transfer function*).

The *CIE* settled the standards for *illuminants*. An *illuminant* is a theoretical source of visible light with its spectral power distribution, which is published and established as a universal reference. It provides the basis for comparing image colors. There is one which regards us especially, the *CIE Standard Illuminant D65*. Because it is used in postproduction in different applications, for instance HDR content, as one of the fundamental components of the *Rec2020* color space that will review later in another chapter.

The *D65* theoretically corresponds to the direct sun light at noon, including the reflected light from the sky in Western Europe/Northern Europe. That is why it is included in the series of *daylight illuminants*. There is no actual light source in the world able to emit *exactly* this spectral power distribution, it is just mathematical simulation data that helps align a light source to this ideal point. In color temperature it sits at around 6504 K,[40] slightly above the *Planckian Locus* (that we will discuss later in this book when we break down the elements of color spaces), that is the origin of its name D, for daylight, and 65 for 6504 K (I know the name D65 suggests that the *correlated color temperature*, also known as *CCT*, should be 6500 K, but in truth it is actually closer to 6504 K; there are historical reasons for that discrepancy, after a revision in 1968 involving the position of *Planckian Locus* to be shifted after the D65 illuminant was already defined, hey, its science, and sometimes adjustments are required, remember the *scientific method*!).

For us, the *CIE Illuminant D65* is quite important because it is used for various standards, including standard dynamic range (SDR) and HDR TV; and, of course, the sRGB color space, the most popular color space used for computer monitors for CGI.

The hardware must be calibrated from its manufacturer for this target D65 specifics, then, when you perform a software calibration to best align the color rendition capabilities of the screen (that varies even with time), it assumes the white point of your monitor must be aligned at the D65 standard, so it balances the white point to be as precise as possible, following the same standards of color temperature and balance magenta/green. Without this factor, the color calibration and alignment could not be possible. So the software (using a color calibration device sampling the colors shown in the display) will make the required adjustments to make the white point as close as possible for the screen.

A note about the quality of the monitor we use: of course we need a good sRGB monitor for regular SDR images or Rec2020 for HDR, but let's address for a second the needs for different types of artists and tasks required. For instance, for compositing, and VFX in general, we do not have the same needs for color accuracy as colorists, because a colorist needs to grade color in *absolute terms*, so their display must be as accurate in the rendition of the color as the standards for cinema projection, or final display targeted for distribution, as possible to guarantee the decisions you are making during the grading process would represent the final artistic direction of the filmmakers. Compositors, and VFX in general, work in a "slightly more relaxed" color accuracy scale, because their reference is not always absolute, they need to integrate different layers from different sources: live action and CGI (or even CGI alone to look photoreal). The key point for them is that they all look coherent with one other, usually having the live-action *plate* (*scan*) as the reference for color, but sometimes there are other reference points, or if you do not have an internal reference in the plate maybe you have it in another plate or even on an external reference ... we do not need to worry "much" about color in "absolute" terms for VFX because a colorist will do that for the whole film, still the image should be coherent and precise in terms of alignment to the reference and the filmmakers artistic intent, as we are trusting data readings (values). Once said that, and in order to clarify your ideas, in case you had any doubts or misunderstanding that could mislead you to think "color accuracy is not important for VFX purposes", no, that is not what I meant. What I mean is that, as we are going to review in the next section below, color precision in *reference* monitors and projectors can be extremely expensive, because they are submitted to an extremely high standard of manufacturing for color precision. And rightly so, because what you see in a reference display, in a controlled environment (like for instance a screening room), becomes the gold standard for the final approval of the whole show: *what you see is what you get*. On the other hand, in practical terms, regular VFX people should work with the best display possible, able to represent a perceptually accurate image for the color space(s) required for their work. That is why sometimes, from the grading suite, we receive some VFX shots, *kicked-back*, because during the grading process certain mismatches in areas of color were shown after certain manipulations of the color or in a perfectly "absolute" calibrated environment. So, monitors really matter for VFX artists as much as anyone else, of course, but this does not mean that in order to work in compositing or lighting you need to spend a fortune in order to be able to work. You need to know that the more accurate your display is, the more control you have over the image you are observing and the more you can trust what you see without unlikely surprises.

Monitor Types

We can classify monitors into three categories, depending on the fidelity of its imaging rendition: A, B, C.

A grade (or grade 1), the true reference display. It is the kind of monitor a colorist needs, the most accurate. The only able to perform a *Quality Control (QC)*.

At the other side of the spectrum there are the *C grade* monitors (or grade 3), in this category they are included with the consumer TVs and some monitors at consumer level. Usually displays (monitors, TVs or projectors) you can find in a "supermarket" (next to the clothing section). Please, try not to use these for operations involving color accurate evaluation.

In the middle the *B grade* (or grade 2) computer and broadcast monitors for professionals, the right for us. Inside this category there are plenty of models and companies to choose. Just some piece of advice, carefully choose your monitor for work, you will spend many hours in front of it. Of course, now you are questioning: "*How can I choose a good monitor?*" and "*What should I look for in a monitor?*", there are many factors to consider, but for me, the most important is the *Delta E* level (also shown as ΔE, or dE).

The CIE developed the standard measurement known as Delta E to measure the difference between two colors that display on a screen. The idea is that you should go for a monitor (or projector) with a Delta E level as low as possible, as close to 0 as you can.

The mathematical difference – known as Delta – between the values of the color that is presented on the screen (displayed) and the color values of the original standard color sent to the display to be presented, is known as the *delta E level*. Greater precision is shown by lower Delta E values, whereas a large mismatch is indicated by higher Delta E values. As a rule of thumb, I would discourage you from working on a display with a delta E value higher than 2.

Empfindung is the German term for "*sensation*", and it is what the letter "E" in *Delta E* stands for. The Greek word *delta* (Δ) refers to a variable's gradual shift. Hence the phrase "Delta E" refers to a *difference in sensation*.

On a typical scale,[41] the Delta E value will range from 0 to 100:

- Not visible to the human eye ($\Delta E \leq 1.0$) (*this is good as a reference monitor*)
- ΔE between 1 and 2: Visible at close inspection (*this is good enough for VFX*)
- ΔE between 2 and 10: Immediately apparent (*please don't use it, try to avoid it. At your own risk*)

- Colors are more comparable than the contrary is true in the range of ΔE between 11 and 49 (*absolutely not!*)
- $\Delta E = 100$: The opposite is true for colors (*that is not a monitor, that is a washing machine, leave it where you found it!*)

As a piece of advice, remember this formula: $\Delta E \leq 2$ is good enough for us.

Another good point to consider is a 10-bit monitor over the traditional 8-bit, the accuracy available will be much better, in theory, because a 10-bit could display more values (gradients). They are becoming more and more popular. However, bit depth alone does not guarantee anything, follow the *Delta E level* as a trustable indicator. In any case, just to be clear, it is just a question of visualization of the image; the quality of the data stored and processed will be the same, and the data does not suffer because of the quality of your display; but be advised: how you handle that data, manipulating the values, is based on your perception, so yes, it will definitely affect the "quality" of your work.

Once we are sure about the "quality" of our display and our hardware and software are calibrated and ready, the second stage is to ensure the color pipeline is aligned. This task is not, strictly speaking, for the artists to do, but for engineers, facilities technicians, and color scientists. Still, it is essential that you understand the whole color management process and your role in it to ensure you play your part accordingly.

I wanted to end this chapter making a more software-oriented consideration. I know I said the book is software-agnostic but I believe it does not hurt to look into the specifics of widely used software to illustrate certain points that otherwise would be trickier to explain and understand in the abstract of the absence of a target software. The next – and last – section of this chapter is oriented to Nuke users.

Input Process & Viewer Process

Between the image data retrieved in a file and the image shown in the display there are a few processes in order to render the image with an artistic intent. Here we are going to discuss two of these processes that will become useful to understand the flow of color processing to render the image on the screen.

In Nuke there are two main image processes applied to the *viewer*[42]: the *viewer process*, and the *input process*. Neither of them changes the actual values of the image, but just the way they are interpreted before being displayed in your *viewer*.

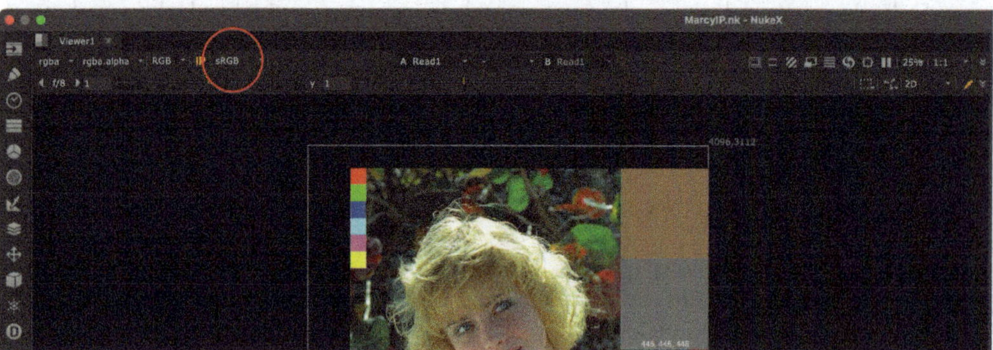

Figure 2.45 Nuke viewer process

The *viewer process*, sometimes generally referred as just an LUT of the viewer, is typically used to convert from the workspace (typically from Nuke *linear* workspace) to the display color space (commonly *sRGB*). Further adjustments to the LUT could be applied in the *viewer process* to "enhance" the display of the image based on arbitrary factors to better represent the *curve* of the target footage (Figure 2.45).

I do not need to tell you this is a very delicate matter, because the wrong LUT could change the appearance of the image and make you have a false impression of it, applying color corrections in a wrong way. For instance, if the LUT in your *viewer process* is too magenta you will attempt to correct your image by adding more green to view your image "correctly" in your *viewer*, and wrongly compensate for the error in the LUT by adding the same error the right LUT should be compensating. At this point we are in a so-called *display referred* workflow, we will discuss about it in a later chapter.

By default, if you do not have different instructions, work with the default *sRGB* for computer monitors or *rec709* if you are displaying your viewer in a TV or projector (*HDTV*).[43] Like the case of *sRGB* standard destined for computer monitors, the *rec709* standard was settled by the *International Telecommunication Union* (*ITU*). The full name of this standard is *ITU-R Recommendation BT.709*, and commonly known simply as *Rec 709* (for recommendation 709). The key points of this standard, in relation with color display, are:

- 8-Bit color-depth.
- The black point is settled at value 16 and the white point at 235 in broadcast. Value 0 and value 255 are used for synchronization and are prohibited to be used for video data (so-called *illegal*). So, in the $Y'C_BC_R$ signal, the range is limited to 16–235 for luma and 16–240 for Chroma.
- This standard was specifically created for the digital *HDTV*.[44]

The other process option available in Nuke to be discussed here is the *input process*.

The *input process* consist of a group of operations that are performed on the image before it is processed by the viewer, they can be not only color manipulations but also spatial transformations or filters. Like in the *viewer process*, this correction does not modify the actual values in the image, just the way the *viewer* is going to display the image.

The Input Process in Nuke™

You can create your own *input process* by selecting a node, a *gizmo* or a group. Just go to the menu: *Edit > Node > Use as input process*. As soon as you have an active *input process* you will notice the "*IP*" button on top of the *Viewer* to highlight. The *input process* is very useful to set any primary grade (which is an overall *look* color correction) or even perform image transformations, such as crop or pan-scan; and other filters help you to have a closer look at the final aspect of the film as the filmmakers intended it to be shown, or simply display a manipulation that might help you in any way, being it a color manipulation, the application of LUTs, technical visualizations (like, for instance, a False-Color LUT, very useful to monitor the exposure of your image), or to simply disregard certain areas of the image. This Input Process can be very helpful on a color managed pipeline to place, for instance, the look modification transforms (LMTs),[45] which we will discuss on the chapter regarding ACES (Figures 2.46 and 2.47).

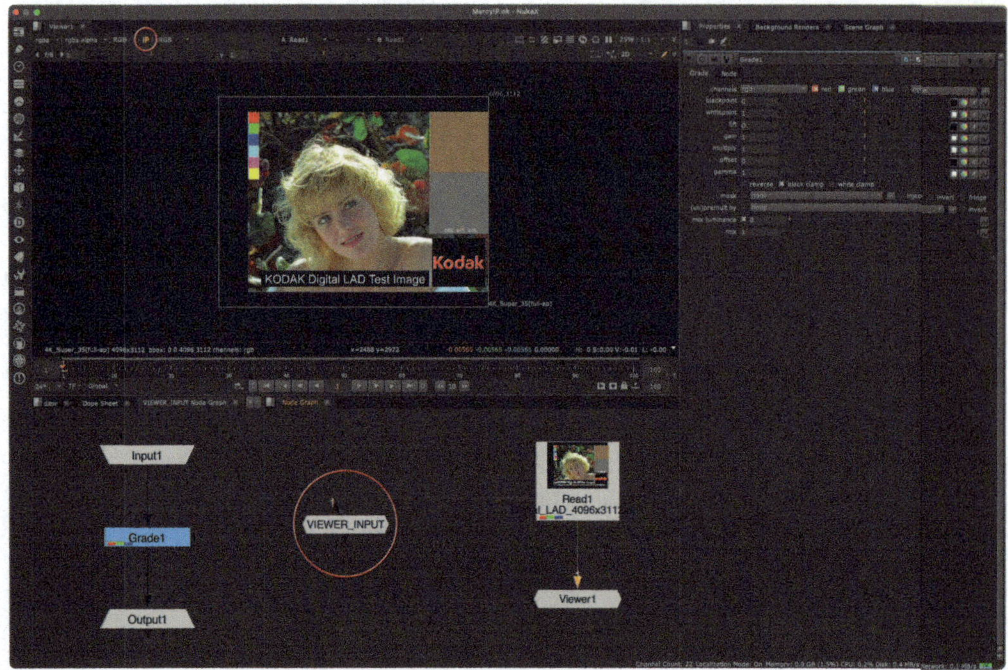

Figure 2.46 Nuke input process

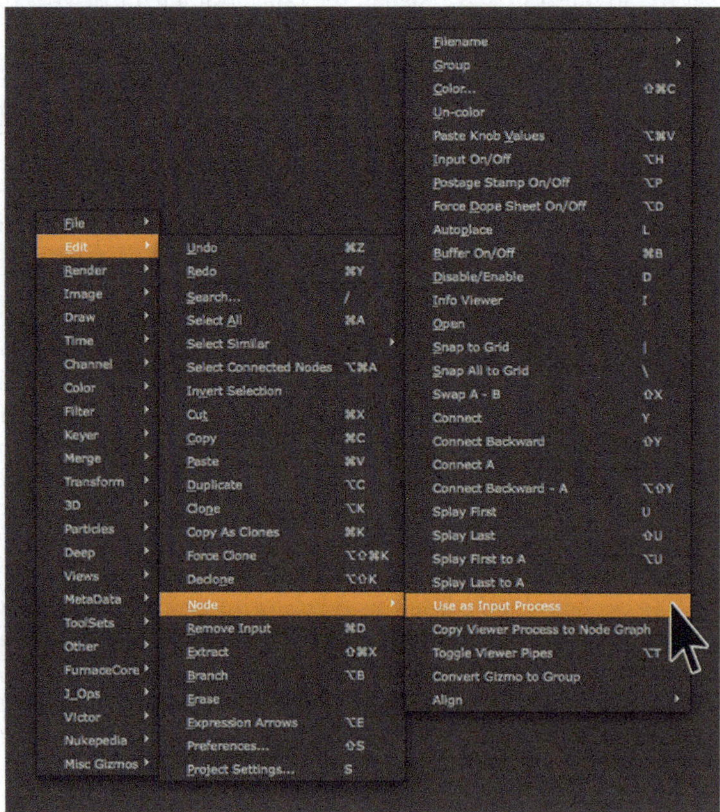

Figure 2.47 Setting the input process node in Nuke

Notes

1 The reason I am placing *color* between quotes ("") here is because I am hypothetically using only one channel to represent levels of intensity as color is the result of the combination of the three RGB channels. I know it would be more correct to refer to it as the intensity levels of a hypothetical monochrome channel or register, but since I do not want to complicate things unnecessarily for this explanation I am going to define as *colors* every possible value of the bit (or combination of them) to be achievable by the defined number of bits.

2 *IEC*: An international standards organization that prepares and publishes international standards for all electrical, electronic, and related technologies, collectively known as *electrotechnology* (in French: *Commission Electrotechniqeu*).

3 Without any nonlinear encoding and decoding luminance or tristimulus values typically used in video or still image systems (such as, for instance, *gamma correction* or logarithmic distribution of luminance samples, a.k.a. *log* encoding).

4 An *integer* is a whole number – not a fractional number – that can be positive, negative, or zero. A few examples of integers are: −1, 0, 1, 23, 45, 678. Just to avoid confusion let me put a few examples of numbers that are not integers: −1.2, 4/5, 6.78, 0.009.

5 *Fixed-point* is a method of representing fractional or decimal – non-integer – computing numbers by storing a *fixed* number of digits of their fractional part. Like, for instance, the price in a supermarket displayed in dollar amounts, often stored with exactly two fractional digits, representing the cents (0.01 of dollar), for example: "$3.99", "$2.65" or "$1.00". In general, the term refers to representing fractional values as integer multiples of some fixed small unit like using *dimes* or the *cents* of the dollar.

6 *IEEE*: The *IEEE* is a professional association for electronic engineering, electrical engineering, and associated disciplines, dedicated to advancing technology.

7 Which means *approximately 340,282,350,000,000,000,000,000,000,000,000,000,000* (against the "mere" 2,147,483,647 of the 32-bit integer variable).

8 Indicated with a *period* character (.) or a *comma* character (,) depending on your regional system.

9 *Scientific notation*: A way of expressing numbers that are too large or too small, resulting in a long string of digits, to be conveniently written in decimal form. For instance: 5×10^6 is the scientific notation of 5,000,000; and 5×10^{-6} is the scientific notation of 0.000005.

10 The term *curve* is used to refer to the representation of the resulting values of a given mathematical *function* – which is an assignment of an element of y to each element of x – so, we can say "a straight *curve*" or "a linear *curve*" referring to a straight line to be the graphic representation of the function, even if it sounds like an oxymoron.

11 The number (2.2 in this case) represents the slope, which is a derivative operator. A gamma value less than 1 ($\gamma < 1$) is usually referred to as *encoding gamma*, and the process of encoding with this "compressive" power-law nonlinear operation is called *gamma compression*; on the other hand a gamma value greater than 1 ($\gamma > 1$), like in this case, is usually referred to as *decoding gamma*, and the application of the expansive power-law nonlinearity is called *gamma expansion*.

12 The term *tagging* (using *tags*) refers to optional color space information parameters written in the metadata of a media that describe the content. Tags describe image colorimetry in a simplified way and can be used by the software to interpret the instructions to properly display the content as intended.

13 In Nuke you force this kind of nonlinear behavior using the *Log2lin* node (going from linear to logarithmic: "lin2log") before the operation; and another *Log2lin* node in reverse (going from logarithmic to linear again: "log2lin"); and setting the appropriate parameters in the other knobs (usually: *black* = "0" (minimum); *white* = "1023" (maximum); and *gamma* = "1") for a natural logarithmic progression.

14 For this to be true: x is *Real number* greater than 0.

15 *Base plus fog* density is the optical density of a film due to its base density plus any action of the developer on the unexposed silver halide crystals. It represents the darkest black level archivable where dark details get lost (flattened) under the minimum level of exposure to achieve any brightness variations in the dark areas. The *base plus fog* density can be measured by developing an unexposed film strip through the entire processing cycle and measuring the resultant optical density.

16 *ICC profile* is a set of data that characterizes a color input or output device, or a color space, according to the standards proclaimed by the ICC.

17   The Oscars for technology.
18   «Developed in partnership by the Academy of Motion Picture Arts and Sciences and the Linux Foundation, the Academy Software Foundation provides a neutral forum for open source software developers in the motion picture and broader media industries to share resources and collaborate on technologies for image creation, visual effects, animation and sound. The Foundation is home to OpenVDB, OpenColorIO, OpenEXR and OpenCue.» Olin, E. (May 1, 2019). *Open-EXR and OpenCue Become Academy Software Foundation Projects*. Academy Software Foundation. https://www.aswf.io/news/openexr-and-opencue-join-aswf/
19   *Color quantization,* in general in computer graphics, is referred to the simplification of a color space, using a process that reduces the number of individual colors used in an image, typically with the purpose that the resulting image should be as visually similar as possible to the original image. The word "quantize", intends the restriction of the number of possible values of "a quantity" so that certain variables can assume only certain discrete (fixed defined) magnitudes.
20   This process is known as *indexation.*
21   *Dither* is the process of application of randomization noise with the purpose to prevent large-scale patterns such as color banding in images.
22   *True color* usually refers to 24-bit images – meaning 8-bit per channel (8 for Red, 8 for Green and 8 for Blue = 24 bits in total) – and reaching, in this case 16,777,216 color variations. Since the human eye can discriminate up to about ten million colors, this means this should cover a greater range of color than can be perceived by humans, so in other words, enough color information to be perceived with its true original colors. We refer to True color images those that have a bit depth containing color information that is over the color perception of humans.
23   A *codec* is a software (or a hardware) that encodes or decodes a data stream or signal. The word codec comes from the contraction of the two words indicating the directions of encoding: coder and decoder.
24   *MOS* presumably stands for *Mute Of Sound,* which means the video contains no sound. It is a conventional way of expressing video clips without audio track in the postproduction industry in general. If the video has sound it could be described as: "*Sound: Mono*", "*Sound: 5.1(LR-ClfeLsRs)*" (for surround, indicating the order of the sound channels), "*Sound: Stereo*" (make sure you specify the word "*Sound*" next to the *stereo* specifically to avoid any misunderstandings with stereography – the *3D stereo* "for the glasses" – this feature should be indicated under "*Multiview*" key only if applicable). As a fun fact, there is no clear history for the origin of the abbreviation MOS, some say it is an acronym that comes from German "*mit-out sound*", others from "*motor only shot*". Regardless of the history of the word, it always signifies the same: silent shot.
25   Apple Inc. (2018, April 9). *About Apple ProRes.* Apple. Retrieved December 2, 2022, from https://support.apple.com/en-us/HT202410
26   When the color subsampling is composed by a ratio of 4 numbers instead of the usual 3 the last digit, in the fourth position, indicates the sample ratio of the Alpha channel: R:G:B:A. When the color subsampling ratio indicates 4:4:4:4 it means all data for luma and chroma has been preserved and the Alpha channel too. Codecs indicating this ratios allow RGBA channels.
27   *Apple ProRes 4444 XQ* features a target data rate of approximately 500 Mbps for 4:4:4 sources at 1920 × 1080 and 29.97 fps. Apple Inc. (2018, April 9). *About Apple ProRes.* Apple. Retrieved December 2, 2022, from https://support.apple.com/en-us/HT202410
28   *Apple ProRes 4444* has a target data rate of approximately 330 Mbps for 4:4:4 sources at 1920 × 1080 and 29.97 fps. It also offers direct encoding of and decoding to both RGB and Y'CBCR pixel formats. Apple Inc. (2018, April 9). *About Apple ProRes.* Apple. Retrieved December 2, 2022, from https://support.apple.com/en-us/HT202410
29   The target data rate is approximately 220 Mbps at 1920 × 1080 and 29.97 fps. Apple Inc. (2018, April 9). *About Apple ProRes.* Apple. Retrieved December 2, 2022, from https://support.apple.com/en-us/HT202410.
30   The target data rate is approximately 147 Mbps at 1920 × 1080 and 29.97 fps. Apple Inc. (2018, April 9). *About Apple ProRes.* Apple. Retrieved December 2, 2022, from https://support.apple.com/en-us/HT202410.

31 The target data rate is approximately 102 Mbps at 1920 × 1080 and 29.97 fps. Apple Inc. (2018, April 9). *About Apple ProRes*. Apple. Retrieved December 2, 2022, from https://support.apple.com/en-us/HT202410.

32 Avid DNxHD codec profiles specify their bitrates (per second), ranging from 440 Mbps down to 36 Mbps.

33 SDTV: Standard Definition TV (*PAL, NTSC*).

34 *DVB*: Digital Video Broadcasting is a set of international open standards for digital TV.

35 *HDTV* (also known as HD): HDTV refers to resolution formats such as 720p, 1080i, 1080p).

36 *UHD*: Also known as *Ultra HD* or *UHDTV*, it includes *4K UHD* and *8K UHD*, which are two digital video formats with an aspect ratio of 16:9 (not to be confused with the *DCI 4K* and *DCI 8K* that are different resolutions with different aspect ratio).

37 *Metadata* is the data that lies behind other data, in this case the media. It is a type of descriptive data that assists a person or computer in identifying the properties of a file. For instance, the metadata could contain the information about the camera model and the lenses used to capture that clip. There is an infinity of properties that could be described in the metadata of an image or video, both visible and hidden. To learn to preserve that metadata through the pipeline, when needed, is an important aspect to keep in mind, as metadata can be destroyed with certain processes or simply not stored in certain containers (file formats).

38 *Raster Image*: *Raster* (or *bitmap*) images are generally what you think about when thinking of digital pictures. In other words, to simplify the subject, any image made of pixels is a *raster image*, also known as *bitmap* (for instance JPG, TIF, PNG …). There are other kind of images that are not made of pixels, hence not raster images, for instance a vector image (EPS, SVG…).

39 *YUV* is a color model usually utilized as part of a color image pipeline. The YUV model distinguishes between two *chrominance* components, U (blue projection) and V (red projection), as well as one *luminance* component (Y), which refers to physical linear-space brightness. It can be used to convert between other color spaces and the *RGB* model.

40 *K*: the unit symbol of the *Kelvin* scale.

41 Schuessler, Z. (2020). *Delta E 101*. Quantifying Color Difference. http://zschuessler.github.io/DeltaE/learn/

42 *Viewer*: The *viewer* is Nuke's *Graphic User Interface* "viewport", where the result of the selected stream of operations is displayed in the monitor.

43 Make sure you are using the right color space of your display where the Viewer is positioned.

44 Please do not confuse the *Rec709* with the *Rec609*. The *Rec609* was originally issued in 1982 for encoding interlaced analog video signals in digital video. They are two different things.

45 *LMT*: in an ACES color-managed pipeline, the *LMTs* are very versatile fixed color manipulations, let's say, for the time being for you to understand a simplified version of this concept, that an LMT act in a similar way to an LUT within the ACES workflow. No worries, I expand this subject properly on the chapter dedicated to ACES.

Color Management

3

The Importance of Color Management

In the coming sections you are going to understand the elements of color workflow at a more scientific level in order to setup a simple but consistent pipeline according to the project, in relation with other departments, inside and outside visual effects environments, from camera to screen, so everybody is aligned to the same standards, preserving color qualities and consistency and maintaining the artistic intent.

We are now talking about *color management*, so let's be clear about this concept up front:

Color management is a protocol of controlled conversion between the color representations of various devices to keep all departments aligned to a common vision, by providing consistency in image reproduction and creative intent. I know, that is a very "wordy" explanation, but it is exactly that indeed. Let me elaborate it in simple terms: It is a way to ensure everybody, everywhere, is seeing the same image on their respective screens, and not just in any way, but the way <u>the artists</u> working on those images (the filmmakers) intended to show. So, the principle is quite simple: you *see* what I *see* and we both *see* the right image. It may seem trivial but, believe me, for many reasons – even historical reasons – it is quite a complex subject that requires a good precise understanding of many different aspects of the image processing and displaying (Figure 3.1).

Maybe you are asking: "Why?"

Well, let's wind back our clocks a few years, at the times when digital film cameras were not invented yet, so we simply used film negative to shoot movies, a filmstrip that was later developed and then scanned (that is already "modern"): stored as *Cineon* files – do you remember that time? If not, maybe I am getting old; then, on the other hand you had computers, generating renders: usually linear images; and other digital media, coming from Photoshop or other sources, generally all using the same standard sRGB format. Time where the color spaces in use were essentially: log, lin, and gamma encoded media that you composited together; and then that content was delivered either for cinema or broadcast, that is it. And frankly, at the time, we thought that was already complicated because you had to keep in mind we were mixing those three different color spaces and usually different bit-depths as well … and other elements.

Today things are radically different – brace yourself – even though the tools we use today allow us to work smarter, <u>you need to know</u> clearly what to do and how to do it. As always, the artist is in command, there are things that you simply cannot skip: and color management is one of those (Figure 3.2).

Yes, it is true that we are still using film negative cameras combined with computer images as we did back then, however, the element that has truly revolutionized the media entertainment industry – from the point of view of acquiring images – is the digital camera.

DOI: 10.4324/b23222-5

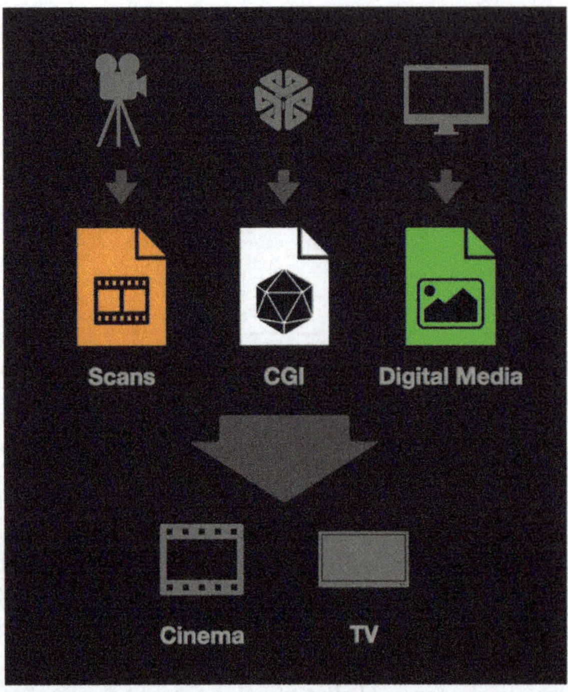

Figure 3.1 Scans, computer-generated imagery (CGI) and other digital media in the "analog era"

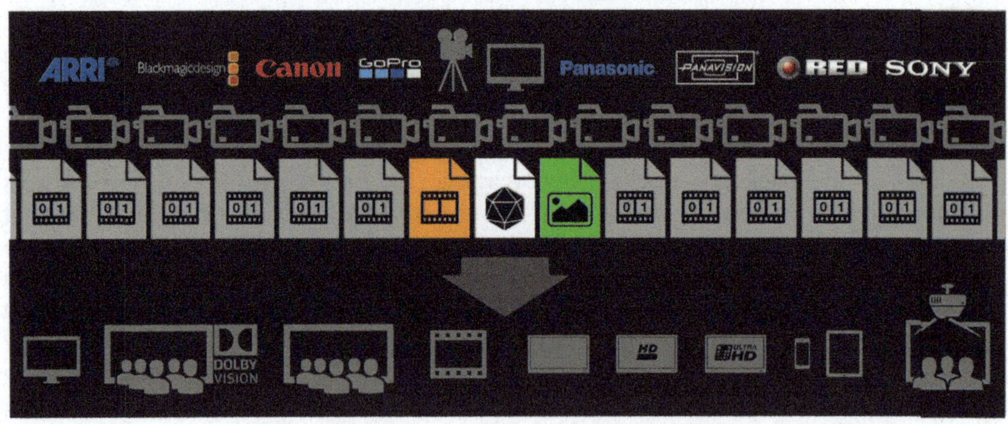

Figure 3.2 Some digital cinema cameras and different media platforms and displays result in multiple color spaces and the organic need for color management

There are so many different manufacturers and camera models, each one with their own way to encode light, and I mean different color *gamuts* and *transfer functions*, in other words: different *color spaces*, that we have to add to the previous ones I mentioned above from a few years ago. No worries, we are going to demystify all those concepts I just mentioned. But cameras are not the only innovation from this new era of digital media. How we watch content has evolved as well. Analog cinema projections still exist, if you do not trust me, you can ask Mr. Christopher Nolan about it. However, I think we all can

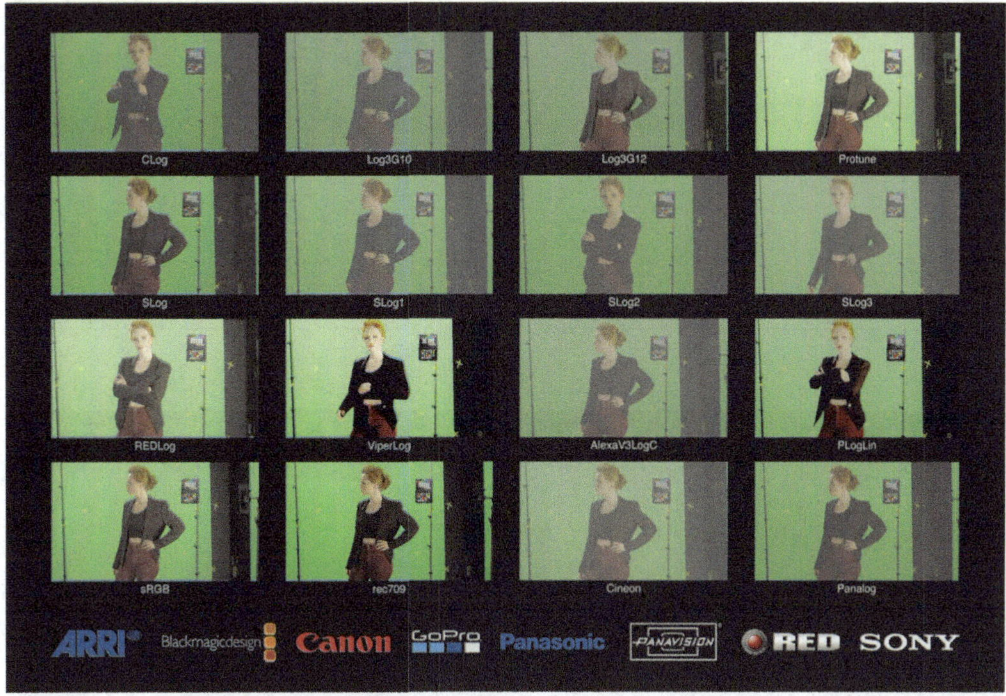

Figure 3.3 **Different color spaces results**

agree the mainstream of cinema projection – as well as other devices for watching media entertainment – is digital. Cinema, or TV (that, by the way, is now digital as well) and not only *just* digital, there are different versions coexisting: Standard Definition, HD, UHD … each of those standards with their own color spaces; and then HDR TVs and projectors, both for home theatre and cinema … and then computers of course … and the superstar of all devices: mobile phones and tablets, that now stream content directly from the various media streaming services and platforms, whose standards need to meet all the above at once.

We have to ensure everybody delivers the same high-quality standards. An even more complicated task when you have different facilities working on the same show or even on the same shot. Every color counts. So, let's start breaking down the problem from the top: how we capture images. Film scans are always "the same", so, then let's focus on digital cameras (Figure 3.3).

These are a few examples of the most popular digital film cameras; the first thing you are going to notice is each one has a different representation of light. Those are the clips without any correction applied to remap the colors to their right places and see the image as intended by the manufacturer, what we can call, the "right color". Each clip has its own color space, specifically designed by the manufacturer to optimize the fidelity of the colors the sensor is able to reproduce, mapping the linear tristimulus values and the non-linear electronic signal. See the difference? It is because every image has its own color space and that is going to determine the input point of the color-managed pipeline.

Time to dive deep into the color space.

4

Understanding Color Spaces

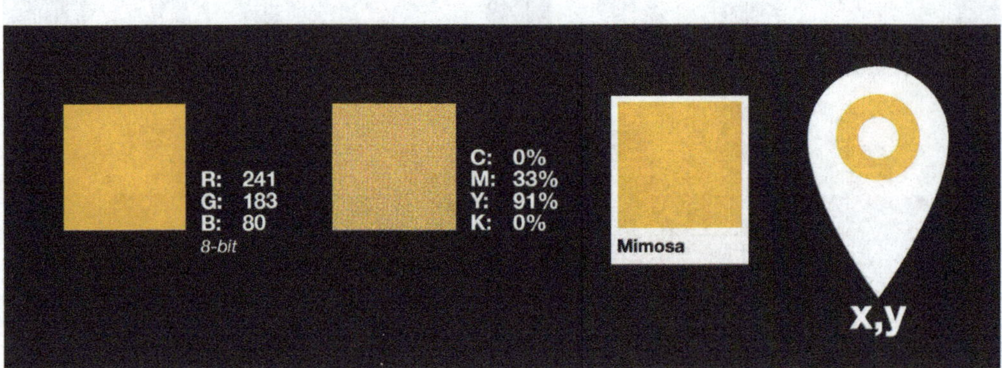

Figure 4.1 Same color in different color space denominations

In order to really understand color management, the first things that needs to be clear are the Foundations of color spaces (Figure 4.1).

A color space is a specific organization of colors originated from the combinations of the color components from a color model. It can be arbitrary, by assigning just a "name", like, for instance, in the Pantone collection, or defined within a mathematical structure, for instance a set of coordinates. So, we must see color spaces as that, a space to layout the "address" and identification to each single color available to be reproduced by a given device, either to capture or to reproduce. Where is that space, how it is defined, and the elements that constitute it, are the subject of this chapter.

Color Models

There are several color models, depending on their use (Figure 4.2). Like, for instance, the *CIE* that studies the human perception; the *CMY* – or *CMYK* – for inks (which means printing purposes), uses a subtractive synthesis, meaning all the components together give you black – as opposite to *RGB* that altogether gives you white; the *RYB*, used for painting pigments in art and design, the one that they teach us in primary school that mixing yellow and blue makes green; other color spaces are more familiar for us VFX artists, like hue, saturation, and value (*HSV*) – or hue, saturation, and luminance (*HSL*)– that

DOI: 10.4324/b23222-6

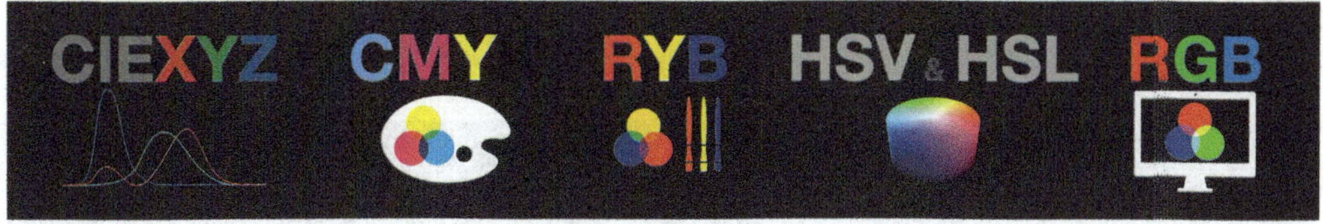

Figure 4.2 Examples of color models

is structured in polar coordinates on a *cylinder*; and finally, the instance that interest us the most for our purpose, the RGB model, the additive synthesis of light, where all colors together give you white. The color spaces for displays, cameras, and postproduction, all use the RGB model.

The Visible Spectrum

The reason we use the RGB model is because cameras and displays had been created using the human perception of color as a reference. Time to get to the bottom of how humans *see* color.

Inside the human eye we have three different photosensitive cells that capture different wavelengths of light, as I mentioned in the first chapter. The span of those wavelengths of light is what we call the visible spectrum, the average range goes from 380 to 700 nanometers. So, if we lay out the wavelengths as a continuous mix of colors we have the ability to navigate through this spectrum in one dimension, one line (Figure 4.3).

However, we are missing a group of colors in that line: Where are my purples? Did you notice those were missing? No worries, it is completely normal, they just are not represented by a single wavelength of light. Actually *magenta* is what our brain visualizes when the small cone cells (that capture what we perceive primarily as blue) are stimulated together with the large cone cells (that capture what we perceive primarily as red), with no, or very little, stimulation of the medium cone cells (in charge of visualizing the green); that is when magenta appears in our brain. Then, if we want to mix the stimuli from all three cones – what we call Tristimuli – we have to put it in a way we can have all colors able to be represented. Let's convert then the visible spectrum into a color wheel so we can move in two dimensions (Figure 4.4).

I am sure you are way more familiar with this visualization of color. And by the way, notice the arc in the figure containing the purples section we were talking about above.

What we have in the circumference are all the available colors at their maximum intensity, called: *hue* (I am sure you have seen this before, you can find this color manipulator, for instance, in any RGB knob set in Nuke or other image processors). So, in this model, we can define the first line of the address of a color by a degree angle of this circle. Where 0 degrees is red, 110 degrees is green, 220 degrees is blue, and at 360 degrees we obviously are back at red again. Still, the address is incomplete because we are just running on the edge of the color wheel, so we need another control to move in the direction of the center, to mix our samples with the other opposite colors, this control is the *saturation* and it is the second piece of information of the address of the color sample, and yes, you have this control next to the *hue* in the *HSV* sliders, those are the manipulations based on

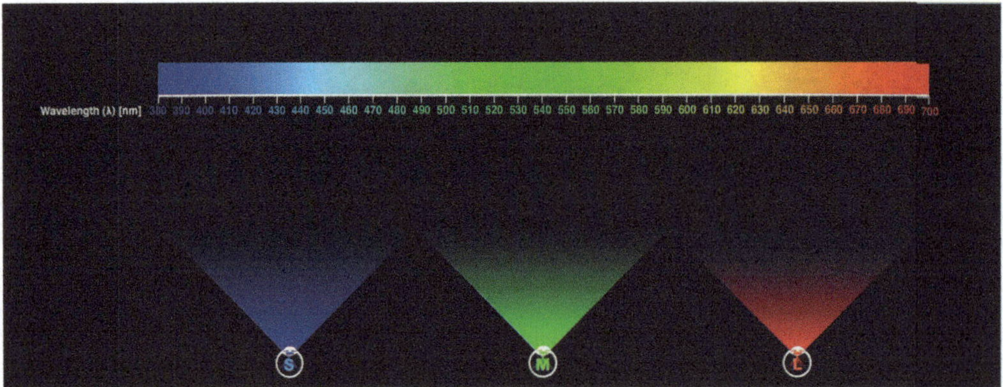

Figure 4.3 The visible spectrum of light

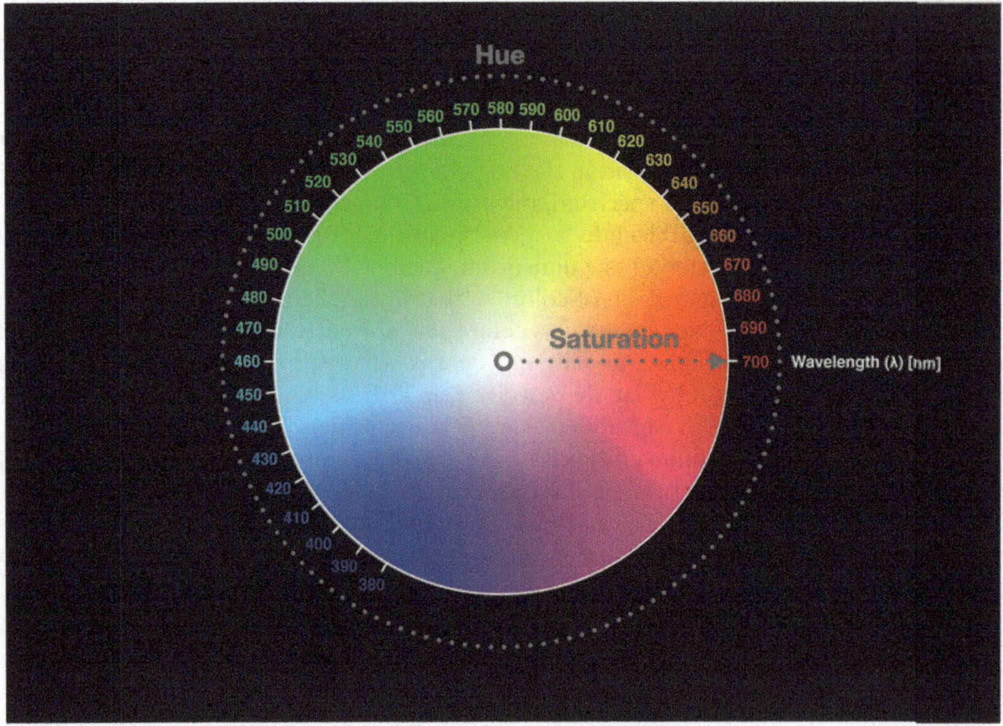

Figure 4.4 Color wheel with the indications for hue and saturation

the *hue*, *saturation* and *value* model. Notice that we are talking about color without taking in consideration the luminance or brightness of the sample, just purely color, no matter how dark or how bright it is, we refer to these luminance-agnostic colors as *chromaticity*; a 2D coordinates sample. In this instance, a *hue* and *saturation* sample without the brightness component.

The only problem is that, if we want to represent colors based on human perception, we need to face the fact that we do not perceive all colors the same way, we are more sensitive to certain wavelengths than others, and that directly affects the luminance of each color. So instead of using the color wheel, which is a theoretical and mathematical representation of chromaticity with an equal distribution of *hue* and *saturation* of the *RGB model*, let's organize these colors in a *space* that has been studied to accommodate the wavelengths of light from the visible spectrum, keeping in consideration the perception of amount of colors and their respective luminance component.

The International Commission on Illumination (CIE) xy Chromaticity Diagram

This is a Cartesian diagram, with both its x and y axes formatted from 0 to 1 (Figure 4.5). So, we can recall a sample based on its x and y coordinates; that set of two coordinates, by the way, is called a *tuple*. The y axis, the vertical one, will be used for two different purposes: one is to be coupled with the x axis coordinate to define a point mapped in this diagram, and the other use is to indicate the luminance of the sample.

The higher the luminance, the higher value in the y axis (Figure 4.6). This is the reason why you will repeatedly see the luminance component in different systems referred to as Y (upper case) when talking about certain color spaces. For instance $Y'C_bC_r$ (by the way, the apostrophe next to the Y denotes the fact it is a non-linear component) to cite just one. Some diagrams even state these particular sets of coordinates as xyY (with the last letter upper case) to evidence the double purpose of the y axis, even though the position of the samples will be reported with just a tuple of two coordinates as expected. Let's go ahead and place all the wavelengths of the visible spectrum according to this diagram of human perception of color (Figure 4.7).

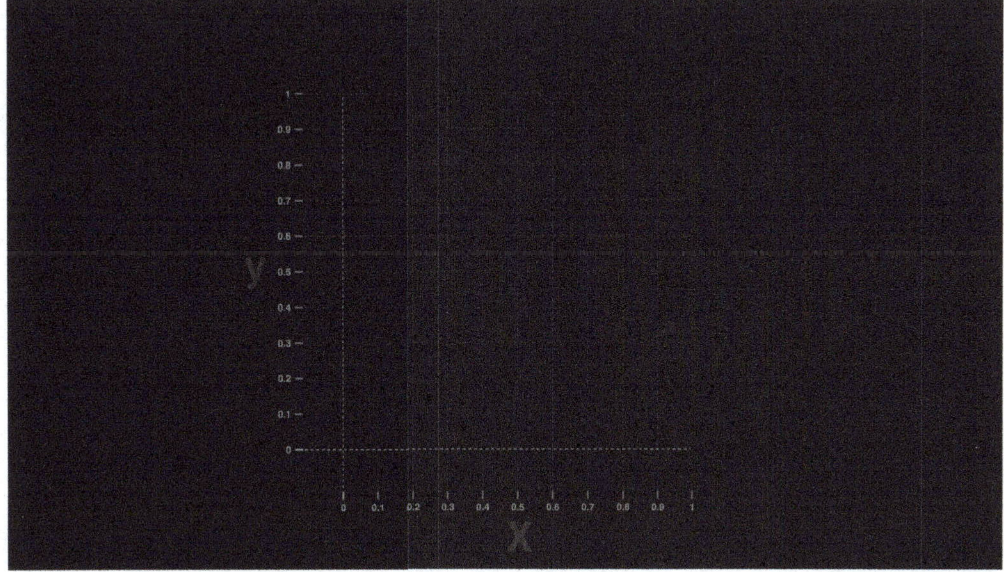

Figure 4.5 Cartesian diagram

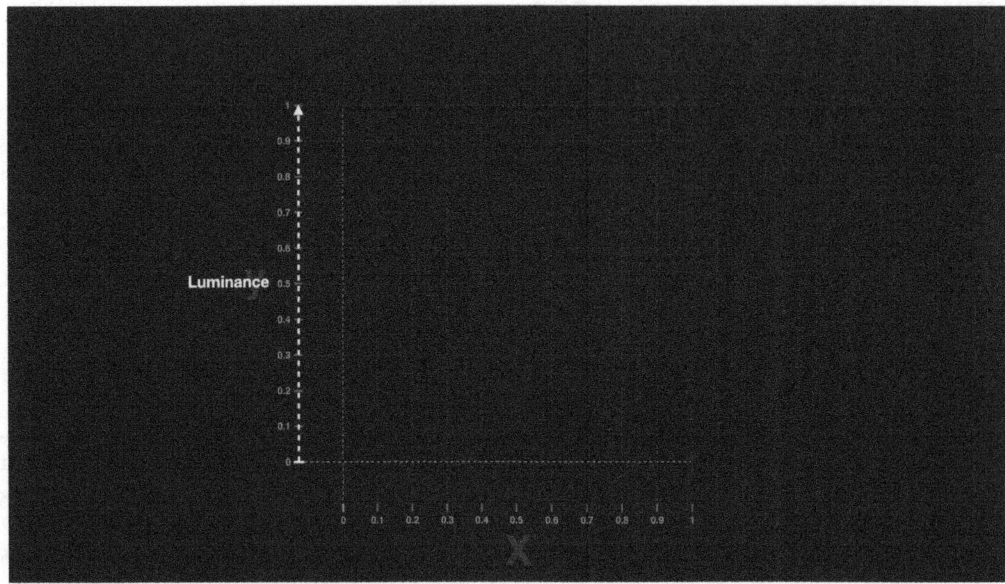

Figure 4.6 The double purpose of the y (vertical) axis

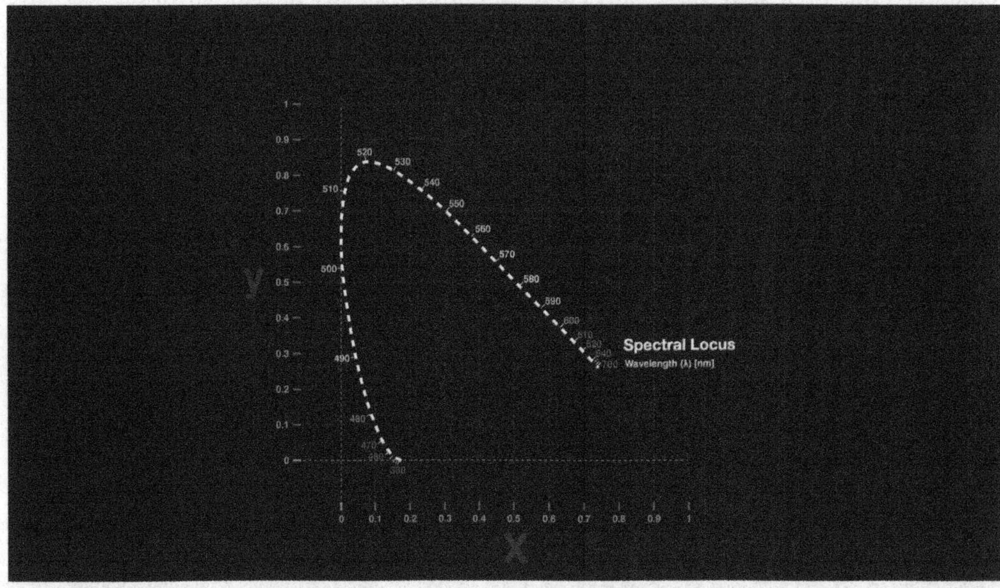

Figure 4.7 Spectral locus

This horseshoe-shaped line that joins the position of all visible wavelengths is known as the *spectral locus*. Therefore, if we combine all those wavelengths we will define all visible colors by the standardized average human vision and their luminance contribution (Figure 4.8).

This diagram was the result of research done in 1931 by the International Commission on Illumination (CIE). So this is called *CIE xy chromaticity diagram*, and it is going to put

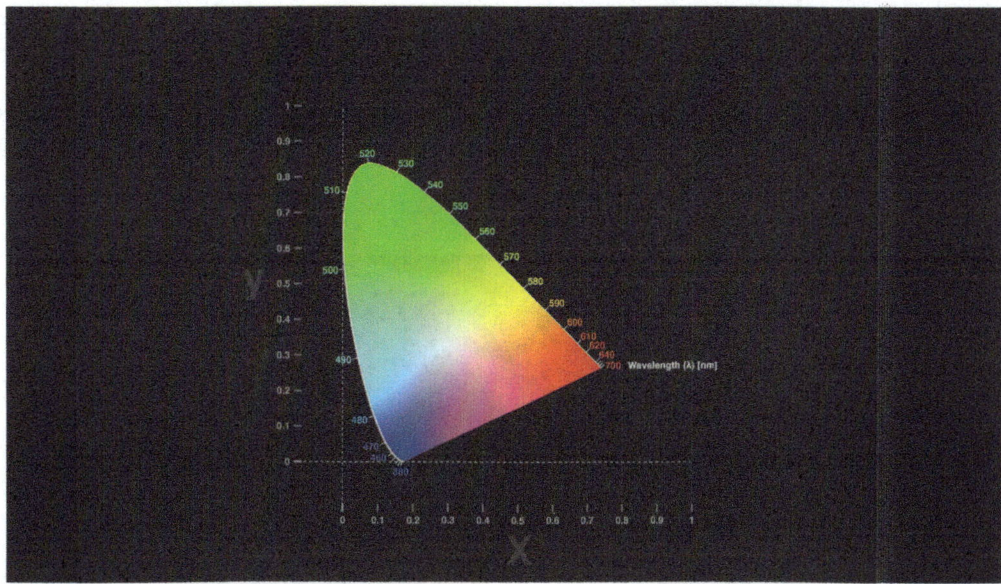

Figure 4.8 International Commission on Illumination (CIE) xy chromaticity diagram

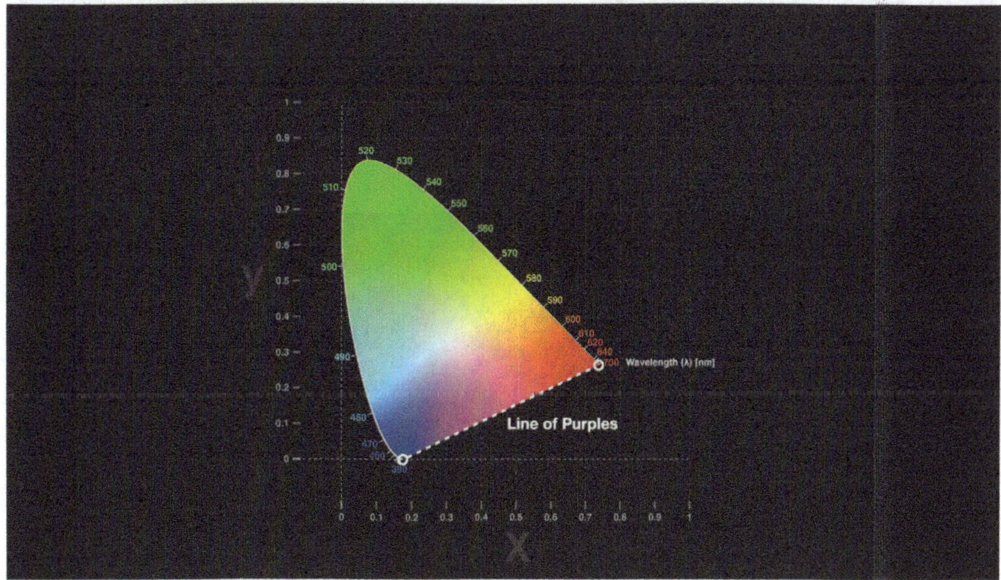

Figure 4.9 Line of purples

us, and our color spaces, in the context of human vision. First of all, remember I mentioned there was a specific portion of the color wheel that does not correspond to any wavelength, and still there is color there, this line at the bottom is named Line of Purples: the color does exist, the wavelength does not (Figure 4.9).

Another thing that is going to seem familiar is the *hue*, that runs around on the edges of the spectral locus but, unlike the color wheel that is a perfect circle, in here we have to arbitrarily define where the center is (we will talk about this later) (Figure 4.10).

From that center to the edges we have something quite similar to the concept of *saturation*, but in the *spectral locus* we call it *purity*, which refers to the predominance of one single "pure" wavelength (Figure 4.11).

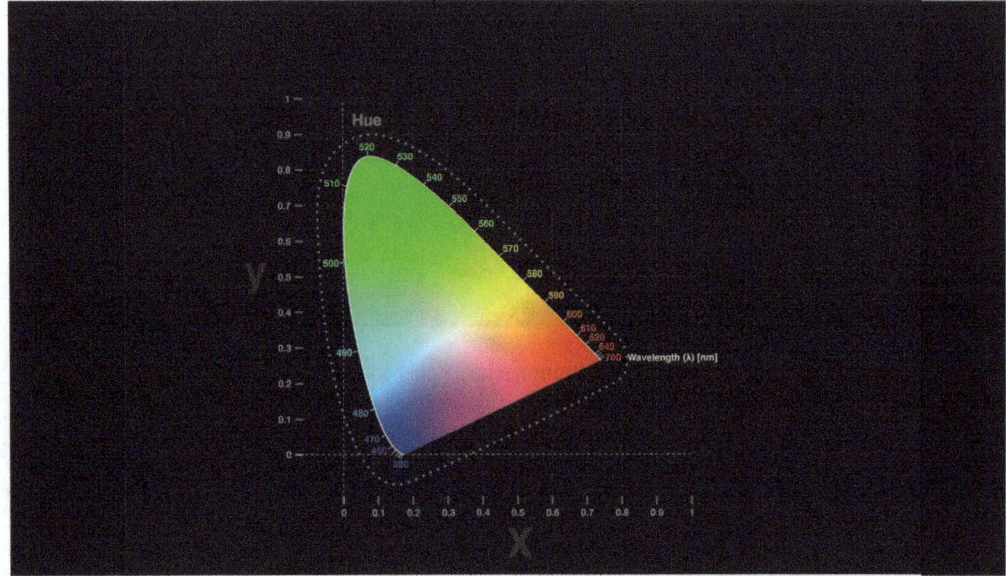

Figure 4.10　Hue

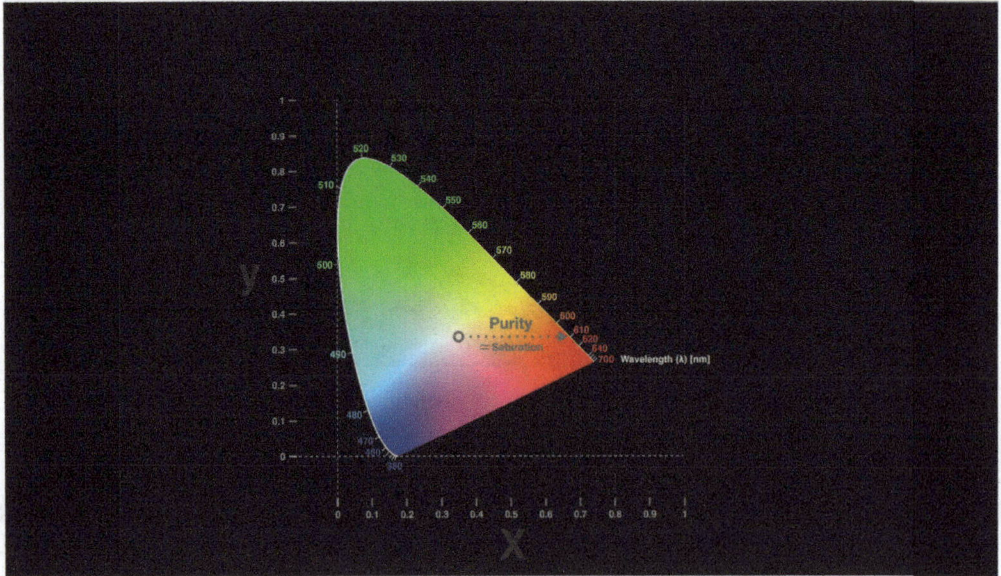

Figure 4.11　Purity

By the way, you cannot have purity toward the Line of Purples (magenta), because there is no wavelength corresponding to that line, but on the other hand you can have *saturation*, see the difference?

The *chromaticity diagram* is actually in itself a color space, and not just any color space, it is our Reference Color Space that we will use to put our RGB color spaces in relation to the human vision.

I think it is time to introduce a concept we are going to use a lot for color management: *gamut*. The *spectral locus* of the *CIE xy chromaticity diagram* represents all colors that are within the visible spectrum, in other words, wavelength combinations resulting in colors we can *see*. And those samples that are not inside the delimited area bounded by the *spectral locus* will be *out* of the Gamut, still those samples may *exist*, in a mathematical way, we just cannot see them. This is an important concept to understand as we will study color gamuts for certain color spaces that will comprehend values outside the *spectral locus*.

Color Gamut

I think it's a good idea we briefly discuss what exactly is a gamut. In plain English, the word "gamut" does not refer just to color, if you search on any dictionary it will say something like: *A gamut is the whole available range of something defined*, and it means all the elements contained in the span, from end to end, for instance "the gamut of human emotions" from happiness to sadness, anger, fear, disgust … they are all part of that particular gamut. In our case the subject is <u>color</u> gamut, so we should use the following definition provided by the *CIE*: A color gamut expresses «*volume, area, or solid in a colour space, consisting of all those colours that are either: present in a specific scene, artwork, photograph, photomechanical or other reproduction; or capable of being created using a particular output device and/or medium*»,[1] but in the following examples I will use just numbers to describe a gamut in mathematical terms, just make it easier to understand before we move ahead and describe color gamuts (Figure 4.12).

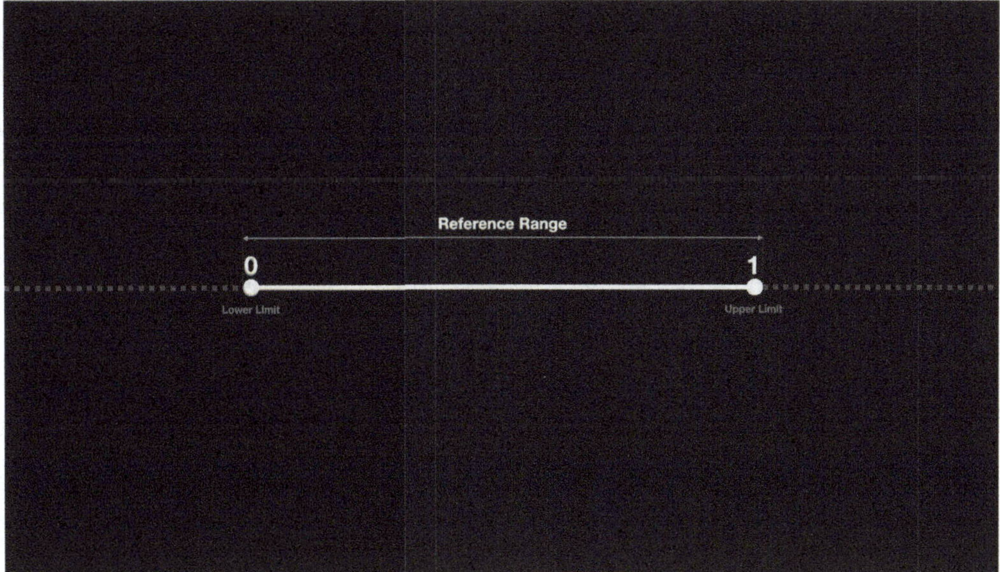

Figure 4.12 Reference range to contextualize our given gamut

The dotted trace represents an *infinite* straight line. From that line, we are going to define a segment to set us in a scale; so, we have a lower limit, and an upper limit. Let's assign value 0 as the lowest and value 1 as the highest. This is going to be our reference range: this defines our scale (Figure 4.13).

Once we have the layout of scale, we are going to establish the range of our target gamut. For instance: from value 0.35 up to 0.65, this red segment will be our gamut (Figure 4.14).

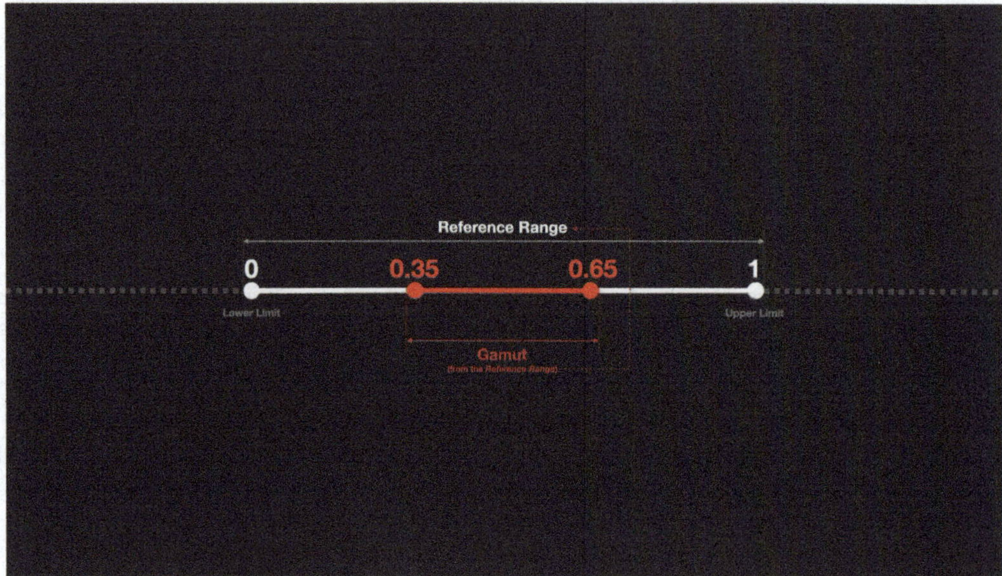

Figure 4.13 Our given gamut

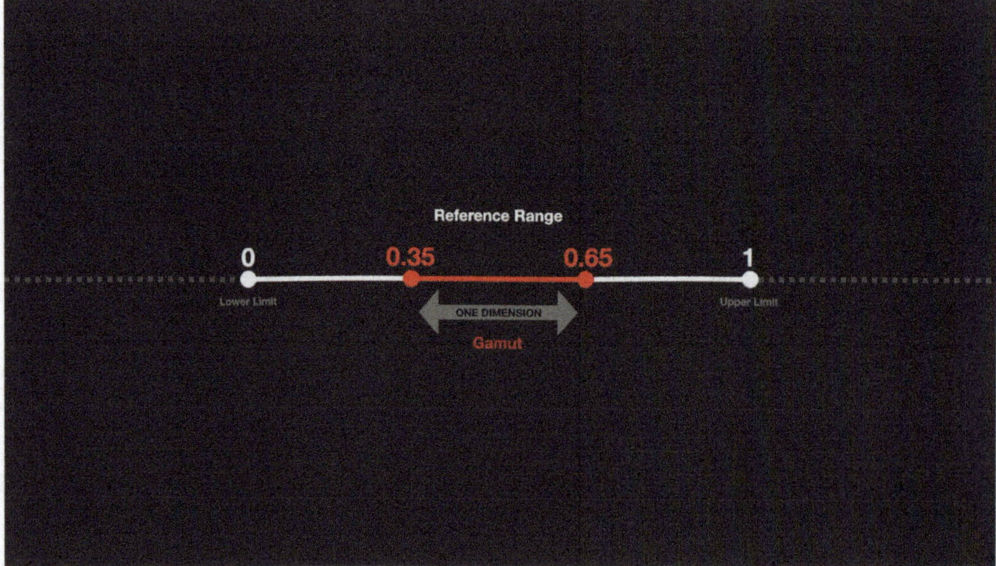

Figure 4.14 One-dimensional gamut

As you can see, it is expressed in absolute terms as we are using a defined numerical scope specified by the scaled reference, and so all values between 0.35 and 0.65 conform to our gamut. In this instance we have a one-dimensional representation, a progression of numbers in one single axis, a line.

Now, let me point out something interesting to note: think about what we called the reference range ... is it not itself a gamut referenced to the first grey dashed straight line? (Figure 4.15).

The only difference is that our reference range, the white one, was *relative*, because we positioned the values arbitrarily in relation to the dashed line; while the red gamut was established in *absolute* terms, using the numerical scale we defined for the reference range ... So, let's do something, instead of calling the white one "reference range", we can call it: *reference gamut*. This setup is very similar to the way we express color gamuts in relation to the chromaticity diagram you will see in a moment. But right now, we are using only one dimension, and our diagram for chromaticity is two-dimensional. So, let's have a look at 2D gamuts (Figure 4.16).

Now, our *reference gamut* – or reference range – is defined by two axes intersecting at the center. Therefore, we have all directions of the 2D plane available. The gamut now would not be a line, but an area, defined by coordinate points originated from the center (0,0). Those points will establish the vertices of a polygon: its area is our gamut. In this case, the polygon has three vertices: a triangle. Hence, all coordinates of this diagram that are inside the red triangle belong to our gamut (Figure 4.17).

Let's apply this principle to color spaces, and so we talk about *color gamut*.

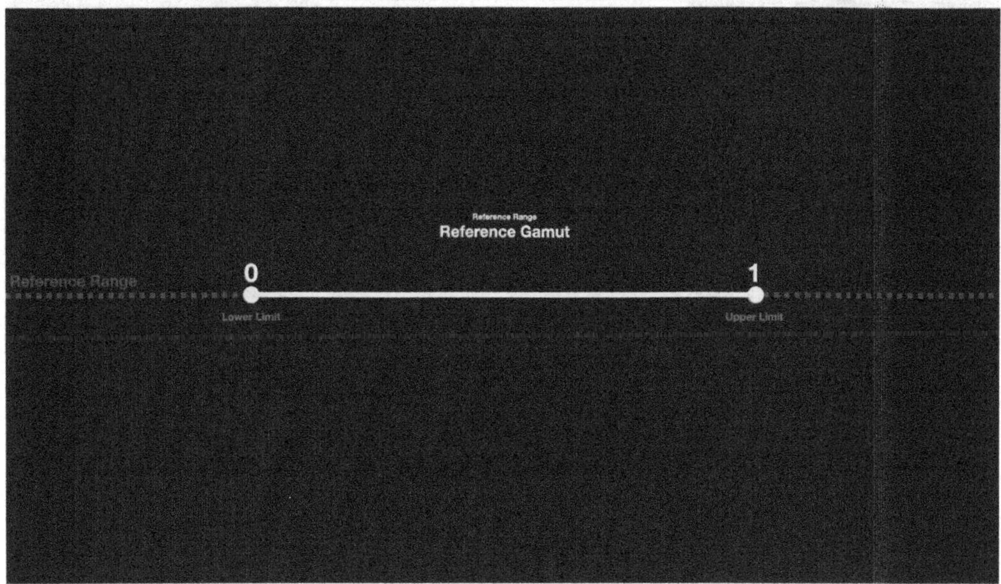

Figure 4.15 1D reference gamut

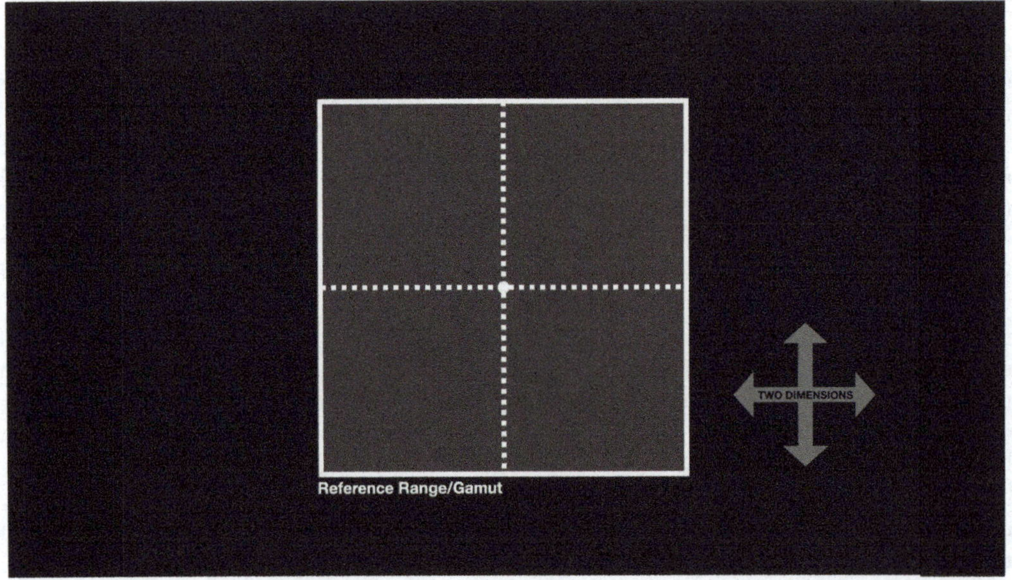

Figure 4.16 Two-dimensional gamut

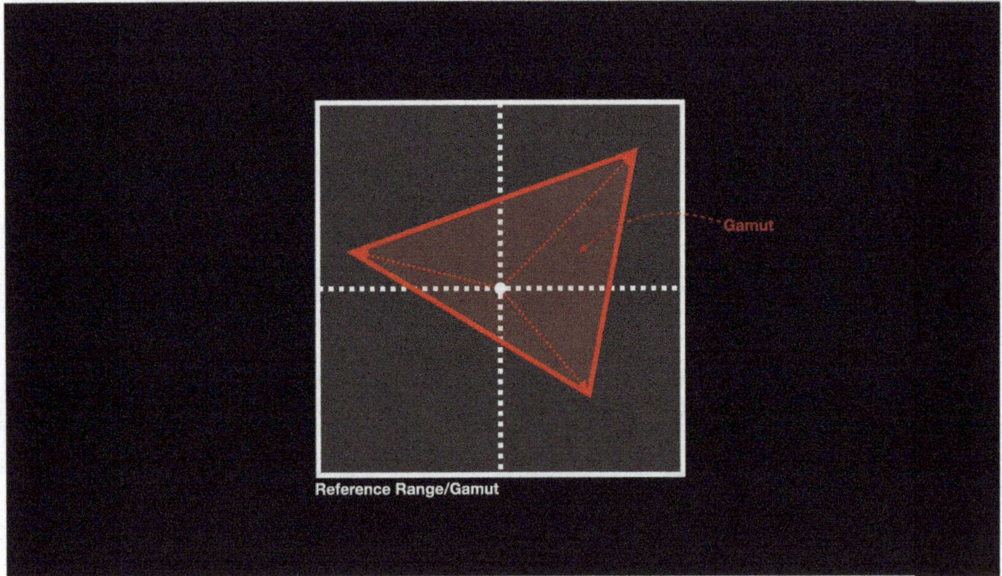

Figure 4.17 2D gamut

The color gamut is going to represent the colors from the chromaticity diagram that a certain device can capture or reproduce. This is going to be the area of the given color space (Figure 4.18).

A gamut is defined by three points. However, this color gamut is going to be incomplete if we do not define a fourth point that is going to set "its center", the point of lowest

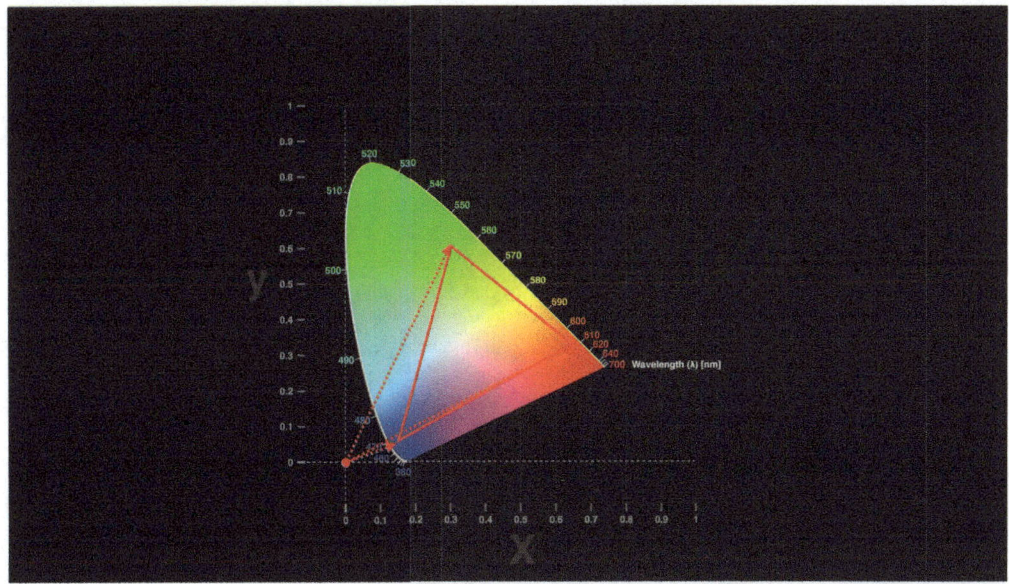

Figure 4.18 Color gamut traced from the origin of coordinates of the cartesian diagram

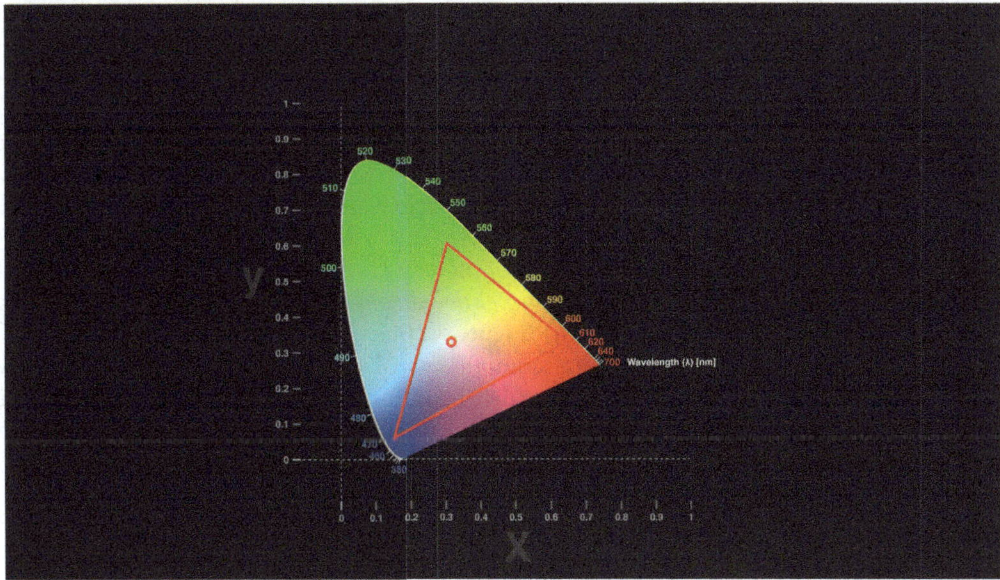

Figure 4.19 Color space gamut and white point

saturation of the color space, which we will call the *white point*, something we are going to discuss later (Figure 4.19).

We have the *chromaticity diagram* that is the *reference gamut* and we have the Triangle we defined as our *color gamut*, which is, by the way, within the *spectral locus*, that means this color gamut is entirely visible by humans.

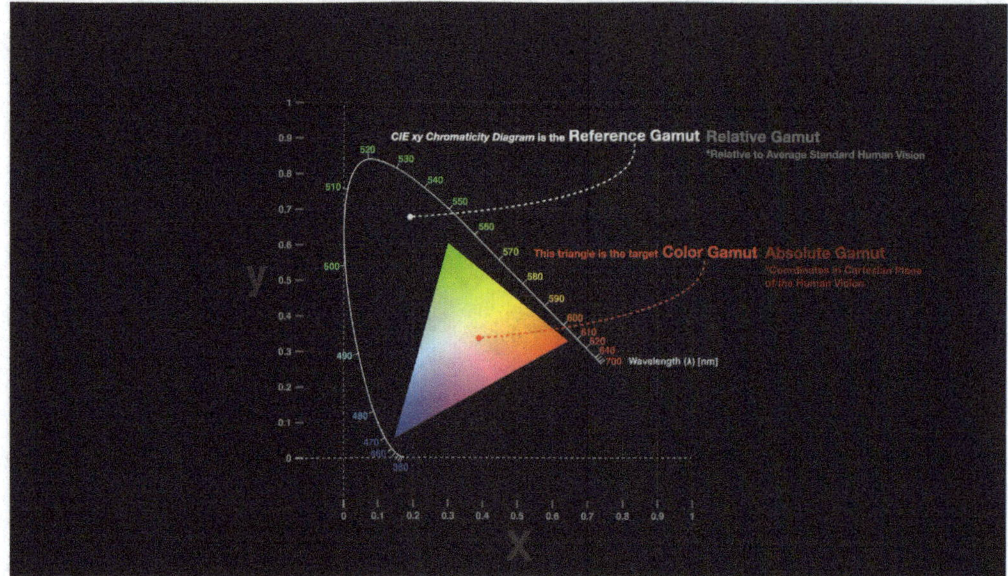

Figure 4.20 Relative (to human perception) and absolute (defined in the framework of the diagram) color gamuts

Then, we have the *reference color gamut*, which is a *relative gamut*, but relative to what? Relative to the *average standard human vision*, and we have the *target color gamut* which is an *absolute gamut*, because it is laid out in mathematical values in the Cartesian Plane defined by the *chromaticity diagram*.

In brief, a *color gamut*: Indicates *chromatic intensity* (which we have called *chromaticity*); Sets the limits for the *reproduction ranges of color*; and it defines two things: one is the *potential chromaticity reproduction capability of a given output device* (for instance a monitor, a TV or a projector); or the other, the *potential chromaticity processing capability of a given input device* (for instance a camera) (Figure 4.20).

The gamut is one of the fundamental components of the color space, as it defines the actual space boundaries. But before going deeper into our RGB color spaces I think we should analyze further the *chromaticity diagram* as it will define several aspects of our color spaces.

White Point

Before I mentioned the center of the color space, the point of lowest saturation, it will define the aspect of the white color, which is, as you probably know, all colors manifesting at their maximum intensity. However, that center is arbitrary. And usually it is going to be located within a particular range of values, the arc known as the *Planckian locus* (Figure 4.21).

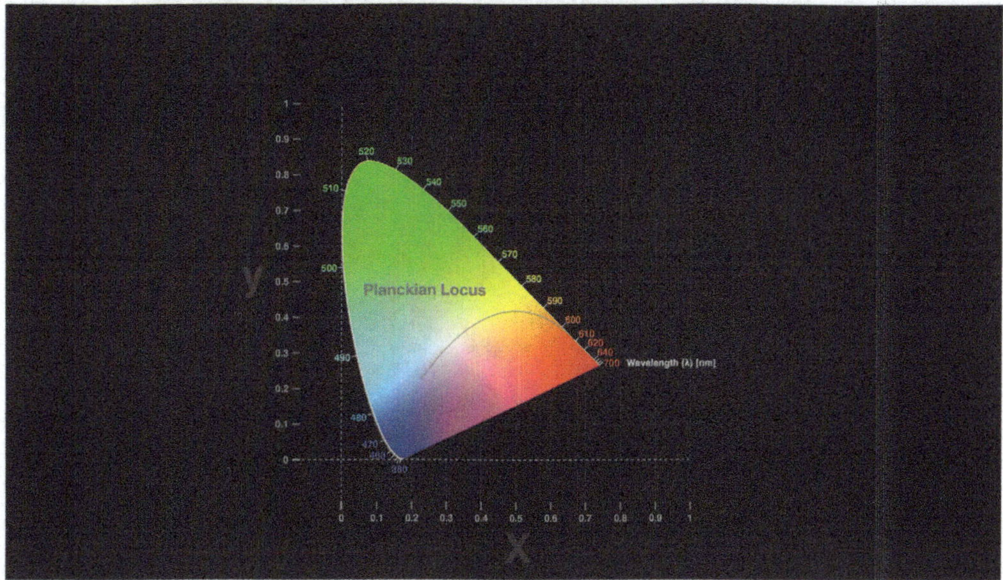

Figure 4.21 Planckian locus

The *Planckian locus* represents, within the *spectral locus*, the path that the color of an incandescent black body would take as its temperature changes. To refresh your memory, in thermodynamics a so called "black body" is an idealized opaque, non-reflective body; something like … what happens to a needle when you heat it up with a flame: it becomes initially red, then orange, and then if you keep applying heat it become bluish … (please kids don't try this at home without the presence of an adult to supervise you) (Figure 4.22).

These lines are *called isotherm lines*, which show the direction in which samples could change color while still preserving the same color temperature. Remember the color temperature is measured in the *Kelvin* scale: the higher the temperature the more bluish the color, and at the other end, the lower the reddish. We are talking about another way of navigating color, using *temperature* and *magenta*. The *Planckian locus* arc defines the changes in color temperature, while moving in the direction of the *isotherm lines* will affect the magenta component while preserving the color temperature.[2] Humans are quite used to this color temperature shift as our eyes are constantly balancing the temperature of the light we are receiving to adapt and make sense of the environment in a continuous, constant way – *white balance* – and so define the *white point* of our perception, and we do not even notice it. But in order for everybody to perceive the same aspect of all color transformations, this point must be established and standardized, so the CIE started defining different standards to represent what we perceive as *white* under different lighting conditions. The *white light*, or *illuminant*. One of the most important for us, using RGB color spaces, is this one (Figure 4.23):

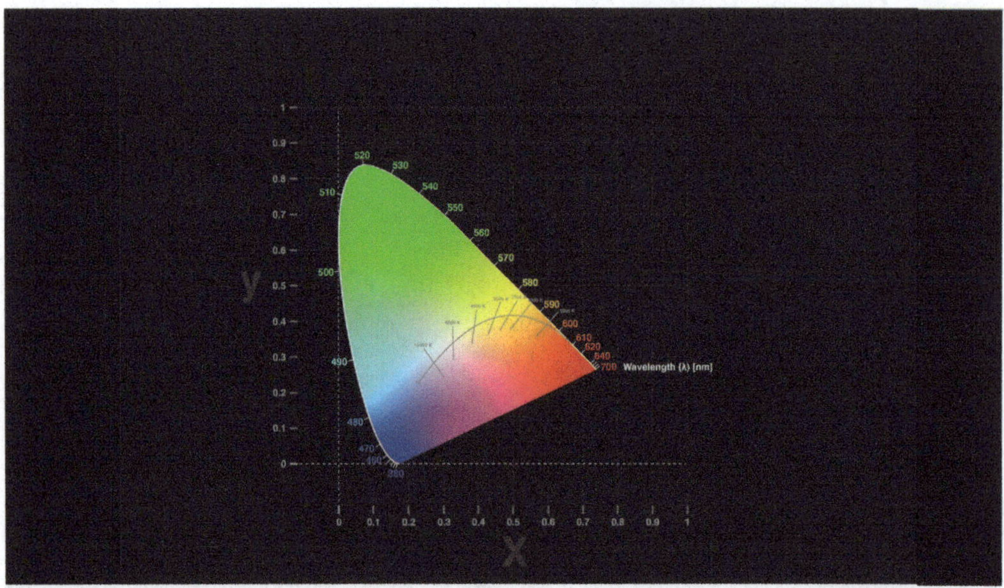

Figure 4.22 Isotherm lines

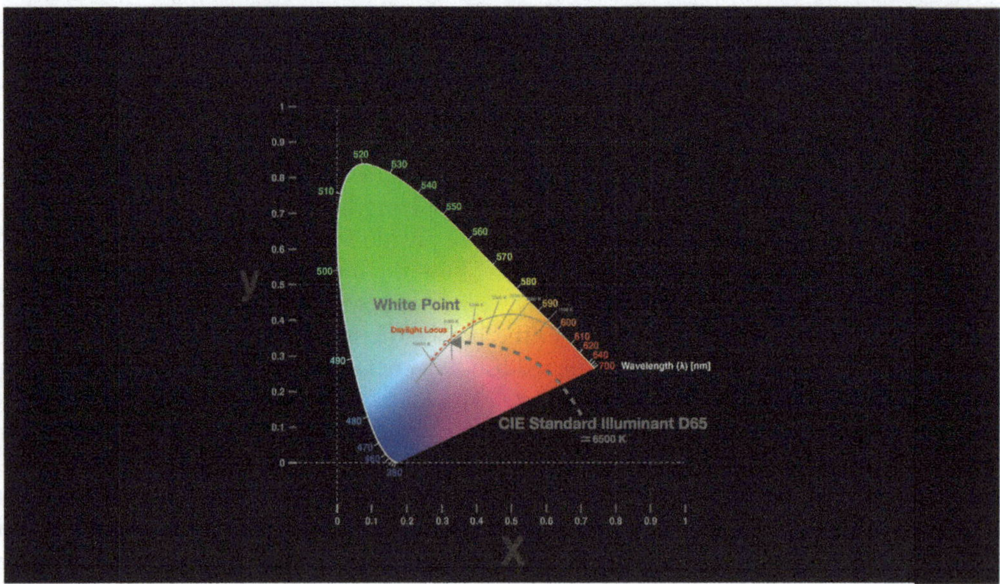

Figure 4.23 Daylight locus and International Commission on Illumination (CIE) standard illuminant D65

The *CIE standard illuminant D65* which is found at approximately 6500 K (actually closer to 6504 K) and slightly above the *Planckian locus* and it corresponds roughly to the average midday light in North Western Europe (comprising both direct sunlight and the light diffused by a clear sky), hence it is also called a daylight illuminant, which is why they put the D before the 65 (that represents 6500 K, even if it is 6504 K as you know).

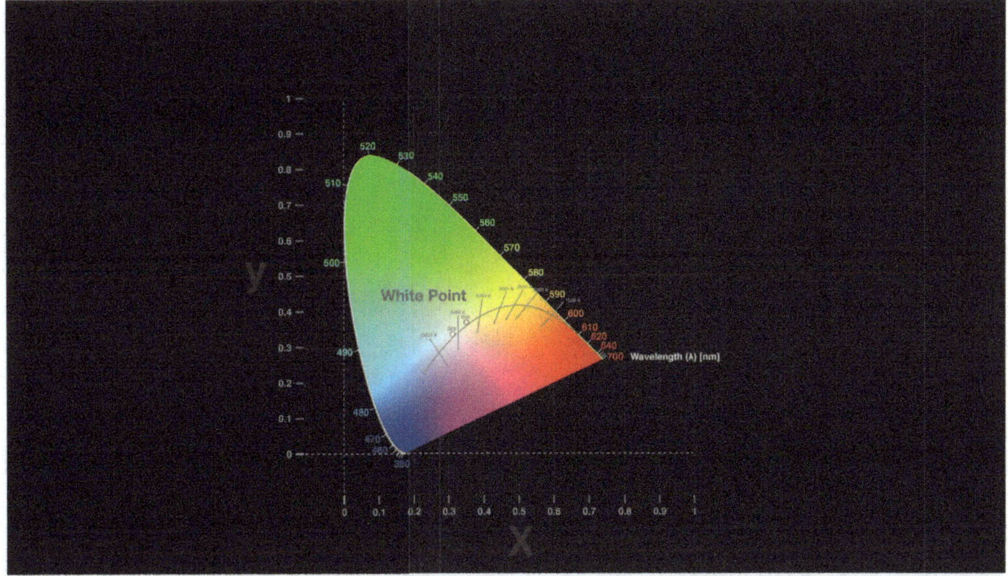

Figure 4.24 D65 and D50 illuminants

This is the arc where all *daylight illuminants* are located, which is called the *daylight locus.*

[0.31271, 0.32902] are the coordinates[3] in the *chromaticity diagram* for the *D65 illuminant*, that represents the *white point* on several color spaces we use. But it is not the only one relevant for us, we also have the *D50*, slightly warmer white at 0.33242, 0.34743; and others not standardized by the CIE but specifically calculated for certain color spaces as we will see later (Figure 4.24).

So now that we understand fully the *CIE xy chromaticity diagram* and how to calculate a *color gamut*, it is time to focus on the fundamental features of the *color space.*

Primaries

Cameras and displays have been created to reproduce images using a similar process to the way the human eye perceives light and color, a tristimulus signal based on the wavelengths of light our cone cells recognize: red, green and blue: RGB. Those three colors are the three components that are going to be combined to define all the colors in the space (Figure 4.25).

The three vertices of the triangle traced by the gamut will be represented by each of these R, G, and B components, which we call *primaries*, the signals (light sources) that combine to originate the colors. The position of each Primary defines its Purity. The closer to the edge, the purer the sample. Keep in mind that the wider and more distant the primaries are from each other, the bigger the gamut (the "triangle") hence the more colors it will contain.

So, in this figure, when we connect the primaries, the resulting triangle is the *color gamut* for this given *color space*. Now that we have the *gamut*, let's establish the white point (Figure 4.26).

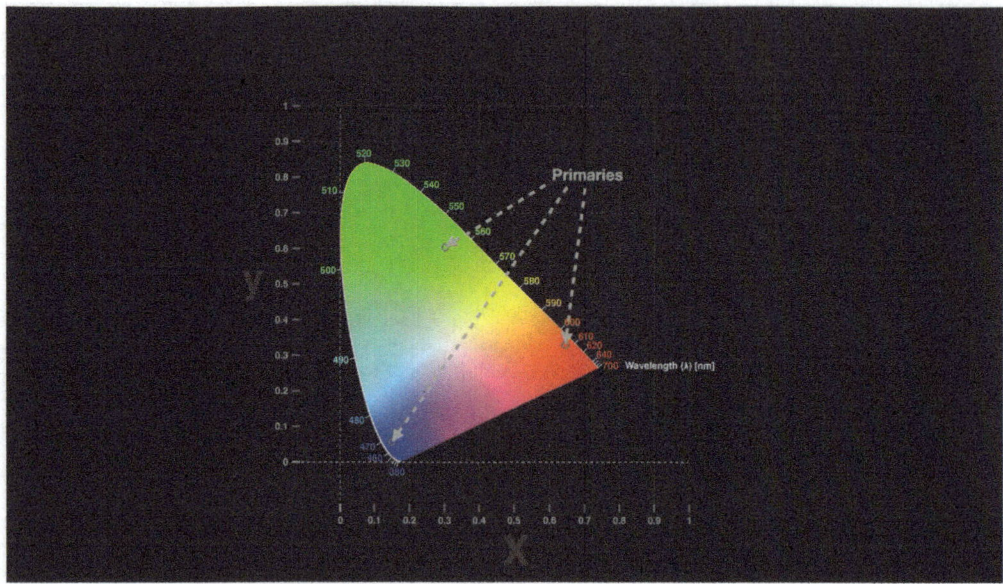

Figure 4.25 Primaries

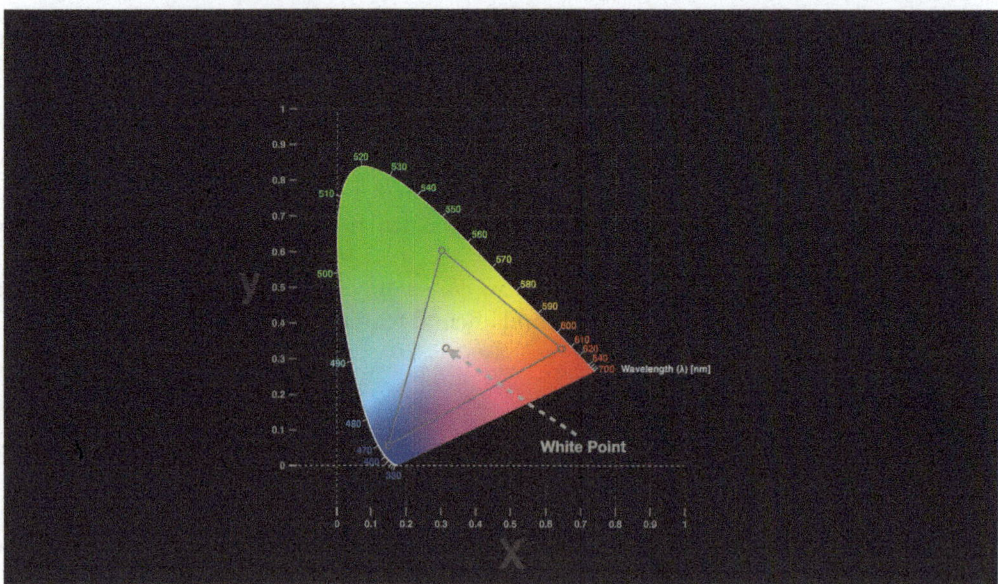

Figure 4.26 White point

There, on the *white point*, the coordinate where the saturation is equals to 0 (as there is no prevalence of any primary over any other, therefore the appearance of the White light.

The color space that is presented in the figure below represents the famous sRGB. In *CIE xy chromaticity* coordinates the position of its primaries are as follow: red is at [0.6400,

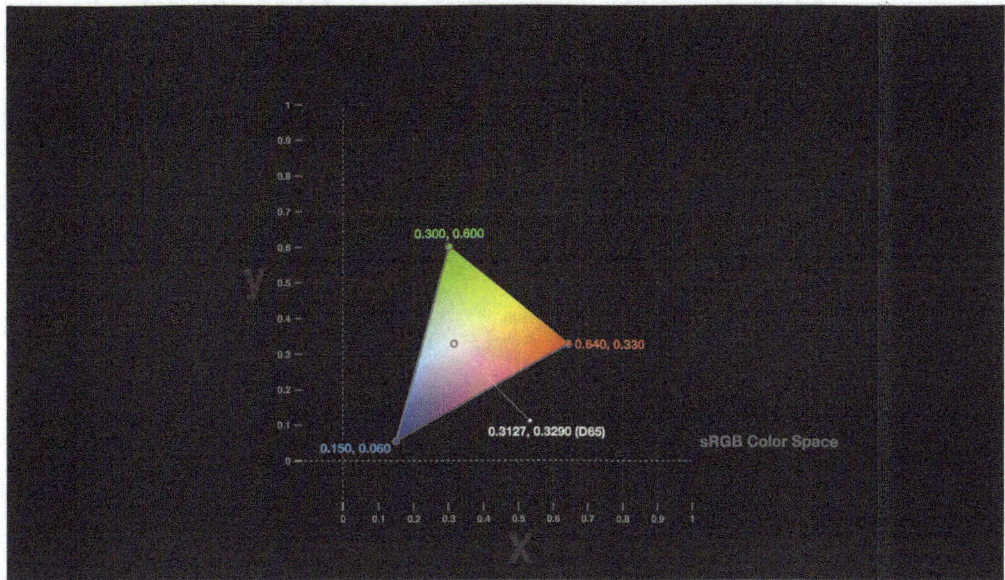

Figure 4.27 sRGB color gamut and white point

0.3300], green at [0.3000, 0.6000], and blue is at [0.1500, 0.0600]; and the white point, that by the way, is precisely the *D65*, at [0.3127, 0.3290] as we discussed earlier. This is the color space ruling, still today, by most of the computer monitors in the world. Which is why this color space is so important for us, it is an industry standard. The sRGB was developed in 1996 by HP and Microsoft for monitors, printers and of course the web. It was then standardized by the *International Electrotechnical Commission* in 1999, and since then it has been an industry standard for VFX (Figure 4.27).

I believe that at this point there is a question that needs to be demystified about how a software displays an image on your screen, a subject that will introduce the next section of this chapter. I think this is one of those cases where an example is going to make it easier to understand instead of an abstract explanation, and I will try to be as generic as possible so you can apply the theory behind it to any software of your choice to manipulate images. In my case, I will use Nuke because the processes are clearly isolated.

If you are working with Nuke using a monitor with an sRGB color space your *viewer process* should be set on *sRGB* as shown in the figure below (Figure 4.28).

However, this does not mean Nuke operates the image in this color space, this is merely a transformation, based on an LUT, to convert the image from the software internal working space to be ready to be correctly displayed on your screen, operating the necessary compensations to translate the color date to the specifics of the standards your monitor color space complies. If instead of your sRGB monitor, you were using, for instance an HDTV, with its Rec709 color space, your viewer process should be set on Rec709 instead of the default sRGB option, so the viewer would be adapted to that display. Easy, isn't it? But this takes us to another question: "*What is the color space that Nuke uses to process the image then?*" First of all, I think it would be more interesting to ask for the *working space* instead of the *color space*. The internal *working space* is a compendium of specifics that

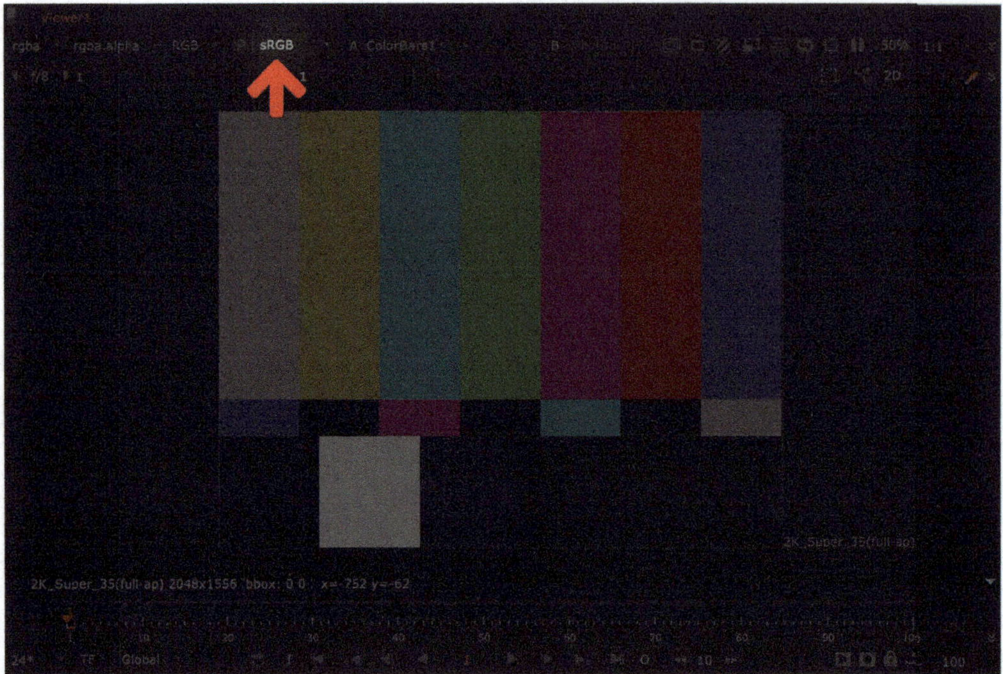

Figure 4.28 Nuke viewer process color space

will better define how the software operate the processes at its core, its framework. Nuke color management <u>by default</u>[4] does not define a set of primaries for its working space; instead, it uses something called *linear light* … but we will discuss this in depth later in the next chapters.

Back to our color spaces, now that we understand what the *gamut* is, that is based on the three primaries and completed by the white point, let's go ahead and study the last element that conforms a color space: the *transfer function*.

The Transfer Function

In color management, there is a *function*[5] that is an essential part of the *color space*, which is the *transfer function*. In this case, it's used to encode the image into the color space and so the *transfer function* defines the mapping between linear tristimulus values and non-linear electronic signal values of the image capturing device. So, it distributes every sample of light, or exposure, captured by the camera (or any other acquisition device) into its right position in the color space. And on the other hand, a *transfer function* can be operated also as a decoding function to distribute the color samples into a target display device. We will see the types of *transfer functions* in the next part of this course. So, this way, every sensor manufacturer creates a specific *transfer function* for every model of sensor to optimize its performance to render photographic results and so the overall ability of the camera to

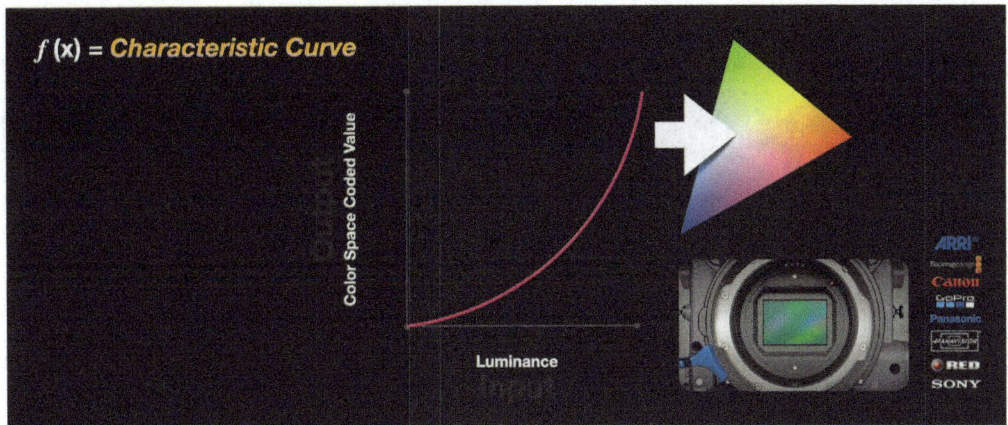

Figure 4.29 Characteristic curve example curve

reproduce color. In other words, how the sensor (or the display) is going to distribute the color data to be rightly positioned within the color space.

The *transfer function* for a capturing device is called *input transfer*; and as you can imagine, there are also *output transfer* functions, designed to convert the values of an image for a target display, same process but the other way around (Figure 4.29).

By the way, the trace resulting from that function, for all three components of the color model, is known as the *characteristic curve*; and defines the ability and features of the camera to capture light, which means: the characteristics of that particular digital camera, or any other particular capturing device.

There are different categories of *transfer functions* depending on the mathematical operations used to correspond to the data. Let's visualize them in the graphic form of the *output transform* (Figure 4.30).

- The first one is the *linear*, also known as lin, where the input and the output are the same, it means the signal is not altered. When you visualize something "RAW", with no conversion into a certain color space you are actually seeing its perceptually linear distribution of samples, from normalized 0 to normalized 1 – and beyond – in an arithmetic progression. Computers usually generate images linearly, as they do not have any electronic signal to be converted, but a mathematical calculation of light. A mathematically perfect linear light.
- Then you have the *logarithmic*, or *log*, functions. They are used for cameras and film scanners as they accurately represent the behavior of light in relation to sensitivity and the perception of detail for the different expositions. The classic *Cineon*, developed for film scans, and the newer *Alexa log C* are part of this category.
- The *gamma function* was originally developed for correcting CRT monitors and then evolved for other displays. It maintains the end points of the curve intact (normalized 0 and 1) but remaps the values in between. Examples of this function can be found in the *sRGB* for computer monitors and the *Rec709* for HDTV. This function sometimes is referred as *gamma encoding*.

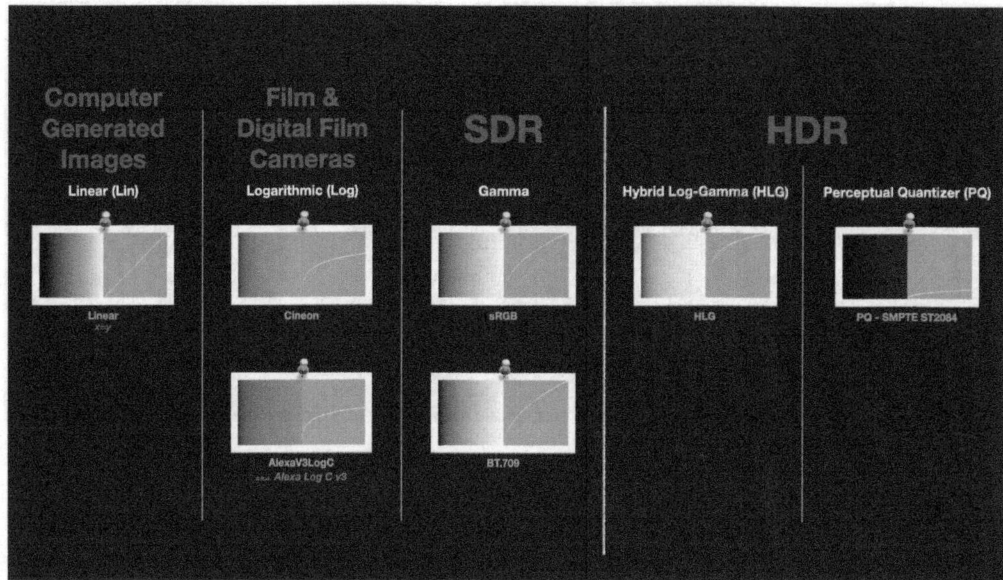

Figure 4.30 Transfer functions (EOTF)

Those ones above belong to the *SDR* world. But now, with modern displays, we are adding new categories that are going to keep in consideration the signals for values brighter than the usual white point of an SDR monitor, so with a brighter white we need special *transfer functions*, so that's why our next two categories fall under the HDR group, and they are:

- *Hybrid log-gamma (HLG)*, combining both functions: the *logarithmic* and the *gamma* in one curve, and the *perceptual quantizer (PQ)*, which is an *electro-optical transfer function* that allows an HDR signal with a luminance up to 10,000 *nits*, or *candelas per square meter (cd/m²)*. The use of either function combined with the *Rec.2020 primaries* has been standardized as *Rec.2100*.

Just to show you the difference between the SDR displays *transfer functions* and the HDR ones, here is a sneak peek of something we will study later in this series, to put in relation the light levels of HDR and the *signal value* distribution (Figure 4.31).

With these groups of LUT's you have an overview of some different *transfer functions* that are used to encode images.

The question now, to avoid misunderstanding, is to separate the concept of *transfer function* from the common so called *look up table* (LUT) as they are similar concepts but certainly not the same.

LUT's have been part of color handling since the beginning, especially when you have to convert the color space of an image to be visualized into a different display device with a different color space, and even more relevant when you are working with an image based on the color capabilities of a particular display ... I think it is time to explore *look up tables*.

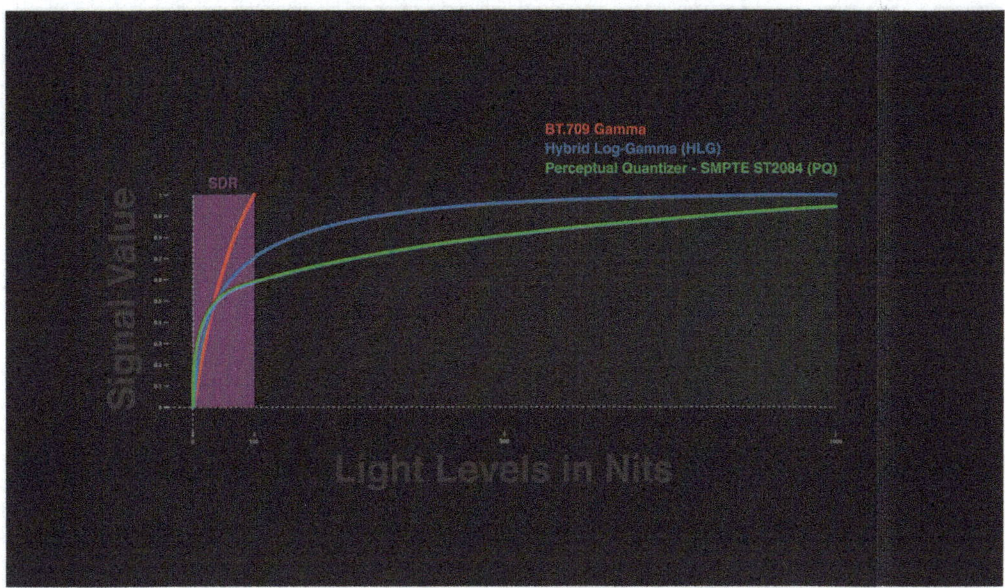

Figure 4.31 High dynamic range (HDR) vs standard dynamic range (SDR) EOTFs (transfer functions)

Look Up Table

First of all: "*What is an LUT (also known as look up table)?*" It is simply an array of data structured by correspondence – like in a dictionary, for every word you have an explanation, in an LUT for every given input value you have a given output value – and it replaces runtime calculations by the computer (which is what actually happens in a *Function*). In other words, it is a list of instructions to convert the given values (or input values) into a desired target value (or output) for every single pixel. In terms of color, it transforms your input color values into other output color values, in what is called a *remapping operation*. LUT's could be pre-calculated in an array resulting from a function, or just arbitrary values stored in the array, so the computer just reads and re-assigns the values for every pixel of the image. So, we can say the *transfer function* could be the source of a particular type of LUT, but not all LUT's are *transfer functions*. For example, some LUT's are meant to transform from one color space into another; others simply to apply a "creative look", and any other uses you like for any "fixed transformation" of color based on a correspondence for every given value on every pixel in the image.

Let's have a look at an easy example for both versions: the pre-calculated LUT and its original function, so I can make a point on a peculiar aspect of LUT's, which is the linear interpolation between its resulting values (Figure 4.32).

This is our given RGB image – and for RGB I just mean color image; but before we continue, let me introduce you to this "girl", her name is Marcy Rylan, I'm sure it is not the first time you have seen her. This image is very famous in the post-production industry, its technical name is *Laboratory Aim Density (LAD) Test Image*. The purpose of this calibrated set of data, as described by its manufacturer: «*The KODAK Digital LAD Test Image is a digital image that can be used as an aid in setting up digital film recorders to*

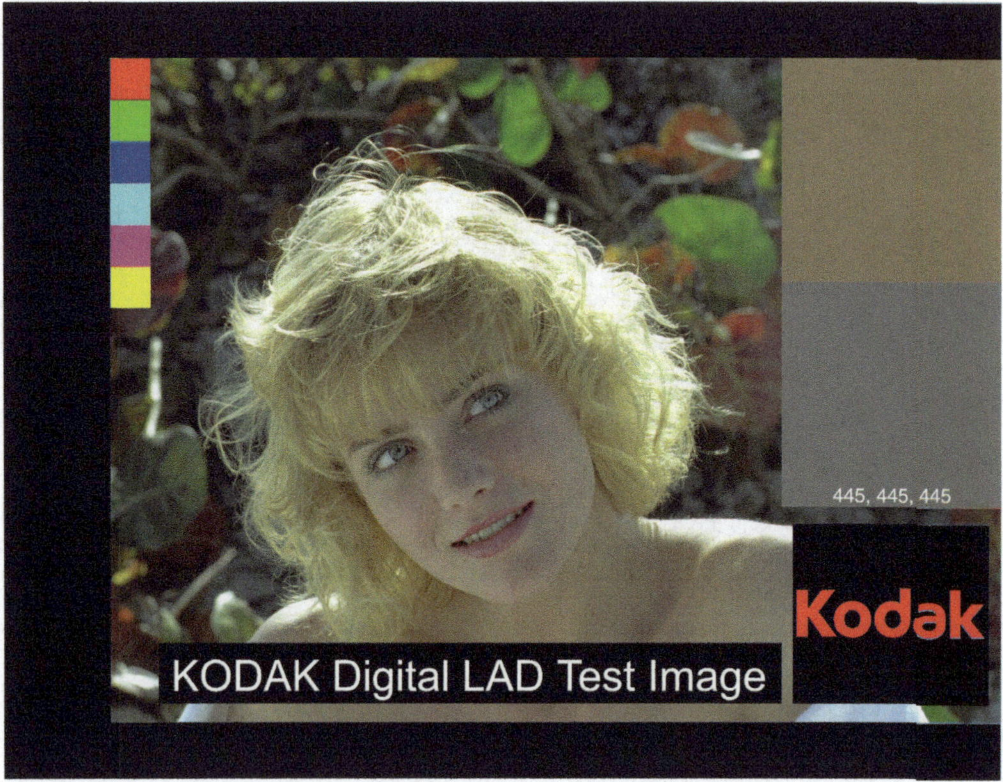

Figure 4.32 KODAK digital laboratory aim density (LAD) test image. Copyright by Kodak™

produce properly exposed digital negatives and in obtaining pleasing prints from those negatives.»[6] Since everybody is very familiar with Marcy – the name by which everyone knows this image – it is widely used to test the calibration of mostly anything in display systems, or even the color aspect of a given sequence of images, placing Marcy at the head of the clip for testing purposes. If you want to know all the details and specifics about the KODAK Digital LAD Test Image or download the image, available in *DPX* and *Cineon*, you can consult the *KODAK Publication No. H-387* that is available – for free – on the website of Kodak.[7]

Now that you are familiar with Marcy, we are going to apply one single array to all three channel-components, so the same correspondence of values for RGB, this means my *look up table* is a *1D LUT*, so only one curve represents the operation for all channels.

We are going to layout all the luminance values of the image, from the darkest, normalized 0, to the brightest, normalized 1 (this is going to make the calculations much easier, instead of using the nominal 10-bits values ranging from 0 to 1023). Now let's create a graphic representation to visualize the LUT (Figure 4.33).

Right, the Cartesian plane again. In both axes the same scale of numbers, placed in an arithmetic progression from 0 to 1. The horizontal axis, the *x*, will represent the *input*,

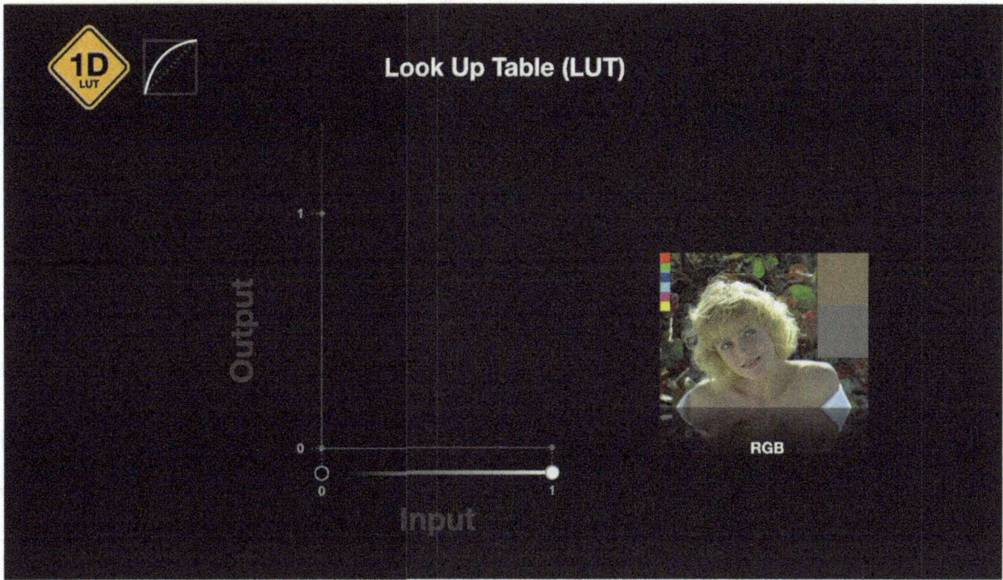

Figure 4.33 1D look-up table (LUT) layout (input values correlated to output values)

the original values; and the vertical, or *y*, will be the *output*, the resulting values of the processed image after the LUT has been applied. Notice that while the Input data states the original values written in the source image file are fully normalized, the highest value cannot be higher than the maximum value allowed by the bit-depth. In other words, for example, in a 10-bit image we say normalized value 1 is the original maximum value, corresponding to the 10-bit 1023 value, so in an 10-bit image you cannot write a value of, for instance, 2000, because it simply does not exist. That is why we are going to have an input from 0 to 1 (the maximum "normalized" value). However, the output is a different story, you can create a correspondence above the normalized 1 (which is, by the way, quite common and widely used by certain file formats, like the *log* ones), as a commodity to represent the darkest black and the brightest white in relation to an sRGB monitor. The normalization of the *y* axis refers to the range of values able to be displayed by an 8-bit *sRGB* color space. Does it mean you cannot have an LUT with input values above 1, well, yes, and even more, with values less than 0, but those LUTs are meant for more "creative" purposes while in here we are focusing on the LUT's and *transfer functions* to remap color values within a certain color space for its proper distribution, so for these examples I'm assuming just the nominal bit-depth color positions (bit combination), of a raw image for the output luminance of a normalized display. Remember, it is just an example, the important point here is to understand the correspondence and interpolation. In any case, strictly speaking, all LUT's behave the same, input values remapped into output values. That's it.

The first instance is going to be a linear pre-calculated array (Figure 4.34).

Here you have the values. This example LUT has only three keys, meaning the rest of the values will be interpolated linearly between the key values by the computer.

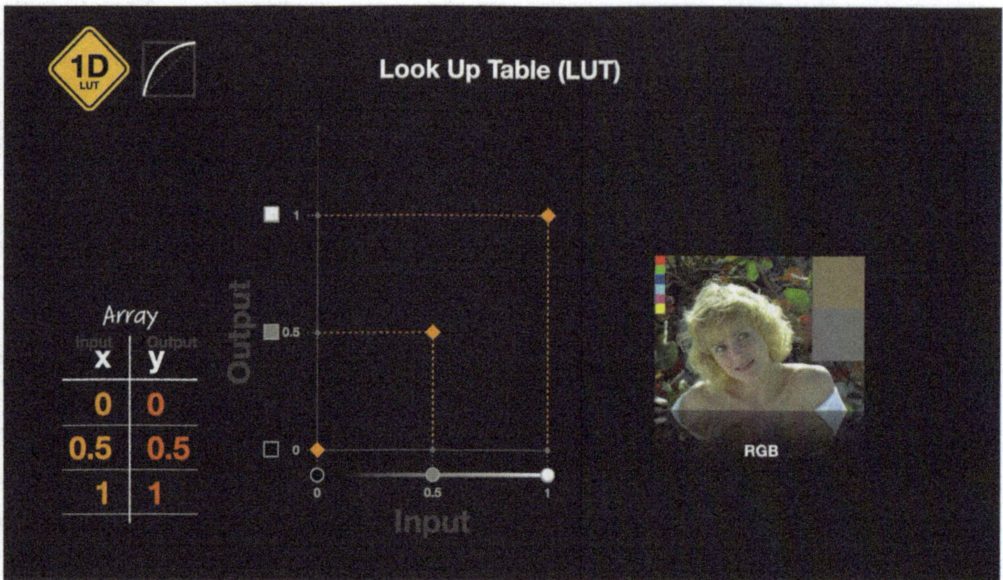

Figure 4.34 The three values of 1D look-up table (LUT) in the instance 1

Let's locate the first array in the graphic: Input value 0, the *black point* goes up to value 0 in the y axis. So, it stays where it was. The next one, the original value 0.5 – the midpoint – goes up to result in 0.5, ending in the middle of the vertical axis. And value 1, the *white point*, is mapped into the output value 1, the same level of white as you can see. So, if we connect those points the result is this (Figure 4.35):

A linear arithmetic progression between the input and the output, in other words, the image remains unchanged. We can call this LUT at "rest", meaning, it is not changing the image that it is being applied to. In other words, it is doing nothing. This is what happens to an image with a *linear* color space when it is ingested into the same *linear* workspace: no transformation is required for the linearization of the image because the image was already linear. I think this concept is linearly clear (yes, pun intended).

Precision and Interpolation

The precision of the LUT will depend on the number of keys in the pre-calculated array. In an 8-bit LUT you will have up to 256 keys, so an 8-bit image will have all its possible values pre-calculated, while the same 8-bit LUT applied to a 10-bit image (with its 1024 values) will have only a quarter of values pre-calculated and the others will be interpolated linearly, resulting in a loss of precision. So, on the hand we have the fast computational option, the *Array*, and on the other a formula that is going to be mathematically precise for every value, regardless of the bit-depth of the image that is being applied to (the *function*) but needs to be applied in runtime (on the fly), as opposed to as a pre-calculated transformation.

Let's have a look at the difference between both methods in this case (Figure 4.36).

The mathematical *function* for this *linear* LUT is f of x equals x. So, the coordinates are $[x, f(x)]$ (the function of x), where $f(x)$ is equals to y, and in this case: $f(x) = x$. It means

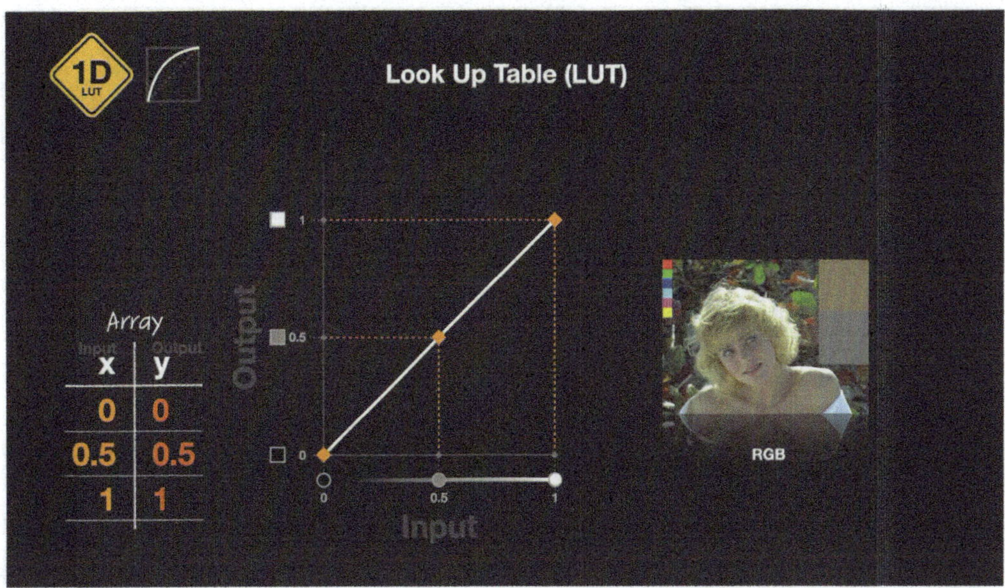

Figure 4.35 Linearly interpolated values of 1D look-up table (LUT) in the instance 1

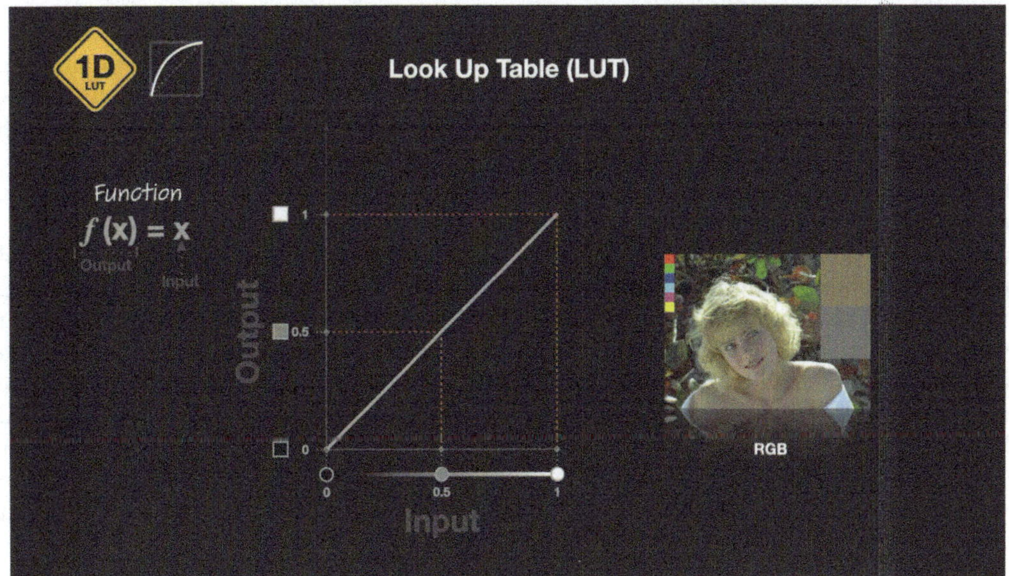

Figure 4.36 Function of instance 1

every input value, and what is after the equal sign is the formula to calculate the resulting value for every given input value, the output, or in this case *y*. So, if we apply this formula where the output is equal to the input, here you have the result.

Exactly as before, you can check using the same values we pre-calculated for the array and the resulting image: same as before. This is the *linear* LUT.

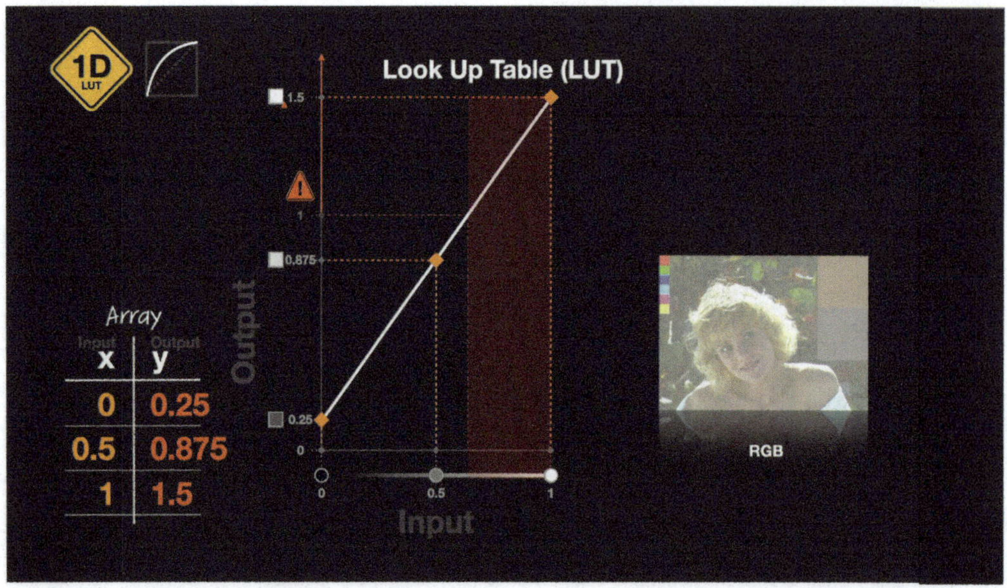

Figure 4.37 Linearly interpolated values of 1D look-up table (LUT) in the instance 2

Let's have a look at a more interesting and complex example.

We are still using a 1D LUT. Let's position the values: input 0, the *black point*, goes up to 0.25, so this means the darkest black we will have in our resulting image will be this grey, a so called "milky" black point. Next, the midpoint, 0.5 is going up to 0.875, which means the mid areas of luminance are going to be very bright. And my original value one, the brightest of my input is going beyond the output value 1, exactly at value 1.5, meaning it is on the *super-whites*[8] area, the values my monitor cannot display, and they will be reproduced by the *8-bit sRGB* monitor as just value one, together with everything that is equal to or higher than the output value one. Have a look at the resulting image: Very bright, milky blacks, and the highlights would be displayed in the monitor as merely white, but we know there is data on those bright areas (trust the values, not just your eyes). So having this LUT associated with the original data written on the file is actually a good way to store normalized values that represent light beyond value one, and still be encoded in a contained bit-depth. If you are hearing the term bit-depth a lot, and you are unsure about why it is so important in relation to LUTs and human perception for certain *transfer functions*, no worries, we will talk about it later more in depth. Now let's have a look at the Function that defined that pre-calculated array (Figure 4.38):

As you can see, the formula for the *function* is quite different: now we have to take the input value, expressed as you know as x, and multiply it by 1.25, and then (after the multiplication, as we learned in school), add 0.25. This is the function: $f(x) = x \times 1.25 + 0.25$. Same result as the LUT because this function expresses an arithmetic progression that coincides with the linear interpolation between values (that is equally arithmetic). But things are going to get complicated in the next example (Figure 4.39).

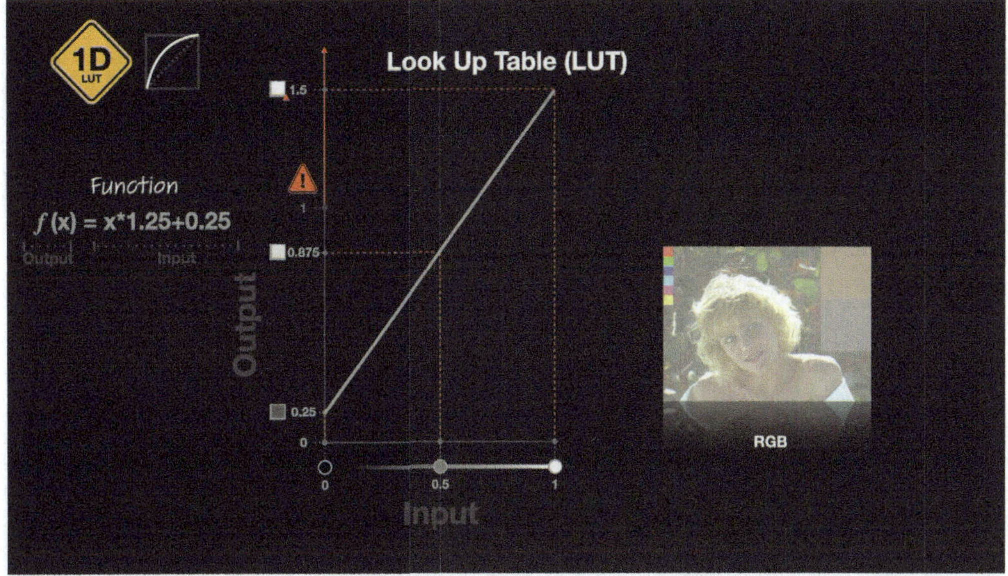

Figure 4.38 Function of instance 2

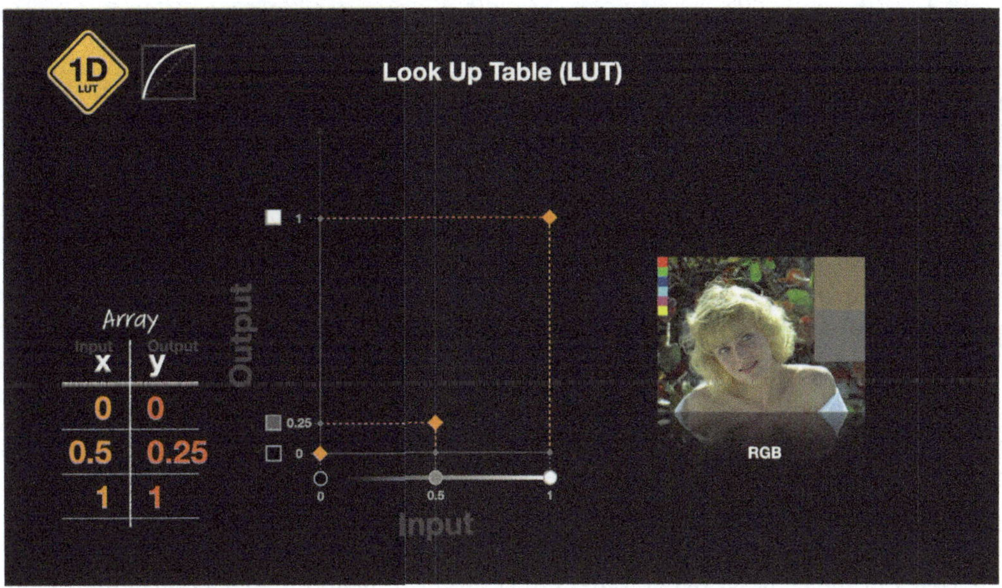

Figure 4.39 The three values of 1D look-up table (LUT) in the instance 3

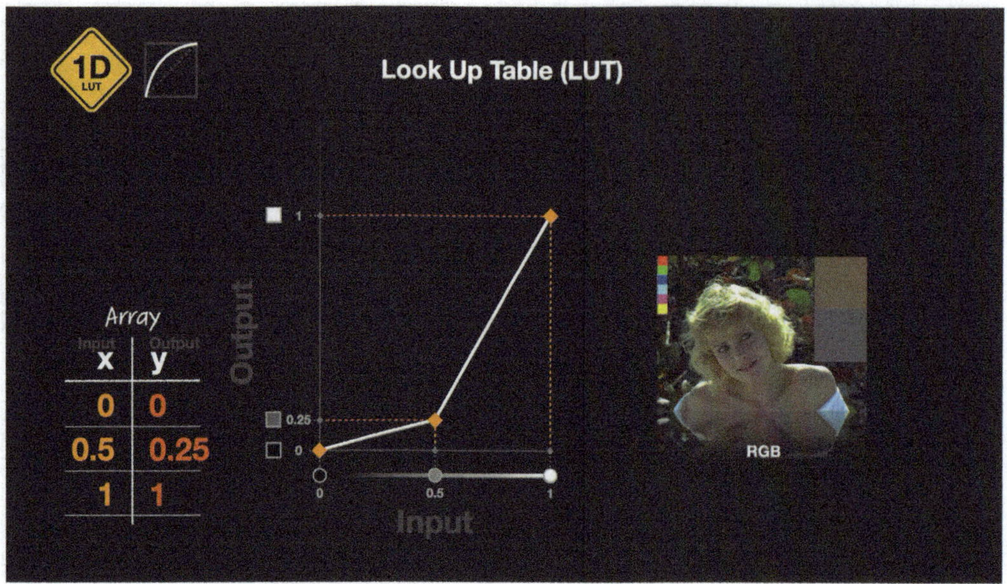

Figure 4.40 Linearly interpolated values of 1D look-up table (LUT) in the instance 3

In this other example, we have a very different progression. 0 remains unchanged, 0.5 goes up to 0.25, visible darker mid-tones, and value 1 remains unchanged as well (Figure 4.40).

Look, if we interpolate the results our line appears to be "broken" or "discontinuous" (not a smooth curve at all), and not a continuous straight line as in the previous examples, it means the progression of contrast in the first half of values is different from the progression of contrast in the second half of the output (in both cases constant progression but different slopes),[9] and that doesn't look very "physically plausible". The reason the linear interpolation here is not working well is because we don't have enough *density* of data, I mean number of keys in the array is very little, to populate the LUT. So instead of using a pre-calculated LUT with a limited number of points, let's have a look at the *function* that I used to generate those three points (Figure 4.41):

The function is a *power function* of x, hence $f(x) = x^2$, therefore the result is not linear, it is exponential. Not a straight line anymore, but a curve. Have a look at the resulting image of the figure above. The "mid-tones" had changed the most, values below 1 and above 0, with those two ends remaining unvaried. Notice the color chips in the image of Marcy are intact, as they have either value 1 or 0 on each RGB channel, therefore applying this function: value 0 and value 1 always remain unchanged[10] (Figure 4.42).

The figure above shows the overlap of the LUT array against the Function graphic representations. Quite different, aren't they?

So, "*How do you bake (precalculate) the results of this curve into an array?*" I am glad you ask, because you have to get an LUT array with the pre-computed result of a key for every single available value in the target bit-depth of the image: which means 256 keys with their respective values for 8-bit images, 1024 for 10-bits images and so on … maybe we can express the LUT simply with the Function and avoid having to read and write so

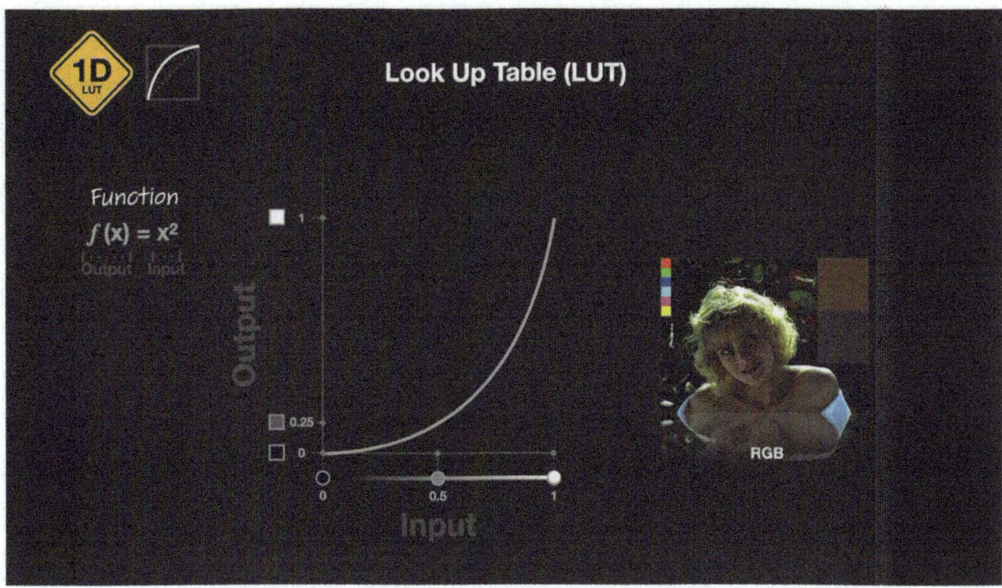

Figure 4.41 Function of instance 3

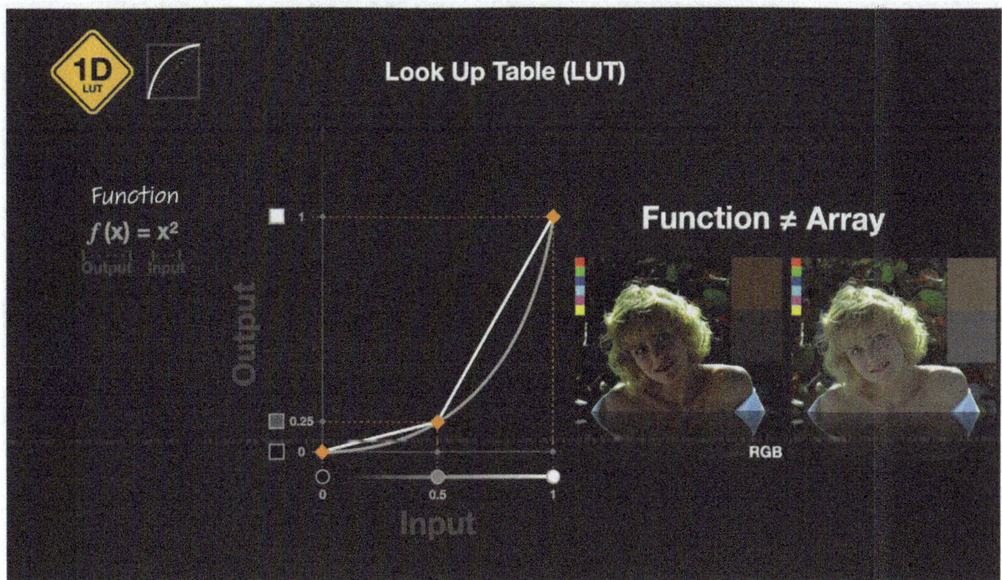

Figure 4.42 Linearly interpolated values of 1D look-up table (LUTs) vs the function of the instance 3

much data – imagine a 32-bit LUT – besides, a function is universal for any bit-depth, and things are going to get big when you get an array for a 3D LUT, meaning you have an array (or function) for every channel. Like a cube in 3D, each of the three axes of the three-dimensional space represents a color, therefore each component of the RGB will have their own specific array or function (Figure 4.43).

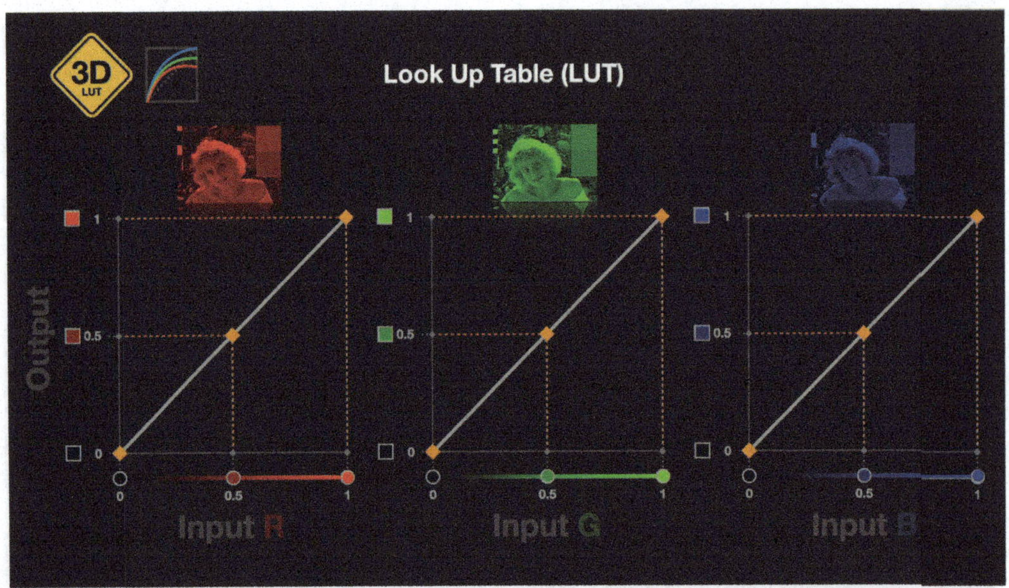

Figure 4.43 3D look-up table (LUT) indicate independent transformations for each RGB

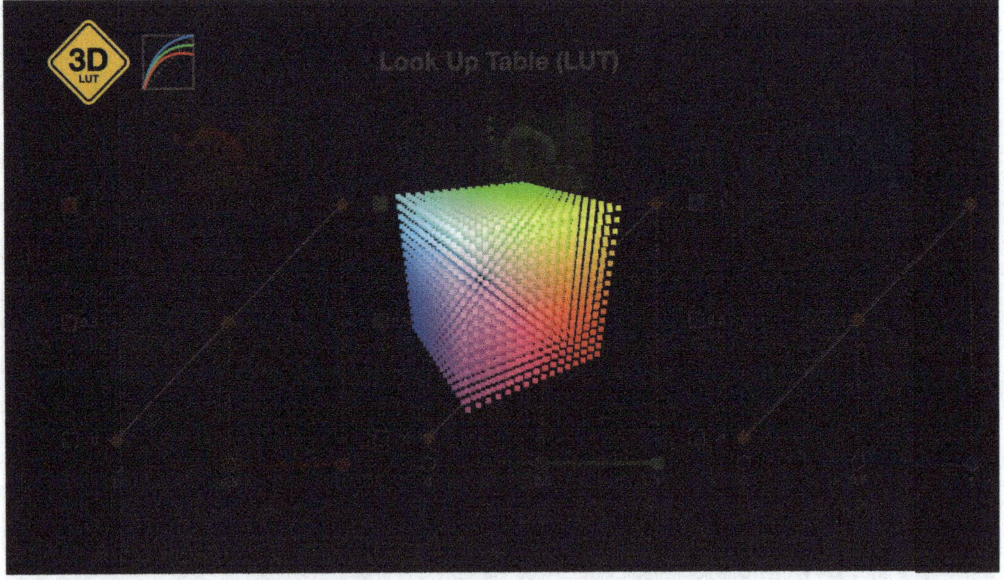

Figure 4.44 3D visualization of the RGB components

This is a view of a different 3D color transformation illustrated in an LUT. As I said before, LUT's can be used also to define a certain creative look, to apply any kind of primary color transformation. By the way *primary color transformation* refers to color transformations that are applied to every pixel, and this is in opposition to *secondary color transformations* where the color manipulation is applied to just an isolated group of pixels, based on a certain criteria (such as a mask, a range of luminance or saturation; or any other discriminatory process of selection of areas of the image). So, an LUT is a fixed color transformation based on a remap of the given values of every pixel in the image, and used for different purposes (Figure 4.44).

I think we should go back in time again to understand how we have been managing color traditionally: by applying LUTs to convert from one color space to another, also known as color transfers. With this, you are going to get an overview of why the change is necessary. Brace yourself.

Display Referred Workflows

Welcome to the "*Brief (and over-simplified) History of the Color Transfer Odyssey*". You are going to see the "problem" very quickly, you will see. If you don't, I promise an illustration at the end that will make the point.

In the beginning there were film cameras, and they shot in film negative stocks. All you needed to do was to develop the film negative and convert it into positive, apply a light to it and voilà: cinema projection. The whole process was analog – a physical support and a chemical process – and everybody was happy.

However, if we wanted to put a film on TV, we then needed to convert the physical support into an electronic signal, so we use a *telecine* (practically a video-camera that taped the negative recording against a light). So, we have a magnetic support that is still analog, not perfect for a few reasons, but still everybody was quite happy with it.

But then people started getting personal computers, accompanied, of course, by CRT monitors – which, by the way, stands for *cathode-ray tube* (CRT) – roughly the same technology as the TVs of the time, so the image capabilities of both TVs and PCs behaved more or less the same. Meaning that any image document required a correction made by the software attempting to visualize it, more or less correctly, in the CRT monitor, and I mean "more or less" because every CRT monitor was built without a standard criteria for color, and every software was doing its own thing to represent color.

Then computers and monitors evolved and finally everything complied with the newly established *sRGB* Color Space (yay!), so my image is going to be displayed correctly as the monitor and the software are aligned in terms of color, and so the websites full of images I browse on the super-slow Internet. In the meantime –we are still in the 90s – the film scanner has been invented, the *digital intermediate* is born. Used for the first time to digitally restore and remaster Walt Disney's 1937 classic *Snow White and the Seven Dwarves*. The process is also known as *DI* as we scan the original negative, converting it into Cineon file sequences in gorgeous 10-bit – higher bit-depth than the 8-bit <u>sRGB</u> we use for watching videos of cats on the Internet. Everything was processed in digital after the scan … but at the end, cough-cough, for the delivery we print it back again in a film strip to be projected in analog as before, so the digital part was just in the middle (hence *intermediate*). Until digital projectors became good enough, affordable, and popular (without mentioning the contribution of the stereoscopic boom created by James Cameron's *Avatar*). *Digital cinema* changed the rules also in the chain of distribution, as film rolls did not need to travel anymore. The new *digital cinema packages* were transmitted over the Internet. Cinema was becoming entirely digital. But not end-to-end just yet, until *digital cameras* landed. No longer did we need to scan film negatives, cough-cough, images from digital cameras though were converted to the same *Cineon* file sequences we used for film scans to keep a consistent workflow.

And then the TV became digital and abandoned the less ecological CRT to become LCD, but during the times of transition to digital, they had to build inside the software of the digital TV the same "defects" of the image reproduction that CRTs had naturally so everybody could see the same corrected signal able to be reproduced by a crap old system, a problem that the LCD did not have natively but had to be embedded for compatibility purposes, a smart move for consistency but a headache for everything else. And since the TVs became digital – meaning they have a computer inside – TV contents started evolving with the same speed as computers. Very quickly we stepped from *standard definition* – remember the old NTSC and PAL systems? – to the new world of unified *High Definition* (with their three versions: 720p, 1080i and 1080p). Yet, all of them had the same color space, which is a tweaked version of the sRGB used for computers. This color space for the TVs was standardized from a recommendation made by the *International Telecommunication Union* and became the standard for HDTVs: the *Recommendation number 709 or ITU-R BT.709* – that is a long and complicated name, let's just call it *Rec709*. The *Rec709* maintains the same *primaries* and *white point* of the sRGB but changing slightly the *gamma encoding* (its transfer function) to represent the images with a better color quality in these new devices.'

But why stop evolution here if we can get bigger resolutions, bigger color spaces, and higher bit depth? Computers get better and more affordable, technology evolves, the pursuit of image quality never stops and here we are at *4K HDR UHD TV*, but just when the trend was "*bigger is better*" and while the market was so focused on making bigger screens and more powerful projectors ... people decided to watch contents on their phones and tablets: the war of devices was on: *portability* vs *bigger screens*.

So, the process that was once called *digital intermediate* became significantly more complex, with elements coming from very different sources, and needed to be visualized for processing on the same *sRGB* monitors but to be delivered for displays with the same capabilities of the computer monitors and for better screens, so how can you work colors, bit-depths and dynamic ranges that you cannot visualize? Of course! Using LUT's to convert from a device to another device, depending on where the image was generated and where we want to transfer it now! Yep ... that is a lot of LUTs. Furthermore, once the project is finished and

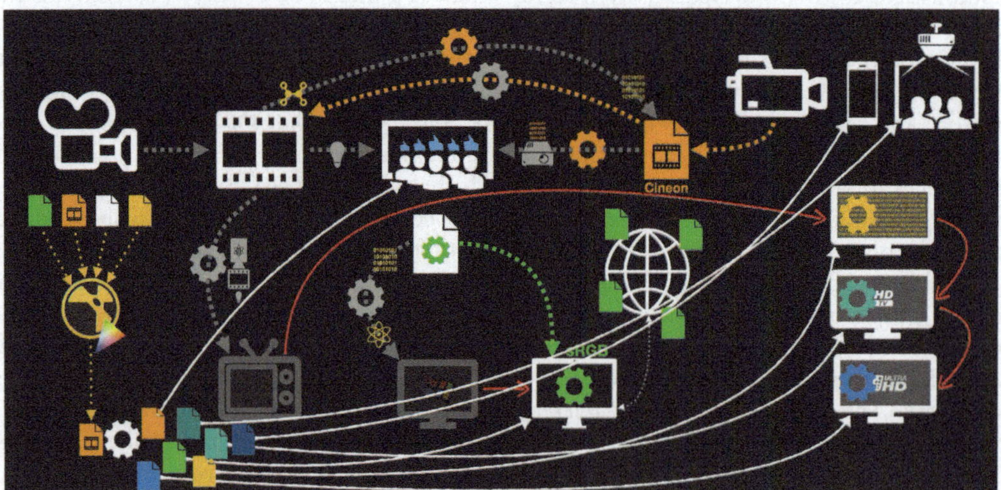

Figure 4.45 Brief and oversimplified history of the color transfer odyssey in a nutshell

the master final delivery is archived, what would happen in a few years when displays get even better? Our precious materials that came at a high cost will become simply obsolete. This mess relies on one single issue: *all corrections to adapt the content to be correctly visualized on the screen implied changing the actual data of the images to be adapted to every display*, so as soon as the technology changes, our files must change every time to adapt to that new technology, to the display (Figure 4.45).

This is known as *display referred workflow*. But there is another way … and it is called *scene referred*. Let's have a look.

Scene Referred Workflows

Let's have a look now at how the *scene referred workflow* actually works. The first thing is to choose the master color space, one wide enough to contain all the gamuts of the files we are going to ingest, HDR compatible these days is a must, so you should keep that in mind as well (Figure 4.46).

The *unified color space* does not depend on any display, it is just a mathematical container of color data, a workspace. It is time to ingest our footages (Figure 4.47).

We will need to apply an *input transform* to convert the *raw video data* or the *source material* from each device into the *unified color space*. Notice that CGI could be rendered, encoding its color values directly into the target *unified color space* (so the color values do not need to be converted from any other color space). However – even if it is not, strictly speaking, recommended – you could always convert the color values of any CGI into that target *unified color space*, in the case, for instance, that you already rendered it in any other color space, by simply using a conversion LUT. The thing is, if you can render it directly into the *unified color space*, please do not make any useless conversions. We will discuss color transformations in Nuke in another section so you can see a practical example.

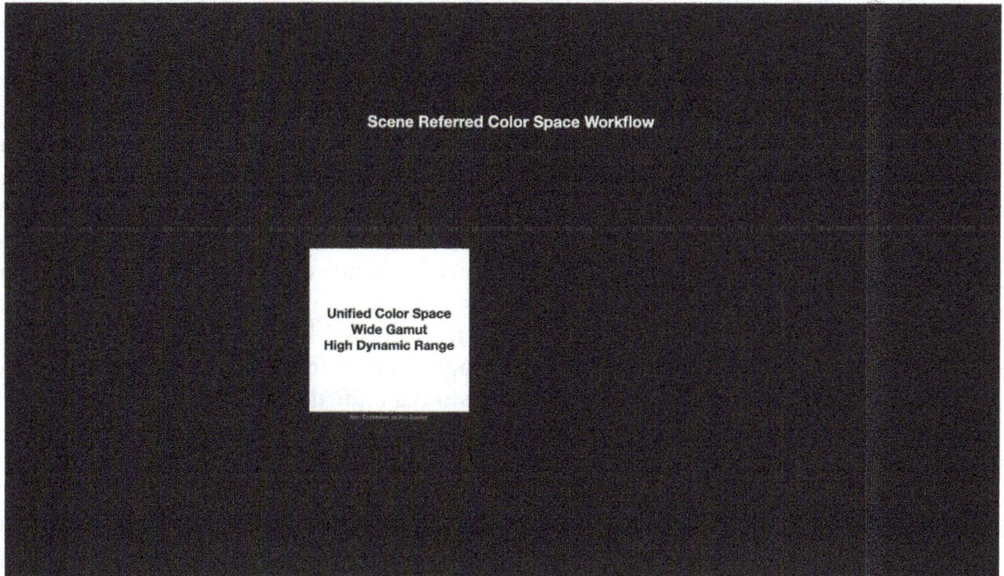

Figure 4.46 Unified scene referred color space

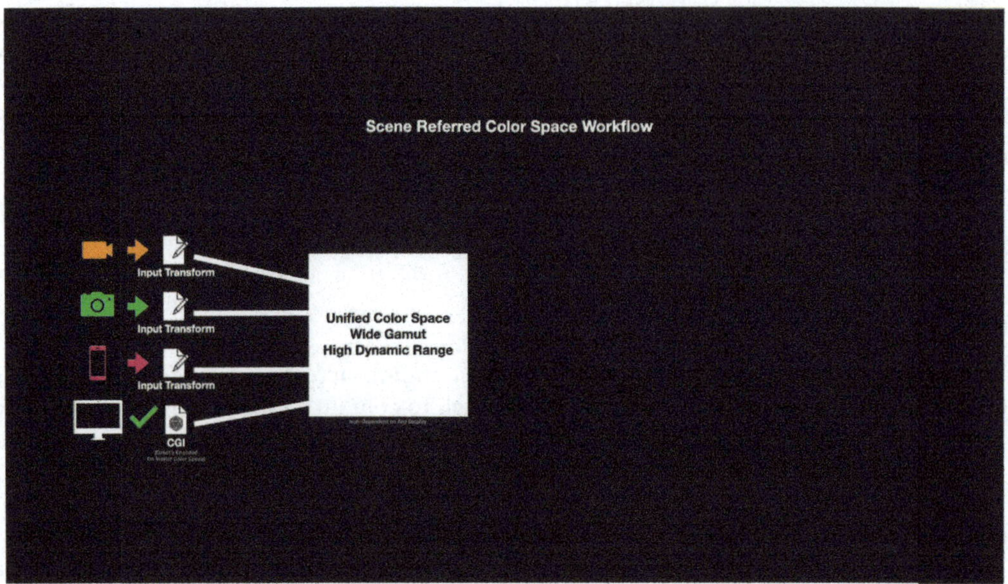

Figure 4.47 Footage and CGI imported into the unified scene referred color space with an input transform

Now everything is in the same unified color space, so they all obey the same rules: same *gamut*, same *white point* and same *transfer function*, this last one expected to be *linear* to facilitate arithmetical operations and color manipulations, but we will talk about that later.

Please, keep in mind that the fact that all footages – coming from different sources – are placed inside the same gamut does not mean they need to cover the entire gamut of that color space. For instance, a video recorded with an iPhone will be allocated a smaller area within the master color space compared to footage captured with, for instance, an ARRI Alexa. Laying out the color data into a bigger color space, should not alter the original qualities of the source image, it will only change the "address" of those colors. To be clear, the original color capabilities of the image do not get either better or worst. By coexisting in the same master Unified Color Space, all color values are placed to correlate their position between all image sources. All colors behave the same way regardless of their origin. Therefore, the process of placing all images in one single color will make the handling of color the same as any other capturing device, no special rules needed. Like what happens inside Nuke when you work with images with different bit-depths: all images handled within Nuke workspace are automatically converted into 32-bit floating-point, regardless of its original source bit-depth so you can mix them without needing to align their bit depths. That is another feature of Nuke workspace. Which means the artist could apply a look from an external file that obeys the rules of this master color space to any image in the unified color space, at this point any color transformation to the images will behave the same for the iPhone images or the ARRI Alexa captures I mentioned above (respecting each source capabilities, but in terms of color manipulation they all behave the same way) (Figure 4.48).

We have all the data intact in our master footages together with the look intent so when the footage moves to other departments, they are all aligned in terms of what everybody sees on their screens and they have access to the footage in the same color space, always maintaining the creative look intent (Figure 4.49).

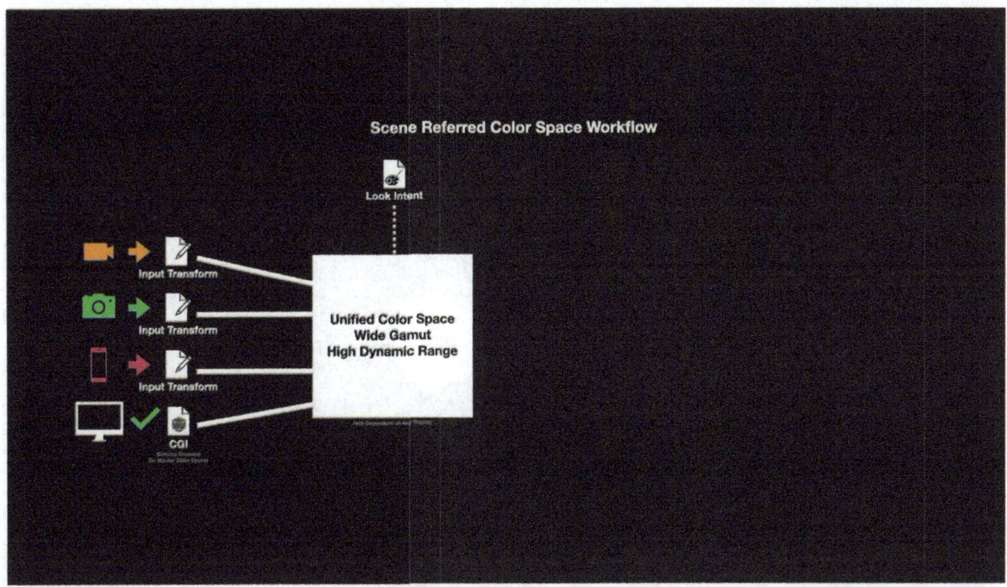

Figure 4.48 Look intent stored as color transformations using the unified scene referred color space rules

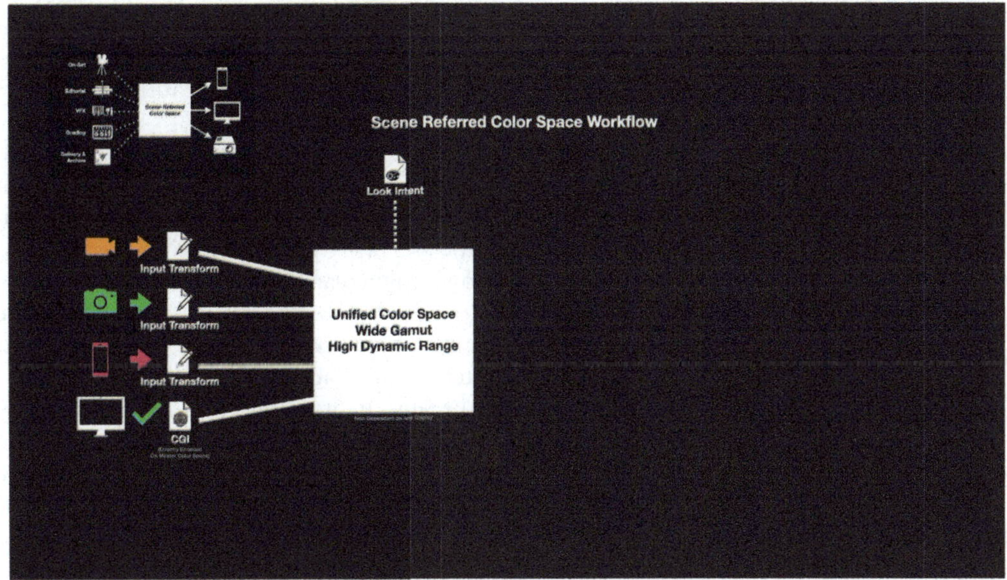

Figure 4.49 All departments use the common unified scene referred color spaces

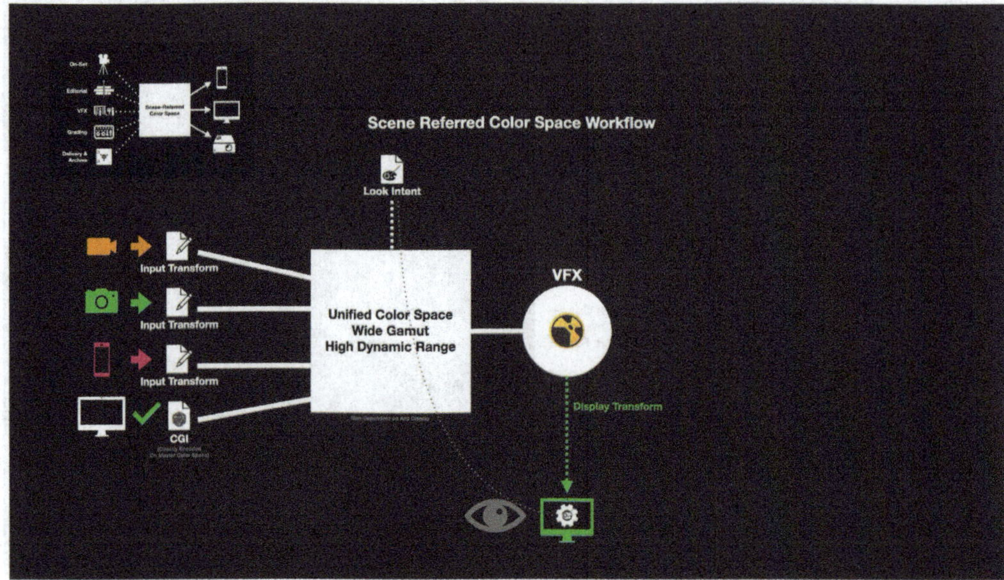

Figure 4.50 Virtual effects (VFX) relates to the unified scene referred color space

In our case, for the VFX department, we can, for instance, read the footage in Nuke, apply to our *viewer* the appropriate *display transform* according to the monitor or projector, or TV we are using to visualize the composition, and also apply to the *viewer* the look intent defined for this shot so we are going to have on our screen the image as the filmmakers intended it to be … while our footage is still intact. They are just visualization corrections applied to the *viewer*, the data remains the same (Figure 4.50).

After VFX have completed their job, everything moves to *DI* – that by the way, DI still today stands for *digital intermediate*, even though the whole process is digital and not simply an intermediate stage, but it is a reminiscence. There the final grade will be applied, keeping in consideration the *Look Intent* and after the grading process a *display transform* will be applied for every destination display device, each one in their own color space and features (Figure 4.51).

Of course, with the transfer to certain narrower color spaces the grade would need to be tweaked to adapt to that color destination. For instance, Pixar's colorist Mark Dinicola, while working on the film *Cars* (Dir. John Lasseter, 2006), had to make adjustments to the grading of the protagonist *Lightning McQueen* because he was displayed quite differently from the cinema version to the TV as the *primaries* of each *gamut* are different and the car's shiny varnish is purely red. So once the grading is complete and all deliveries have been handled it is time to archive. The masters will be collected in the *unified scene-referred color space*, and the grading sessions (color correction of the whole show) will be saved as color transformations so in the future we could always go back and restore everything and deliver for those devices that are not yet invented. It means this workflow is future proofed (Figure 4.52).

As you can see, in here there are only two color transformations happening to the footage, one at the beginning and another at the end (for each display delivery), what happens in the middle is just a chain of visualization transforms but the footage across the whole pipeline always remains untouched in terms of color space transformations.

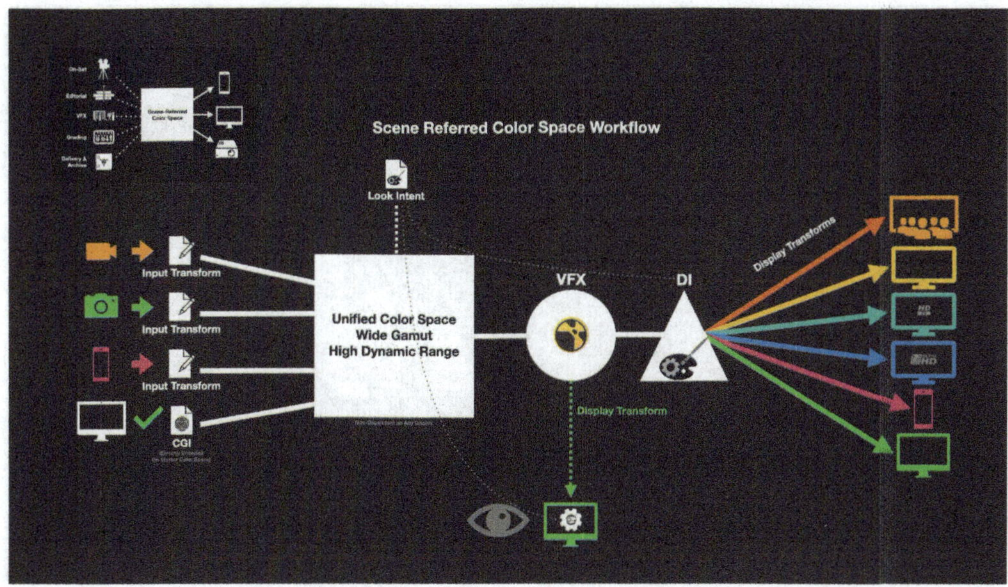

Figure 4.51 DI applies display transforms from the unified scene referred color space to deliver for every display

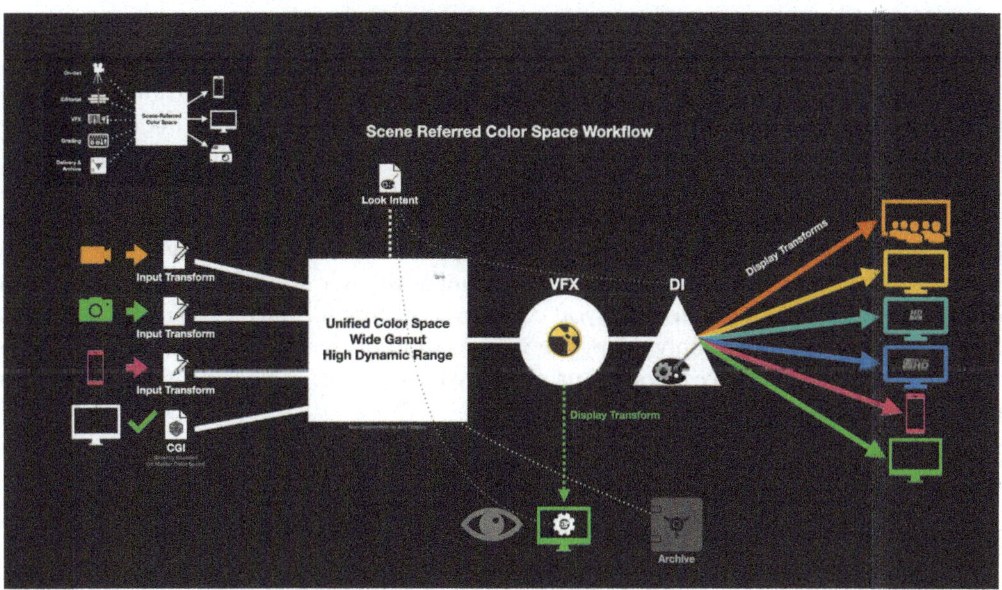

Figure 4.52 Scene referred color space workflow

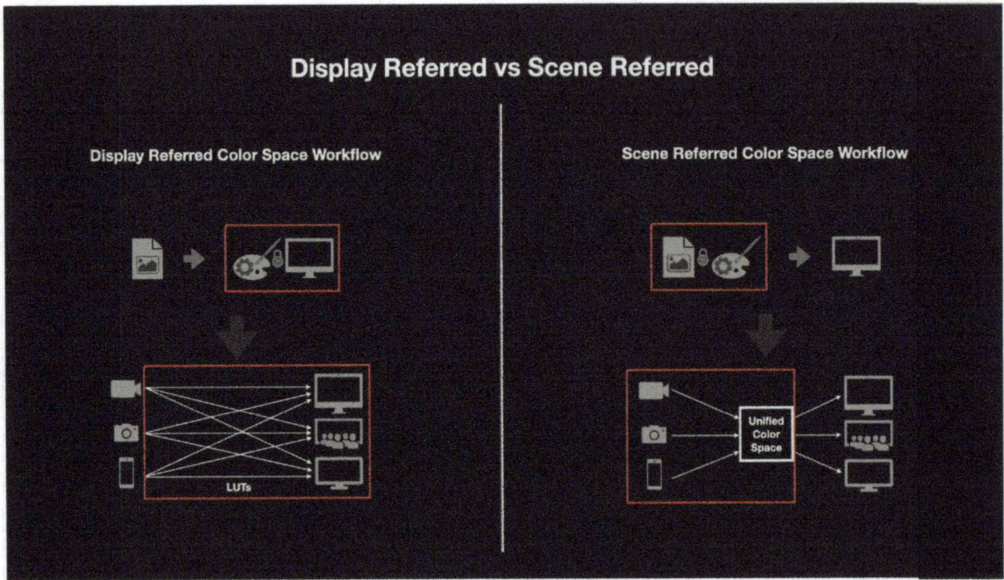

Figure 4.53 Display referred vs scene referred workflows

Display Referred vs Scene Referred Workflows

Essentially the main difference between *display referred* and *scene referred* color space workflows is this (Figure 4.53):

In the display referred instance you have the footage and then the color transformation is applied in relation to the display so it can be shown correctly, modifying the footage every time the display changes. While in the scene-referred instance the color transformation is applied in relation to the footage, once, agnostically from any display.

As a result, in the *display referred* instance you have to apply a *look up table* (a *LUT*) to convert the color from a color space into another, to every footage for every display, ending with a lot of transformations and a high risk of inconsistency and margin for human error. While in the *scene referred* instance you convert every footage into the master color space and from there you can simply adapt the visualization of the footage for a target display, simplifying the whole process and ensuring everyone is on the same page without compromising the footage across the whole pipeline.

The Key Elements of the RGB Color Space

In conclusion, the three key elements of the RGB color space are:

- Three *primaries* to define the *color gamut* of the color space; the vertices of the triangle.
- The *white point*, the point with the lowest chromatic intensity, the minimum saturation, or simply, what we perceive as *white*.
- And the *transfer function*, that defines the mapping between the linear tristimulus values and non-linear electronic signal values, the distribution of the color samples data within the color space (Figure 4.54).

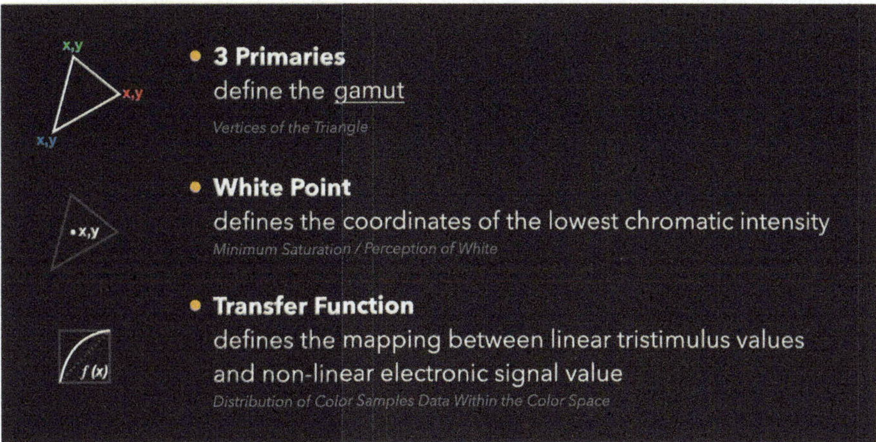

Figure 4.54 Key elements of the RGB color space

Notes

1 CIE (2020, December). *Color Gamut*. IEC 60050 – International Electrotechnical Vocabulary. https://www.electropedia.org/iev/iev.nsf/display?openform&ievref=845-32-007.

2 In Nuke there are color controls for the temperature and the magenta so by moving one slider you still preserve the characteristic of the other. The set of color sliders known as *temperature, magenta* and *intensity (TMI)*.

3 In case you are not familiar reading a tuple of coordinates, the format to interpret the numbers is as follows: [x, y]. Meaning the whole set of coordinates is defined by the square brackets "[ ]" and each component of the set is separated by commas, in this case we have two components, that is why it is called *tuple*, one component for the horizontal axis position and the other for the vertical one. In our tuple of 2D coordinates, the first number – before the comma – stands for the position in the x-axis (horizontal), and the second – after the comma – is the position of our point in the y-axis (vertical). In case of a *triple* (like a tuple but for three coordinates instead of two), a defined 3D position of a point, the reading order is [x, y, z].

4 *By default*: It means it can be changed, however this choice is the vanilla out-of-the-box option. For instance, in Nuke, you can use the default proprietary color management option (as we are discussing in this section), or the *OCIO* option (that we will discuss later in this book).

5 *Function*: In mathematics, a function from a set x to a set y assigns to each element of x exactly one element of y. The set x is known as the function's *domain*, while the set y is known as the function's *codomain*. A function is uniquely represented by the set of all pairings [x, $f (x)$], known as the *function graph*, which is a popular way of visualizing the function. When the *domain* and *codomain* are *Real number* sets, each pair can be thought of as the Cartesian coordinates of a point in the plane.

6 "*KODAK Digital LAD Test Image*". KODAK Publication No. H-387.

7 [Publication] Kodak (2022). *Laboratory Tools and Techniques*. Retrieved December 4, 2022, from https://www.kodak.com/en/motion/page/laboratory-tools-and-techniques

8 *Super-Whites*: Luminance values above normalized value 1.

9 For the "*progression of contrast*" I refer to the angle of inclination of the line (*slope*).

10 $0^2 = 0$, zero to the power of any non-zero number is always zero; and $1^2 = 1$, one to the power of any non-zero number is always one.

High Dynamic Range (HDR)

5

Scene and Display Color Spaces

In the previous section of this book, we focused on understanding the elements that make up color spaces and primary color manipulations. So now that you are familiar with those concepts, I think we are ready to go ahead into the HDR world. But before I proceed, let me tell you that this second part is going to discuss the theory behind those elements in order to create a solid knowledge base – as we did for the previous section of this book– and so after theory we will put into practice everything we learned here in the context of software for the online resources of this book, and you will see how simple every concept becomes once you know the function behind every button we are going to press within the software.

Let's have a look at the end of our journey (Figure 5.1).

This diagram is an example of an ACES scene referred VFX workflow. Every gear represents a color transformation, and every document-clip stands for a key piece of information related to the transform. Therefore, we can go from the source of the image to any display through the whole visual effects pipeline.

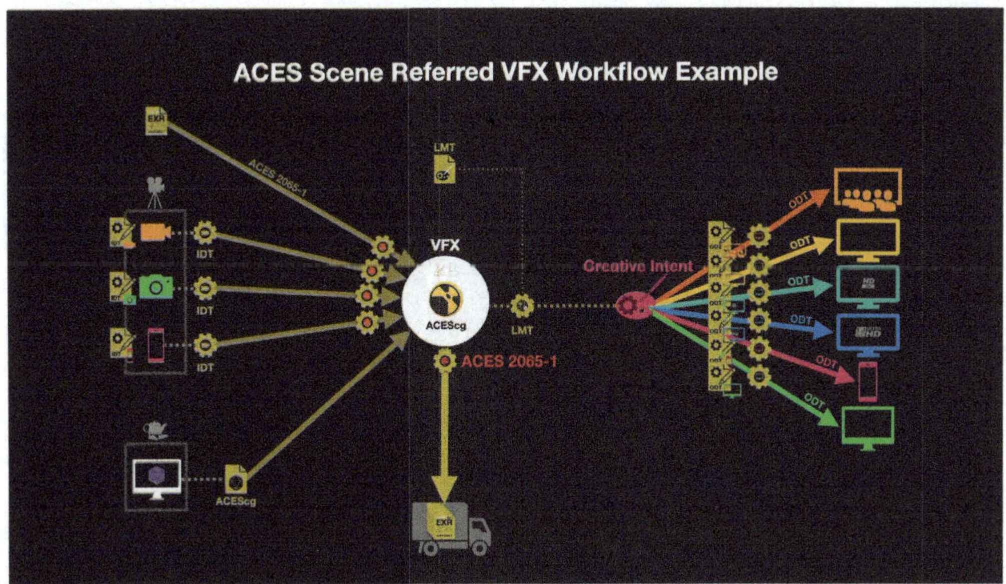

Figure 5.1 Academy color encoding system (ACES) scene referred virtual effects (VFX) workflow example

DOI: 10.4324/b23222-8

Scene and Display Color Spaces

Let's start from the beginning, and this journey starts, of course, with the *CIE xy chromaticity diagram*, because we are going to analyze two different groups of color spaces that we are going to handle quite frequently.

In the first group, I am going to pick 4 common color spaces (Figure 5.2). *sRGB* – that we already discussed in previous chapters; The *Rec709* – that we mentioned as well – notice that the gamut and the white point of both the sRGB and the Rec709 are the same, the difference between them is the transfer function (that is not represented in the diagram), those are traditionally the color spaces for computer monitors, HD TVs and HD Home Projectors; Then we have the *DCI-P3* (name that stands for *Digital Cinema Initiative – Protocol 3*), which comprises a wider gamut than the previous ones, covering 45.5% of the whole chromaticity in this diagram, its blue primary is the same of the *sRGB*; and the red primary is a pure monochromatic light source at a wavelength of 615 nm, and it's used for traditional digital cinema projection. Another one is the *Rec2020*, that we are going to discuss in depth later in this section of the book as it is the standardized color space for HDR, notice that its primaries are located exactly on the *spectral locus*, so they are pure colors from the visible wavelengths of light. However, in theory, only lasers can reproduce those pure wavelengths, and at the present time there are only a few high-end displays that can reproduce the entire gamut. However, as soon as displays become more accessible, this color space will maintain all those colors we are not able to display at the moment, which means that this color space has been created to be a future-proof container of color for displays. Think about it, its three primaries are located at the maximum expanse within the *spectral locus*, keeping all the samples contained in its gamut visible to the human eye, which would be an optimal "possible" gamut for any display, now or in the future. Yet, these days the *Rec2020* is used more as a container of color information for mastering, this is called a "wrapper", so you put inside any other color gamuts that could be contained within.

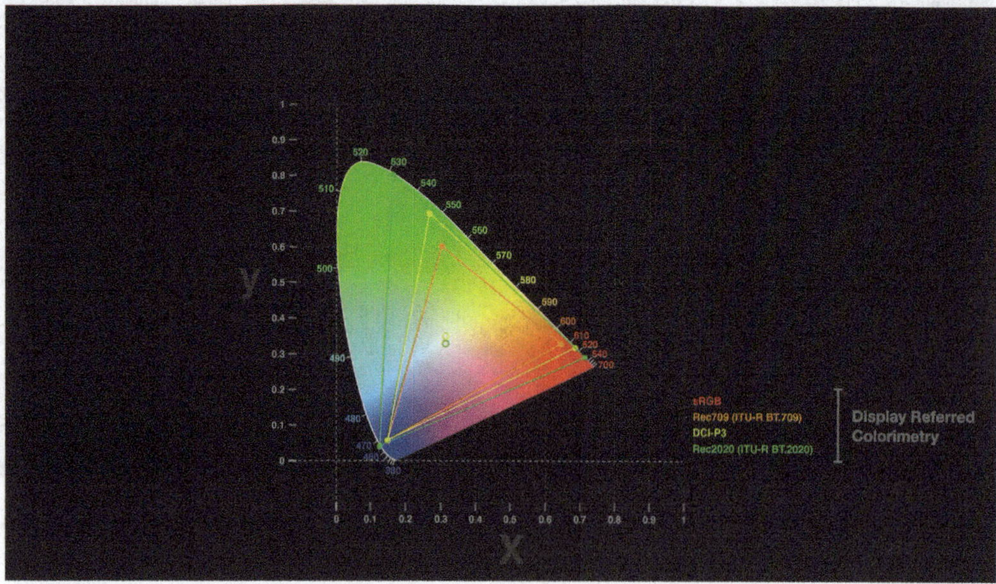

Figure 5.2 Display referred colorimetry color spaces

Those four color spaces are related to displays and so we are going to put them in the group of *display referred colorimetry*.

Now let's have a look at the other group (Figure 5.3). The first color space is the *ARRI ALEXA wide gamut*, and the first thing you are going to notice is that this color space captures more chromaticities that can be visualized by the human eye, and hence by any display. Those areas of the gamut that are outside the *spectral locus* is normal, and it is going to allow a certain margin to manipulate color without losing information (especially saturation and brightness related transforms); The *Canon Cinema Gamut*, see? This one is also wider than the Spectral Locus; *GoPro Protune Native* … another camera, another wider gamut; *REDWideGamutRGB*, this one is so big that the green primary went off the top of the space of the figure; *Sony S-Gamut/S-Gamut3* and *Sony S-Gamut3.Cine*; and the *Panasonic V-Gamut*. All these color spaces are related to cameras, so we are going to group them under the *scene referred colorimetry*, in these cases they are all *camera color spaces*. However, there are other non-camera color spaces that still are *scene referred colorimetry*, like for instance the *ACES 2065-1* – that we will discuss later on the chapter dedicated to ACES. The term "Scene" here, is related to the place where the camera is filming, the *scene*, that is why all cameras color spaces are *scene referred*. On the one hand we have *display referred colorimetry* where the reference is a certain type of monitor or projector; and the *scene referred colorimetry*, where the reference is the defined capture format from the scene (either the camera color space or a master container such as ACES).

As you can imagine, we need to apply color transformations that convert with mathematical precision from one color space to another in order to move the color data from one system to another. One of the key aspects of this transformation is going to be defined by the arrangement and distribution of the color samples within the gamut. Yes, we are talking about the *transfer function*.

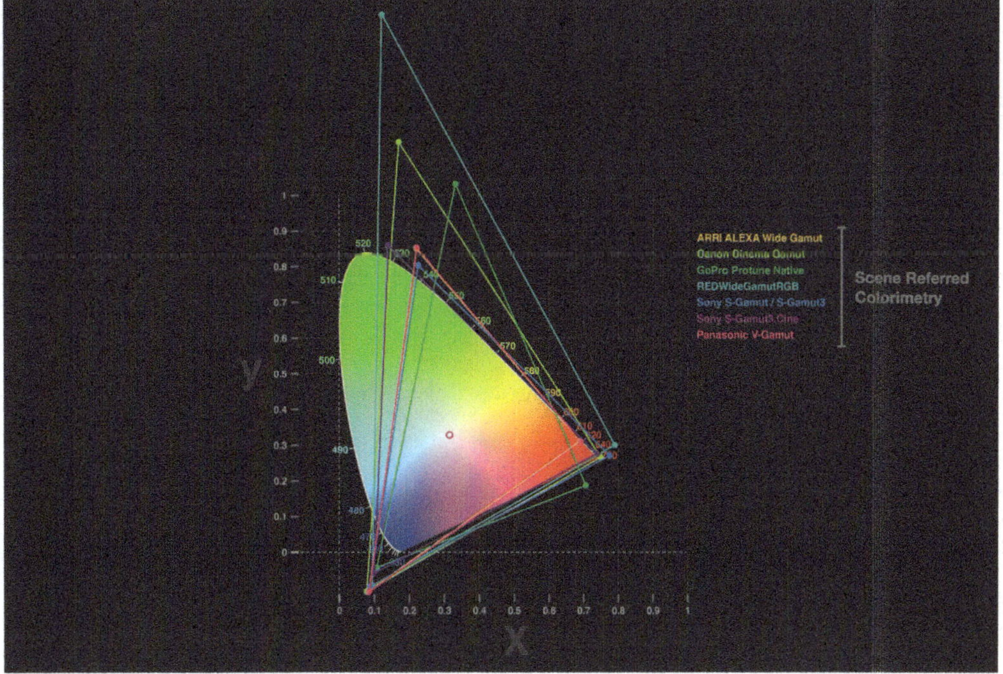

Figure 5.3 Types of transfer functions

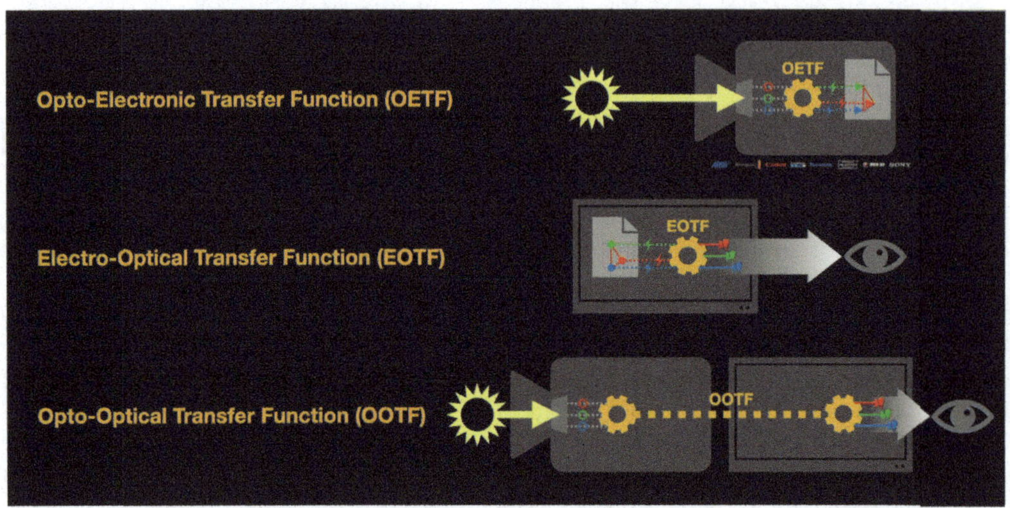

Figure 5.4 Types of transfer functions

Types of Transfer Functions

The transfer function describes the relationship between *electrical signal, scene light* and *displayed light*. We can classify the *transfer functions* into three categories (Figure 5.4).

- The first type is going to ingest the *scene light* as input, and convert it into the *picture* or *video signal*, the output. This is called *opto-electronic transfer function*, or *opto-electronic transfer function (OETF)*. This is typically done within the camera.
- The second instance takes the *picture* or *video signal* as input and converts it into the *linear light output of the display*. This is called *electro-optical transfer function*, or *Electro-optical transfer function (EOTF)*. This is normally done within the display device.
- The third case has the *scene light* as input and the *display light* as output. This is called *opto-optical transfer function*, or *OOTF* and it is the result of the OETF and the EOTF, which is usually non-linear. This is usually done within the display device.

As you can see it is essential to understand the purpose of each type of *transfer function*. For us, in brief: *OETF* for ingesting footage; and *EOTF* to put it into a display.

6

Color Volume

Now that we have discussed the subject of chromaticity at large, it's time to talk about other aspects of color that are going to condition our perception of the image, especially working with high bit-depth images. Let's focus on *color volume*.

Color Samples

The first element we shall discuss is *color samples*. Think about color samples as every unique color that can be identified and labelled within our available colors in the space. I like to think of samples as color balls, and so the volume will be represented by a box containing all those color balls in an ordered way, using, for instance, a criterion of order by primaries combined with brightness. The size, or more precisely, the capacity of that box will represent our color volume.

Color Density

However, as happens with liquids, we have to consider the density of the content, in the case of our example, using balls, "how big are the color balls?" Because we could fit more colored balls in the same space if they were smaller. Let me show you graphically with this example (Figure 6.1).

This is our given gamut, the container of chromaticities. Now I'm going to make a discrete selection of colors to cover the entire gamut (Figure 6.2).

See, now I have identified a certain number of chromaticities, as you can imagine this would not result in a very accurate representation of colors, even if I am filling up the whole available space I do not have many samples to define precise shades of color combining the primaries. Well, let's increase the number of samples (Figure 6.3).

Now we have more definition of chromaticities. Let's go deeper (Figure 6.4).

And deeper (Figure 6.5).

Now the gaps between the samples are very tiny, but we could still be more precise (Figure 6.6).

How deep can we go? In theory we can go infinitely deep. In maths, the distance between two points can be always subdivided infinitely – but only in theory, in the real world we have restrictions – and so happens with color precision, but every sample will occupy space in the data storage, and that space is not infinity (I mean the disk space in your drives is not infinite even in theory), and the data has to be processed as well, so we better find a finite number that will fulfil the purpose of our color volume.

DOI: 10.4324/b23222-9

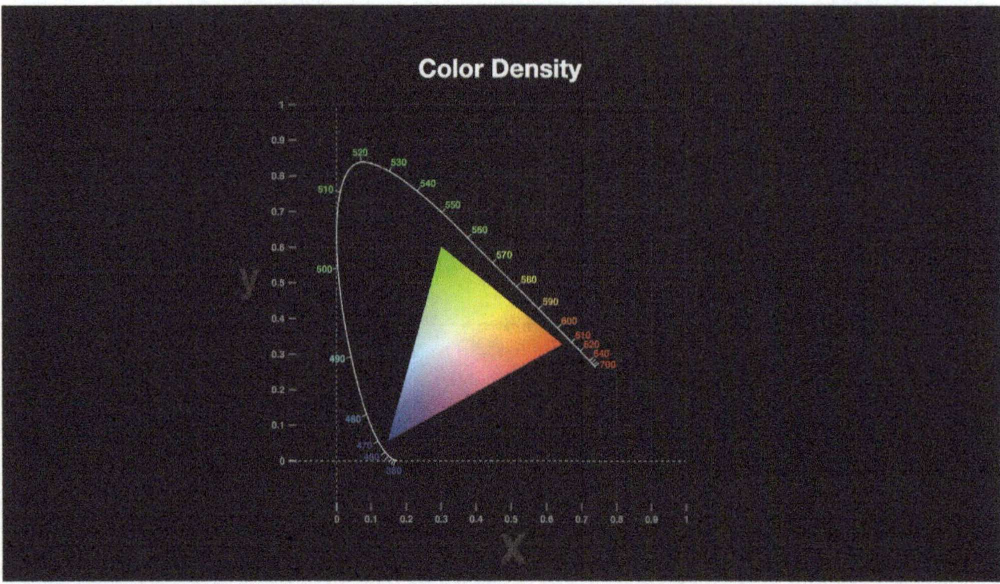

Figure 6.1 The gamut intent

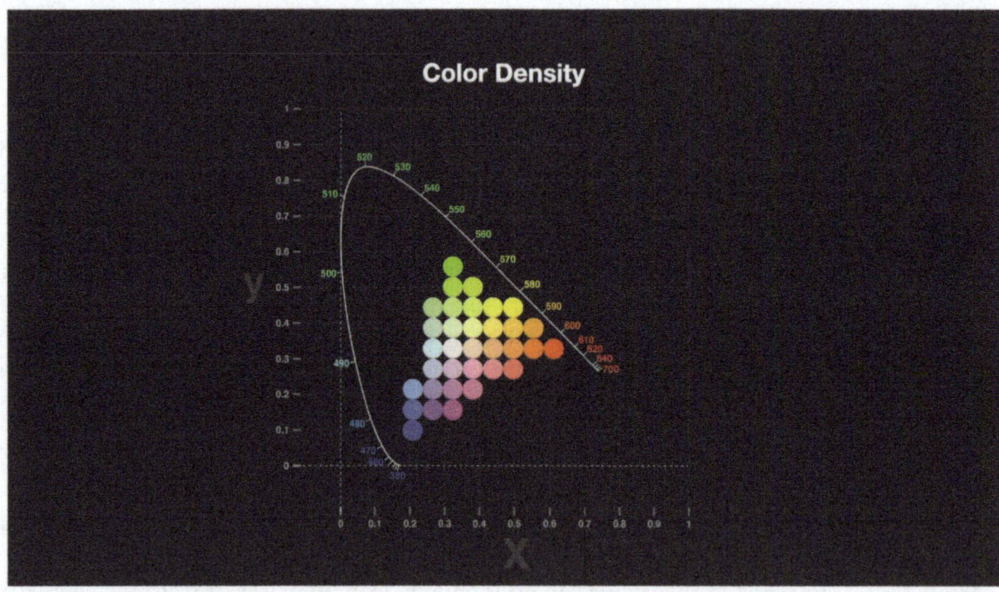

Figure 6.2 A discrete selection of chromaticity samples (extremely low density)

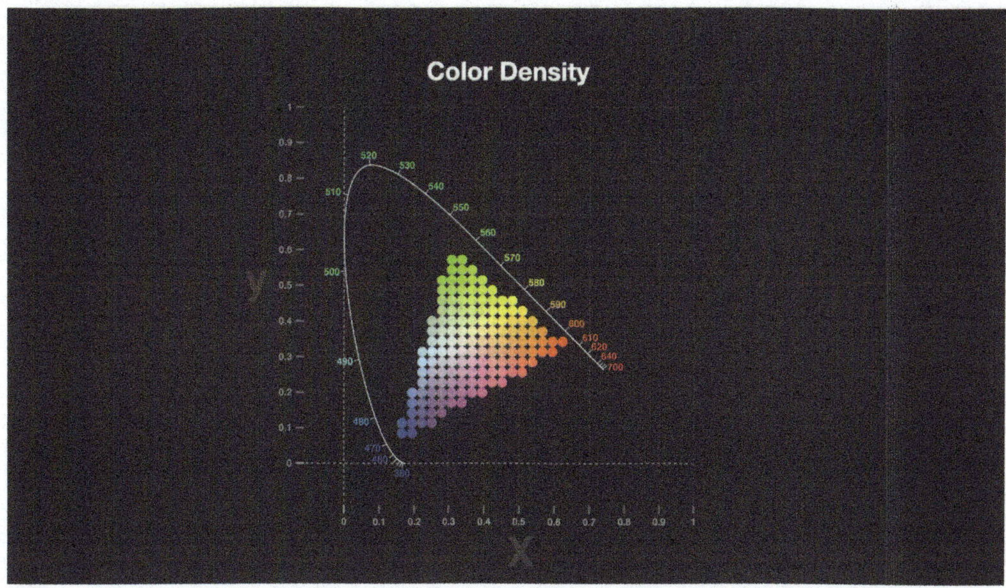

Figure 6.3 A discrete selection of chromaticity samples (very low density)

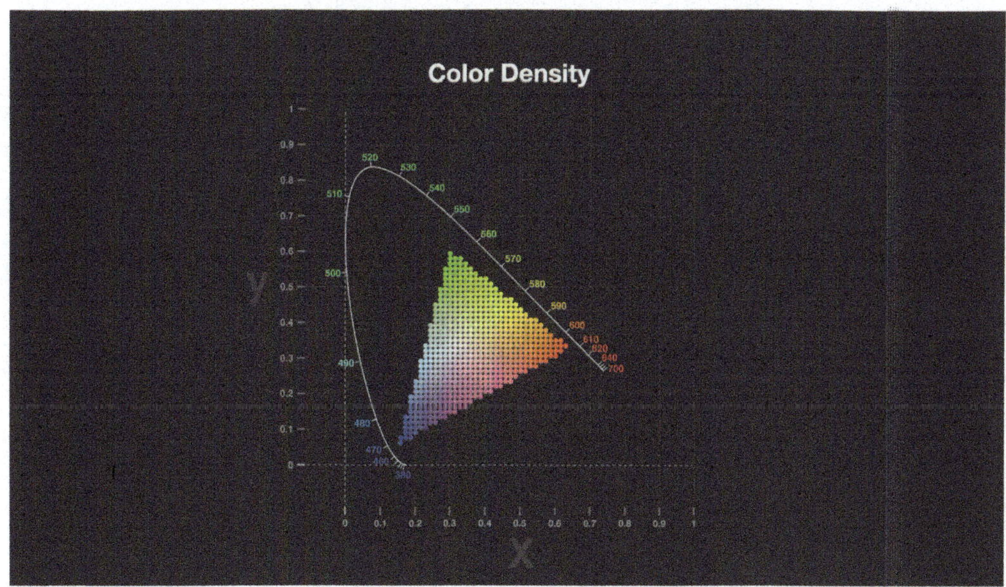

Figure 6.4 A discrete selection of chromaticity samples (still low density)

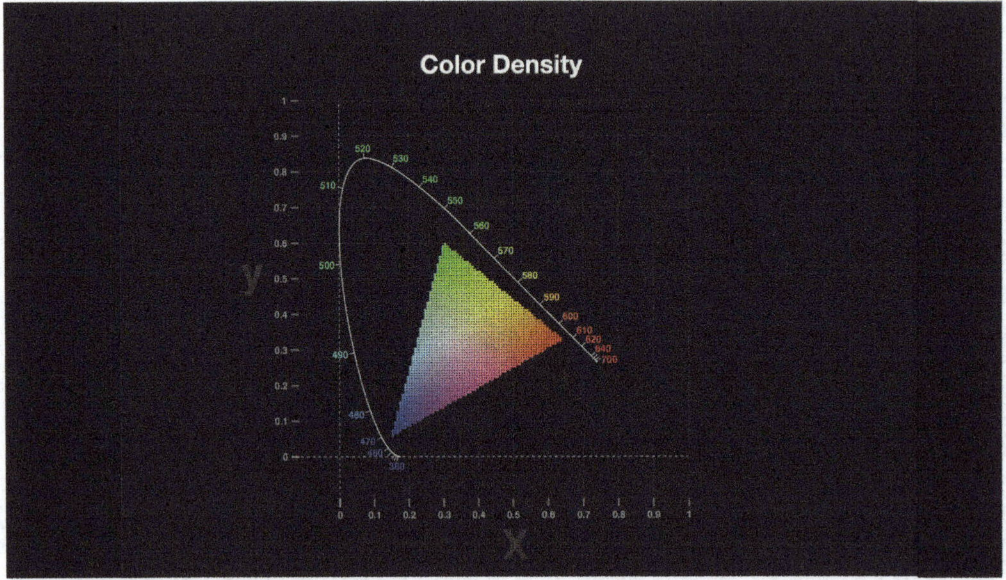

Figure 6.5 A discrete selection of chromaticity samples (low density)

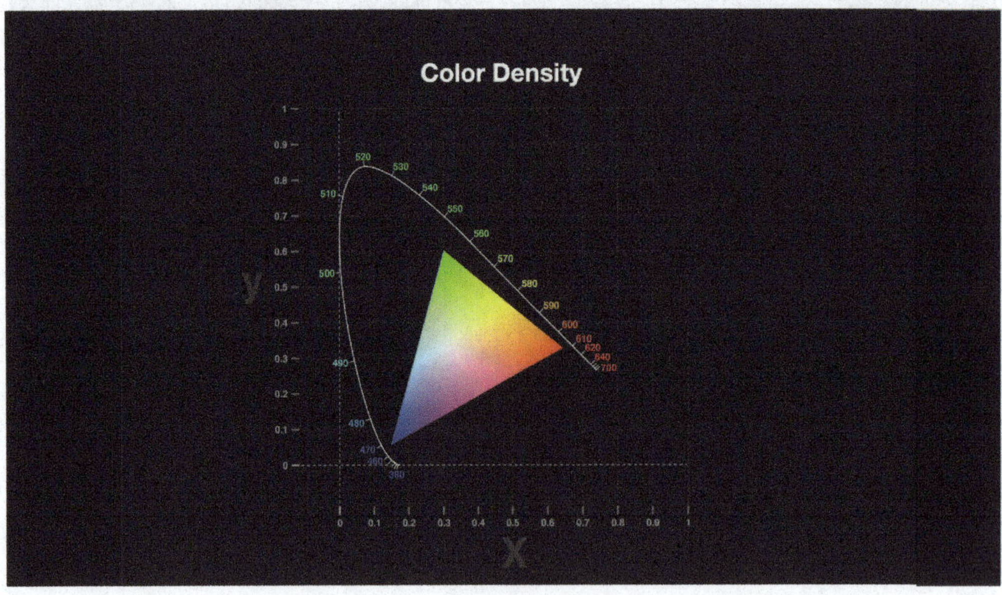

Figure 6.6 A discrete selection of chromaticity samples (dense enough)

By the way, we are talking about volume as the capacity to contain color samples, so it is not just the size of the space, but the number of colors contained. Notice that if I take a certain number of samples and I make the space bigger, the number of samples still remains the same, as does the precision to represent color. So when we are talking about color density we refer to the number of samples in a given space.

Color Bit Depth

We discussed this subject earlier. Now it is time to go to the bottom of this subject as it will condition the rest of our process. I will repeat a few concepts I know I already mentioned but I believe it is essential we recall the process to build upon your new stages of learning, as I had to omit a few important details for the sake of clarity in the previous chapter when discussing bit depth.

When talking about bit depth in relation to color we approach the question about how to label and store the color information data. Well, the basic unit of information in computer data storage is the *bit*, and so we are talking about bit depth. The term "bit" is a contraction of two words: "binary digit", *bit*. Not to be confused with "byte", that's something different. The bit represents a logical state with one of two possible values. These values are most represented as either "1" or "0". I'm going to arbitrarily attach a black sample to the state 0, and a white sample to the state 1 of the same bit. So, with one bit of color information for each pixel I could create an image with just black and white, no mid-tones, or greyscale, only pure black or pure white. We are far from a photorealistic result. But bits can be combined to create so-called "words": combinations of logical states of each bit to store data, so the higher the number of bits we put together, the higher the number of available combinations to assign colors. Now I can assign two grey levels between the black and the white. And so, the scale has more precision to represent the gradient between black and white (Figure 6.7).

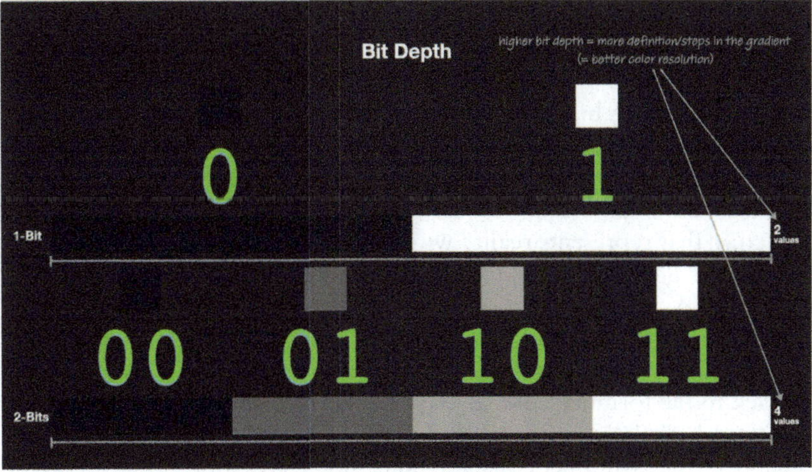

Figure 6.7 Monochrome bit-depth scales for 1-bit and 2-bit with their "words"

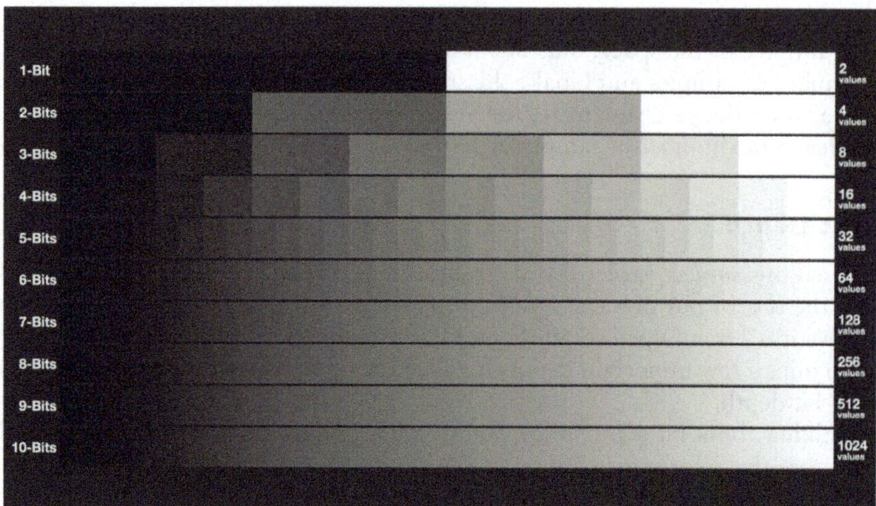

Figure 6.8 Monochrome bit-depth scale of progression

Notice that the black and the white levels are the same as before, so if we compare the scale using the same size for the gradient what we observe is that the samples in the scale of 2-bits are smaller than the scale on top with only one bit, so, yes, we are referring to this as *color resolution*. Allow me to represent the increase of bit-depth in a compared graphic so you can observe the effects of color resolution until the point where your eye cannot see the difference between the intensity of one step to another (Figure 6.8).

See? In the same distance you get smoother gradients, finer definition of the transition from one shade to another. And notice that the increase of values is exponential in relation to the amount of bits, and this is just for a grey scale.

Bits and Colors

Let's have a look at color bit-depth using all three RGB primaries combined, so we can create images in full color. I think it is a good idea to start by understanding the formula to calculate the number of samples, or shades of color, that we can store at a certain bit depth: $(b^n)^{channels}$. This is important because in order to create a photorealistic color result – meaning a picture that represents reality with the same features of color as you can observe in real life – there is one element that is key for color perception of photorealism, which is: how many shades of color can the human eye distinguish? Of course, this depends on the individual, and even on the cultural background,[1] but we can say the number is about ten million different colors. Keep this number in mind.

Let's get back to the formula. The "b" represents the bit logical binary base, so two possible values, 0 or 1. So let's substitute that with the actual number of values available: 2. Then the channels, that's another constant value, because in an RGB image we always have the same amount of channels, red, green and blue: so, 3. So the only variable remaining is the number of bits to represent the color, or color bit depth of the image. Hence the formula for RGB color bit-depth is: $(2^{Bits})^3$ (Figure 6.9).

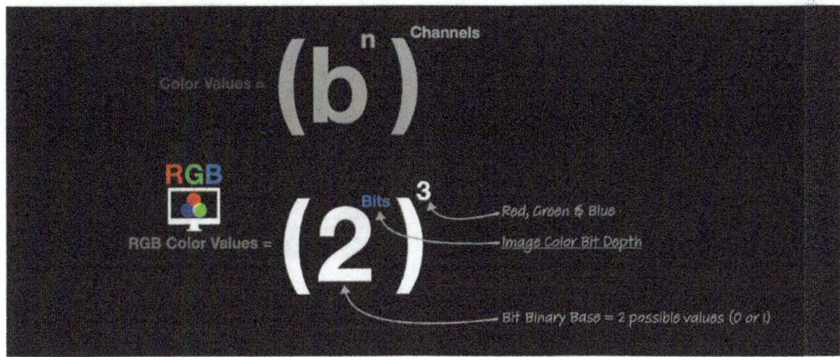

Figure 6.9 Bit-depth available hues calculation formula

To avoid confusion here, I am referring to "bits per channel", for instance, usually, when we say "an 8-bit image" we mean: 8-bit for red, 8-bit for green, and 8-bit for blue. So, in theory the total number of bits to store the color data written in the file, combining all three channels, is 24 bits (what is known as *true color*), but we will refer to these images simply as images with a bit depth of 8-bit <u>per channel</u>, and not as 24-bit images, to avoid confusion.

Let's have a look at the effect of bit depth in the representation of a color image (Figure 6.10).

This is 1 bit per channel. So as we did for the black and white gradient, now we have a gradient for each primary. In this case, the red channel, with only 1 bit, can be either on or off, and so for the other channels. So combining all the available values per channel we have a total of eight color values, or samples … but let's increase the number of bits. Notice that the number of available values per channel are increasing by double the amount of the previous number of bits, and that the total combination is rapidly increasing in an exponential manner: 8, 64, 512, 4,096, 32,768, 262,144, 2,097,152, 16,777,216 … wait a minute! with an 8-bit image we can reach more than 16 million color samples, while with 7-bit slightly more than two millions … mmm, remember when I told you earlier to keep in mind the number of different colors the human eye can distinguish? That is: about ten million, so with just 7-bit we cannot reach this number by a lot, while with 8-bit we are way beyond this threshold. It means an image with a color bit depth of 8-bit per channel can recreate a photographic result. That's one of the reasons the 8-bit per channel was adopted as the standard for consumer computer images. However, for us, professionals of manipulation of images, we need room to transform the colors, to stretch the ranges of luminance, to rescue values from places that are not visible with the naked eye before the manipulation. Therefore, we need more data, at the expense of storage and computational power, because the more colors you have, remember the more data that has to be processed, and then everybody gets grumpy with long render progress bars. So, we have to use the bit depth that suits our needs in order to represent color and depending on the display our image is going to be shown. For instance, traditional digital cinema projection usually operates at 10-bit as a cinema projector can represent a more color-precise image than a regular TV set.

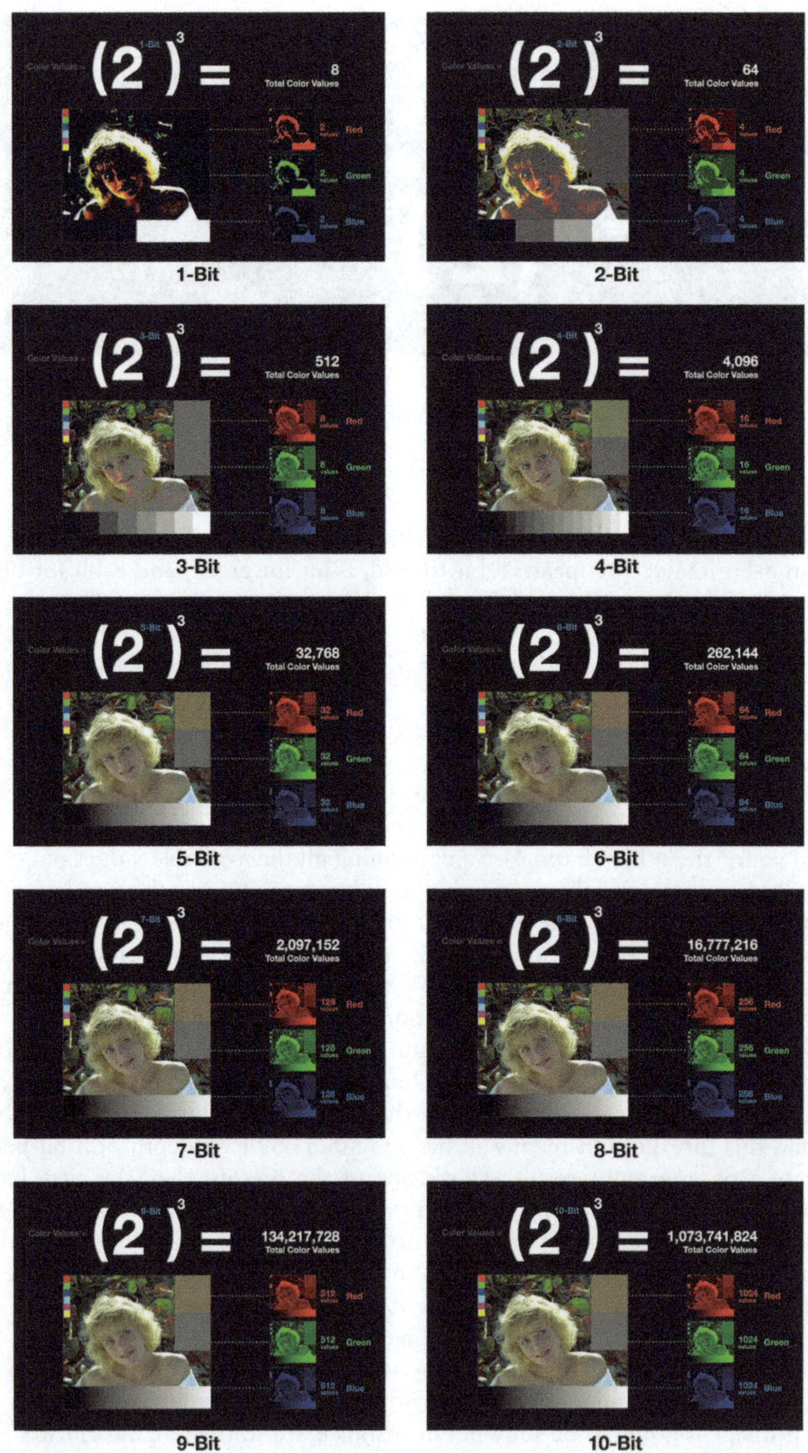

Figure 6.10 RGB bit-depth scale of progression

Linear vs Logarithmic

The number of samples is not the only important point here, because, at the end of the day, human beings do not see colors with the same precision across the whole range of brightness. Let me elaborate a bit more the concept of the *linear* distribution of samples against the *logarithmic* distribution.

Let's put a greyscale gradient of 4-bits – the only reason I'm using 4-bits is to illustrate this concept with a manageable number of samples and make it easier to understand – so in this scale we have 16 samples, from pure black to pure white.

As you can see, the size of all samples is the same, so they are equally distributed across the range, in an arithmetically *linear* progression (Figure 6.11).

I am going to show you three ways of referring to the color samples. For instance, we can use their *binary denomination*, the way the actual data is written corresponding a color sample to its bit-depth *word*. Of course, this is not something we, artists, work with, but it is important to know the correspondence of the bit depth concept we discussed earlier (Figure 6.12).

Then we have the *decimal numeric* representation of the samples in the ramp. Where 0 means the darkest black, and depending on the bit depth, the brightest white will be, in any case, the last numerical assignment. For instance, in this case, a 4-bit image has 16 available samples, so if the first one is 0, the last one will be 15. In case you got lost on why 15 and not 16, it is because in this scale I am counting 0 as the first value, not 1. Same thing happens with the 8-bit decimal scale, that maybe you are more familiar with, black is 0 and white is 255. Things get tricky when you combine different bit-depths and you have to align the samples. Following the same examples I just explained: if we combine a 4-bit image with a 8-bit image, referring to decimal values, 0 is always going to be black in both cases, but value 15 in each instance represent different colors: in the 4-bit, 15 is the brightest white, while in the 8-bit scale, value 15 is a just very dark shade of grey. So, in order to put them together and aligned, both ranges should be converted into the same scale, or bit-depth. That implies different levels of color precision mixed, therefore, instead of using the decimal scale, we are going to refer to the color samples using a normalized scale, that is going to indicate the equivalent aligned values regardless of their bit-depth: the white point of 4-bit aligned with white point of 8-bit, and the black point of the 4-bit scale aligned with the black point of the 8-bit scale; both represent the same range of luminance, but the 8-bit will have more information than the 4-bit to describe the gradient between the same black to white grayscale.

The meaning of the *normalized scale* is quite simple, the lowest value is 0 and the highest reference is 1. Therefore, all the values in the middle are going to be decimal positions,

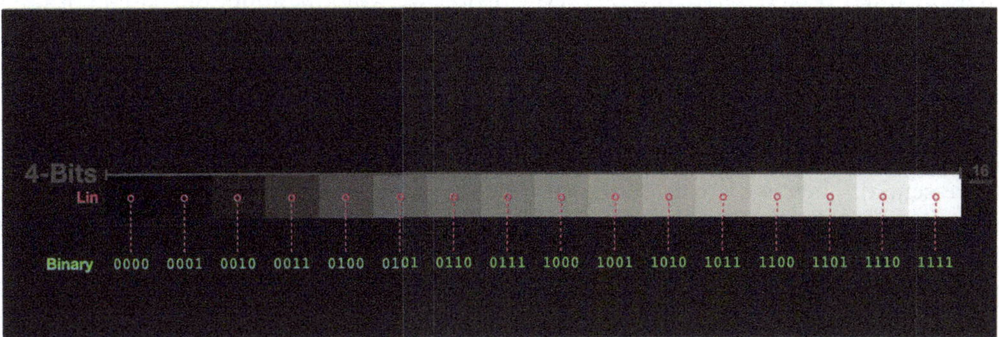

Figure 6.11 Linear distribution of 4-bit monochrome scale with its bit words

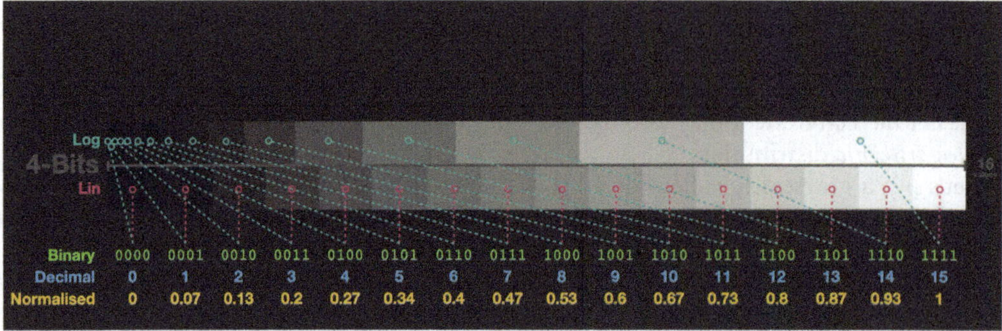

Figure 6.12 Linear distribution of 4-bit monochrome scale with their value assignment using different systems

and it is universal for all bit-depths. For instance, in an 8-bit image, the middle grey value would be 127 – I guess it took you a few seconds to think about that number – but on a normalized scale, the middle is just 0.5, easy, right? The nice thing about this system is that you always can have as many decimal positions as you require, for instance, a value as small as 0.0000001 to indicate precision. Nuke uses normalized values. The way to calculate a normalized scale is quite straightforward: divide every value by the highest value in the range. For instance, in this example of the normalized scale of 4-bits we are dividing every value by 15 … so 15 divided by 15 is 1, the maximum value of the range, and so on for the values in the middle.

The question now is <u>how</u> we distribute the samples in the range.

Why is this important? Well, because the human eye does not perceive color with the same precision across the whole range of brightness. We can identify more shades of color around the dark areas rather than the bright areas. By distributing samples linearly, we have the same amount of density in the areas where we can identify more gradients of color and in those where we are less sensitive. In order to reach photographic results, we just populate the whole range with more samples to cover the critical areas of brightness (the dark areas) with enough density … but, consequently, we are going to end with an overpopulation of samples in the bright areas, where that amount of detail is not required. In the case of the common 8-bit images – that travel through the Internet – is not much of a problem, as the range is fixed between black and a white level of brightness aligned with your monitor that is going to represent a flat clipped white to compress all the high brightness levels into a limited dynamic range, also known as SDR, that has been fixed at 100 nits (no worries, we will talk about nits and light levels later). However, there are devices able to represent a wider dynamic range by expanding the amount of detail in the dark areas and increasing the luminosity of the bright areas, like, for instance, digital cinema projectors – or even film negative for that matter – the problem is that to increase the amount of density of data in those critical areas, with an arithmetic progression we are going to end up wasting plenty of samples in areas that are not essential. Then, we can do something similar to what happens in lossy compression – that discards information where it is not perceived, but in the case of the distribution of samples we do the other way around by adding more data where needed. So we are not going to capture density of samples where it is not that relevant (bright area of the curve), while in the darkest side of the curve we are going to capture extra data, where we need it the most. Therefore, instead of capturing the data in a linear fashion, we are going to create a scale that is going to prioritize the number of samples in the dark areas. This is a

Figure 6.13 Linear vs Logarithmic distributions of 4-bit monochrome scale

system we have been using for many years in order to optimize the amount of computer data – and processing – to the representation of light densities. I am talking about the log (or logarithmic) encoding.

As you can see, you have the same amount of bits for color – same bit-depth – in both gradients, but we have more shades of grey in the dark areas – small samples – and less samples up in the ramp. The *linear* progression is arithmetical, while the *log* progression is exponential, and it better reflects the way we perceive light. It is normally used for 10-bit or 12-bit files. Why not for 8-bit? Well, because you do not have enough data to spread, and the samples will be too big and will result in posterization artefacts in the bright areas. And why it is not a regular practice to use *log* encoding for 16-bit? Because at 16-bit you have enough density of samples to keep a linear distribution and so you have color detail everywhere, regardless of its position in the curve, of course at the expense of the amount of data written but having the advantage of linear calculations (and data to be rescued from the bright areas if needed) (Figure 6.13).

Nuke Workspace Color Bit Depth

As I mentioned earlier, I'm going to use Nuke's workspace to showcase features of the color management, but this can be applied to any software (respecting their own specs).

In order to combine different bit-depths without losing precision, Nuke operates a conversion of any image imported in its environment into the highest working bit-depth available at the moment: 32-bit Float, and, by default, all images are going to converted into a *linear light workspace* – we are going to explore this concept after a few pages – so all images, regardless of their bit-depth are going to be allocated in an arithmetic progression of luminance. Do you want to know the level of precision of the 32-bits Float workspace? Practically this: 3.4028235×10^{38} if you want to see the full number: 340,282,350,000,000, 000,000,000,000,000,000,000, to put in to perspective the available color values. So, no worries, you are not going to lose any precision on any image you read inside Nuke (just make sure you interpret the data the right way).

It is worth mentioning that the *linear light* is not the only *linear workspace* available in Nuke, and this is a very important point of interest for the subject of color management, as we can use a *standardized linear Workspace* with a standardized set of color transformations. This is the case of *ACEScg* for instance, that relies on a set of *primaries* called *AP1* that are built within the *OCIO* system. We are going to get deep into this later in the next section of this book about ACES.

Nuke Native Color Working Space

But to demystify a bit the concept of *linear light* and to understand why we need a standardized Workspace for color management, let's see how exactly the *linear light* workspace operates in Nuke. In a previous chapter I told you that every color space has a set of *primaries* (that define a *gamut*), a *white point* and *transfer function*. So, where are the *primaries* of Nuke's default color space? Well – brace yourself – *linear light* does not have *primaries* nor *white point*! Because it is not a standard color space. The *linear light* is actually a *transfer function* operating in Nuke's workspace to handle the images by aligning their own *light intensities* in relation to their original color spaces, so the values are not mapped within a particular targeted color space but just interpreted to be coherent luminance-wise, so you decide the color space at the end of the process (on the *write* node), but along the process – on the *node-graph* cluster of operations – you are not using any standard color space and so the color transformations are sort of "relative" (but nonetheless arithmetically linear). That is why you need a standard color space and a set of standard color operations, as you want results to be *absolute* (and replicable) and align with everybody not just within the VFX department but across other departments as well. That is why we are here!

Let me show you the internal workflow of the linear light process.

Therefore, when you import an image, let's say an *sRGB* file, this is the scene we wanted to display, what we call: *the intent* (Figure 6.14). But the data recorded in the sRGB has a gamma correction encoded. So, the actual data is registered with a gamma curve to "brighten up" the image (so it can be rightly represented in sRGB displays). The intent in the figure below is agnostic of any workspace or display, it represents a simulation of the data written in the file.

This graphic in the figure below represents the linear progression of luminance, the linear light workspace (Figure 6.15). When the image is imported into Nuke's node graph using a read node, we apply a color space transform (by using an LUT) to get the image correctly linearized into the *linear light workspace*, that is the function of the *"input transform"*

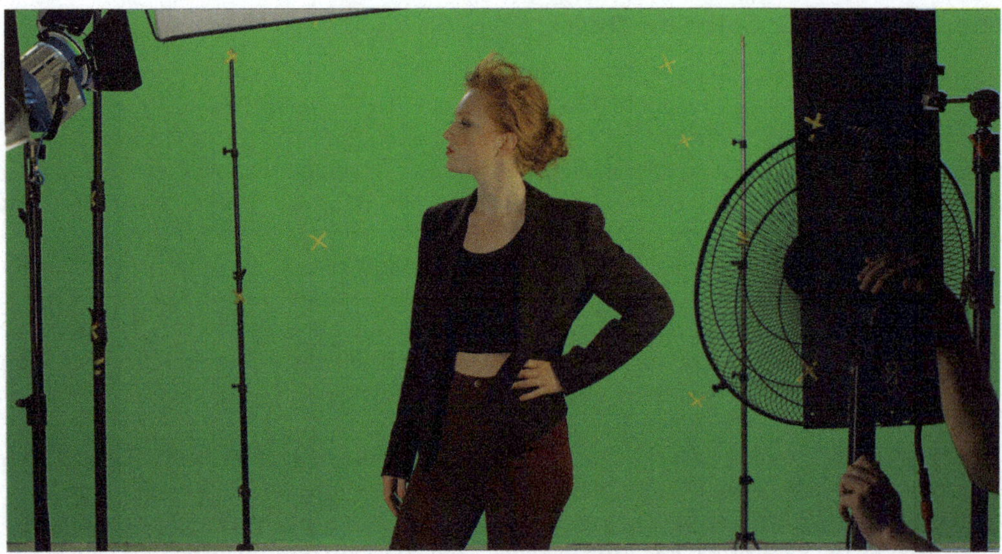

Figure 6.14 **The render intent**

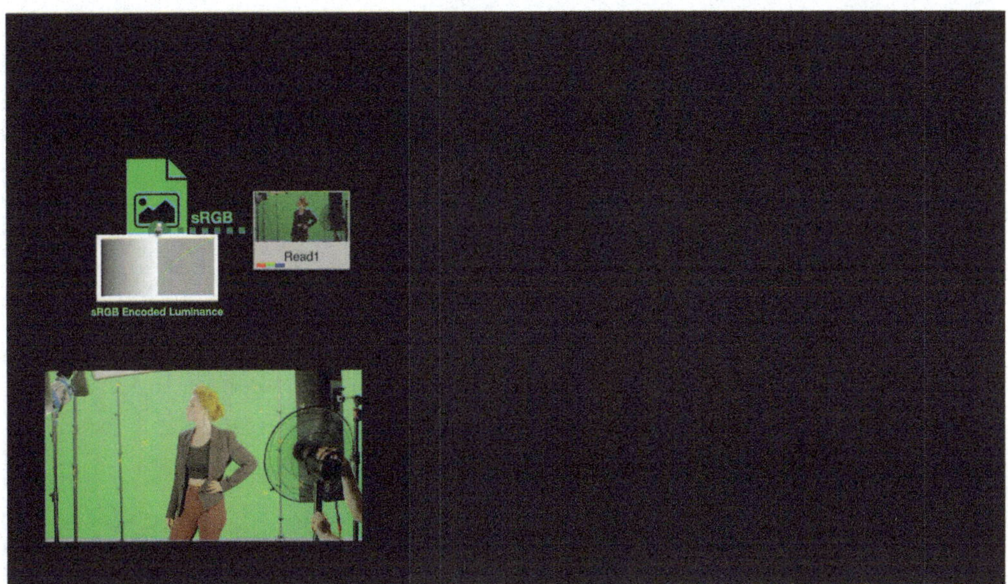

Figure 6.15 sRGB encoded luminance image (the original data)

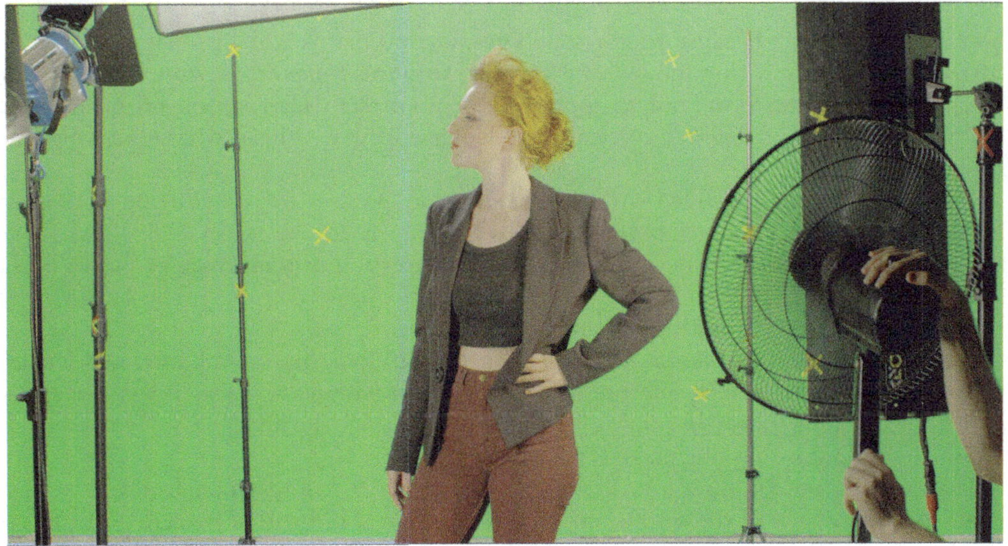

Figure 6.16 sRGB data simulated agnostic of any workspace or display

knob (formerly known as "*colorspace*" in the previous versions of Nuke), as this is the actual transfer function used to encode my *sRGB* image, this is how the image "actually" looks (Figure 6.16).

As you see in the figure above, the gamma encoded in the image makes it look kind of "brighter". That was initially established to be correctly displayed in unmanaged CRT monitors many years ago, part of the standard as we discussed in previous chapters of this

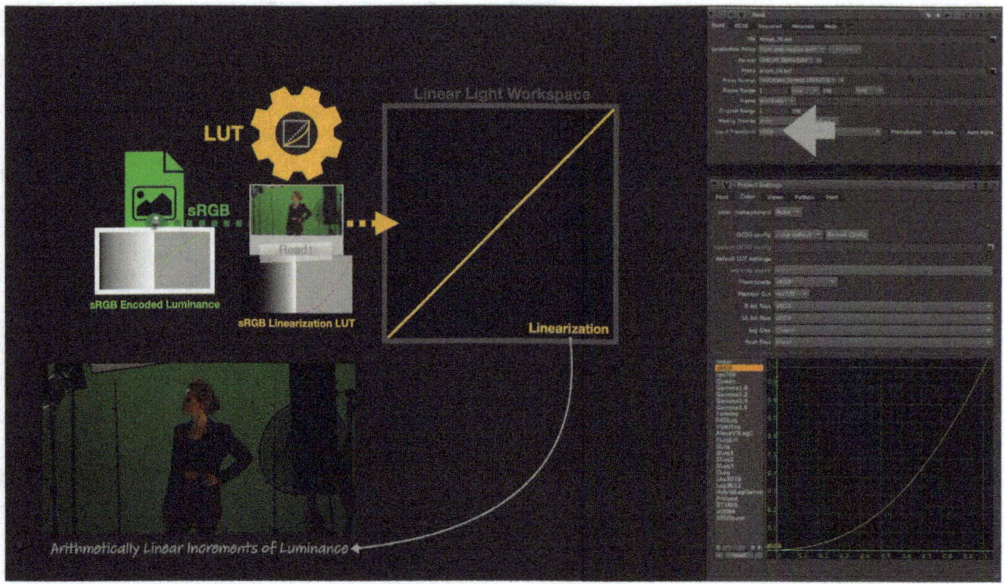

Figure 6.17 Image linearization though an lut to place the image into the linear light workspace

book. But no worries because your system knows it and that is why the image is displayed correctly. So, we know that the *sRGB* is encoded with this *transfer function*, so we need to specify the *input transform* knob to apply an LUT to correctly interpret the image. It means that when the image is ingested correctly into Nuke workspace, this is what is actually happening (Figure 6.17).

The image that was encoded with the *sRGB* color space, is corrected by an LUT using Nuke set of standard *linearization transforms* to compensate the original encoding of Luminance into a *linear light*, resulting in a linear progression of luminance as shown in the graphic above.

Now your image looks like this (Figure 6.18).

I know, I know … that is not how the image should look like – bear with me – that is because the image has been interpreted by the system within the *linear light workspace*, <u>without accounting for the display you are using to visualize the image</u> … we will get there, but the important is that the image is now *linear*.

The question now is how to visualize the image or the composition in order to have good visual feedback of the operations I am performing. So, for that, we are going to use the *viewer process*, and apply another LUT to compensate for the display you are using to view the composition, for instance a computer monitor, that is going to be, probably, *sRGB* as usual. So the image is processed *linearly* but visualized with an LUT appropriate for the display, two different processes: The first one refers to the image and modifies the actual values from the file in order to position them in the right *linear progression of luminance*; while the second one refers to the *display* and is not going to change the actual values of the image but just show them in the "correct way" on your monitor through a *viewer process* (Figure 6.19).

There is still another process. The last color transformation is applied to embed the output color space into the image to be exported. This operation happens in the *write*

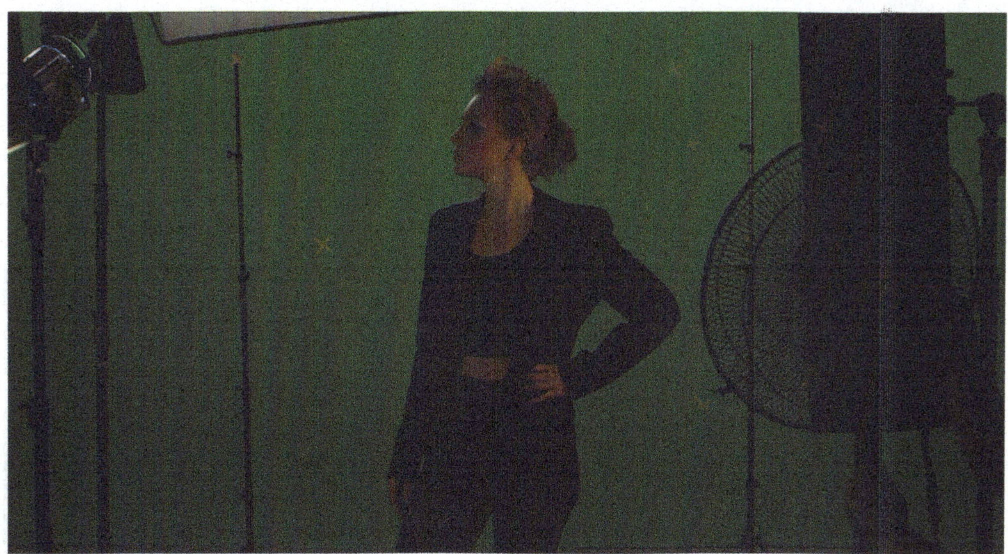

Figure 6.18 The arithmetically linear increments of luminance agnostic of any display

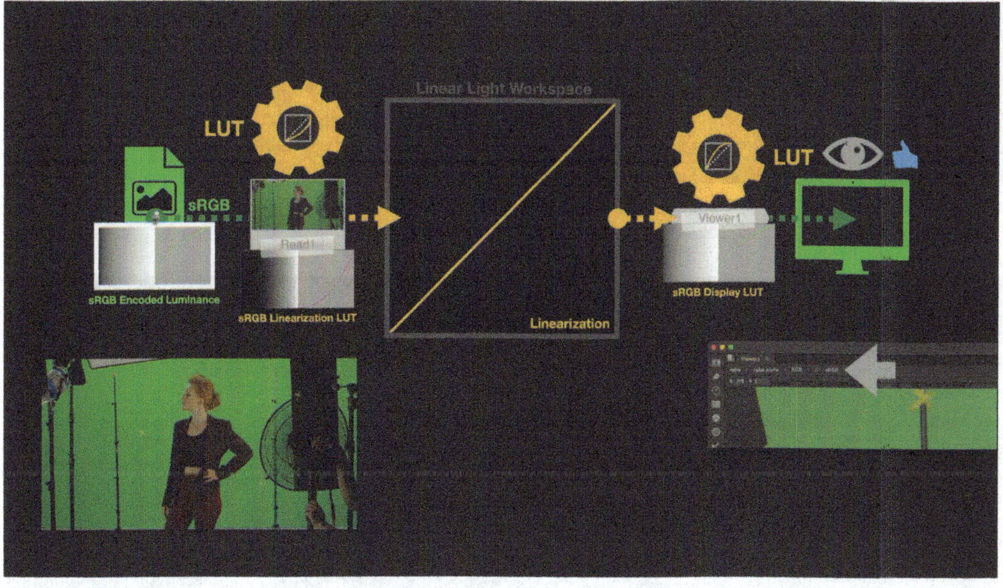

Figure 6.19 sRGB LUT applied for viewing purposes. Gamma encode data > linear light workspace > display color space. The rendered image is displayed as the original render intent

node, and we set it up on the "*output transform*" knob, formerly known as "*colorspace*" in previous versions of Nuke. This LUT is burned into the file in order for the image to be correctly visualized in a target kind of display, from Nuke *linear light workspace* to the color space of our choice. This is a *display referred* operation, since we are adapting the image to the target color space of a certain display. For instance, if the purpose of the file is to be displayed in a regular HDTV we apply the "*rec709*" like in this instance (Figure 6.20).

Three color transforms using the standard transfer functions – that can also be customized as required: one *input transform* (from the image color space to the *linear light workspace*), a *viewer transform* (to visualize the image correctly in your display); and an *output transform* to create the resulting image file with the right color space depending on the destination display delivery (Figure 6.21).

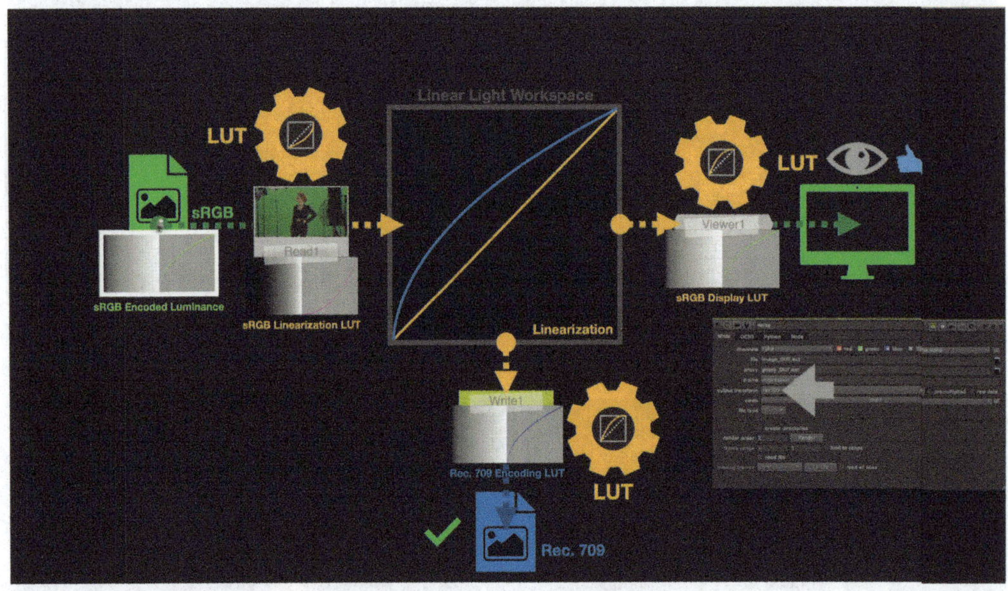

Figure 6.20 Export output transform LUT for the target display

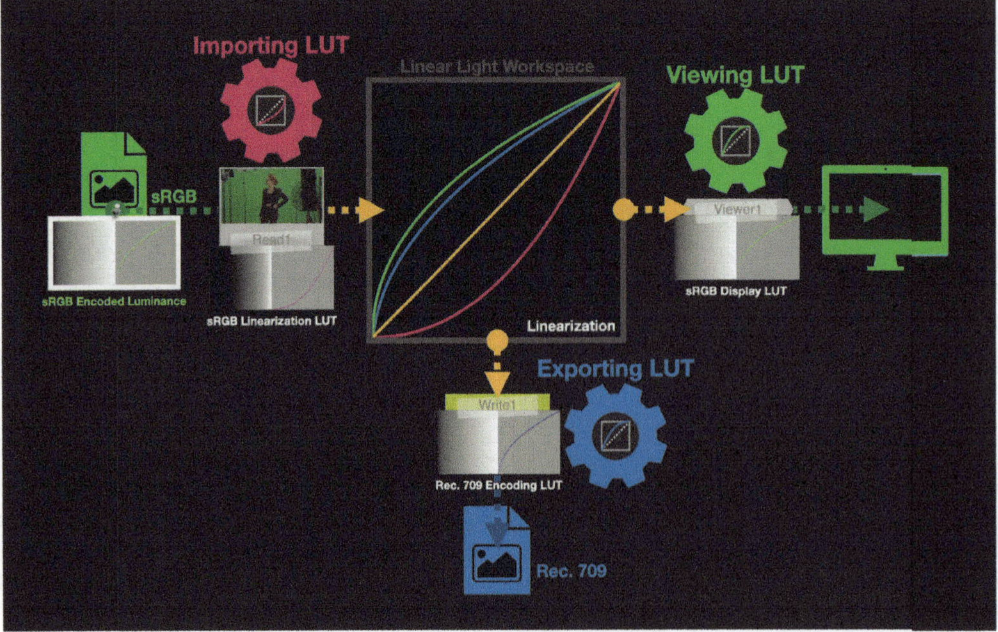

Figure 6.21 Display referred look-up tables (LUTs) (color transformations within Nuke linear light workspace)

But as I said before, the problem with this process is you are not using a set of standardized color transformations within a standard master color space; therefore, this can be a problem when relating with other systems that use other ways of handling color as we can end with different results applying what apparently seems to be the same operation (Figure 6.22).

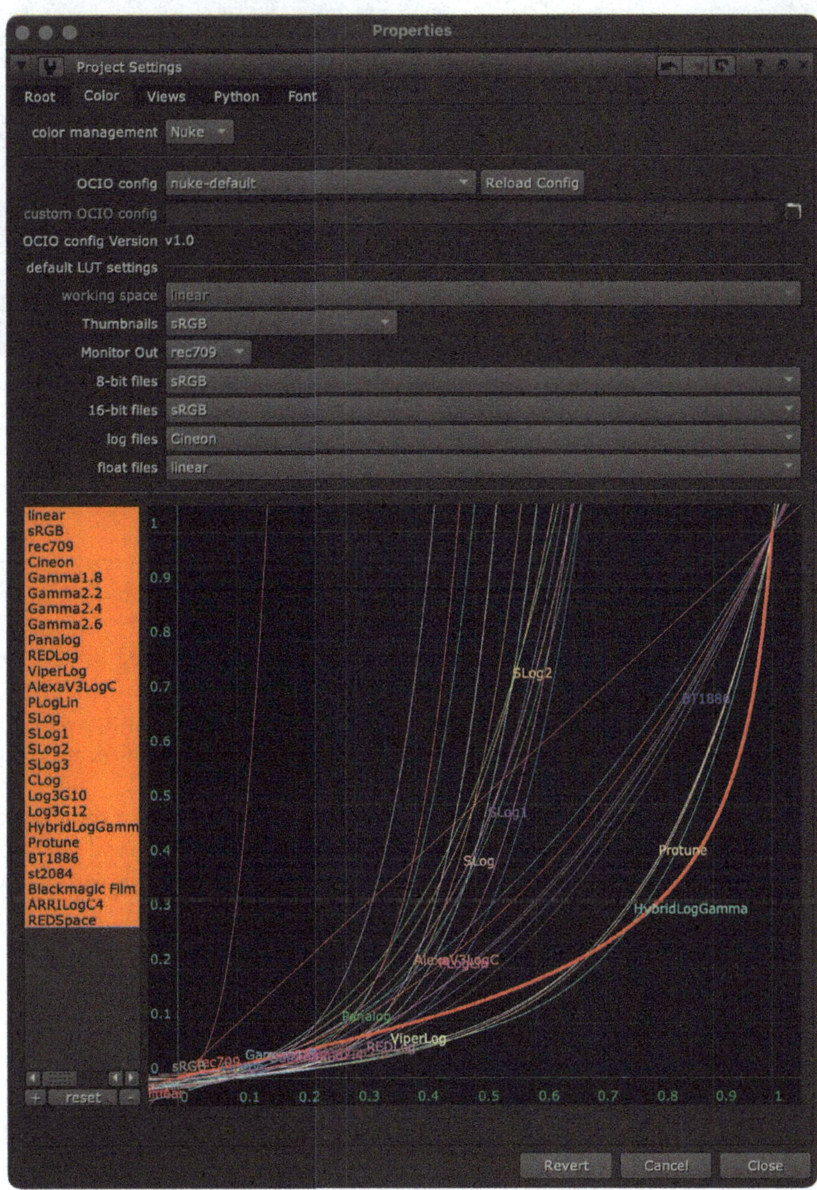

Figure 6.22 Nuke set of default LUTs for the linearization process (in a Nuke-default color managed project)

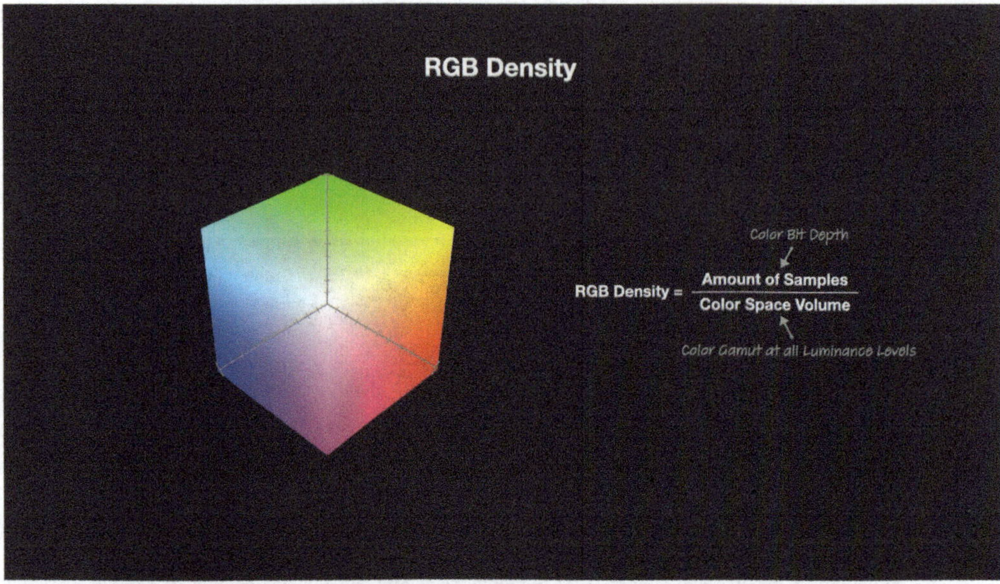

Figure 6.23 RGB density and the color cube

RGB Density

Let's get back to the subject of sample density. By definition, in general terms, density is the *mass* divided by the *volume*. More samples in the same area implies a higher density of the chromaticity. But if we apply the concept of density to color, we can say that the *RGB density* is the amount of *color samples* (Color bit-depth) available divided by the color space volume (its color gamut at all *luminance levels*), so not just chromaticities but actual color with all their shades of intensity. The best way to represent the RGB samples as a tridimensional volume, where every primary color stands for a spatial dimension, like XYZ in the 3D space (Figure 6.23).

Here you have the *color cube*, which from this perspective looks like the gradients from the color wheel as the maximum intensity of each primary can be observed at the end of the normalized axis, but this is actually a spatial volume that contains all the samples addressed as triplets (three coordinates, like points in the 3D space) (Figure 6.24).

As you can see, the density is directly related to the bit-depth. The more samples you have in the space the more density you get. As you can imagine, the bigger the space, the more samples you need to increase the density of colors.

Display Color Volume

Let's compare two common color space volumes related to their brightness peaks. When we talk about the brightness capabilities of the color in a defined display color volume, we are not referring just to lighter or darker overall brightness, but the amount of saturation those primaries can reach. So, let's layout the chromaticity diagram on the floor of a display color volume to project up the standardized luminance peaks of the color spaces (Figure 6.25).

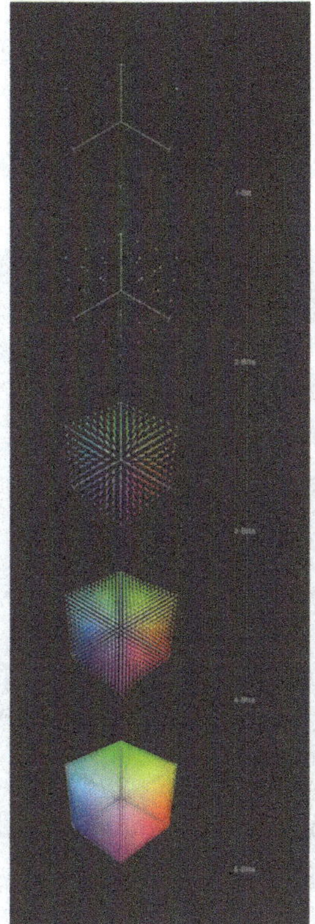

Figure 6.24 Color cube at different bit-depths to represent its RGB density

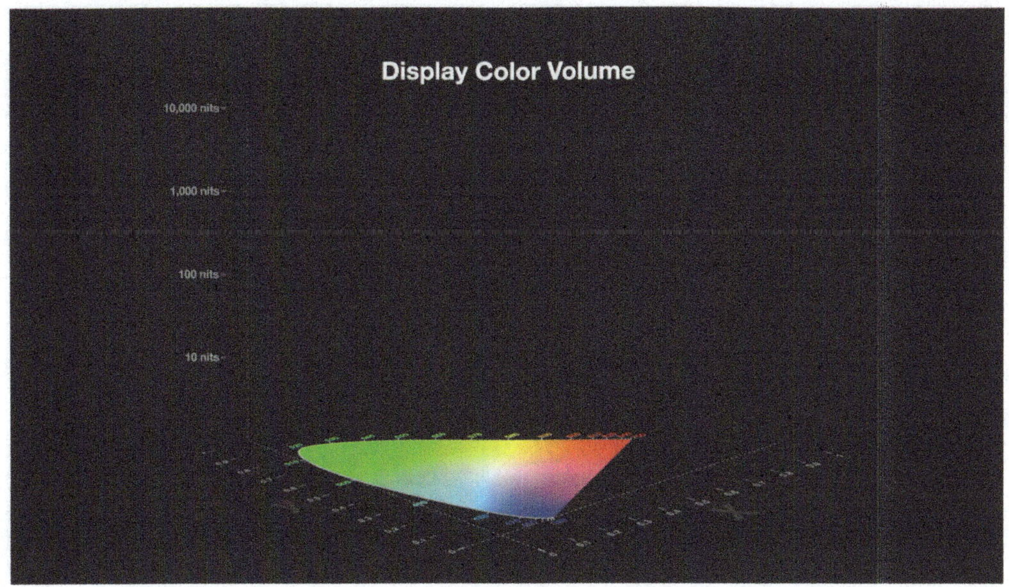

Figure 6.25 Chromaticity diagram with luminance scale for display color volume representation

The first color space we are going to visualize is the *Rec709* (Figure 6.26).

This is the position of its primaries and white point. The vertical axis represents the luminance expressed in *nits*: the higher, the brighter, and so the higher saturation capabilities. The standard SDR *Rec709* peaks at 100 nits.

Now let's layout the gamut of the *Rec2020* (Figure 6.27).

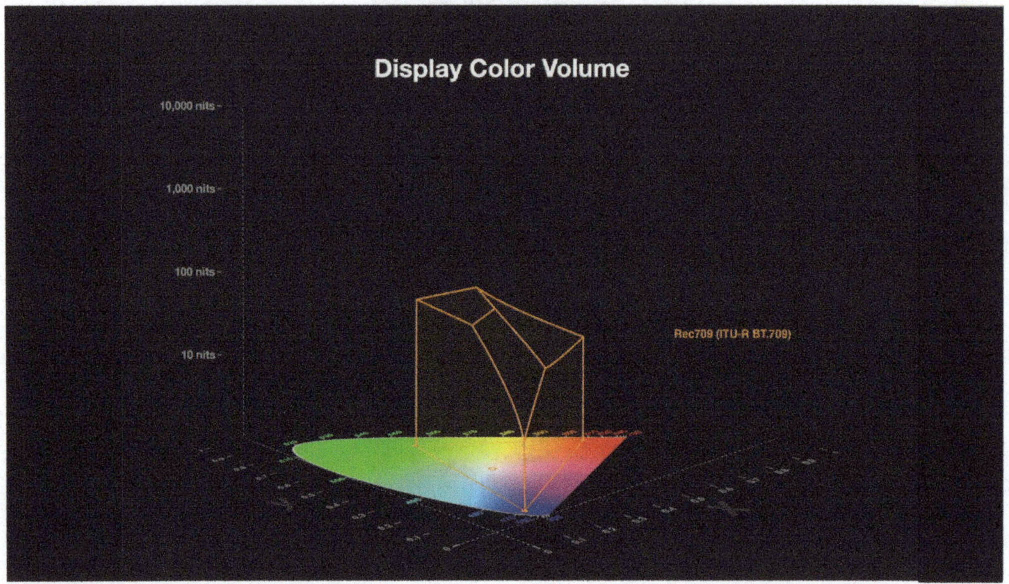

Figure 6.26 Rec709 display volume

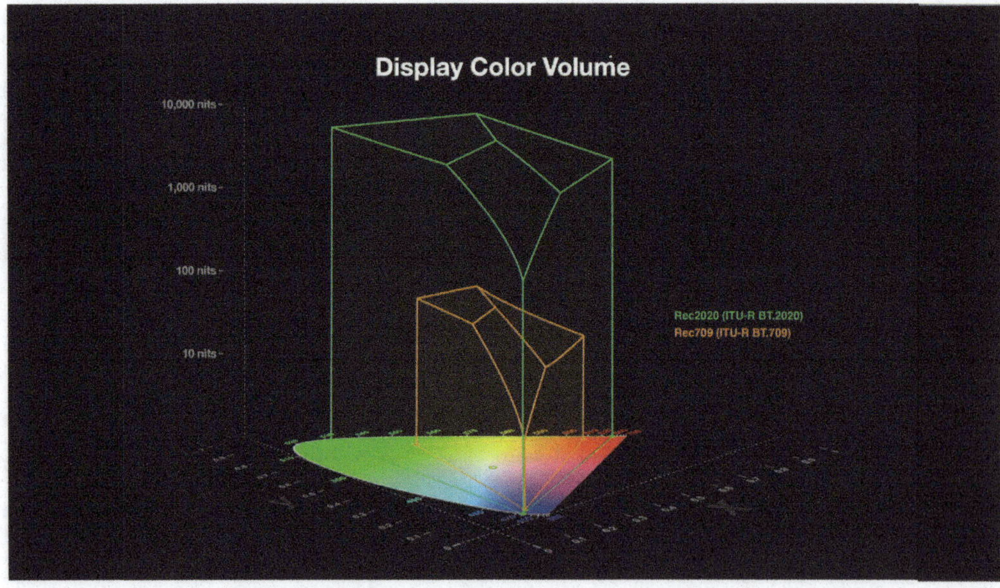

Figure 6.27 Rec709 vs Rec2020 display volumes

And let's compare the *display color volume* of this SDR color space with the HDR one. The first thing we notice is the *color gamut* of the *Rec2020* – corresponding to the HDR Color Volume – is wider than the SDR one, the *Rec709*, so it allows *purer* primaries and way more colors. But not only HDR images can reach up to <u>10,000 nits</u> of luminance (against the only 100 nits of the SDR). It means each primary can achieve a very bright intensity and consequently a very vivid color (closer to the perception of color in real life).

But in order to "fill up" this big volume with a good density of samples, without experiencing any color artefacts relative to *color volume*, as for instance "banding" (posterization) – which happens when you notice the steps of a gradient between the shades of the color, instead of visualizing just a progressive and unnoticeable ramp of tonalities (as we discussed a few pages back with the example of the bit depth) – we need a vast amount of color samples. The 8-bit, that was more than enough to populate the *Rec709* color space, is definitively insufficient for this HDR instance using the *Rec2020* color space. So, to put this in other words, using the instance of colored balls to represent color samples: SDR would be like having a bucket full of colored balls, while HDR would be like having a pool full of colored balls (each one in any case made of a different unique color). As you can imagine, HDR is way more fun!

Note

1 Jules Davidoff conducted a series of color perception experiments with the *Himba* tribe in northern Namibia. In comparison to the 11 typical words in English, the Himba have only five words to describe color. The divides are also drawn differently. The sky is black, the ocean is white, and the words blue and green are interchangeable. Himba participants were taking part in a study on how people discern between colors. The participants were shown a series of color swatches and asked to identify the odd one out. When shown a various equal sample of a particular shade of green and, in the middle a – clearly different for us – shade of blue, Himba participants would struggle to discern the two colors since they had spent their lives describing blue and green with the same color. However, because of how the Himba language divides color, they can readily distinguish between these two tones of nearly identical green that for the generic western population would look the same as another experiment with the other set of color demonstrated. Dr Davidoff explains it was weird to witness someone struggle to distinguish between two colors that were so strikingly distinct to him. However, he explains, surely the feeling would be mutual with the Himba people if the roles were reversed, and he had to pick the "odd" green out.

   Robinson, S. (Director). (2011). *Do You See What I See?* [Film]. BBC.

   That experiment is similar to the *Sapir-Whorf Hypothesis*, which claims that the structure of language determines how we think and behave. For example, if your language contains a single term for both blue and green, you see them as the same color. It is easy to believe that what I see when I look at a pink flamingo is not the same as what you see. However, fresh studies have called that into question.

   More information about cultural backgrounds conditioning the perception of color can be found on: (myl) D. Roberson et al. (2004). The development of color categories in two languages: A longitudinal study. *Journal of Experimental Psychology*; and D. Roberson et al. (2005). Color categories: Evidence for the cultural relativity hypothesis. *Cognitive Psychology*.

7

HDR

Well, I think you have all the fundamental knowledge to start exploring the foundations of HDR.

Standards Concerning HRD

The first thing you need to know is that HDR has been standardized so all parts involved in the production and reproduction of the HDR images are aligned with the same specifics, this includes: display manufacturers, distribution and streaming services, software companies, production studios, and so on. Of course, we are going to focus on those that concern us the most for a color-managed workflow manipulating the images, softwarewise, but we need to keep an eye on *display* specifics as they are a key part of our work. Let's review the five top standards:

The first one is the **ITU-R Recommendation BT.2020** (also known as **Rec. 2020**). It defines various aspects of *UHDTV* with *SDR* and *Wide Color Gamut*, including picture resolutions, frame rates with progressive scan, bit depths, chroma subsamplings, **color primaries**, RGB and luma-chroma color representations, and an *OETF*. Something worth mentioning is that the *Rec. 2020* gamut is used as a *UHD Premium* container but effectively it is limited to a *DCI-P3* enclosed, and an *OETF*.

Please do not confused the *OETF* with the *EOTF*. Remember the OETF refers how the capturing device stores the light data, while the *EOTF* refers to how the display interprets the data.

So, the *Rec. 2020* defines a color space we use as a container for HDR, what we call a color space *"wrapper"*.

The second standard is the **SMPTE ST.2084**. It defines the *PQ*, a *transfer function* that allows for the display of HDR video with a luminance level of up to 10,000 nits and can be used with the *Rec. 2020* color space. *PQ* is a non-linear *EOTF*.

The third is the **ITU-R Recommendation BT.2100**, is also known as **Rec. 2100**. It introduces *HDRTV* by recommending the use of *PQ* or *HGL* transfer functions instead of *BT.1886 EOTF* and other transfer functions previously recommended for SDR-TV. The *hybrid log-gamma* was designed for live TV as it does not require metadata. And, by the way, the *BT.1886* refers to the transfer function of the *Rec. 709* color space, its *"gamma correction"*.

The forth one is the **SMPTE ST.2086** and refers to *static metadata*. It defines mastering display color volume metadata supporting high luminance and wide color gamut images.

DOI: 10.4324/b23222-10

Aimed for describing the scenes as they appear on the mastering display for consumer displays that have a limited color volume. For instance, a TV that does not provide peak brightness/contrast and color gamut required by the standards, this metadata allows the display to change the signal to be adapted and displayed accordingly.

The fifth is the **SMPTE ST.2094** and refers to *dynamic metadata*. It defines *content-dependent* metadata for color volume transformation of high luminance and wide color gamut images. It includes dynamic metadata that can change from scene to scene. This includes the *Dolby Vision* format (further specified on the standard *ST.2094-10*), and Samsung's *HDR10+* (defined in the *ST.2094-40*).

In order to understand HDR images we have to comprehend the specifics of HDR displays.

What do we mean with *dynamic range*? The *dynamic range* is the ratio of the largest to the smallest intensity of brightness that can be reliably transmitted or reproduced by a particular imaging system (Figure 7.1).

We can express it by dividing the brightest white by the darkest black values. Therefore, the brighter the white peaks the more details in the bright areas and so the better, but still maintaining the ability to show details in the darkest areas of the image, so the darkest black, the better. So HDR is not just having brighter values but having very detailed brighter values while preserving very dark detailed values, the higher the ratio the better. For the way the human eye works, little variations of brightness in the dark areas are very noticeable while a great increase of the whites results in a more accurate representation of light. In a display system such as a projector or a monitor, this property is referred as *contrast ratio*, the ratio of the luminance of the brightest color (white or maximum value for every channel) to that of the darkest color (black, or minimum value for every channel) that the

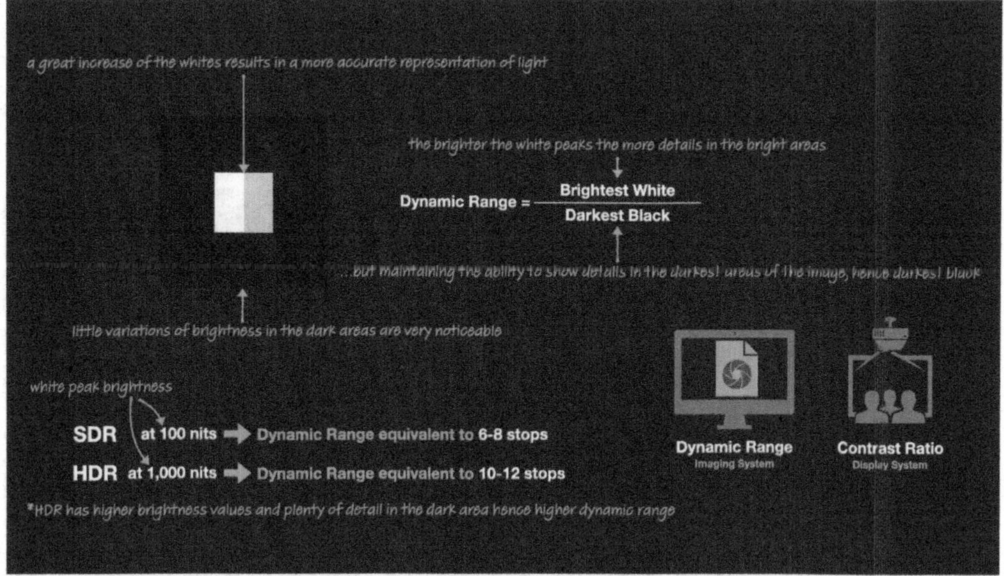

Figure 7.1 Imaging system dynamic range (SDR)

system is capable of producing. On the other hand, the *dynamic range* is a property of the *imaging system*. So, they both refer to the same concept but they are actually independent, which means you can still work an HDR image in an SDR monitor … but that would be like saying: you can work a color image using a black and white monitor, it is not appropriate (maybe this example is a bit hyperbolic but I think it renders the idea). That is why your monitor should reflect the specs necessary to work with HDR.

In terms of brightness, SDR peaks at 100 nits with a *dynamic range* equivalent to about six to eight stops of light; while HDR monitors usually peak at 1,000 nits for an equivalent *Dynamic Range* of ten to twelve stops of light. HDR has higher brightness values and plenty of detail in the dark area hence the higher dynamic range. By the way, you may have noticed I am using two different units of light: *nits* and *stops*. *Stops* are the measure of light in the scene, it is the traditional unit that cinematographers use on set; *nits*, on the other hand, is the unit we use to measure the amount of light a display can emit. As the word *nit* is a term we will use a lot in HDR, I think it worth spending a few words about it (Figure 7.2).

1 *nit* is equal to 1 *candela per square meter*, which is the derived *international system* (or *SI*) unit of *luminance*. The *candela* is the unit of *luminous intensity*, and the *square meter* is the *SI* unit of *area*. The *nit* does not belong to the *international system* of units but it is the standard unit to measure the *luminance* in *display systems* and *imaging systems*, and we will use it a lot, especially when working with HDR images. *luminance* is a photometric measure of the luminous intensity per unit area of light travelling in a given direction. It describes the *amount of light* that passes through, is emitted from, or is reflected from a particular area, and falls within a given *solid angle*.[1] It is important we understand how to read the instruments, like the RGB parade, to recognize the luminance of regions that are not visualized by the display or simply to have an analytical perception of the luminance data contained in the image, either in input or in output. Keep in mind HDR can contain luminance values up to 10,000 *nits*, but currently the displaying technology can reach up to 4,000, although in the future this is very likely to change, so the data will be available. *scene* and *camera dynamic range* is usually measured in *stops* and does not correlate linearly with *displays*, that is the unit used on set to measure the actual light to be captured by the camera and adjust exposition parameters.

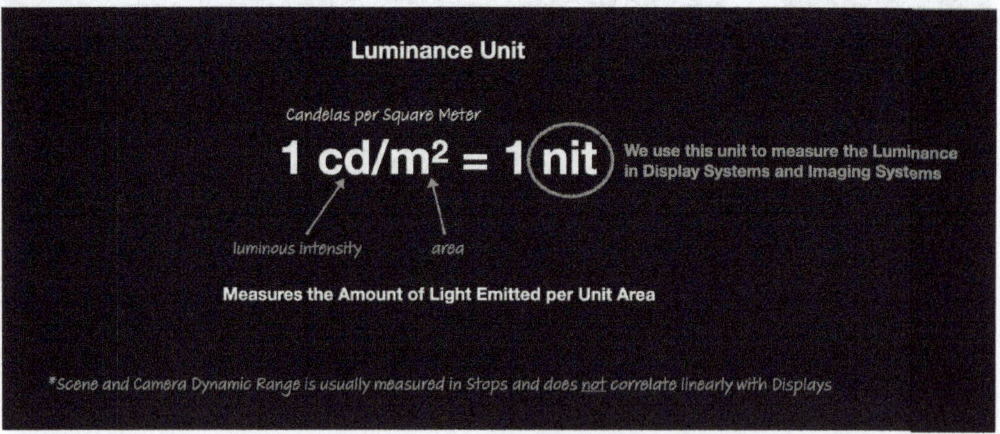

Figure 7.2 Nits

To have a clear understanding about the relation between brightness and HDR let me elaborate it visually: I'm going to illustrate the whole range of luminance in SDR, by brightness zones (Figure 7.3).

The standardized maximum level of luminance, what we call the reference peak level, is 100 nits. So, this way we can assign a percentage of the maximum peak to label all the brightness levels in the image. However, what happens to all those elements that are exposed brighter than the maximum peak of 100 nits? Well, they will be just clipped, nothing can get brighter than the brightest level, so that information will be flattened down up to the maximum white allowed by the SDR levels: 100 nits; and those details will be forever lost since SDR has no super-whites. It means any 8-bit monitor will be able to visualize the whole range, then, of course, if you want to work into the reference range you have to ensure your monitor is calibrated to display the white peak at 100 nits. At this point, someone mistakenly could think that to increase the span of the SDR you can just take the luminance values of the SDR and stretch them up to make the image brighter. Absolutely not, have a look at the figure below (Figure 7.4).

By stretching the SDR level, the only thing you will achieve will be just a brighter stretched SDR with the white point off the reference calibration, but the number of values and the actual level of the signal would not improve, and even worse you are destroying the artistic intent: you stretch the bright values as much as the dark ones, so the real contrast ratio of the image remains the same. Please don't do that.

One of the huge advantages of HDR is not only the ability to display more detail in the bright areas with brighter values available, but at the same time the access to very deep

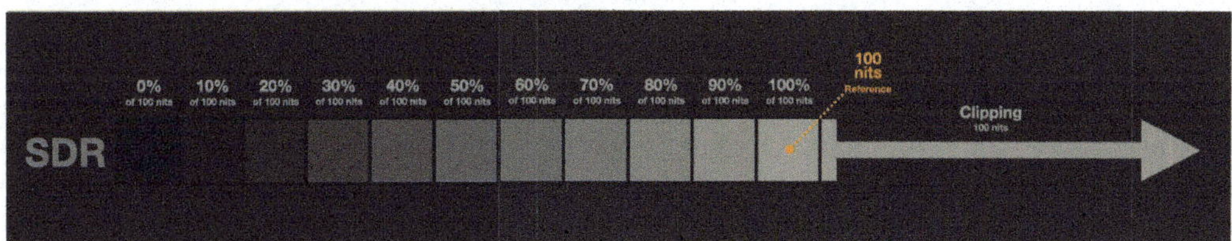

Figure 7.3 Standard dynamic range (SDR) by "Brightness Zones" (A simplistic representation of luminance levels to be compared against HDR luminance capabilities)

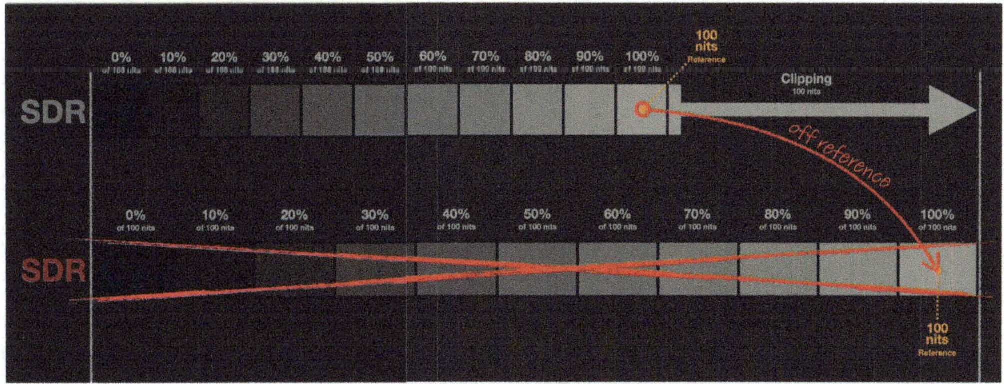

Figure 7.4 Stretched luminance zones does not convert standard dynamic range (SDR) into high dynamic range (HDR)

blacks with plenty of detail in the dark areas. So, in HDR you can have brightness levels beyond the 100 nits reference level of the SDR, adding more brightness zones. Therefore, instead of measuring the luminance of the image by the relative white peak of reference with percentages of that maximum brightness we are going to use a system that is calibrated to render the luminance in "absolute terms"[2] between the imaging system and the display, by using the *PQ* (Figure 7.5).

We call the luminance levels by its standardized unit of luminance: nits. And because the whole system is standardized end-to-end with a huge color volume and with a high density of values to represent more dark luminance levels, we can achieve deeper blacks, and brighter and more saturated colors; with the ability to store more color data that is able to be displayed at the present time by the current technology. HDR is future proof. Unlike other imaging technologies, this one is here to stay, so you better prepare.

I am going to simulate the differences between SDR and HDR. In order to make the differences easy to understand I have exaggerated them a notch just for demonstrating purposes. Please keep in mind the image printed in this book showcasing this point is clearly not a HDR video image (you cannot print HDR, it is a display medium, not a printed one), but I can simulate for you the main features you need to understand here. I will use the same image in two different versions: on the left you have the simulated SDR version, and on the right the simulated HDR. Let's overlap the two versions and split the picture (Figure 7.6).

The first thing you are going to notice is probably the level of saturation. The HDR image has richer colors and is more saturated because, as we saw a few pages back, the brightness of the primaries can reach brighter values than the SDR version; and still related to the brightness levels, have a look at the highlights, especially shown in this picture next to the eye. In the SDR version you have a clipped white where the detail of the highlights gets flattened. By contrast, in the HDR version - since you can reach higher values in its color volume - clipping is not happening and you have way more available levels of brightness to be represented. The same thing happens in the fine details of the glitter, which affects the perception of sharpness because the high-frequencies of the image (the little detail in the highlights) get flattened in SDR. This is another collateral effect of HDR: the increased appearance of sharpness due to the higher contrast in the high frequencies[3] of the image. When *clipping* happens, you lose details in the clipping area: imagine this, if you have a Red value of 100 nits, a Green value of 200 nits and a Blue value of 800 nits, in SDR that will be displayed as flat 100% white (100 nits top white), while in HDR that will be a very vivid Blue

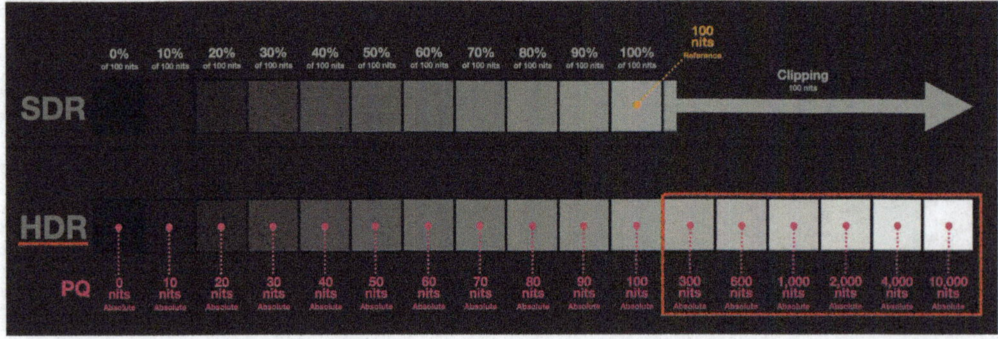

Figure 7.5 Standard dynamic range (SDR) vs high dynamic range (HDR) "Brightness Zones"

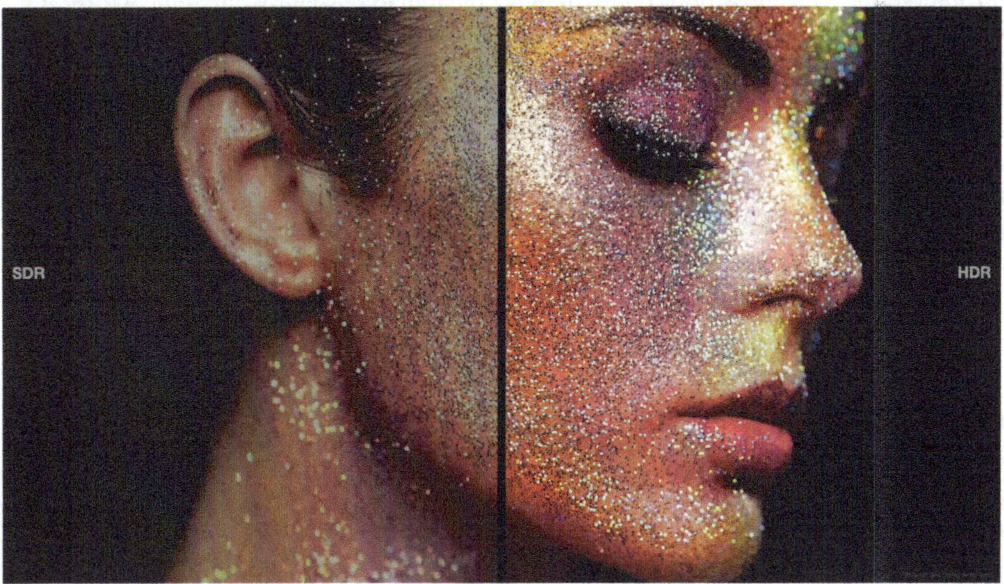

Figure 7.6 Simulation of standard dynamic range (SDR) vs high dynamic range (HDR) render
intent

(with a few notes of violet in it). So, in creative terms you can reach colors that were impossible to display in SDR. Another artifact you can observe in this simulation is *posterizing* (also known as *banding*). Have a look at the neck of the girl, in the HDR version you have a smooth gradient of shadows that provide detail in the shape of the jaw, while on the left side, the lack of a dense amount of samples makes it difficult to understand when the jaw ends and when the neck begins. That is banding, this artifact can be created by the image compression as well, but that is another story. This is related to color issues, and the purpose of this simulation is for you to understand the concept. The last point to be compared is the black levels, which is one of the strengths of HDR. Part of the perception of a rich and contrasted image is how dark the black levels are in relation to how bright the white levels are, and the ability to define details in the shadows by little noticeable differences. In the HDR version you can see the profile is very well defined and you have very deep details in the eyelashes, or the nostrils, or even the mouth. While in the left side, the SDR, the black background and the hair are the same value, the neck shadow fades into the background without providing information of the neck. Therefore, if you compare the luminance levels of both black levels for the background in the HDR and the SDR versions, the one on the left looks "milky".

SDR and HDR are different creative mediums, so films usually have two separate grading treatments, one for each system as what works in one dynamic range probably would not work in the other, so, in order to maintain the creative intent (or the closest possible to it within the restrictions of SDR) they have to do everything twice. But, which one is the golden master and the first one to define the directions in terms of color is a question that these days depends of the filmmakers; some prefer to start with the SDR version with its limitations and then transfer it to the HDR medium so you have two versions that look quite similar; and, on another hand, other filmmakers prefer to start working on the HDR version and then they leave to the colorist the task to transfer it into SDR, working around the limitations with corrections that will make the film look slightly different. We are still in the process of transition. But as VFX artists we must preserve all the color information we receive and ensure the creative intent end-to-end, the artistic decisions they do in the color suite are not our concern, as far as we are providing all the information required.

I believe it would be a good idea that you understand the HDR standards relative to the different *video formats* and *transfer functions*, that we will refer to as *EOTF* so you get how the image will be displayed on the screen. There is so much information out there and it is good to have clear ideas and not to be confused.

Video Formats

The signal to be decoded by the HDR display (Figure 7.7).

HDR10 Media Profile

The first one is the most common: *HDR10 media profile*, or simple *HDR10*. It is open source, which means it is free and anybody can use it. Its bit-depth is 10-bit (so up to 1024 value levels per channel, for a total of more than a billion hues; remember that the 8-bit contains "only" over 16 million hues). Its *EOTF* is *PQ* (I will discuss this one later as it is a very important feature we need to analyze in depth). The *white point* is *D65* (you are already familiar with this, as we discussed it in a previous chapter). The *peak brightness* is 1,000 nits (against the mere 100 nits available in SDR images); remember that I told you that HDR can store up to 10,000 nits of information, well, we refer to the Master image

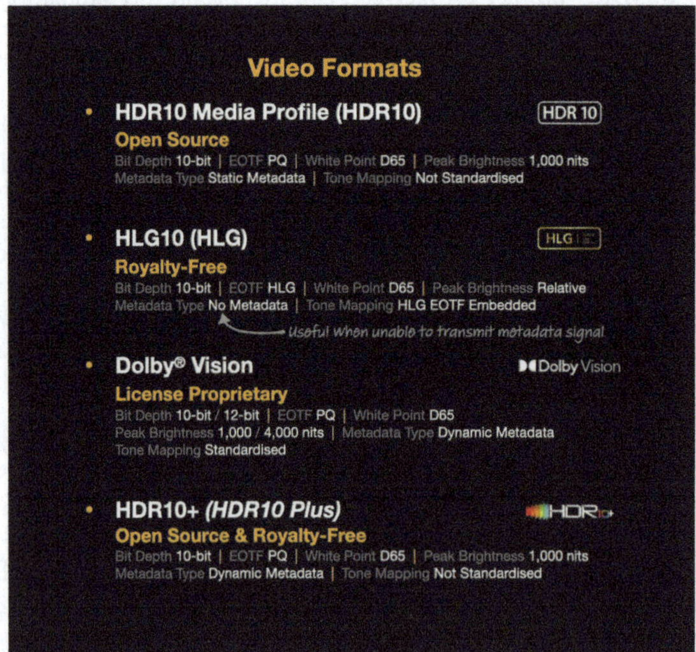

Figure 7.7 High dynamic range (HDR) Electro-optical transfer functions (EOTFs). and Video formats

data, the specific data here – 1,000 nits – refers to the display signal, so a display that is decoding a HDR10 video format would not get any luminance value above 1,000 nits (regardless the image maximum peak of white or whatever was stored in the Master HDR image). Any brightness value above 1,000 nits will be downgraded to 1,000 nits (clipping). Well, let's say that, right now, many consumer displays would not reach even to 1,000 nits mark of brightness peak, so *right now* this limitation *is not a big deal*, and, in any case, there is another standard right now that goes way higher than this, and for sure, in the future new ones will arise as the displays get *better*.

Metadata

The purpose of HDR metadata is to aid the display device to show the content in an optimal manner. It contains the HDR content and mastering device properties, so the display device uses it to map the content according to its own color gamut and peak brightness. You know all displays are different, so the metadata adapts the contents to the limitations of every display, therefore the image looks as good as it gets for that display. Let me put an example: imagine that you have two different HDR TVs, one is *cheap*, with a peak brightness of 600 nits and a limited color gamut due to a not so *good* LED panel; then, on the other hand, you have an *expensive* one with a maximum peak of 1,000 nits, with deep blacks and a very nice and wider color gamut; the metadata will be used to adapt the image to have the "same render intent". So, in theory the general appearance of the same image on both TV's will be *the same*, but of course, on the *good* TV you will appreciate the details where the *cheap* TV cannot reach; without the metadata, each TV would stretch the values of the image arbitrarily, resulting in a very different appearance of blacks, whites, midtones, colors, contrast ... without maintaining any logic. That is why the standard is important, so everybody stands by the same rules.

There are two kinds of HDR Metadata: *static* and *dynamic*. The *static metadata* describes a setting that must be applied to the whole program or movie. It will average the render to conceal all the different levels for dark scenes and bright scenes, and all the different color instances in the whole program. Of course the average will require sacrificing certain particular moments of the movie for the greater good of the whole video. That is why the other version of HDR metadata exists: the *dynamic metadata* allows a different setting for intervals of the program, even down to a frame-by-frame different set of metadata, this way the metadata can describe the best render performance for that particular part of the program that requires different needs than others without the sacrifice of the average.

HDR10 has static metadata.

Tone Mapping

Tone mapping is the process of adapting digital signals to appropriate light levels based on the HDR metadata, so in other words, how the metadata is applied (I will discuss this later in more detail, so you get a clearer overview of the process). Right now, you just need to know that the *tone mapping* of HDR10 is not standardized so each manufacturer does their own thing, resulting in different results depending on the manufacturer. Well, I guess it is the "price" to pay for the freedom of open-source technology, it takes time to reach a consensus.

Hybrid Log-Gamma

The next format is the *HLG10*, also known as simple *HLG*, which stands for *hybrid log-gamma*, taking the name from its characteristic *transfer function (EOTF)*. Developed by the *BBC* and the *Japan Broadcasting Corporation*, it is the system used for HDR live broadcasting where metadata cannot be transmitted. Keep in mind the air signal does not have the band capabilities of the latest generation HDMI which allows the metadata to define the render of the content in relation with the display. So, the engineers at the BBC and the NHK developed a transfer function that was backwards compatible with SDR, combining a *gamma curve* and *logarithmic curve* in the same EOTF, a limited signal that works for all, accepting certain compromises. Its license is royalty free, so you would not have to pay to use it, but you have to request the license to be authorized to use it. Its bit-depth is 10-bit, the white point is D65, the peak brightness is *relative* to the parameters of the content broadcasted, and as I said before it has no metadata. The tone mapping is inherently *embedded* in the *HLG EOTF* itself.

Dolby® Vision

Then we have the *Dolby Vision*, which requires a proprietary license from *Dolby Laboratories*. Today it is one of the highest quality standards for HDR. It can use 10-bit or 12-bit, the EOTF is PQ and the white point is, as always, D65. Another big difference is the peak brightness that can go from 1,000 to 4,000 nits. The metadata is dynamic, allowing the image signal to be modulated as precisely as a per frame basis. And the tone mapping is standardized. The *Dolby Vision* has become very popular and widely distributed.

HDR10+

And the last one on this list is the *HDR10+*, which is practically the same as the HDR10 but with the addition of dynamic metadata.

Do any of these video formats influence the way we handle HDR? Not really, just simply make sure you work with a managed color workflow that will preserve all the qualities of the HDR Master without losing any data or modifying the artistic intent. Well, that is why we are here, aren't we? But it is important you know these standards as the signal your monitor will receive to visualize HDR content should comply with any of those standards. The imaging system and the display systems should be aligned.

Electro-optical transfer function (EOTF) for HDR

Let's have a closer look now at the transfer functions for HDR, or EOTFs (Figure 7.8).

Perceptual Quantizer (PQ)

I would say this one is most important for us, as it is the universal mastering one, also referred to as PQ. It uses a non-linear distribution of the values based on what is called *just noticeable differences* (JND), in other words, the human perception of increments of light, hence the name *PQ*. This EOTF can reach a maximum luminance of 10,000 nits. As this one is very important for us VFX artists, we will discuss it in depth in a separate

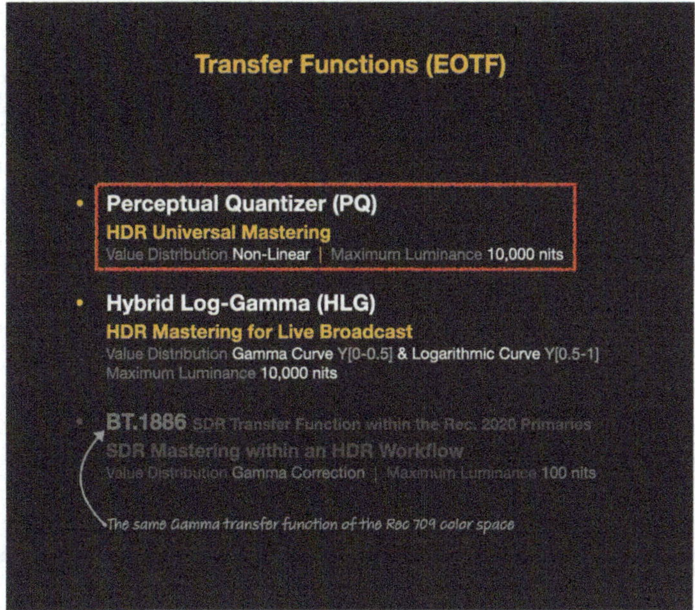

Figure 7.8 High dynamic range (HDR) standard electro-optical transfer functions (EOTFs).

section to understand all its features. The PQ is the EOTF of *HDR10*, *HDR10+*, and *Dolby Vision*.

Hybrid Log-Gamma EOTF

The other one is the *hybrid log-gamma EOTF*, that consists in a *gamma curve* for the first section of the function, and a *logarithmic curve* for the second part. As I mentioned before, it is retro-compatible with SDR systems. This EOTF is used in the *HLG10* video format and can be translated from the PQ one.

BT.1886

And the last one is the *BT.1886*, which is the *transfer function* of the SDR, the same as the *Rec709* but allocated within the *Rec.2020 primaries*. Hence, it is the SDR mastering option within a HDR workflow. It preserves all the features of SDR: the *gamma correction* and the maximum luminance for a *peak brightness* of 100 nits, this also can be extrapolated sourcing from the *PQ*.

The main transfer function for us, for mastering HDR purposes to be displayed is the PQ.

HDR TV vs HDR Cinema

To put all this information about HDR standards in context, let's compare different specs of HDR Cinema and TV.

I am going to use the *Dolby* HDR standards for both, TV (*Dolby Vision*) – quite popular these days – and cinema (*Dolby Cinema*), just to show how the same *branded* standard can vary from the way the content is rendered on the screen and what factors make them different, and what are the same. To be clear, the *Dolby Cinema* is a bespoke cinema, the standards do not apply just to the image that is going to be projected, so not just the content, but also, and foremost, the controlled environment inside the room, from the color and materials of the walls to the specifics of the surface of the screen, everything that conditions the image in a cinema is kept in consideration by the *Dolby Cinema* standard. It uses *Christie* customized digital cinema projectors. This means that the content branded *Dolby Cinema* can be graded and mastered only on a *mastering Dolby Cinema*.

Of course, there are other HDR Cinema systems, like *Eclair Color™* (that uses *Sony & Barco* modified projectors) or *Samsung Onyx™ Cinema* (that uses LED screens), but I am going to refer just to the *Dolby Cinema* standard to keep features easy to be compared.

And then, let's add to our comparative the open standard *Ultra HD Premium™*, defined by the *UHD Alliance*, that comprises the world's leading consumer electronics manufacturers, film and TV studios, content distributors and technology companies. This standard establishes performance requirements for resolution, HDR, color and other video and audio attributes with an eye toward giving consumers the best possible 4K UHD with HDR experience.

So, we have two TV standards and one for cinema. Let's compare them (Figure 7.9).

Primaries

The first thing: the *primaries*. The minimum requirement for *Ultra HD Premium* is at least to reach 90% of *P3* gamut, the more the better. For the *Dolby Vision* TV standard

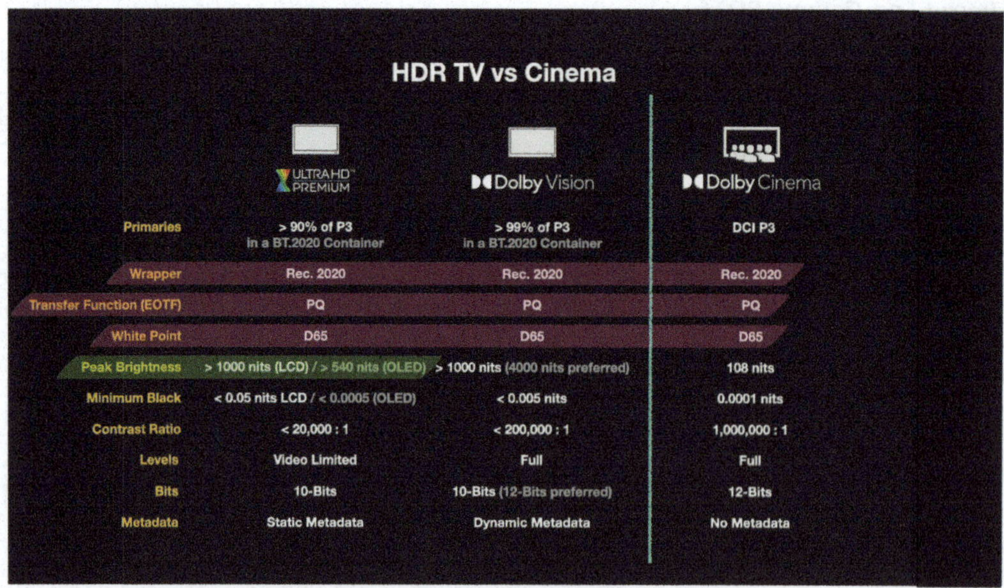

	ULTRAHD PREMIUM	Dolby Vision	Dolby Cinema
Primaries	> 90% of P3 in a BT.2020 Container	> 99% of P3 in a BT.2020 Container	DCI P3
Wrapper	Rec. 2020	Rec. 2020	Rec. 2020
Transfer Function (EOTF)	PQ	PQ	PQ
White Point	D65	D65	D65
Peak Brightness	> 1000 nits (LCD) / > 540 nits (OLED)	> 1000 nits (4000 nits preferred)	108 nits
Minimum Black	< 0.05 nits LCD / < 0.0005 (OLED)	< 0.005 nits	0.0001 nits
Contrast Ratio	< 20,000 : 1	< 200,000 : 1	1,000,000 : 1
Levels	Video Limited	Full	Full
Bits	10-Bits	10-Bits (12-Bits preferred)	12-Bits
Metadata	Static Metadata	Dynamic Metadata	No Metadata

Figure 7.9 Comparison table of high dynamic range (HDR) TV vs HDR cinema common standards

the minimum of the *P3* gamut is 99%, so as you can see, in this regard *Dolby Vision* is more restrictive to raise the standard. For *Dolby Cinema* the requirement is the full *DCI P3* (the name *DCI P3* stands for *digital cinema initiatives – protocol 3*). *P3* and *DCI P3* refer to the same color gamut but *P3*, that can also be referred as *display P3*, has a different transfer function compared to the *DCI P3* one. The *DCI P3* was specified by *SMPTE* for *digital cinema* applications defining a series of recommendations for the *reference projector* and its controlled environment, along with the acceptable tolerances around critical image parameters for *review room* and *theatre* applications.

Wrapper

The *wrapper*, meaning the color space containing the gamut specified by the *primaries* above, is consistent across all HDR standards: *Rec.2020*. Remember the *Rec.2020* set of *primaries* stand on the *spectral locus*, meaning they are theoretically 100% *pure*, allowing any other display color space to be allocated within its gamut. And just to put you in context with the non-HDR content, SDR uses the *Rec.709* color space.

Transfer Function

The *"display" transfer function*, or *EOTF* is another constant: *PQ*. Again, for context, SDR uses the usual *Rec.709 gamma correction* as *EOTF*.

White Point

Another important point is the *White Point* which is going to be the same for all HDR standards: the *CIE daylight illuminant D65*.

Peak Brightness

Now let's move to one of the most recognizable features of HDR, the *peak brightness*. For *Ultra HD Premium* requires at least 1,000 nits for LCD, and 540 nits for organic light-emitting diode (OLED) screens.[4] The reason why OLED screens are allowed to have a lower peak brightness relies on the fact that the black levels of OLED screens are darker than LCD and what really matters here is the contrast ratio. Remember you can get a higher contrast ratio by increasing the *peak brightness* or reducing the *minimum black*. For *Dolby Vision*, the standardized *minimum peak brightness* is at least 1,000 nits, but they recommend 4,000 nits to master the content. And here we have one of the massive differences between TV and cinema: The *Dolby Cinema* requires 108 nits of *peak brightness*. As I just mentioned earlier about the contrast aspect, the peak brightness is directly proportional to the minimum black, and I want you to think about a fact: a TV uses a panel of tiny "lights" to create the image, so even if the intensity of those mini light bulbs is very low, they are always emitting some amount of light. However, in a cinema the screen is not emitting any light, it is actually reflecting the light thrown at it by the projector, so having a low intensity light beam will result positively in how the black levels are going to be contaminated by the residual bouncing light in the environment. It is all about contrast ratio. For context, SDR peaks at 100 nits as we saw earlier.

Minimum Black

The *minimum black*. For *Ultra HD Premium* we have a tolerance up to 0.05 nits for the LCD screens, and 0.0005 for OLED. As you can see the OLED can reach deeper blacks than the LCD. For *Dolby Vision* the minimum black is set at 0.005. For *Dolby Cinema* we have an impressive 0.0001 … that is really dark.

Contrast Ratio

It is time we analyze the *contrast ratio*, that TV display standards range from at least 20,000:1 for *Ultra HD Premium*; to 200,000:1 for the *Dolby Vision* standard. But if we observe the *Dolby Cinema* specs, its contrast ratio is 1,000,000:1 representing by far the highest contrast ratio in the table. However, in 2019, an article of the *Society for Information Display Journal* exploring the challenges that must be addressed and the potential solutions that could be incorporated to enable a mainstream rollout of HDR in cinema pointed out that «*Unfortunately, despite the significant impact of a better black level on image quality, most cinemagoers never benefit from it, because of the auditorium's light pollution, including exit signs and reflections off the audience from bright imagery*».[5] Nevertheless, the *Dolby Cinema* has an outstanding contrast ratio intent and their certification expands beyond the specifics of the screen to the whole screening room environment (Figure 7.10).

Levels

The levels are *video limited* for the *Ultra HD Premium* and full for both the instances by *Dolby*.

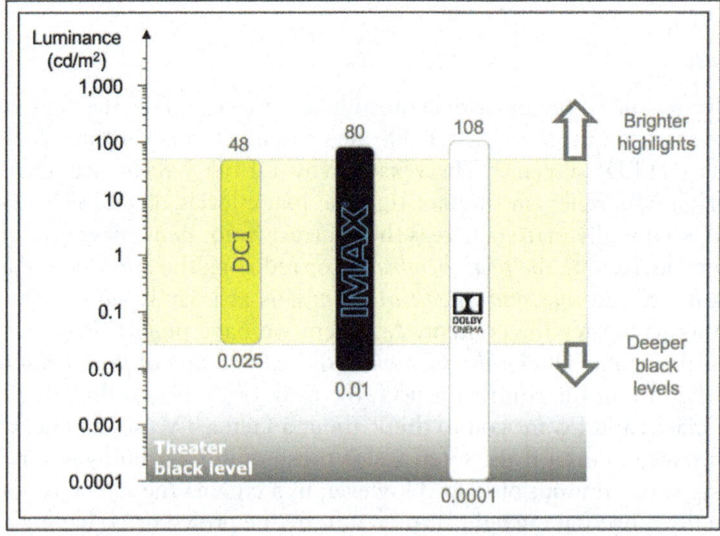

Figure 7.10 Cinema standards comparative [information display, volume: 35, issue: 5, pages: 9–13, first published: 26 september 2019, DOI: (10.1002/msid.1059)]

Bit Depth

Regarding the bit depth, the *Ultra HD Premium* uses 10-bits while the *Dolby Vision* can use 10-bit; or better 12-bit (as they recommend). For *Dolby Cinema* the standard is 12-bits.

Metadata

And the last element to compare on this list, the *metadata*, which is *static* for the *Ultra HD Premium,* and *dynamic* for the *Dolby Vision* standard. Regarding *Dolby Cinema*, obviously there is no need for metadata as the whole chain of displaying the picture is standardized and the projector is always the same calibrated reference, so the metadata is not needed to adapt the render of the image to the "capabilities" of the display, the image is encoded as its required to be displayed.

Just a note regarding the mastering: Theatrical HDR is usually mastered after the SDR, "traditional" is mastered on a *digital cinema projector*.

With this table we can identify key pieces of information for us to keep in mind: The first element to be noticed is that the color space used for HDR is always the *Rec.2020*, even if it is just a wrapper to contain a portion of the *P3*, but the color space remains constant across different systems. The *EOTF* remains constant as well, always *PQ*; and so, the *white point*, that stays at *D65*. Regarding the minimum reference *peak brightness*, the minimum indicated is 1,000 nits (the OLED specs are relative to its especially low minimum black that enhances its contrast ratio, but in order to have a uniformed reference level 1,000 nits is recommended).

So now that you know how HDR images are going to be displayed you can have a clearer idea about your reference specs.

The PQ EOTF

As you already know, the *PQ EOTF* is one of the most important elements of displaying HDR content, so I think it is worth exploring the features of this transfer function and its reference levels (Figure 7.11).

Figure 7.12 represents the scale of brightness between the distribution of 10-bits values and its corresponding luminance level on the display measured in nits. These are different luminance benchmarks that point to different standards. At the top, the 10,000 nits mark the maximum brightness level of the *PQ* container. Let's look at the correspondence between bit and nit values in Figure 7.12.

From the bottom: the first mark, at 48 nits, uses 448 values from the 10-bit scale and corresponds to the traditional *DCI projection*. Above that we have the 100 nits mark that established the *SDR reference luminance* – notice that we are at around halfway to the top, this is because we are more sensitive to observing differences in the dark area than in the bright area so have more intensity samples (bit values) to describe this area of the curve than the very bright area. Above that we have 108 nits for *Dolby Cinema*, and the 1,000 nits mark that defines the *minimum brightness level upper limit* for professional HDR reference displays. Another important benchmark is the 4,000 nits used for mastering *Dolby Vision* content, using the *Dolby Pulsar* monitor. The highest point, the 10,000 nits is just theoretical as at the moment there is no commercial monitor able to reach that level of luminance.

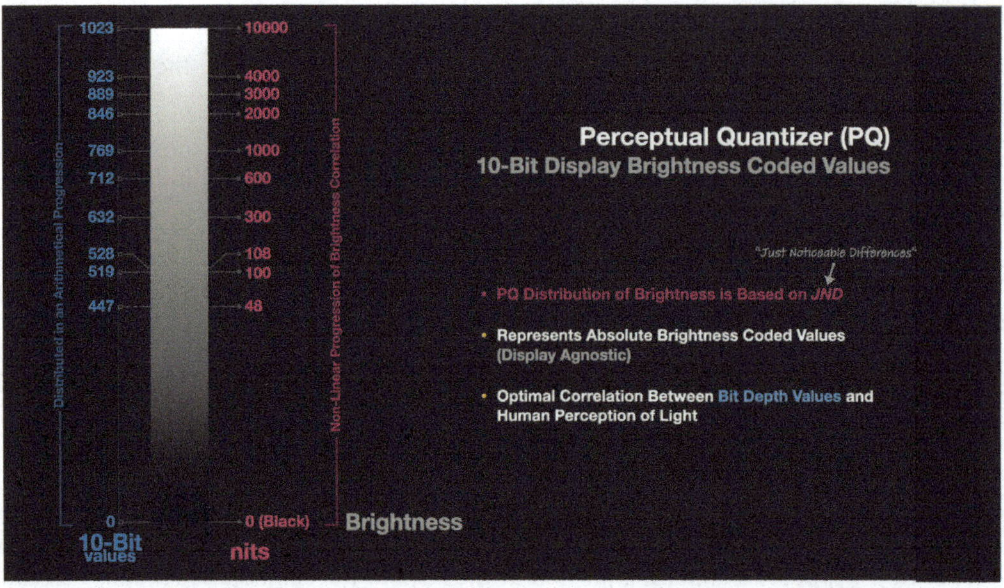

Figure 7.11 10-Bit display brightness coded values

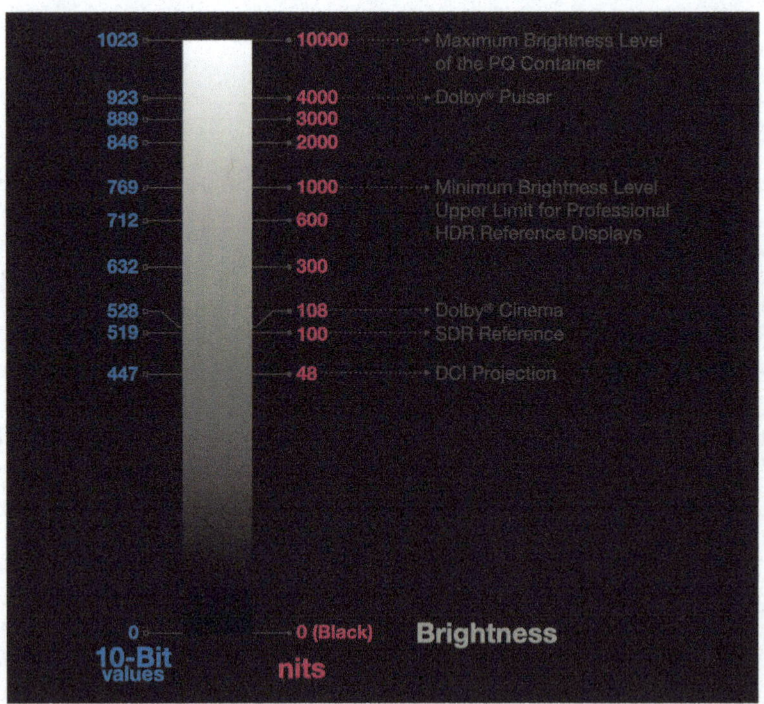

Figure 7.12 High dynamic range (HDR) brightness level benchmarks

On the left, you see the arithmetical progression of the decimal bit values and on the right the distribution of luminance, a scale that is not linear. That progression of correspondence will give the name to this *transfer function*.

This part of the curve represents the values achievable by SDR screens, that reach up to 100 nits. The other part of the curve represents a hundred times more luminance values than the SDR range (Figure 7.13).

This blue area represents the peak brightness achievable by most consumer displays, as you can see, a few reach to the 1,000 mark while most of them are below, reaching between 300 and 600. That is why metadata is required, to adapt the brightness of the content to the specifics of each display. Of course, with a display capability to reach 1,000 nits will be able to show more details in the highlights than one that peaks at 300 nits, but still, the distribution of the luminance below those ranges will look fairly similar, maintaining the mastering intent with as much fidelity as the quality of the screen could render (Figure 7.14).

This top range that goes from 4,000 nits to 10,000 nits (marked in red in the previous figure) is reserved for future compatibility, so when displays get better and able to reach higher peaks of brightness they will be able to reproduce the values on the contents that were mastered using the *PQ EOTF*. So HDR is future proof. You may think that this is a waste of data right now, but notice that the number of decimal values from the 10-bits depth is less than a tenth, and in the low area, where details are really necessary we have plenty of values so it is a conscious compromise for a greater good (Figure 7.14).

The line that is going to establish the minimum HDR reference level is 1,000 nits. So, if your content will be mastered in *Ultra HD Premium* standard – which is quite

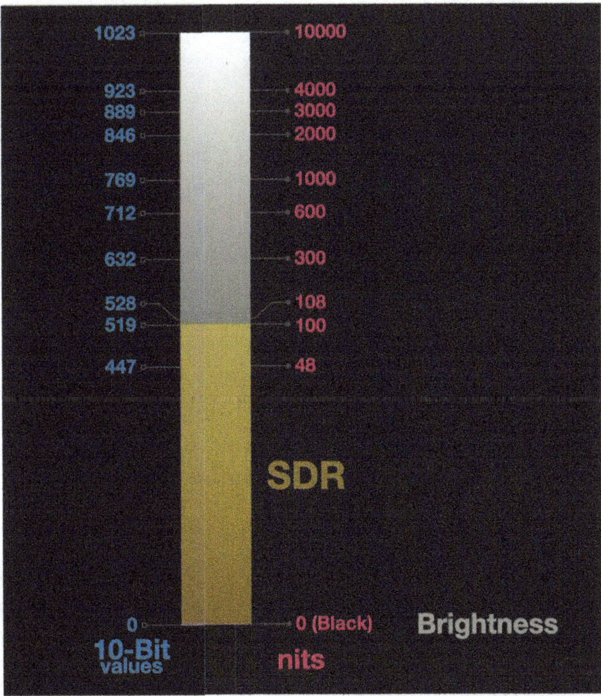

Figure 7.13 Standard dynamic range (SDR) brightness levels in the bit-depth context of the perceptual quantizer (PQ) electro-optical transfer function (EOTF).

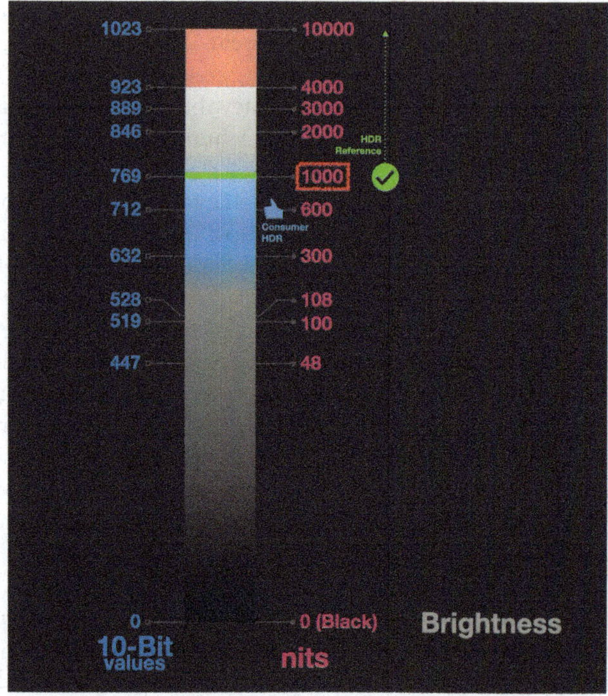

Figure 7.14 Benchmarks of high dynamic range (HDR) displays

common – you should be able to check values at least up to 1,000 nits. For *Dolby Vision* content you can still check up to 1,000 nits but *Dolby* recommends 4,000 nits for this purpose (Figure 7.14).

Then, what is the criteria they used to build the *PQ transfer function*? If it is not linear, is it logarithmic? Well, not exactly. The *PQ* distribution of brightness is based on *JND*, that stands for: *just noticeable differences*. It means every progression to the next decimal bit position has in consideration the way we perceive light, so we quantify the step of brightness based on human perception of light, hence the name *PQ*. As I explained earlier in the book, we perceive little brightness changes in dark, while in order to perceive any noticeable change of light in the bright areas we need a quite substantial increase of brightness.

The *PQ EOTF* represents absolute brightness coded values; hence it is display agnostic.

This establishes an optimal correlation between the values available from the bit depth and how humans perceive light.

Just a note to clarify that the *PQ* can be applied to bit-depths higher than 10-bits, but not less. For instance, *Dolby Cinema* uses 12-bits as it is able to manage a huge contrast ratio in the low light areas needing extra room for tiny differences of brightness.

So, the question now is: if the *PQ* represents absolute brightness coded values but monitors are all different how can the image be represented with the same criteria in all of them? Of course, the metadata will assist a process known as *tone mapping*.

Tone Mapping

Tone mapping is the process of adapting digital signals to appropriate light levels based, in this case, on the HDR metadata. This process is not simply applying the *EOTF* (*electro-optical transfer function*) on the image data, but it is rather trying to map the image data with the display device capabilities using metadata information. Since a broad range of HDR display devices are available in the market, each with their own *nits range* (consequently their own *brightness levels* available), correct *tone mapping* is necessary for a good viewing experience. Since the *tone mapping* is done based on the meta-data in the video stream, presence of correct meta-data is necessary.

Source footage can be shot at HDR with the best of cameras and then mastered on high-end HDR mastering systems, but it still needs to be displayed optimally on the range of HDR televisions available in the market. *Tone mapping* performs an appropriate brightness mapping of the content to the device without significant degradation.

I'm going to show you a very drastic example to make you understand the concept of *tone mapping*.

Imagine that we have a HDR image with all its values, and we just display it on an SDR monitor without any *tone mapping* operation applied. So, the linear correspondence means that the SDR monitor will extract the portion of the HDR curve able to be displayed in the SDR monitor, resulting in a representation of the image that does not preserve the original HDR creative intent (Figure 7.15).

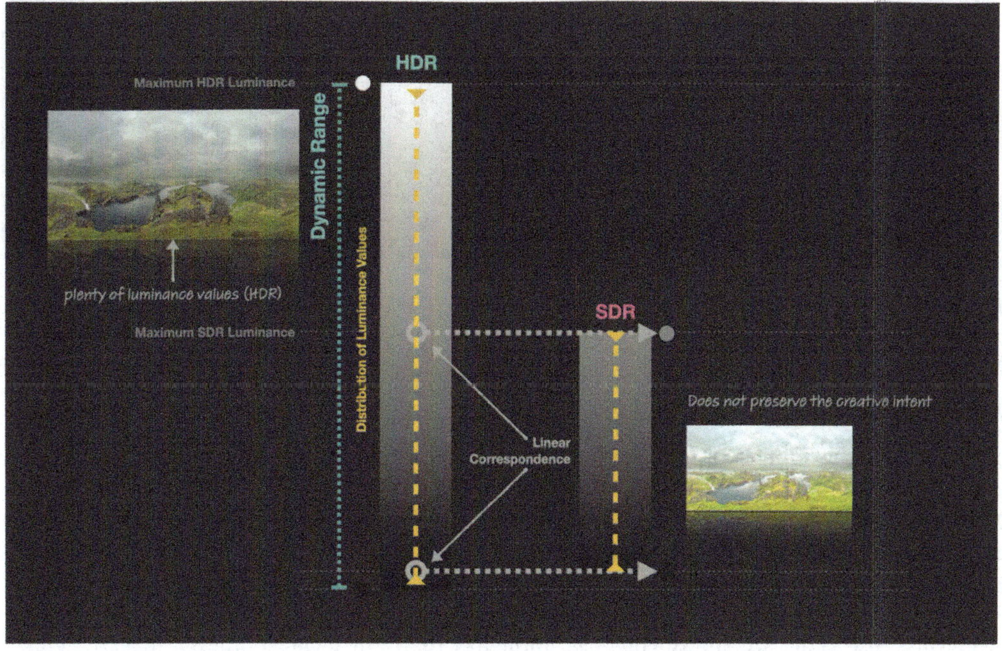

Figure 7.15 Simulation example of linear correspondence of luminance values between high dynamic range (HDR) and standard dynamic range (SDR) (no tone mapping)

The *brightness peak*, the *minimum black*, and the *EOTF* of the SDR system does not correspond with the HDR ones and so the image will be read incorrectly and look weird (Figure 7.16).

Tone mapping will compress the distribution of *luminance* values by discarding discretely certain values and positioning the rest accordingly in a way that preserves the same artistic intent within a lower dynamic range framework.

It is worth mentioning that the *tone mapping* operation does not belong just to HDR to convert to SDR, but for any HDRI to be down-sampled to other lower dynamic ranges, like for instance HDRI panoramic *latlong* radiance maps very commonly used in VFX for lighting purposes. *Tone mapping* refers to the operation of adapting the dynamic range to a lower container, preserving certain aspects of the original image to approximate the artistic intent: such as exposure and gamma, highlight compression, histogram equalization, etc.

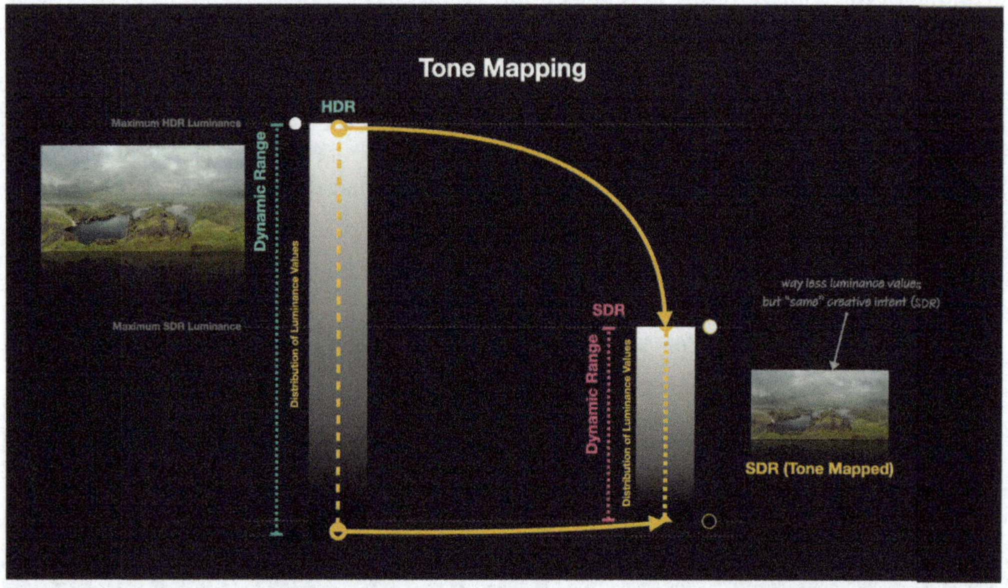

Figure 7.16 Simulation example of high dynamic range (HDR) to standard dynamic range (SDR) tone mapping

HDR Signal Value

And to close the subject of HDR we should compare the *HDR signal value* with the SDR one by putting into context the three main curves (EOTF): *BT.709* (the *gamma curve* of the SDR system), the *hybrid log-gamma*, and the *PQ*. This will help you visualize the actual brightness level capabilities of each system (and also why the *tone mapping* is necessary to change from one to another) (Figure 7.17).

First of all, keep in mind the mark that represents the 100 nits' light level, the reference brightness for SDR. So, the purple area indicates the light levels available in SDR, and so the red curve is the *BT.709 gamma*, as you can see there is no information above 100 nits.

The other mark on the right hand side at the base is the 1,000 nit, which is the reference light level for HDR, but remember the *PQ* signal value can reach up to 10,000 nits, so just

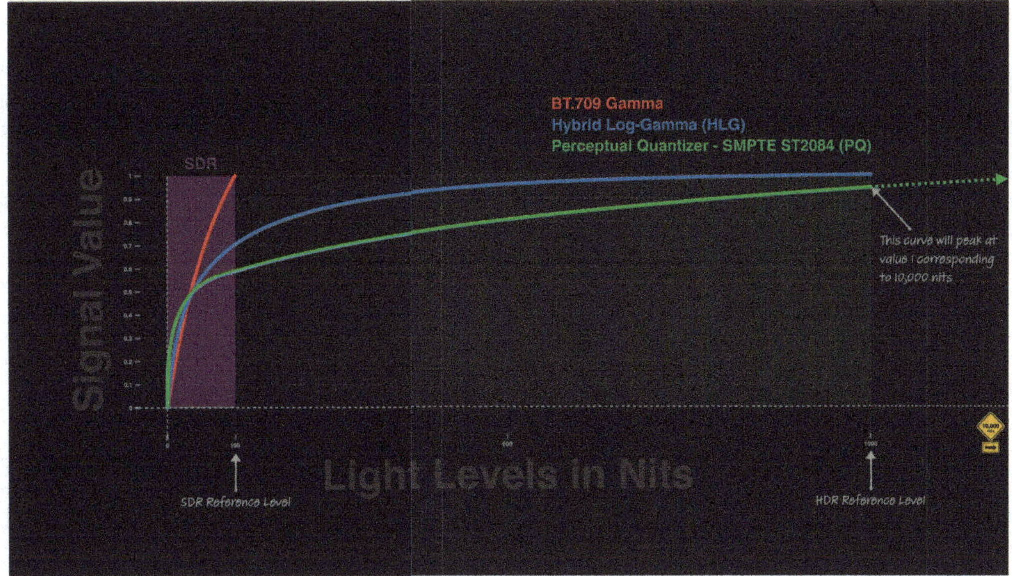

Figure 7.17 High dynamic range (HDR) and standard dynamic range (SDR) signal values

to keep things easy to read I made the graphic up to 1,000 nits, as you can see there is a bit of room for more highlights to develop across the *PQ* curve above the 1,000 nits mark. The *hybrid log-gamma* curve peaks at 1,000 nits and the slope is significantly different from the *PQ*, notice that the more inclined part of the slope of the *HLG* sits on the SDR area, in that region, the progression of brightness behaves quite similarly to the *BT.709* curve (especially if you stretch its 100 nits markup to value 1 on the signal value) this is to maintain a compatibility of the signal between both worlds, the SDR and HDR. Remember the *HLG* was designed not to need metadata for *tone mapping*, the display will adapt the signal to this standardized curve.

I think with this you have enough information to understand how HDR works end-to-end, from the image captured to the image displayed. Now it is time to move into a more practical subject that will allow us to work in a workflow compatible with HDR, or SDR, or practically anything available now or probably in the future. In the next chapter, we study the ACES workflow and its components.

Notes

1 *Solid Angle*: A portion of the 3D space projected from a point describing the solid region comprised within that solid projection. In *geometry*, a solid angle is a measure of the amount of the field of view from some particular point that a given object covers. For instance, the frustrum of a camera – what the camera sees – described by a *pyramid* with the top vertex on the lenses, is a solid angle.
2 Based on the human perception of luminance changes. As it will be explained later in this chapter.
3 *Frequency*: Image frequency refers to the rate of change in intensity per pixel. Assume you have a section in your image that shifts from white to black. It is low frequency if it takes several pixels to change. The higher the frequency, the fewer pixels it takes to express that intensity fluctuation. To picture a simple example: by blurring an image you are reducing its frequency.

4   «LED stands for light-emitting diode. These are little solid-state devices that make light because of the movement of electrons through a semi-conductor. LEDs are relatively small compared to compact fluorescent and incandescent light bulbs, but they can get extremely bright. However, LEDs aren't small enough to be used as the pixels of a TV – they're way too big for that. That's why LEDs are only used as the backlight for LCD televisions. OLED stands for organic light-emitting diode. Very simply put, an OLED is made with organic compounds that light up when fed electricity. That may not seem like a huge difference when compared to LED, but OLEDs can be made to be extremely thin, small and remarkably flexible. On an OLED TV, each pixel lights itself up independently of the others. [...] The differences between LED and OLED TVs include illumination methods, price points, and energy efficiency levels. The list below documents these differences: 1. The main difference between an LED TV and an OLED TV is that the pixels of an OLED TV are self-illuminating, whereas the LEDs in an LED TV are used to light an LCD display; 2. LED TVs are currently less expensive than OLED displays, though eventually experts expect OLED TVs to drop significantly in price; 3. OLED TVs feature a wider viewing angle than do LED TVs. With OLED, the colors do not get washed out when viewers watch from extreme angles; 4. OLED technology offers the ability to develop lighter and thinner displays than LED TVs do; 5. OLED TVs offer the deepest blacks of any type of flat-screen diode TV available; 6. OLED TVs have the ability to make a greater number of colors, though this advantage is miniscule when compared to the current level of HDTV technology, limiting the number of colors that can be utilized; 7. OLED TVs are more energy efficient when compared to their LED counterparts.» Bagher, A. M. (2016). Comparison of LED and OLED. Scholars Journal of Engineering and Technology (SJET) 4(4):206–210. ISSN 2347-9523.

5   Ballestad, A., Boitard, R., Damberg, G., & Stojmenovik, G. (2019). Taking HDR Cinema Mainstream. *Society for Information Display*. https://doi.org/10.1002/msid.1059

Academy Color Encoding System (ACES) Workflows

8

ACES

A Future-Proof Color Management System

This part of the book is entirely dedicated to the ACES. So, what is it exactly?

ACES is the industry standard for managing color throughout the life cycle of a motion picture or TV production. From image capture through editing, VFX, mastering, public presentation, archiving and future remastering, *ACES* ensures a consistent color experience that preserves the filmmaker's creative vision. In addition to the creative benefits, *ACES* addresses and solves a number of significant production, post-production, delivery, and archiving problems that have arisen with the increasing variety of digital cameras and formats in use, as well as the surge in the number of productions that rely on worldwide collaboration using shared digital image files.

ACES is a free, open, device-independent color management and image interchange system that can be applied to almost any current or future workflow. It was developed by hundreds of the industry's top scientists, engineers, and end users, working together under the auspices of the Academy of Motion Picture Arts and Sciences.

Let's analyze its specs (Figure 8.1).

Resolution

Image resolution? *Multiformat resolution.* Just any format. *ACES* is resolution independent so you can have any number of pixels distributed in any aspect ratio. It does not change. So even resolutions not yet developed will be compatible with *ACES*.

Frame Rate

The *Frame Rate* is the same thing as per the resolution, any FPS (also known as *frame per second*) is compatible with ACES. It is defined as *frame rate independent*. Hence, if in the future they decided to go for higher frame rates, they will always be compatible with ACES.

Color Gamut

In relation to the *visible spectrum* … how many visible colors can *ACES* handle? The answer is: all of them. The ACES color space has been designed to contain all display referred

DOI: 10.4324/b23222-12

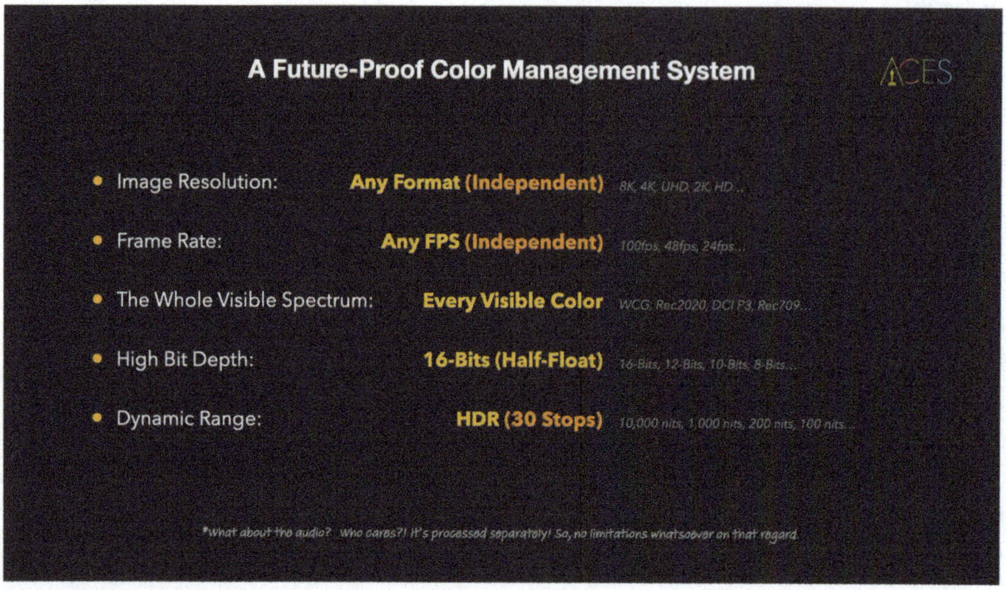

A Future-Proof Color Management System   ACES

Image Resolution: **Any Format (Independent)**   8K, 4K, UHD, 2K, HD...

Frame Rate: **Any FPS (Independent)**   100fps, 48fps, 24fps...

The Whole Visible Spectrum: **Every Visible Color**   WCG, Rec2020, DCI P3, Rec709...

High Bit Depth: **16-Bits (Half-Float)**   16-Bits, 12-Bits, 10-Bits, 8-Bits...

Dynamic Range: **HDR (30 Stops)**   10,000 nits, 1,000 nits, 200 nits, 100 nits...

*What about the audio? Who cares?! It's processed separately! So, no limitations whatsoever on that regard.

Figure 8.1 Academy color encoding system (ACES) specs

gamuts, such as *Rec2020*, *P3*, *Rec709* … and even more, the whole *CIE xy chromaticity diagram* is contained, so basically, if you can see it, *ACES* can reproduce it. The thing is, all display referred *gamuts* are, as you know, contextualized in a set of primaries within the chromaticities defined by the *spectral locus*, so in the future, any possible new gamut will be contained in it, hence it will be able to be reproduce by the ACES.

Bit Depth

The *ACES compliant* container is defined at 16-bit, half-float. Why? Because it is enough to handle the visible spectrum with enough density for very high precision. Someone could be asking why not 32-bits? Well, it would have more density for precision, but files will become unnecessarily heavy. 32-bit is a great bit depth for processing color operations and maybe for some specific CGI AOVs, but for representing color and still having great room for stretching certain areas of color without generating artifacts 16-bit is optimal. This is directly related to the next point.

Dynamic Range

ACES is HDR compatible, able to store up to 30 stops of light. To put yourself in context you need to know that, by some estimates, the human eye can distinguish up to 24 *f*-stops of dynamic range. Therefore, 30 stops is way above this range, and as I mentioned before this is related to the bit depth due to the color density. Keep in mind that a *stop* of light is not a fundamental unit, but a method of measuring the increase or decrease of light in a photographic exposure. One light *stop* is either double – plus one stop – or half – minus one stop. So, irrespective of your initial exposure, increasing it by one *stop* means twice as much light, and decreasing it by one *stop* means half the amount of light. It represents an exponential scale, so two *stops* are double of double, or half of half: hence, four times more light or four times less light ... and so on. The thirty *stops* of *dynamic range* in *ACES* is more than enough to reach the 10,000 nits mark of HDR (that are still unreachable by any commercial monitor by the way).

If someone is asking about the audio ... who cares? Audio is processed separately. ACES handles just the image and exchanged in frame sequences (on EXR containers as I will explain later). So audio is completely unrelated to this color management process, it just travel on another lane.

ACES Standards: The ST.2065 Family

If you want to know all the technical specifics about ACES let me guide you through the list of Standards that rule ACES. The most critical is the *ST.2065 family* standardized by *SMPTE*. I am going to flag five here:

- SMPTE ST.2065-1:2012 (Academy Color Encoding Specification)
  The standard defines the Academy Color Encoding Specification (ACES).

- SMPTE ST.2065-2:2012 (APD Academy Printing Density)
  This standard defines Academy Printing Density (APD) by specifying the spectral responsivities, APD and the APD reference measurement device.

- SMPTE ST.2065-3:2012 (ADX Academy Density Exchange Encoding)
  This standard defines the Academy Density Exchange Encoding (ADX) including the encoding method, the 16-bit and 10-bit component value encoding metrics, and the method for converting between the 16-bit and 10-bit component value encoding metrics.

- SMPTE ST.2065-4:2013 (ACES Image Container File Layout)
  This standard specifies the layout of, and metadata in, files containing images that conform to SMPTE ST 2065-1, Academy Color Encoding Specification (ACES).

- SMPTE ST.2065-5:2016 (MXF Wrapped EXRs)
  This standard specifies frame and clip-based mappings of a sequence of monoscopic ACES coded still pictures, as specified in SMPTE ST 2065-4, into the MXF generic container, as defined in SMPTE ST 379-2. This standard specifies the key, the length, and the value fields of the ACES coded picture element. This standard also defines the essence container and label values and the essence descriptor.

SMPTE ST.2065-1:2012 specifies the ACES Color Spaces. We will use the ACES 2065-1 a lot in this section of the book. Then, the *SMPTE ST.2065-2:2012* and the *SMPTE ST.2065-3:2012* refer to film densities encoding metrics; the *SMPTE ST.2065-4:2013* and the *SMPTE ST.2065-5:2016* are subject of the container to store this data, being the last one dedicated to the EXR. We will discuss every subject in different sections of this part of the book. Now let's go ahead and review the *ACES Working Spaces* Standards.
ACES WORKING SPACES STANDARDS

There are four dedicated color-working spaces in ACES with their respective standard denomination on the left.

- S-2013-001 *ACESproxy*: An Integer Log Encoding of ACES Image Data
- S-2014-003 *ACEScc*: A Logarithmic Encoding of ACES Data for use within Color Grading Systems
- S-2014-004 *ACEScg*: A Working Space for CGI Render and Compositing
- S-2016-001 *ACEScct*: A Quasi-Logarithmic Encoding of ACES Data for use within Color Grading Systems

We have the *ACES proxy color space*, used mainly on set or editorial for monitoring purposes only; the *ACES color correction space* (or *ACEScc*), which is *Log*, specifically design for *DI* (*digital intermediate*), the point of this working space is that grading software and colorists are used to work with *Log* encoded images, so *ACES* has adapted to these systems to reproduce the same response; there is a variation of this space that is the *ACEScct* (or *ACES color correction space with toe*), that has a more natural feeling by including the *toe* (a critical lower region of the *characteristic curve* which behavior defines the look of the black levels and darkest areas of the image), the *toe* is one of the most characteristic features of the film negative support. *ACEScct* provides colorists a more familiar feel for grading compared to *ACEScc*.

However, the one that interest us the most here is the *ACEScg* or *ACES computer graphics space*, which is the only one in this list that is linear. This was conceived for CGI renders and compositing. This is the working space that substitutes the old *"linear"* color space. For your information, when you setup Nuke to use ACES for color management, *ACEScg* is *Nuke working space*, instead of the *default linear light* that has no primaries – as I mentioned in a previous part of this book. The *ACEScg* has defined primaries and a gamut so wide that contains even more than the *Rec2020*, that as you know is required for HDR, and because it is linear our operations behave linearly as we are used to, so this *working space* is perfect for us.

Of course, *ACES* is alive and grows organically, hence many color scientists and image engineers are continually working to improve the system. If you want to stay current with the latest updates or simply dig deeper into different aspect of *ACES*, or simply ask your questions to the community, the best place to go is to the source: *ACES central*.

www.acescentral.com is the place to expand your *ACES* knowledge and join the community forum. It is the most comprehensive and up-to-date website for all things *ACES*. Active *ACES* users, equipment manufacturers, and *academy* staff are available to answer questions and share their experience. As I mentioned earlier, *ACES* is open, free and device-independent, so you should know the platform over which ACES is built, it is called *OpenColorIO*.

OpenColorIO

OCIO is a complete color management solution geared toward motion picture production with an emphasis on visual effects and computer animation. It is free and open-source software. *OCIO* provides a straightforward and consistent user experience across all supporting applications while allowing for sophisticated back-end configuration options suitable for high-end production usage. *OCIO* is LUT-format agnostic, supporting many popular formats. It is governed by the *ASWF*.

OpenColorIO was originally developed and made open-source by *Sony Pictures Imageworks*, and released in 2010. The core design, and the majority of *OCIO 1.0* code, was authored by *Imageworks*, who continue to support and contribute to *OCIO 2.0* development. The design and development of *OpenColorIO 2.0* is being led by *Autodesk*. *Autodesk* submitted a proposal to revitalize the project in 2017, and have authored the majority of *OCIO 2.0* code in the years since. Significant contributions have also been made by *Industrial Light & Magic, Dneg*, and many individuals.

OpenColorIO aims to: be stable, secure, and thoroughly tested on *Linux, macOS*, and *Windows*; be performant on modern *CPUs* and *GPUs*; be simple, scalable, and well documented; be compatible with critical color and imaging standards; provide lossless color processing wherever possible; maintain config backwards compatibility across major versions; have every new feature carefully reviewed by leaders from the motion picture, VFX, animation, and video game industries; have a healthy and active community; receive wide industry adoption.

In brief, *OpenColorIO* is a color management platform made by the people in the VFX & Animation Industry, for the people in the VFX & Animation Industry.

VFX Focused ACES Colorspaces

Let's focus on our area of interest: VFX. So, let's have a look at the two color spaces that we will be handling within our department (Figure 8.2).

The first one is the main ACES color space, and it is defined by its own set of color primaries called *AP0* (*AP* stands for *ACES primaries*, the *0* is to indicate the original set). It completely encompasses the whole visible spectral locus as defined by the *CIE xyY specification*. The *white point* is approximate to the *CIE D60 standard illuminant*, which is the same for all the *ACES working spaces*. This color space is the *ACES 2065-1*, every *ACES compliant* set of images will be encoded into this *color space*.

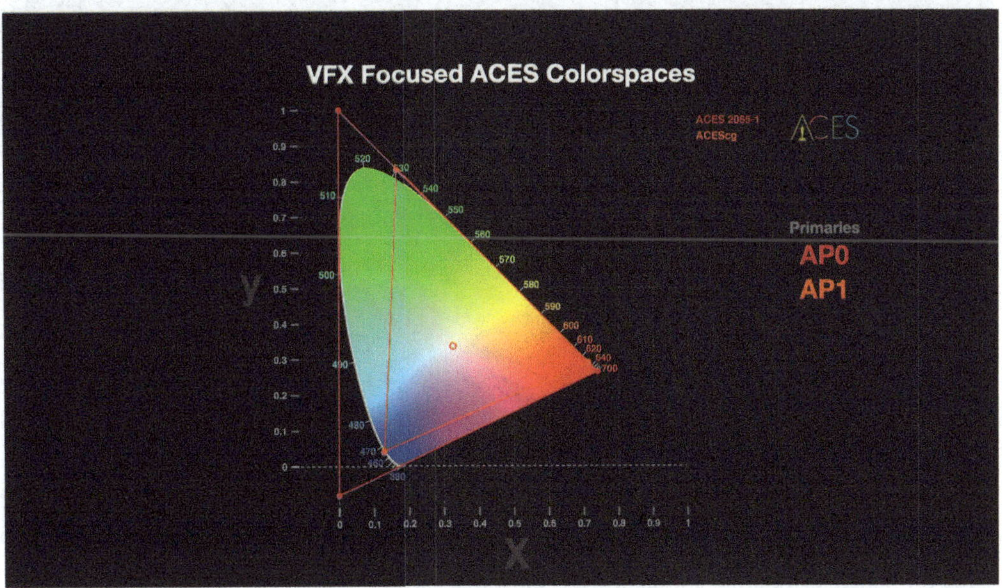

Figure 8.2 Virtual effects (VFX) Focused academy color encoding system (ACES) Color spaces

Then there is another particular set of primaries that defines a color space very relevant for us VFX artists, the *AP1* that describes the *gamut* of the *ACEScg*, the linear color working space used widely in the VFX and animation pipeline. Let me show you something. Let's put this color space in relation to the *Rec2020* that we studied in the previous part of this book (Figure 8.3).

As you can see, *ACEScg* is slightly wider, so we can affirm that the *Rec2020* is contained within the *ACEScg* which is wider and so respects all the color capabilities of the *Rec2020*, and more. To contextualize this, remember the Rec2020 is a display color space, so it was designed to reproduce visible wavelengths of light that could be generated by a display, even if just in theory, but *ACEScg* is not a *display referred color Space*, it is a *color working space* (non-physically realizable) specifically designed to handle CGI, so it does not have the restrictions of a display gamut, hence the *ACEScg* contains the *Rec2020* plus more visible "*yellow*" colors. But why? There are a few reasons, all of them quite technical, as color scientist Thomas Mansencal – one of the most relevant contributors of ACES – explains on *ACESCentral*: it is «*to encompass P3 mostly, ACEScg is a gamut close to BT.2020 but that encompasses P3 and this requires non-physically realizable primaries*». In general, it does not mean that one color space is "better" than another in absolute terms, but it could be more convenient to use one rather than another depending on the purpose. However, the choice of color space and its primaries is critical to achieve a faithful rendering. *ACEScg* encompasses to *P3* which is the actual gamut used in HDR for example (*wrapped* in a *Rec2020* container), so that correlation between *ACEScg* and *P3* makes *AP0* the best available choice for rendering CGI to get results that overall will be closer to a ground truthful spectral rendering.

Just to be clear, you should avoid rendering CGI into *ACES 2065-1*, as it is far from optimal for this kind of light rendering and you will end with undesired values, such as, for instance, negative blue values unable to be handled in a photorealistic manner.

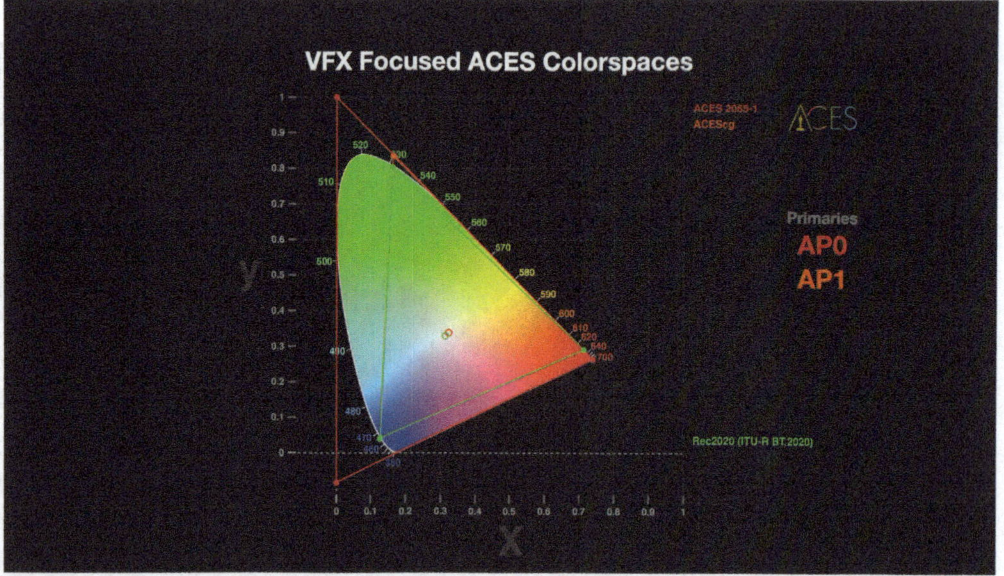

Figure 8.3 Nuke write node academy color encoding system (ACES) compliant EXR settings

Nuke working space, when the color management has been setup to *ACES*, is the *AC-EScg*, this is our "new" *linear color managed work space*.

ACES Compliant EXR

In order to preserve a coherent exchange of files between software, departments or facilities, we have to comply to a standardized methodology to preserve all qualities of the data contained according to our color managed workflow. *SMPTE* defined the standard for the *ACES image container file Layout* in the *ST.2065-4* specifications. But before we get into the specs of the *ACES Compliant OpenEXR*, I think it would be a good idea to understand a bit better the *OpenEXR* file format in itself.

Starting in 1999, *Industrial Light & Magic* developed *OpenEXR*, an HDR image file format for use in digital visual effects production. In early 2003, after using and refining the file format for a few years, *ILM* released *OpenEXR* as an open-source C++ library. In 2013, *Weta Digital* and *ILM* jointly released *OpenEXR* version 2.0, which added support for deep images and multi-part files. The goal of the *OpenEXR Project* is to keep the format reliable and modern and to maintain its place as the preferred image format for entertainment content creation. Major revisions are infrequent, and new features will be carefully weighed against increased complexity. The purpose of the *EXR* format is to accurately and efficiently represent high-dynamic-range scene-linear image data and associated metadata, with strong support for multi-part, multi-channel use cases. The library is widely used in host application software where accuracy is critical, such as photorealistic rendering, texture access, image compositing, deep compositing, and *DI*.

The key features of the EXR are:

- Conceived as a Linear Data Container for VFX Purposes
- Multi-Channel and Multi-View *(monoscopic, stereoscopic, multi-cam)*

  o Available Bit Depths:
  o 16-bit half-floating point
  o 32-bit floating point
  o 32-bit integer

- HDR
- Metadata
- Available Compression Methods:

  o Uncompressed
  o Lossless:

    - Run Length Encoding (RLE)
    - Zip (per scanline or 16 scanline blocks)
    - Wavelet (PIZ)

  o Lossy:

    - B44
    - B44A
    - DWAA
    - DWAB

Since it can store arbitrary channels – *specular*, *diffuse*, *alpha*, *normals*, and various other types – in one file, it takes away the need to store this information in separate files. A good instance to understand key features of having multiple channels is that it also reduces the necessity to *bake-in*[1] the light components data to the final image, also known as *beauty pass*. If a compositor, for instance, is not happy with the current level of specularity, they can adjust that specific channel using the different passes rendered inside the file: this practice is known as multipass compositing. But you can even store other renders that are not meant to reproduce light, such as *AOVs*. Furthermore, you not only have *multi-channel*, but also multi-views, for instance stereoscopic images or even other camera angles. *Multipart*: ability to encode separate, but related, images in one file. This allows for access to individual parts without the need to read other parts in the file.

Support for *16-bit floating-point, 32-bit floating-point*, and – not very common – 32-bit integer pixels, with HDR and *color precision*. Of course, it can also store *metadata*. And flexible support for deep data as well: pixels can store a variable-length list of samples and, thus, it is possible to store multiple values at different depths for each pixel. Hard surfaces and volumetric data representations are accommodated.

Multiple image compression algorithms, both *lossless* and *lossy*. Remember, *lossy* means you reduce the size of the file by discarding information, resulting in a loss of quality; while *lossless* refers to compacting data to save space without losing anything but resulting in an increase of processing (which means time and computer resources). Some of the included codecs can achieve *2:1 lossless compression ratio* on images with film grain. The lossy codecs have been tuned for visual quality and decoding performance.

And many more features you can consult on the OpenEXR Project website: www.openexr.com.

Key Specs of ACES Compliant OpenEXR

- OpenEXR file format

  1 file per frame

- RGB or RGBA

  either mono or stereoscopic

- 16-bit Half Float
- Uncompressed
- Color Encoded in **ACES2065-1 Color Space,** no LUTs to be baked into the data

  no LMT, nor reference rendering transform (RRT), nor output device transform (ODT) baked in the image

- **ST2065-4** Compulsory Metadata Fields in the OpenEXR Header

  Nuke can do this for you!

Now let's focus on the *ACES Compliant* related features, their specifications and, by the way, I will show you how easy is to setup the *write* node to generate an ACES Compliant EXR from Nuke (Figure 8.4).

Let's start with the bit-depth: *ACES* requires 16-bit precision (also known as *half-float*). Completely <u>uncompressed</u>. In Nuke's write node there is a checkbox to write an "*ACES*

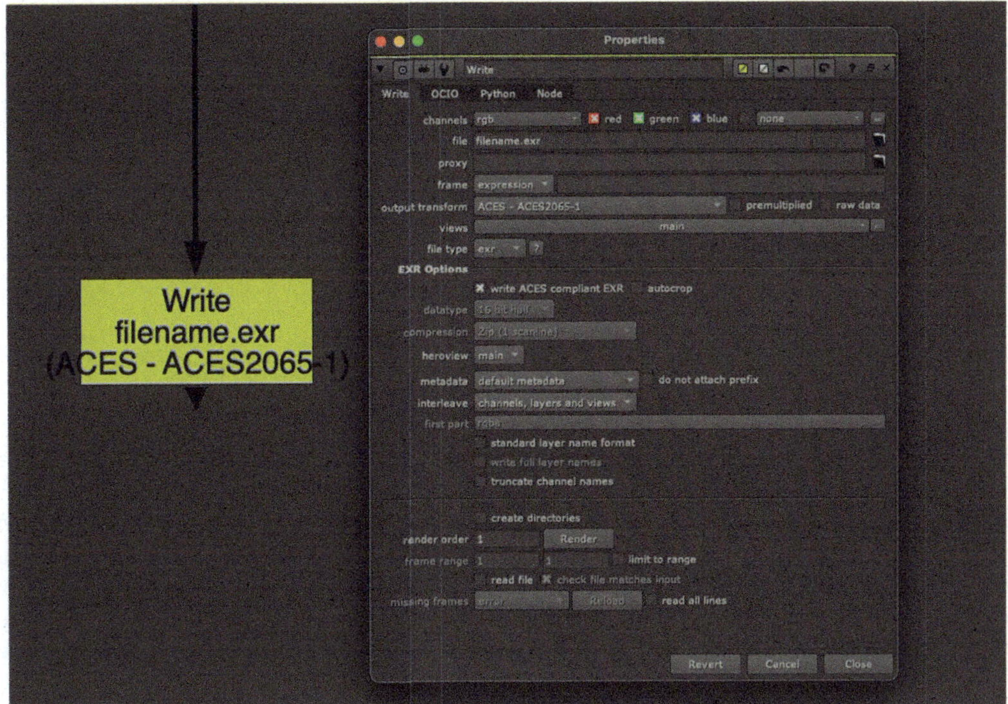

Figure 8.4 Nuke write node academy color encoding system (ACES) Compliant EXR settings

compliant EXR": That will set those two elements I have just mentioned above, but keep in mind you have to specify yourself the channels to be written, *ACES compliant EXRs* accept *RGB* and *RGBA* either *mono-view* or *stereoscopic*. Another advantage of the *ACES compliant EXR* checkbox is that Nuke will write the required metadata to meet the ACES standards in that regard.

That's it. Those are all the key specifics you need to keep in mind for *ACES compliant EXRs*: one file per frame (obviously), no restrictions for naming conventions or frame padding number – but please be wise with your choices – *RGB* or *RGBA* channels, either *mono* or *stereoscopic*; *16-bit half-float* bit depth; *uncompressed*; colorspace ACES2065-1, no LUTs or other color transformations backed into the data; and the *compulsory metadata* that, in our case Nuke will handle for us. That is pretty much it:

- Choose the channels
- Put the *output transform* knob to *"ACES2065-1"*
- Tick on the *"write ACES compliant EXR"* checkbox

Press *Render* and you are done!

Note

1 *To Bake Parameters*: Baking is the process of taking the resulting element driven by various controls external to the controlled element, affecting its properties, and *flattening* the results onto the inherent properties of the element.

9

ACES Color Transformations

The last part left to study, before being completely able to fully understand the ACES color workflow diagram, regards the components of the *ACES color transformations*.

The ACES system comprises various types of color transforms which are designed to work together handling color end-to-end to create a uniform workflow. From the camera to the screen with all the stages in between, understanding them is key to preserve the integrity of the color management workflow. It may seem overwhelming, but fear not, the structure of *ACES color transforms* within the color management workflow is quite simple. Let me show you in a straight line, end-to-end (Figure 9.1).

Those are the three kind of components you will be handling on this workflow: an input transform; an output transform; and one or more (or even none) look modification or creative transforms. That's it, those are the building blocks of our color pipeline. In case you wonder, this is where the VFX operate within the color management workflow.

So, let's see all the ACES color transformations.

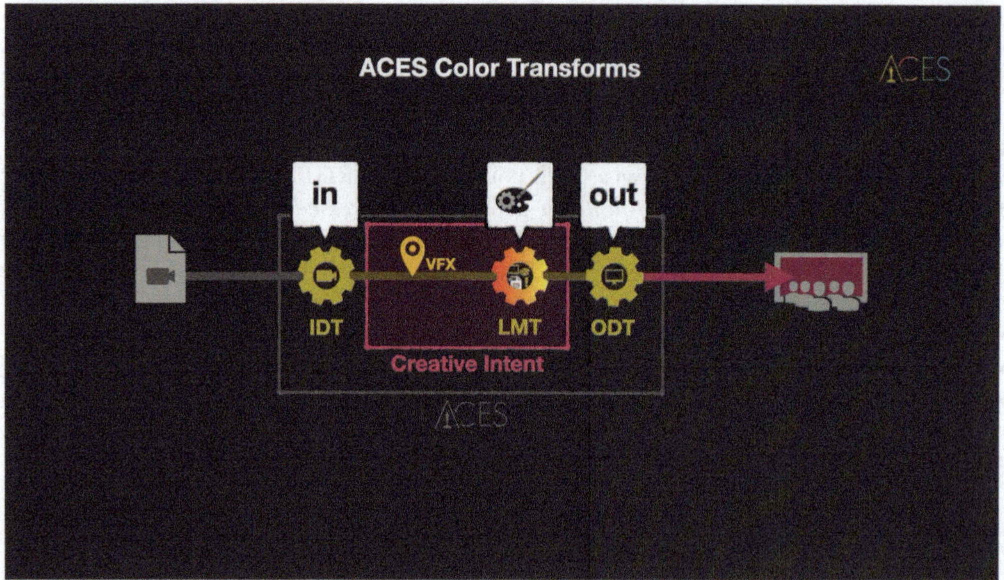

Figure 9.1 Academy color encoding system (ACES) color transforms end-to-end

DOI: 10.4324/b23222-13

Input Device Transform (IDT)

IDT stands for *input device transform*, sometimes referred as just *input transform* (Figure 9.2). The purpose of this operation is to process the original camera data converting the light captured in the scene – and in relation to its established balanced white – into the ACES RGB relative exposure values in the ACES scene linear master color space (*ACES2065-1*).

Camera manufacturers are usually responsible for developing the *IDTs* for their cameras – as nobody knows those cameras better than them – but in the case the manufacturer did not release the *IDT* for a certain camera, the community can develop a *user-derived IDT* to fill the blank. These are the perks of an open-source technology (still creating an *IDT* should be addressed only when the *IDT* is not available by the manufacturer, and not an "*artistic choice*", this is a technical approach, and it is written in CTL programming language). Every footage that needs to enter the ACES pipeline needs an *IDT*, even the same camera can have multiple *IDTs* depending on different camera settings – for different lighting conditions – (for instance, different white balances). It is quite common to find at least two different *IDTs* for the same camera, one optimized for *daylight* (which corresponds to the *CIE illuminant D55*); and another for *tungsten* (corresponding to the *ISO 7589 studio tungsten illuminant*), but the manufacturers are encouraged to provide *IDTs* for other common lighting scenarios in cinematography, like for instance, *overcast daylight*, *fluorescent*, etc.

Keep in mind that the input device color space is regarded as *scene referred colorimetry*, which means the original camera data is acquired in the form of *non-color-rendered RGB* image values from a captured scene lit by an assumed illumination source (the scene adopted white) so it cannot be visualized without a display color transform. In the other hand the *ACES display referred colorimetry*, resembles a traditional film image rendering encoded with the characteristic *s-shaped* curve, but remember the *ACES 2065-1* is not a display color space, it is still *scene referred* for the workflow as it uses the scene relative exposure values.

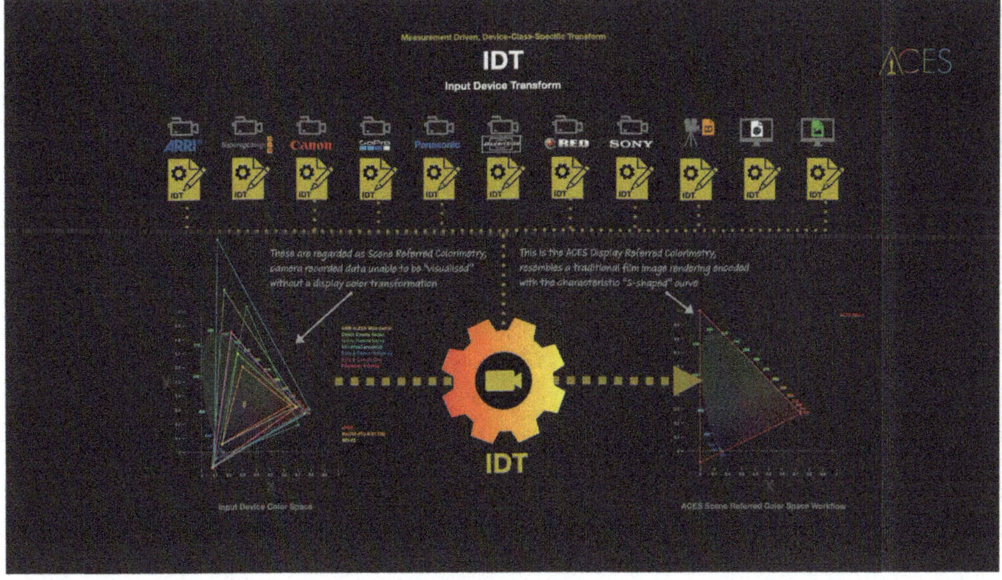

Figure 9.2 Academy color encoding system (ACES) input device transform (IDT)

The question now is: "Do we apply the *IDT* to the raw material before any other process?" Well, not exactly, the *IDT* is expected to be applied after the basic processes of the RAW material, such as: *dark frame subtraction, noise reduction, flat fielding, demosaicing,* conversion to a *device-specific RGB* color space, and/or *deblurring.* If you must apply any of these process to you footage you should do it before applying the *IDT* to get into the ACES workflow, and if *linearization* or *white balance* takes place prior to one of the processes above, then that linearization or *white balance* should obviously be excluded from the *IDT* to avoid reapplying the same operation twice.

Note that there are also *IDTs* for images that are not coming directly from the camera, for instance *film scans,* or *sRGB* images coming, for example, from the Internet, or any other computer-generated image originally not rendered into the ACES color workflow. Those are more generic *IDTs.*

Once an *ACES IDT* is applied, your footage is in the ACES color managed workflow, but in order to be visualized color must be rendered using the *ACES RRT* and *ODT* appropriate for the display used for critical color evaluation. Let's have a look at those transforms.

Reference Rendering Transform (RRT)

Think of RRT (Figure 9.3) it as the *"render engine"* component of the ACES workflow. The *RRT* converts the linear *scene-referred colorimetry* to *display-referred.* It resembles traditional film image rendering with an *s-shaped curve* and has a larger *gamut* and *dynamic range* available to allow for rendering to any output device – even those not yet invented. But the *RRT* alone does not allow you to display the data, in order to be able to put the data on a screen the *RRT* must be combined with the required *ODT* to create viewable data for displays and projectors. The output of the *RRT* is called *output color encoding specifications (OCES)* – Yes,

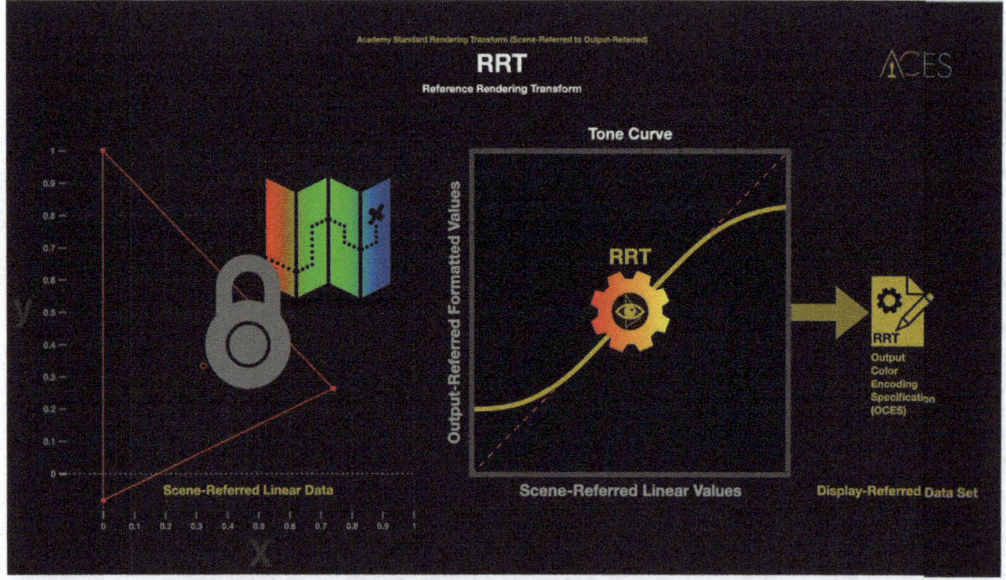

Figure 9.3 Academy color encoding system (ACES) reference rendering transform (RRT)

OCES with an O, it isn't a typo. I know, I know … you have no idea what the *ODT* is, but no worries because I am going to explain it to you in a minute. I just want you to know that in Nuke, as in other software, you do not have to worry about the *RRT* as the software will automatically take care of it, you just need to use the right *ODT* for the target display. The RRT is a technical process that is happening behind the hood, essential for the *ODT* to happen, but essentially you, as an artist, just need to know that it happens together with the *ODT*. Well, let's have a look at this *ODT* then.

Output Device Transform (ODT)

ODT stands for *output device transform*, also known as *ACES output transform* (Figure 9.4). The *output transform* is the final step in the ACES processing pipeline. It takes the RRT with its *ultra-wide gamut* and *HDR data* and adapts it for any screen of choice and their color spaces, such as *P3*, *Rec709*, *Rec2020*, etc. Every kind of monitor, TV or projector has its own color space, just be sure you are outputting the right one for every target screen. For instance, traditional computer monitors, as we had discussed earlier in this course, still use the *sRGB* color space, while an *HDTV* uses a *Rec709*, traditional digital cinema projectors use *P3* … and so on. Know your display well to be sure that the image represented on the screen is the right one.

Just a note about the upcoming diagrams. Since Nuke handles the *RRT* together with the *ODT* under the hood automatically, every time I will refer to the *display output transform* I will recall just the *ODT* assuming you know I mean *RRT* and *ODT* together, just to simplify things in a clear and practical way. In any case, in Nuke, there is nothing you have to do about the *RRT*.

See? Now you know the *transformations* at both ends. It is time we explore the *transformations* in the middle of the workflow. But before getting to the specific *ACES transform* I

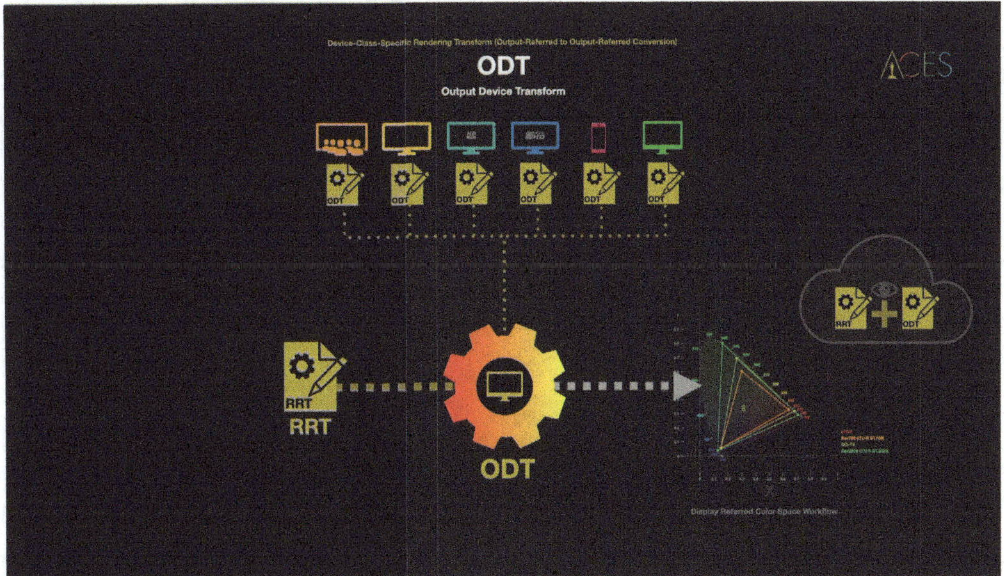

Figure 9.4 Academy color encoding system (ACES) output device transform (ODT)

would like to discuss an element that is widely used by cinematographers, which is not just for ACES workflows but for any color management workflow, I am talking about *CDLs*.

American Society of Cinematographers (ASC) Color Decision List (CDL)

CDLs are not part of the *ACES transforms*, but since they can be used in the ACES workflow as *LMT* (that we will discuss later in the next chapter), and they are very popular, I think it would be important to know *CDLs* well.

The *American Society of Cinematographers Color Decision List (ASC CDL)* is a format for the exchange of basic primary color grading information between equipment and software from different manufacturers. The format defines the math for three functions: *slope*, *offset*, and *power*; and an additional control for the *Saturation*. The ASC CDL allows color corrections made with one device at one location to be applied or modified by other devices elsewhere. For example, a cinematographer filming on location can create a color correction with a small portable device, sending the *ASC CDL* color correction to a colorist in post-production to use as a starting point for final color correction. To communicate "*looks*" usefully in this fashion, *calibrations*, *viewing environments*, *devices*, and any *output transforms* – like for instance the "*film look*" – must be managed very carefully; in general, they should be identical at origination and subsequent viewing. Hence, the importance of consistent and accurate color management from set to post-production. Let's have a look at a visual representation of the mathematical functions.

Slope

The *slope* is the first operation to be applied to the image, as you know the order of the operations matters to the result (Figure 9.5). The Slope multiplies the code values with a

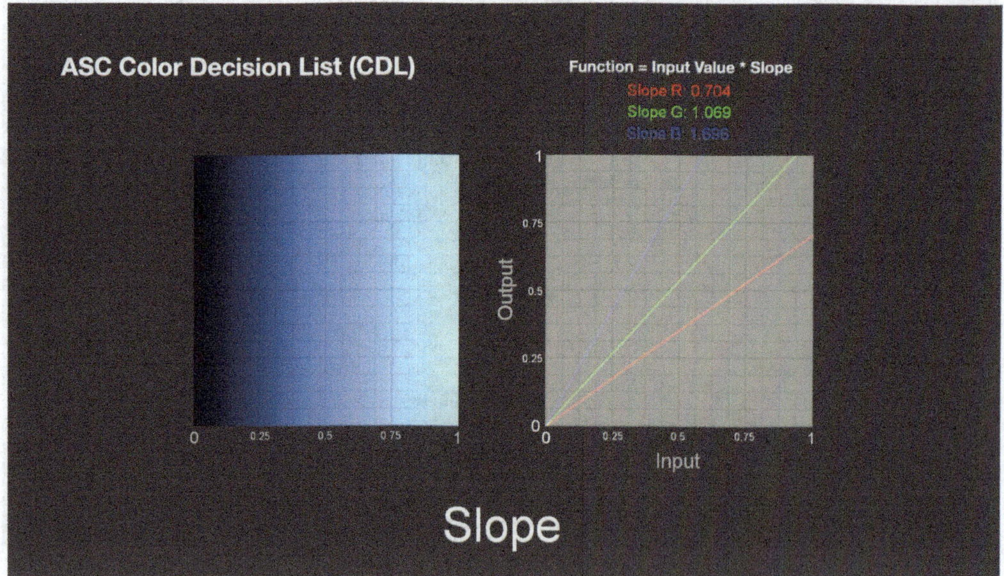

Figure 9.5 American Society of Cinematographers color decision list (ASC CDL) – slope

factor. It means the *slope* is a multiply operation. You can modify every R, G, B parameter separately or altogether. The typical characteristic of the *multiply* operation is that the point 0 – pure black – (the base of the curve), as you can see, remains the same, and the higher the input value, the more it is going to be affected by the multiplication factor. You can use the *slope* to increase or decrease the *amount* of light, as the multiplication can be interpreted as a virtual slider for exposure (to "*multiply*" the amount of light). The default value for the Slope is 1, as you know, when you multiply something by 1 it remains the same.

Offset

After the *slope*, the next operation to be applied is the *offset* (Figure 9.6). The *offset* adds or subtracts a certain value to all codes, or input values. As you can see it modifies all values at the same distance, regardless their distribution on the input curve. It is a *plus* operator. The key point of the offset is that it changes the *black point* and the *black levels* as much as the *bright areas*, in a parallel translation of the whole curve; however, due to a question of perception, the *offset* is more noticeable in the *dark areas* – remember I discussed before the "*noticeable differences*" where little steps in the low areas of the curve are more noticeable than the same increases in a higher area? – so it is often used to modify the *black levels*, with the advantage of not changing the contrast distribution of the image. The contrast is represented in this graphic with the inclination of the line, the more it is inclined, the higher the contrast. The *offset* moves all up or down without modifying the inclination. The default value for the *offset* is 0, because when you add or subtract 0 to any given value it remains always the same. When any of these operations are applying their defaults they are said to be "*at rest*", meaning they are not modifying the result.

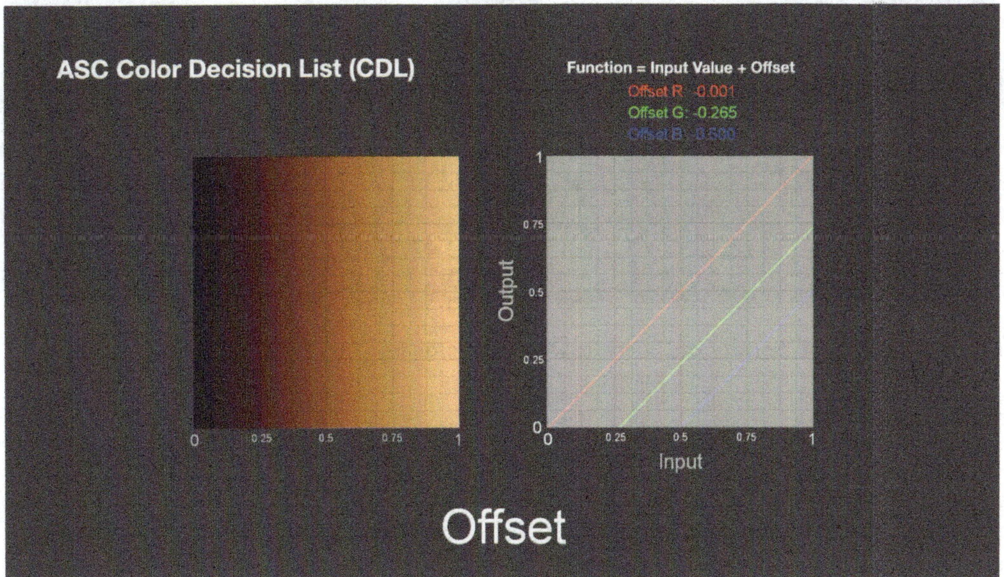

Figure 9.6 American Society of Cinematographers color decision list (ASC CDL) – offset

Power

The third operation applied to the curve, after *slope* and *offset*, is the *power*, which is the *power function* of the resulting values from the previous operations (Figure 9.7). As our input value is normalized, meaning the range of available values goes from 0 to 1, the *power* function will be applied to all the decimal positions in between, and the end points, 0 and 1 will always remain the same. Keep in mind that 0 raised to the power of any number will be 0 and 1 raised to the power of any number will be 1 in any case. So, the *power* function will deal with the values "in the middle". You can say it modifies the "*mid-tones*" of the curve, slightly more emphasized toward the lower-mid area (where our perception notices more details). I like to see the *power* as a balance distribution of the contrast as well. As you can see in the figure, by increasing or decreasing the *power* value, it bends the curve. Notice this can be interpreted as a "*horizontal flattening*" on one section of the curve and an "*vertical rising of the slope*" on the other side, so you increase the contrast in one half, and decrease it on the other half, yet maintaining the *black point* and the *white point* untouched. The *power* function may seem very familiar to the *gamma* operation, but they are not the same, even if their behavior seems to be the same, but they should not be considered the same thing to avoid confusion. By the way, the default value for the *power* is 1, as any number raised to the power of 1 is the same number as before.

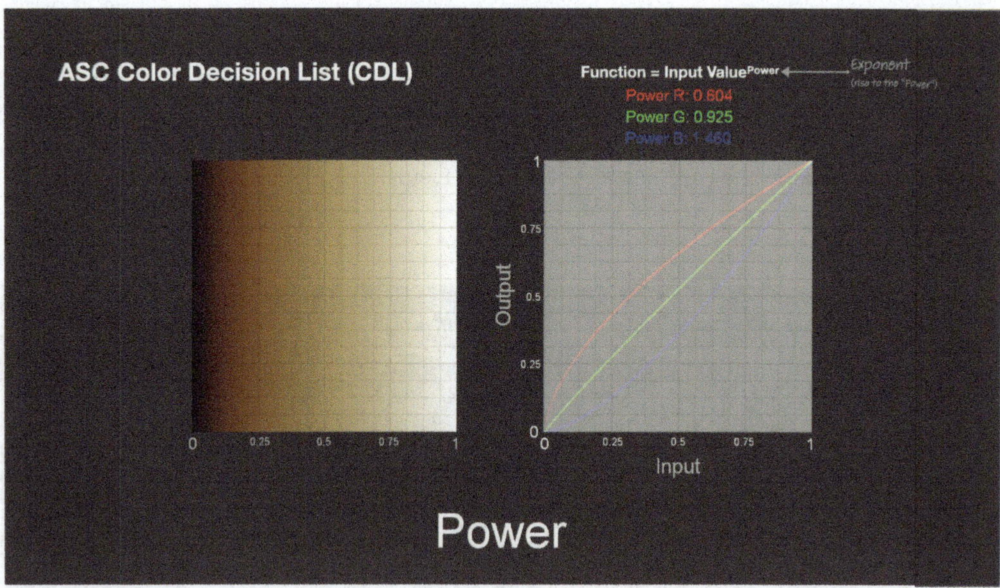

Figure 9.7 American Society of Cinematographers color decision list (ASC CDL) – power

Saturation

After the three core operations: *slope, offset* and *power* are applied, one additional filter and parameter is specified that influences all three color channels at once: the *saturation* (Figure 9.8). The *saturation* affects the balance between the three channels, saturating – creating bigger imbalance between the value peaks of one channel against the others – or de-saturating the colors – reducing that unbalance between channels – (with color components

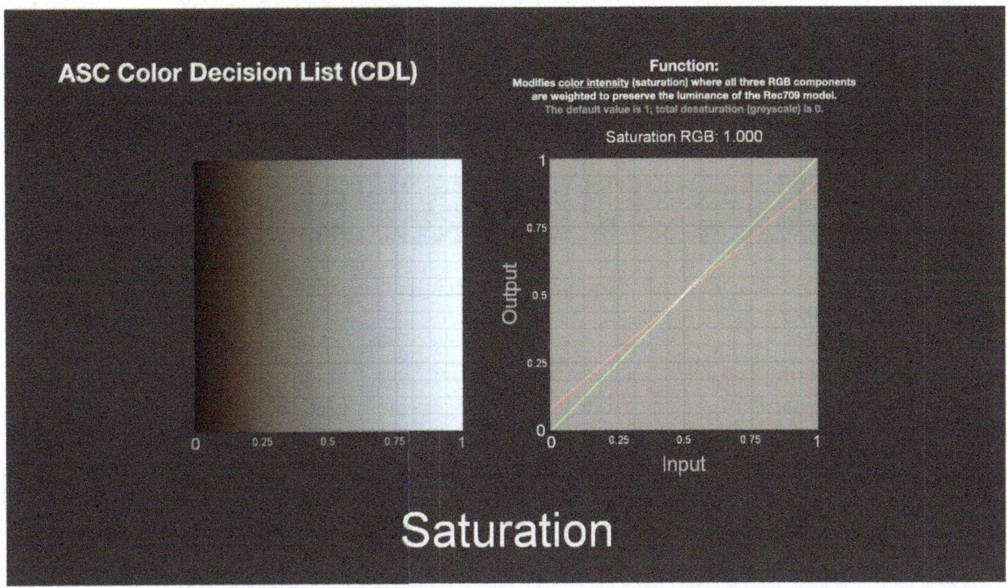

Figure 9.8 American Society of Cinematographers color decision list (ASC CDL) – saturation

weighted with values from the *Rec.709 matrix*. In other words, the intent is to change the saturation without changing the luminance, as you know, each RGB component influences the resulting luminance differently than the others, being the green the maximum influencer and blue the least). Keep in mind that the saturation refers to the imbalance between the input RGB values, more saturation means more separation between the R, G and B values, while no saturation means the RGB values are overlapping. The default saturation value is 1.

ASC CDL File Formats

Let's have a look at the file formats to store our *color decision lists*.

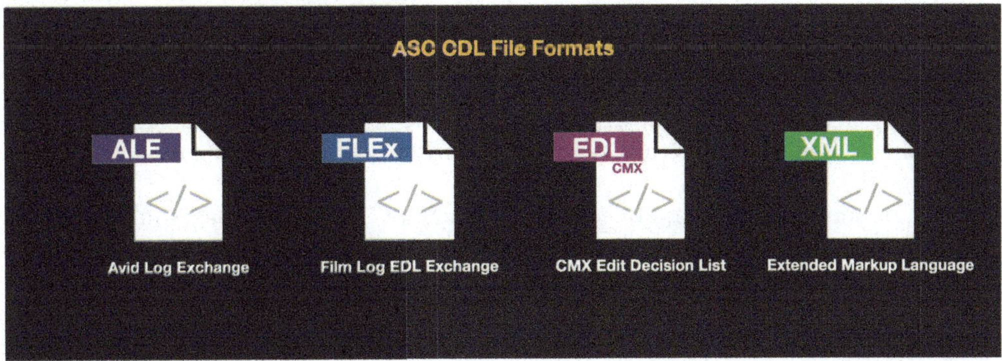

Figure 9.9 American Society of Cinematographers color decision list (ASC CDL) file formats

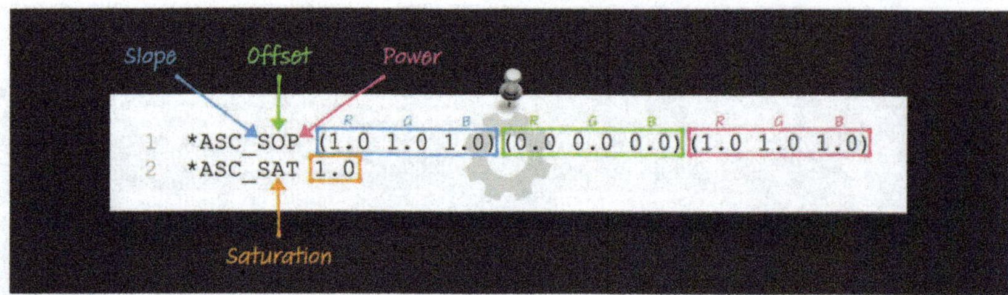

Figure 9.10 American Society of Cinematographers color decision list (ASC CDL) data components

The *ASC* has defined an *XML* schema for exchanging *ASC CDL* data, along with other metadata about what footage the color corrections were applied to, the type of input signal used, and the viewing device and environment (Figure 9.9). They have also standardized methods for using ASC CDL data within the following file formats: *Avid Log Exchange (ALE)*, *Film Log EDL Exchange (FLEx)*, *Edit Decision List (CMX)*, and *Extended Markup Language (XML)*.

Each function uses a number for the red, green, and blue color channels for a total of nine numbers comprising a single-color decision. A tenth number, *Saturation* – specified in the Version 1.2 release – applies to the R, G, and B color channels in combination. This is how the values look written in the file:

As I said before, the CDL is not, strictly speaking, a component of ACES, but it is compatible with this workflow by using the *LMT* within the ACES set of color transformations (Figure 9.10). *CDLs* are very common so I thought you better get familiar with those before we start discussing the last component of the ACES. Let's have a look at the LMT.

Look Modification Transform (LMT)

LMTs are a very powerful component of the *Academy Color Encoding System* and offer extraordinary flexibility in ACES-based workflows. The *LMT* is an ACES-to-ACES transform that systematically change the appearance of ACES-encoded data viewed through an *ACES output transform* (remember *RRT+ODT*). This means the *LMT* must be applied to an ACES workflow, after the footage has been ingested into the ACES pipeline through its correspondent *IDT*. Worth noting that in case of visual effects shots, any *LMTs* are usually applied after the compositing process of the shot, I mean after the VFX are completed, but in Nuke we can integrate *LMTs* within the composing process for visualization purposes, so you see the shot result as it is intended to be seen on the screen, and this is critical to be able to keep in consideration the artistic intent of the filmmakers while creating the VFX, to optimize the attention focus and to avoid "surprises" at the end when the shot is turned around to DI.

LMTs are mechanisms to apply an infinite variety of "*looks*" to images in ACES-based workflows. Any adjustment away from the starting default reference rendering is considered a "*look*" within an ACES framework. By this definition, a "*look*" can be as simple as *ASC CDL* values preserved from set to define a starting grade. They exist because some color manipulations can be complex and having a pre-set for a complex look makes a colorist's work more efficient. A key distinction is interactive image modification, which can either be across the entire frame – *primary grade* or *first light* – or isolated regions of interest –

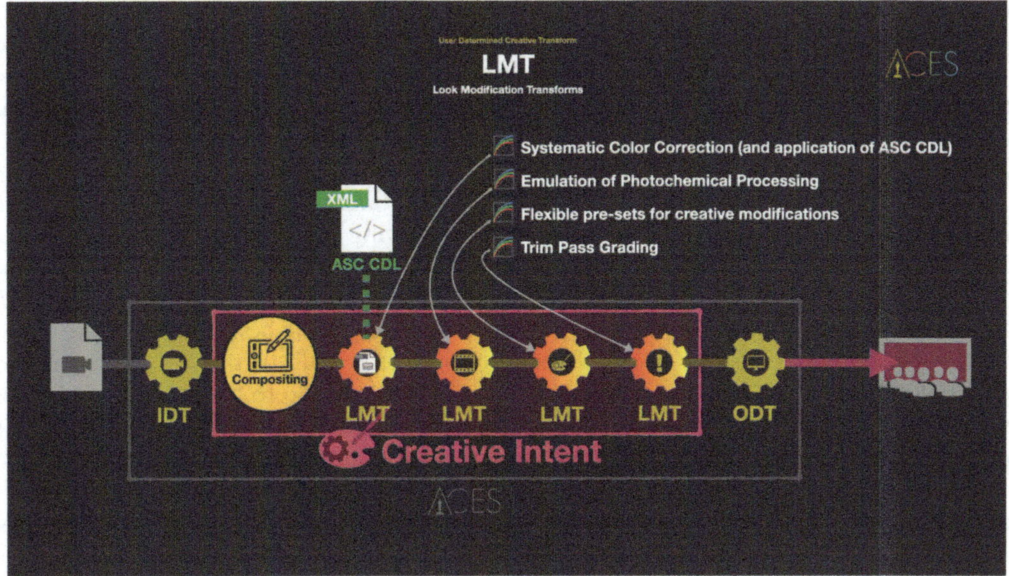

Figure 9.11 ACES look modification transform (LMT)

secondary grade, or more generically just *grading*, as it comprises all types of operations. The ACES term for preset systematic, full-frame – so *primary grade* – image modification is "*look modification*". It allows custom and systematic color changes to a set of clips or entire timeline to realize a chosen creative intent.

LMTs are always ACES-to-ACES transforms, in other words, the *LMTs* are applied to the footage once directly translated from camera-native image data into the *ACES 2065-1* color space (using the correspondent *IDT*). The resulting output of the *LMT* will be still in the *ACES 2065-1* color space (and referred in papers as *ACES'*, to indicate it is *ACES* but it has been modified from its original look), so in order to view this new set of modified data, as usual an *ACES output transform* is required. So *LMTs* happen within the *ACES scene referred working space*.

Once the footage is in *ACES*, *LMTs* can be applied in a variety of ways. Let's see a few common uses (Figure 9.11):

Well, the first one I like to mention is to create a *systematic color correction*, like for instance to apply a *CDL*.

It can be a starting point for *grading*. *LMTs* offer traditional colorists' tools for grading and manipulating images. They can be used project-wide to reduce contrast and saturation across all shots, providing what might be a more preferred starting point for colorists accustomed to flatter and more muted starting images.

They can be used to match or transfer to an existing *look*, like for instance the *emulation of a photochemical process*, a "*bleach bypass*", or a *Technicolor* particular color rendition, etcetera.

One of the most popular uses is to create *presets*. That enables looks to be reusable and applicable within all contexts, regardless of image source. *LMTs* are basically *preset looks*, and one may find it desirable to build up a "*library of looks*" made up of pre-built filters that can be used to quickly decide an initial grade or a "*show LUT*" look on any given project. Further grading adjustments can be made on top of the new starting point. These are very complex creative looks and can make colorists' work more efficient by allowing them to quickly get the creative *look* they (and the filmmaker) want, and to spend more time on shot- and/or region-specific creative color requests from clients. In *ACES*, well-designed *LMTs* are interchangeable.

Another use I would like to mention is the *trim pass grading*. The purpose of the *trim pass* is to "*accentuate*" the image for any non-standard viewing environment. For instance, if a film has been graded in HDR, that is our reference master; then to create the SDR version for TV you use an *ODT* for the *Rec709* color space, which is radically different. The *ODT* has applied a procedural *tone mapping* that, overall, will get the best translation from the HDR look into the SDR, but due to the limitations of the SDR, certain color elements of the HDR grading will be lost in the SDR or even look wrong. So to "correct" these issues, we apply a *trim pass*, which is another final *LMT* that has been designed to work with that particular *ODT* in order to "*accentuate*" the image for that particular medium.

The important thing is that the *LMTs*, within the ACES color managed pipeline, represent the image with its creative intent, that is carried and respected *end-to-end*. For us, VFX artists, this is a very important element of the *color management workflow* as it allows us to visualize the final look of the image we are working with, even if we work with the camera footage just ingested into *ACES*, but able to display it as it would look at the end of the journey.

Here you are, the ACES pipeline end-to-end, from the camera to the screen.

Now, remember when we were talking about the *scene referred workflow* in general terms? You should be confident that you are able to understand the ACES diagram I showed you a few pages back. Time to face the ACES workflow for VFX, and we are going to finish the argument in the next chapter by understanding the actual *ACES Scene Referred VFX workflow* with an example.

10

ACES Scene Referred VFX Workflow Example

And here we are. Everything you have learned with this book has led us to this point.

Let's use the pipeline map we used in a previous chapter for the scene referred color management workflow to be used for comparison with the ACES one (so you can see the similarities and differences) (Figure 10.1).

Now I am going to demonstrate to you now that you actually understand *color management* and how to interpret the following VFX Workflow diagram. Let's start with the base, the software that will act as a hub for our project to deal with all footages and CGI, in this case, as an example, I will use Nuke because it's the industry standard. You will see how versatile it is and how easy it is to setup once you know the fundamentals you learned with this course.

So, the first point in this VFX workflow diagram is Nuke's workspace.

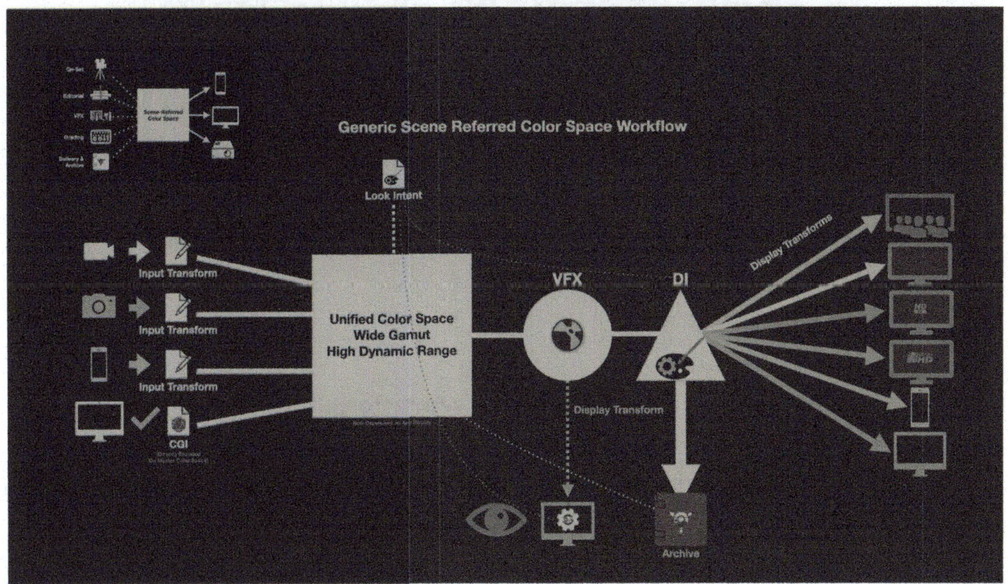

Figure 10.1 Generic scene referred color space workflow

DOI: 10.4324/b23222-14

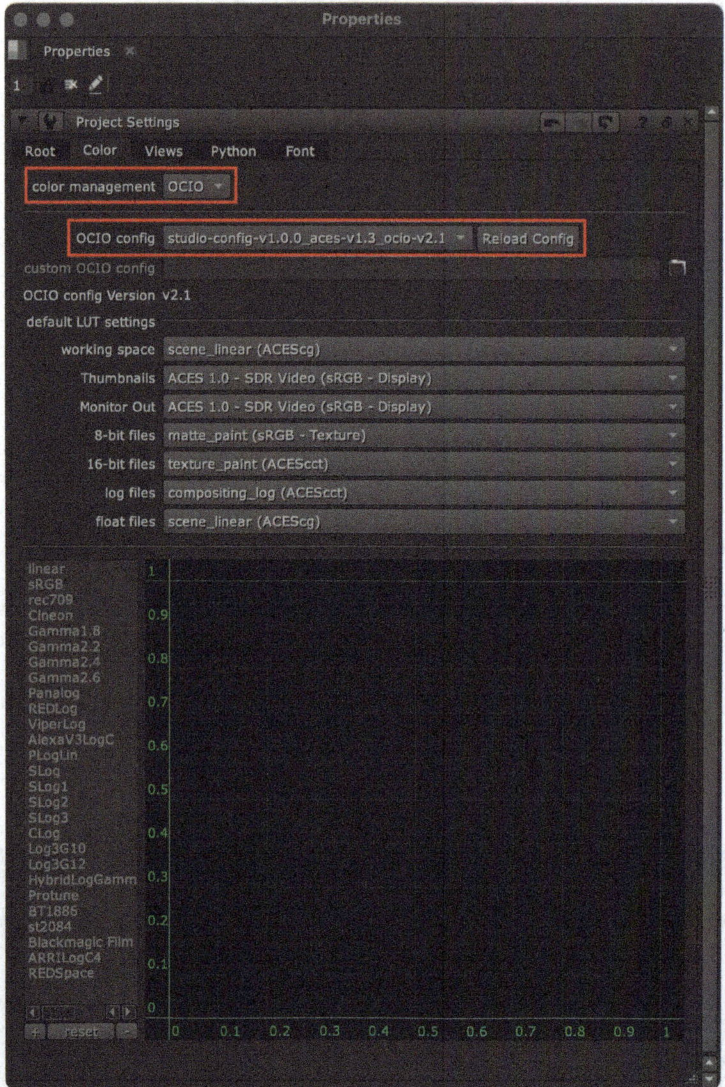

Figure 10.2 Nuke project settings/color

Nuke End-to-End ACES Color Managed Workflow

Here you set the *project settings* to *color manage* using *OpenColorIO*, then select the *OCIO configuration* to *ACES*, and that will automatically set up Nuke Working Space to *ACEScg* and the other default standards and recommended color spaces for the different typologies of images we are going to deal with, as you can see in the panel (Figure 10.2). Nuke is ready. Remember *ACEScg* is linear, not to be confused with *ACES2065-1* which is the main *ACES color space*. *ACEScg* was designed for us, the VFX Department, to work in a *linear color space* within a specific set of primaries framework (Figure 10.3).

Now let's bring in our camera footage (Figure 10.4).

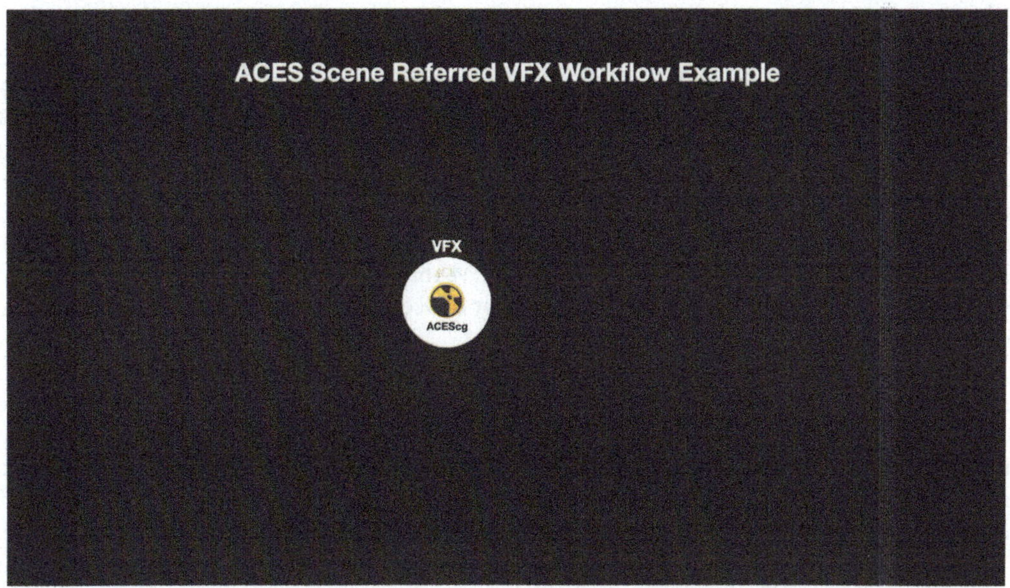

Figure 10.3 Academy color encoding system (ACES) scene referred vfx workflow example – Nuke ACEScg workspace

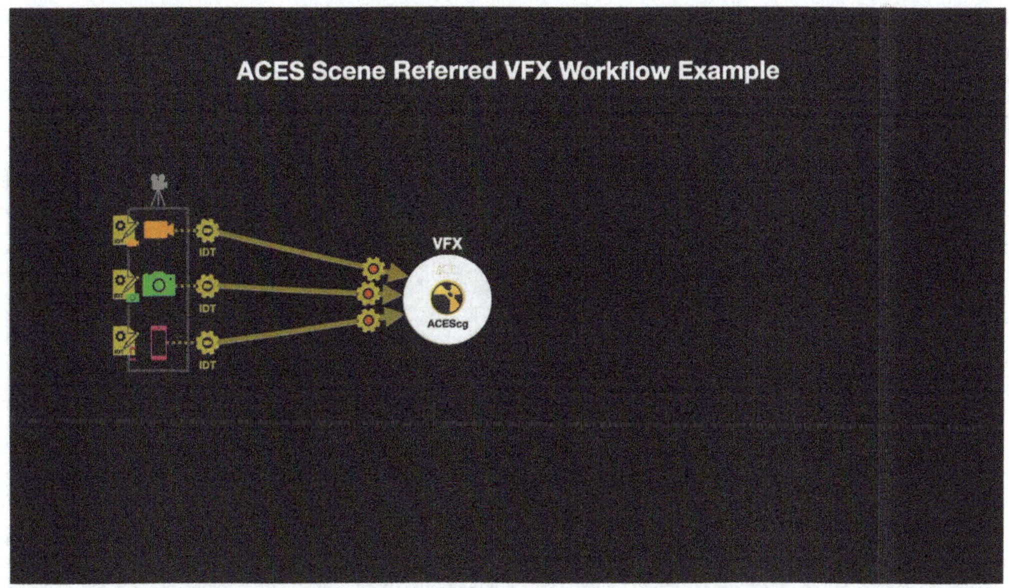

Figure 10.4 Academy color encoding system (ACES) scene referred vfx workflow example – camera footage & input device transform (IDT)

I am going to add different sources, such as a *digital cinema camera*, a *video camera*, and even a *smart phone video*. These are our *camera sources*. So, we just need, for each source to select its respective *IDT*, a knob indicated in the properties of the *read node* as "*input transform*". Once you have done that, Nuke will interpret all footage with its right colorimetry into the *ACES workflow*. Nuke has all the *IDTs* already available, you do not need to import anything, just select it from the menu. And this was the first *color transform* from your ACES workflow. However during the process of compositing, we usually also deal with other kinds of footage other than that coming from the camera from set, for instance *stock footage* from a library. Actually, the process is exactly the same, just select the appropriate "*Input Transform*" to bring it in from its original color space. For instance, if you have a video clip encoded in *Rec709* color space (very common), just use the '*Rec709*' option. If you have a still image from a stock service encoded in *sRGB* (also very common), then choose the '*sRGB*' input transform utility. Yeah, it's really this simple. You can ingest anything; just be sure you apply the right color space as *input transform* to maintain the right colorimetry (Figure 10.5).

What about CGI? They can be rendered directly into the *ACEScg* color space, so they do not need to be converted, just *interpreted*, and this would be the best-case scenario. But in the case you have CGI that is not already in *ACEScg* and just the old fashioned Linear, just ingest it using the *linear* color space – or whatever color space it was encoded for that matter. Do not get me wrong, it can be done for sure, but let's be clear, if you are working in an *ACES color managed pipeline* you are expected to render your CGI directly in *ACEScg* color space.

So now you have camera footage, stock footages and generic images, and CGI ... what is missing to ingest? Well, you are probably not working alone and maybe there are other facilities or other departments providing you with other sources of images that had been pre-processed. In the case of receiving any footage, in a well color-managed pipeline you can expect to receive *ACES compliant EXRs*. This instance is very common if you are working, for example, with a third party laboratory providing you with the scans from the native camera footage, instead of you doing the ingestion of the camera footages. In this case, as you know, those *ACES compliant EXR sequences* are encoded using the *ACES2065-1* color space. Just make sure they are interpreted this way in the *input transform* (Figure 10.6).

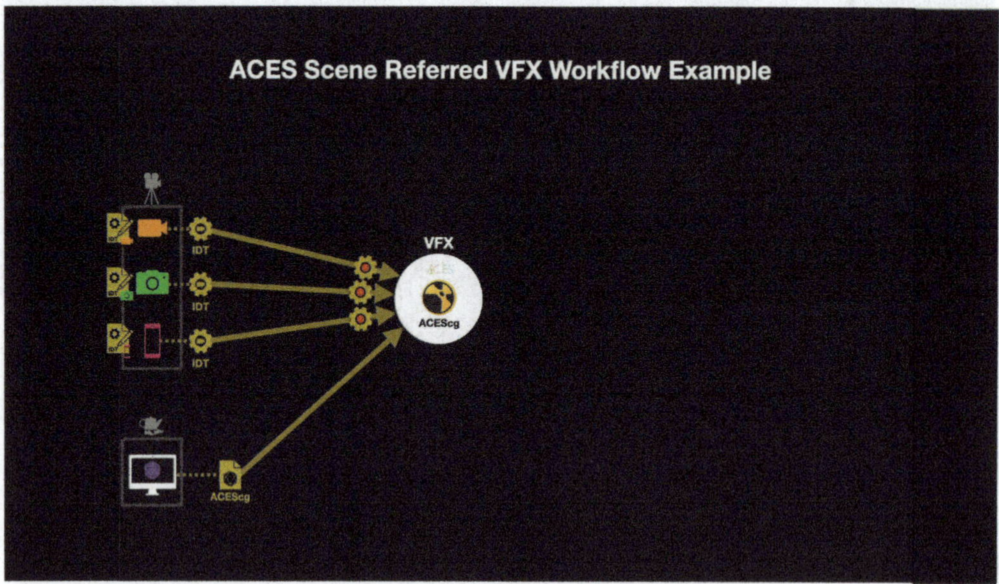

Figure 10.5 Academy color encoding system (ACES) scene referred virtual effects (VFX) workflow example – computer-generated imagery (CGI)

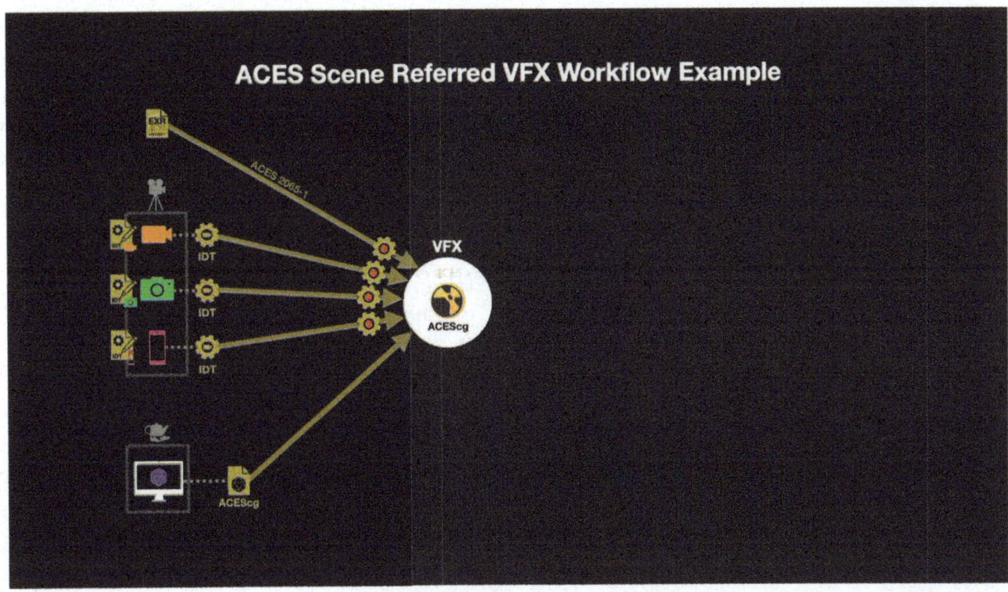

Figure 10.6 Academy color encoding system (ACES) scene referred virtual effects (VFX) workflow example – ACES compliant EXR image sequences

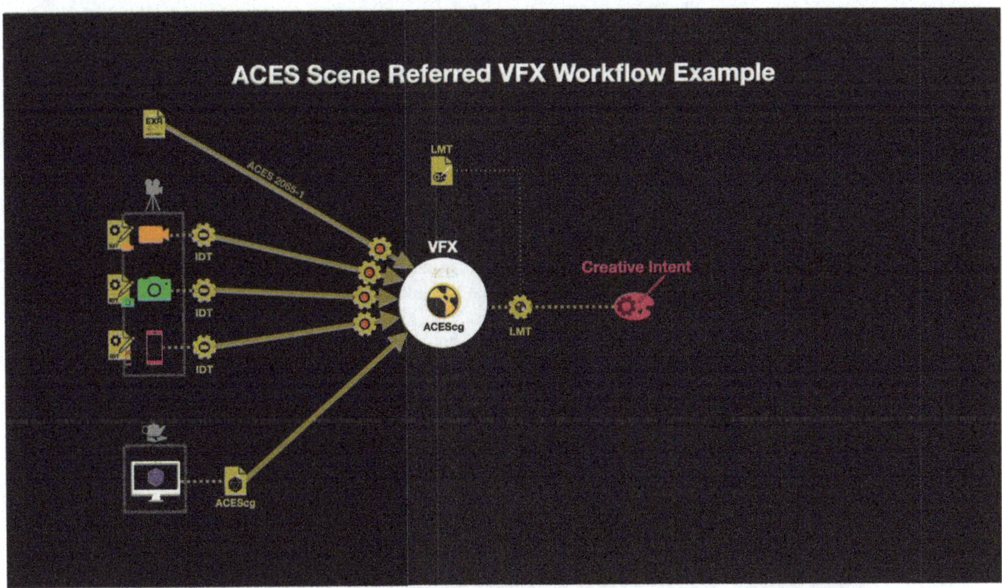

Figure 10.7 Academy color encoding system (ACES) scene referred virtual effects (VFX) workflow example – look modification transform (LMT)

This is the first part of the diagram, that refers to ingesting the materials, as you can see it is all about the *IDT*. Now let's move to the middle section and discuss *looks*, or as ACES call them: *LMTs* (Figure 10.7).

I am going to represent any *LMT* I want to apply to my viewer here with this *LMT* file. I'm going to use one just for clarity but remember you can apply as many as you want, the process will be the same, just keep in mind <u>the order of the color transformations matters</u>, so ensure they are in the right order. To apply the different kinds of LMTs you have a few nodes in Nuke under the *OCIO* menu in the *color nodes* menu, you can use depending on what you need, for instance:

- The *OCIOFileTransform*, that uses the *OpenColorIO* library to load a color space conversion from a file (usually a *1D* or *3D LUT*) and apply it, however you can also load other file-based transformations, for example an *ASC color correction XML* (Figure 10.8);
- The *OCIOCDLtransform*, where you can manually apply *ASC CDL* parameters, and even export your custom *CDL*, or by contrary import a *CDL file* provided (Figure 10.9);
- The *OCIOLookTransform* that offers you a way to apply per-shot color corrections as specified using the *OpenColorIO* look mechanism. It sets which looks to apply, referencing the *OCIO configuration*. You can chain looks together using a list delimited by commas or colons. You can even use this node to reverse a color correction already applied (like the "*reverse*" *knob* within the *grade node*), that is called *direction*, being "*forward*" the application of the transformation, and "*backwards*" the reverse operation (Figure 10.10).

All these operations represent the creative intent in terms of color. You can either *bake-in* the color transformations into the resulting image, if required, or just apply it to the *viewer* as an *input process*, so you work visualizing the color transformations but actually working on the original source material without actually modifying its look. Therefore, the colorist and other technicians from *DI* could apply the same colorimetry parameters as per the non-VFX footage (also referred as *drama shots*). This instance is very common. The *Input process* is just a group of nodes encapsulated in a *group node* named (by default) "*VIEWER_INPUT*", that processes those nodes inside the group just on the *viewer* (Figure 10.11).

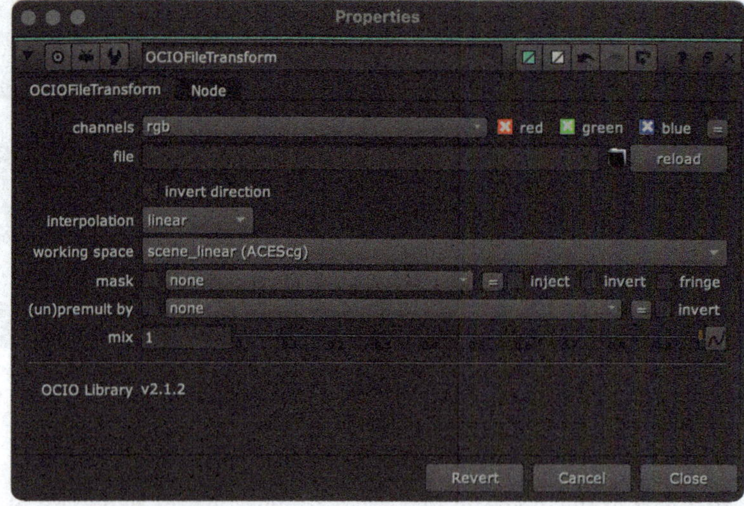

Figure 10.8 Nuke – OCIOFileTransform

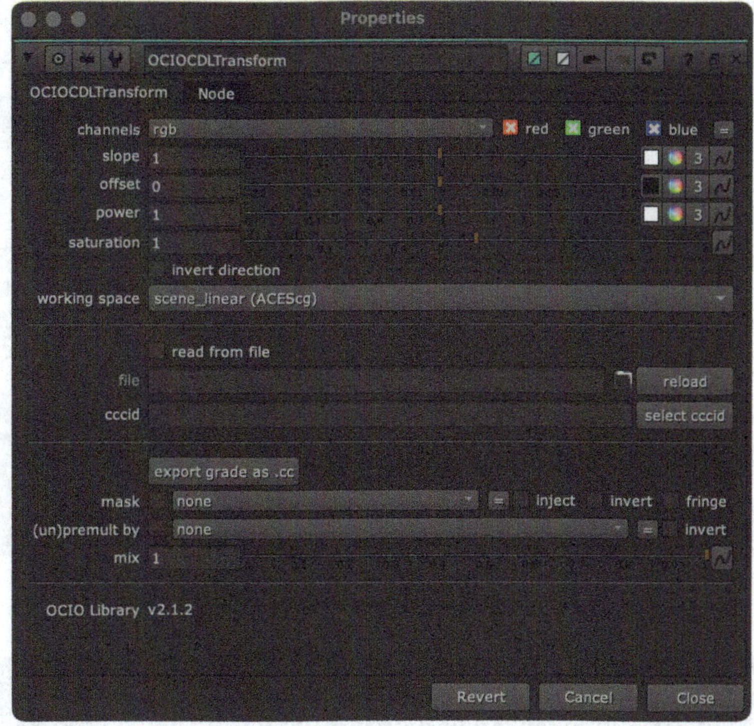

Figure 10.9 Nuke – OCIOCDLTransform

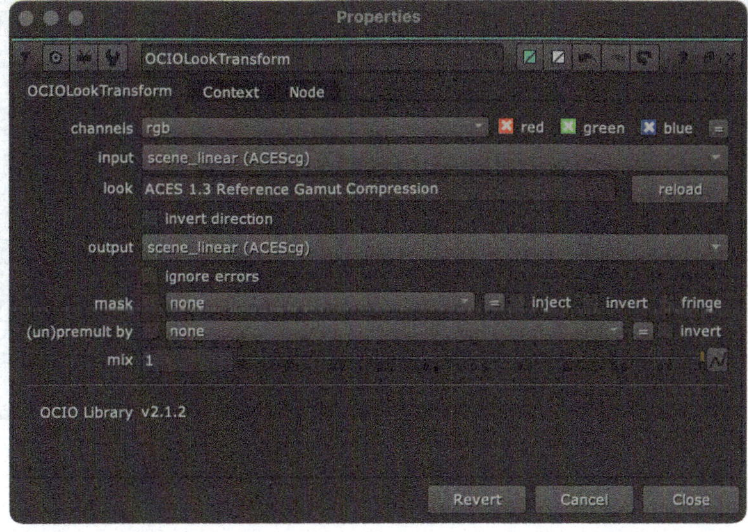

Figure 10.10 Nuke – OCIOLookTransform

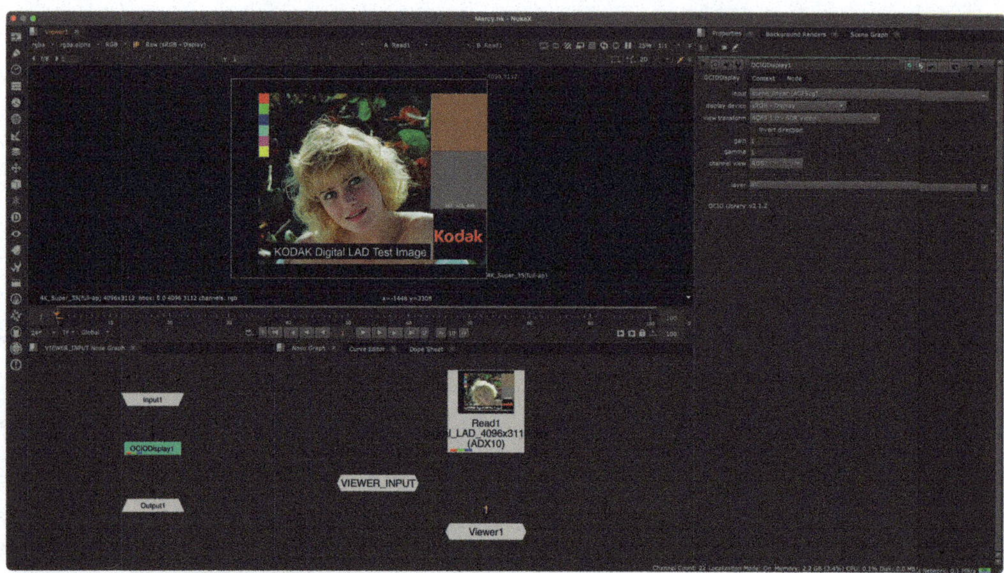

Figure 10.11 Nuke – input process

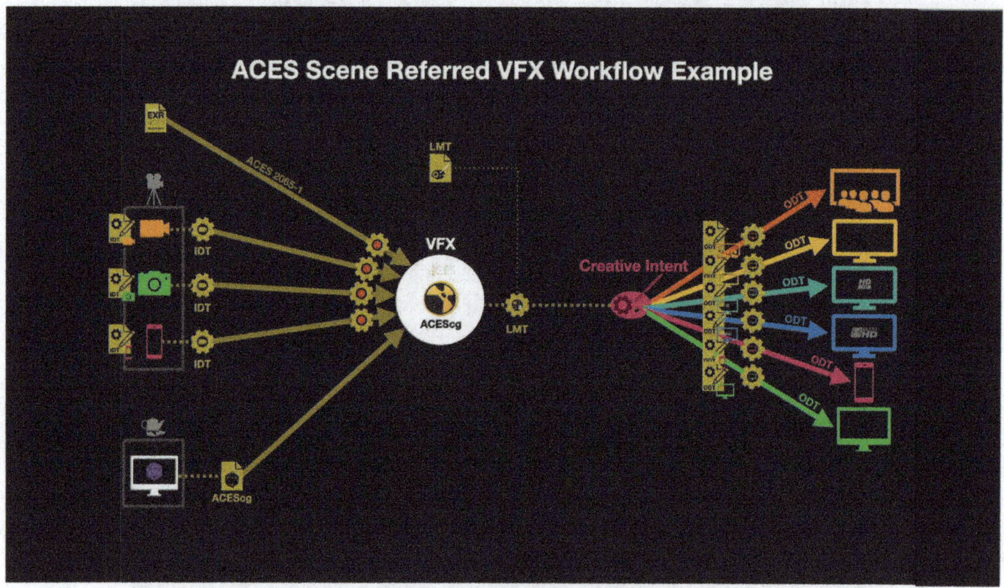

Figure 10.12 Academy color encoding system (ACES) scene referred virtual effects (VFX) work-flow example – output device transform (ODT)

Now we are missing the last part of the *workflow*: how to display the image on your monitor or any other screen, accurately represented. For that we use the right *ODT* that is going to depend on the kind of monitor you are using to display the *viewer*, or external *monitor output*, and select its right color space. For instance, a traditional computer monitor would use the "*sRGB (ACES)*" *ODT* (Figure 10.12).

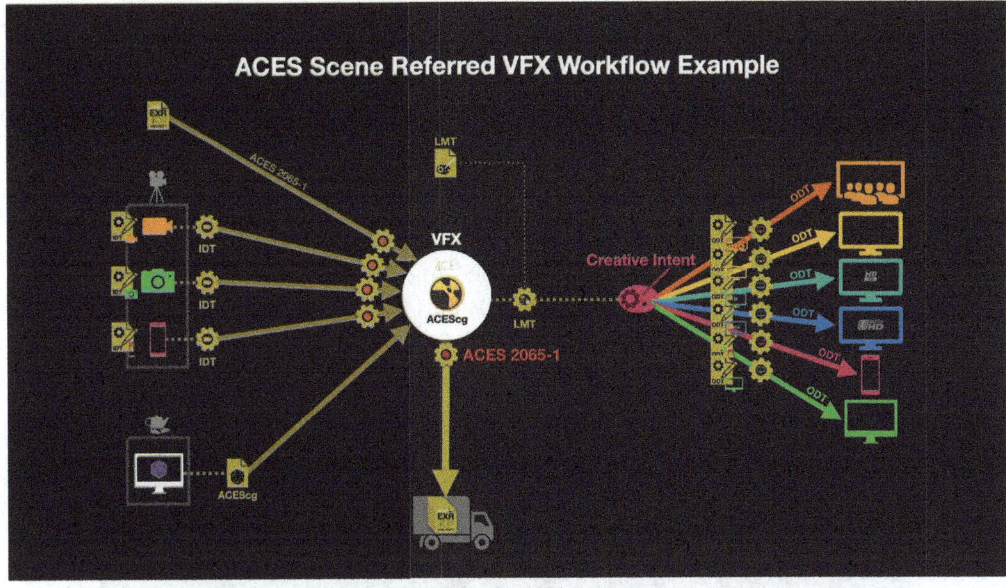

Figure 10.13 Academy color encoding system (ACES) scene referred virtual effects (VFX) work-flow example – ACES compliant deliverables

As you can see there are plenty of options available, and for the most advanced users, you have also the ability to add others or modify the existing ones using the *OCIOdisplay* transform *viewer process* panel ... but honestly, you should have all you may need with the default available options already listed in the *viewer process*. Ah! You do not need to worry about the *RRT*, Nuke is taking care of that for you under the hood.

The last remaining question is: "*How to export in ACES for delivery?*" It is as simple as a *write node*, as usual. Just keep in mind you must render out a sequence of *ACES compliant OpenEXR files*. So, set the *file format* to *EXR*, ensure the *output transform* is set at *ACES2065-1* and that you ticked the "*write ACES compliant EXR*" and that will setup the required parameters and write the *ACES-specific metadata* into the files (Figure 10.13).

And that's it! Let me tell you once more: *ACES color managed files* must move across this workflow, inter departments or between facilities using just *ACES compliant EXRs*, and only that, please make no exceptions.

DaVinci Resolve™ ACES Color Managed Workflow

Let me briefly showcase how to set up another popular software used in postproduction at large so I can show you in four easy steps an example of an ACES color managed workflow. Of course, you might need to adapt them to the pipeline requirements in accordance with the main workflow of the project. However, the standardization of the ACES workflow is so helpful – once you know the "meaning" of the buttons – that adapting or modifying your workflow for improvements is frankly easy. I wanted to explain the setup of DaVinci Resolve as it is widely used for editorial purposes and preparing deliverables, from the smallest independent project to the highest complexity productions … but the principle is always the same that you would find in Nuke, because they both are compliant to the ACES color management workflow.

Here you have a single setup of Resolve™ in four steps:

1 The first thing is to adjust your project settings. In the color management section, select the *color science*: *ACEScct* and the latest version of ACES available (keep in mind everybody involved in this project needs to use the same version of ACES). The *ACES ODT* uses the color space of the display you are using to work, usually *Rec.709* for SDR, or *P3-D65 ST2084* (1000 nits) with *ACES mid gray luminance* at 15.00 nits for HDR (Figure 10.14).

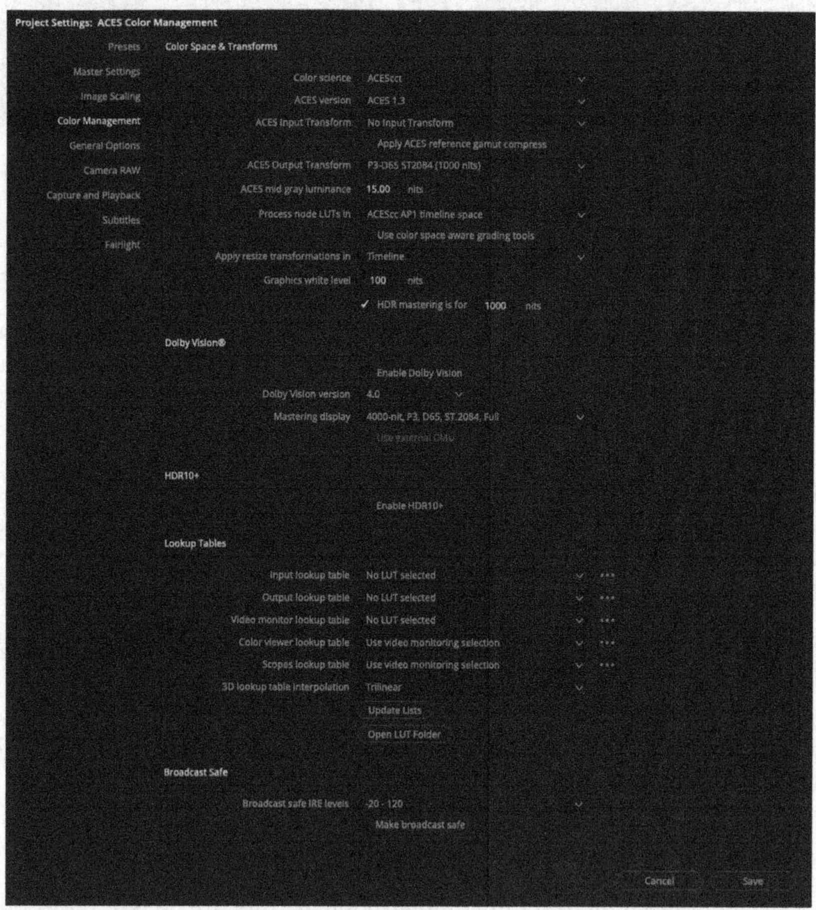

Figure 10.14 DaVinci Resolve project settings/color management

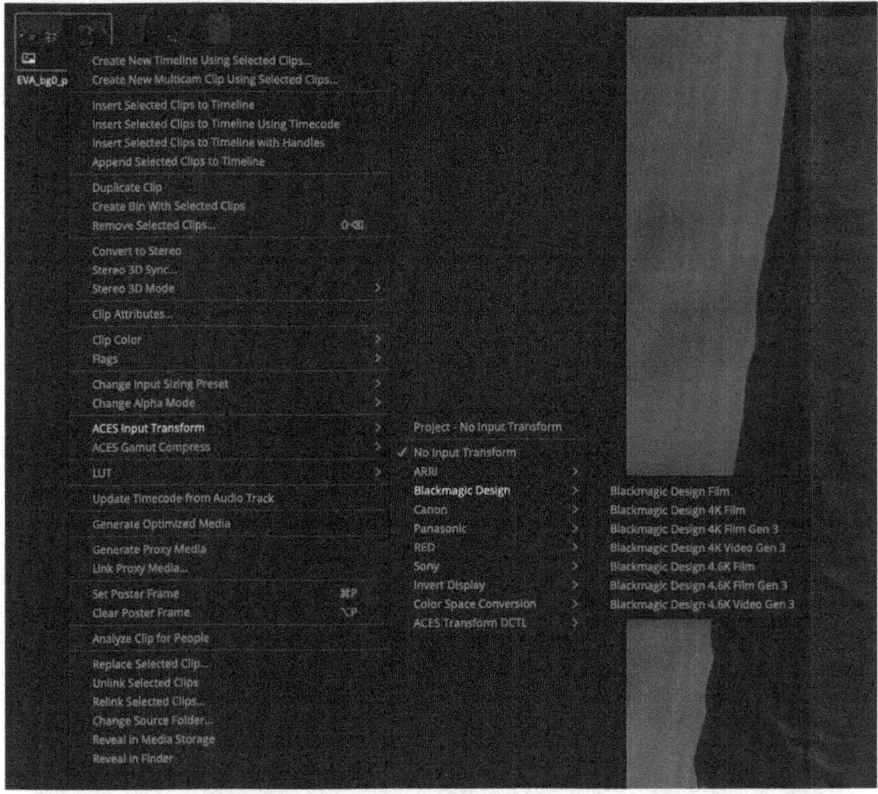

Figure 10.15 DaVinci Resolve – input device transform (IDT)

2 When you are importing your clips into the media pool, Resolve™ should interpret the RAW clips using their required *ACES IDT*. For non-RAW formats (for instance *ProRes*) just right click on the clip (in the *media pool*) and go to *ACES input transform* and select the right one from the list (Figure 10.15).

3 Exporting *intermediate* files (rendering) to work with 3rd parties' software. First of all, consider you should do this on the <u>ungraded master</u> and you want to use the *ACES compliant* way to exchange footage, which is as I explained earlier a specific setting for rendering *EXR file sequences*. The first thing you should do is to reset the *ACES output device transform* of the *color management* tab of the *project settings* to *No output transform*, this way you will export the *Master ACES AP0 primaries* (*ACES2065-1* color space) (Figure 10.16).

4 Lastly, on the *render page* of Resolve™ you need to customize your renders as follows: *render*: "*individual clips*"; *File type*: "*EXR*"; *Codec*: "*RGB half (no compression)*"; *Enable flat pass*: "*always on*" (to ensure you are not applying any grade over the clips you are exporting). Something that might improve your results is the *force*

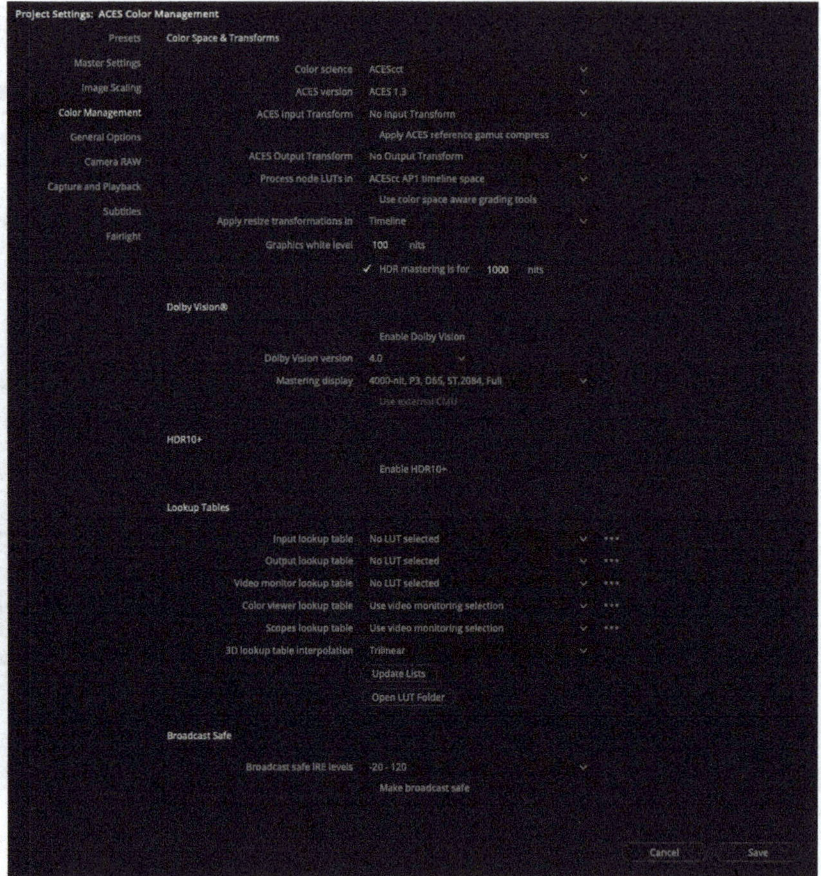

Figure 10.16 DaVinci Resolve project settings/color (Intermediate academy color encoding system (ACES) config)

debayer to *highest quality*. Other parameters you can change as you need are, for instance, the *resolution* (that I would recommend the final delivery resolution for the VFX and maybe the full 6K as well if you are intending to track the camera or other resolution dependent operations) (Figure 10.17).

Hit *render* and collect your folders with the *ACES compliant EXR file sequences* in your destination drive.

So, you do not have to be afraid of color management anymore. Yes, color management has a few critical operations that are crucial to preserve the integrity of the whole workflow, however, as you have seen in these pages we spent together, once you are confident knowing what you are doing, and you know why things are the way they are, and why you should do things the way you are supposed to do them, this subject becomes way less scary and actually quite thrilling!

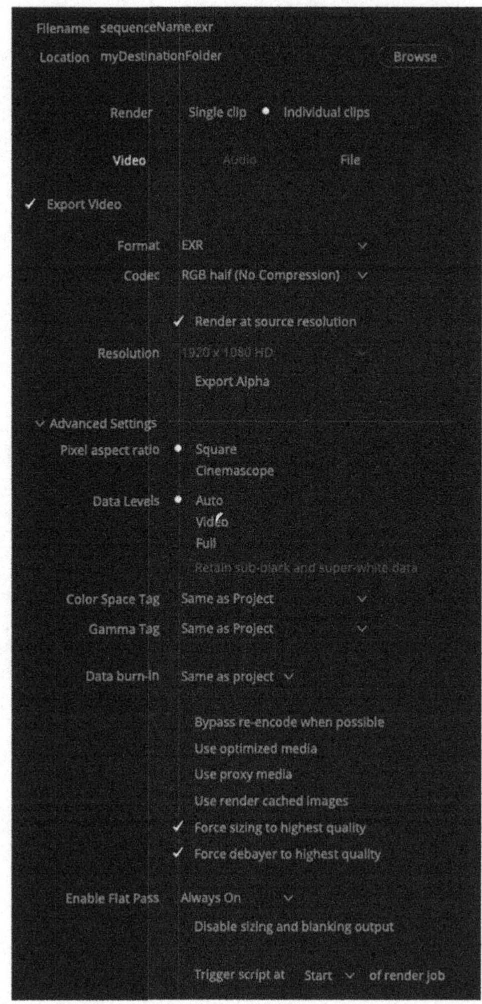

Figure 10.17 DaVinci Resolve – academy color encoding system (ACES) render settings

Index

Note: Page numbers in *italics* refer to figures. Page numbers followed by "n" refer to notes.

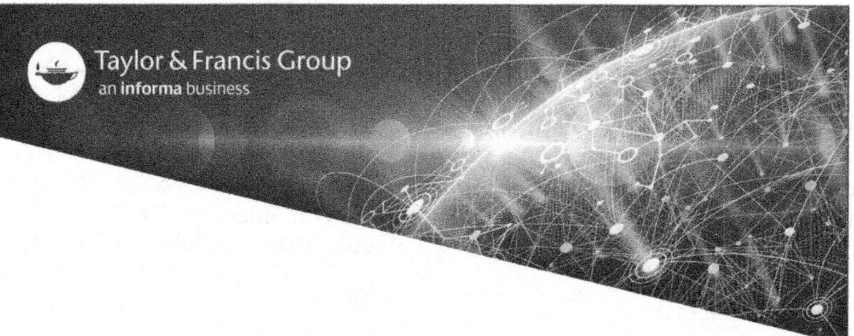

Made in the USA
Coppell, TX
16 February 2024

29022057R10138